Perspectives on Dyslexia
Volume 1

Perspectives on Dyslexia
Volume 1

Neurology, Neuropsychology and Genetics

Edited by

George Th. Pavlidis

George Washington University
Washington D.C., USA

JOHN WILEY & SONS
Chichester · New York · Brisbane · Toronto · Singapore

Other Wiley Editorial Offices

John Wiley & Sons, Inc., 605 Third Avenue,
New York, NY 10158-0012, USA

Jacaranda Wiley Ltd, G.P.O. Box 859, Brisbane,
Queensland 4001, Australia

John Wiley & Sons (Canada) Ltd, 22 Worcester Road,
Rexdale, Ontario M9W 1L1, Canada

John Wiley & Sons (SEA) Pte Ltd, 37 Jalan Pemimpin   05-04,
Block B, Union Industrial Building, Singapore 2057

Library of Congress Cataloging-in-Publication Data:

Perspectives on dyslexia / edited by George Th. Pavlidis.
    p.   cm.
    Contents: Vol. 1. Neurology, neuropsychology and genetics—
v. 2. Cognition, language, and treatment.
    Includes bibliographical references.
    ISBN 0 471 92204 8 (v. 1)—ISBN 0 471 92484 9
(v. 2)
    1. Dyslexia.   I. Pavlidis, George Th.
    [DNLM: 1. Dyslexia.   WM 475 D9977]
RC394.W6D95   1990
616.85'53—dc20
DNLM/DLC
for Library of Congress   89-24793
                                                        CIP

British Library Cataloguing in Publication Data:

Perspectives on dyslexia:
    Vol. 1: Neurology, neuropsychology and genetics
    1. Man. Dyslexia
    I. Pavlidis, George Th.
    616.85'53

    ISBN 0 471 92204 8

Typeset by Acorn Bookwork, Salisbury, Wiltshire
Printed in Great Britain by
Courier International Ltd, Essex

To a person full of love and humanity, to my one and only sister EVA.
Στην Μονάκριβη, Γεμάτη Αγάπη και Ανθρωπιά, Αδελφή μου ΕΥΑ.

G.Th.P.

Contents

Contributors

Dr Alfredo Alvarez *Central Nacional de Investigaciones Científicas de Cuba, La Habana, Cuba*

Dr A. Apicella *Mount Sinai Medical Center, Miami Beach, Florida, USA*

W. W. Barker *Mount Sinai Medical Center, Miami Beach, Florida, USA*

Dr Jacqueline Becker *Universidad Autónoma de Mexico, Mexico, DF*

Dr T. Boothe *University of Miami School of Medicine and Mount Sinai Medical Center, Miami Beach, Florida, USA*

Dr J. Y. Chang *University of Miami School of Medicine, Miami Beach, Florida, USA*

Professor C. Keith Conners *Department of Psychiatry, Duke University Medical Center, Durham, North Carolina 27701, USA*

Professor John C. DeFries *Institute for Behavioral Genetics, University of Colorado, Campus Box 447, Boulder, Colorado 80309, USA*

Dr Ana E. Diaz de Leon *Universidad Autónoma del Estado de Mexico, Mexico, DF*

Dr Charles E. Dodgen *Fair Oaks Hospital, Summit, New Jersey 07902, USA*

Dr R. Duara *Mailman Center for Child Development, University of Miami School of Medicine and Mount Sinai Medical Center, Miami Beach, Florida, USA*

Dr D. Lynn Flowers *Section of Neuropsychology, Bowman Gray School of Medicine, Winston-Salem, North Carolina 27103, USA*

M. S. Fowler *Royal Berkshire Hospital, Reading, Berkshire, UK*

Dr Karen Gross-Glenn *Mailman Center for Child Development, University of Miami School of Medicine, Miami, Florida, USA*

Professor Thalia Harmony *Universidad National Autónoma de Mexico, Mexico, DF*

Dr P. S. Ing *Boys Town National Research Hospital and Creighton University, Omaha, Nebraska 68131, USA*

Professor E. Roy John *Department of Psychiatry, New York University Medical Center, 550 First Avenue, New York, New York 10016, USA*

Dr William J. Kimberling *Center for Human Communications Disorders, Boys Town National Research Hospital and Creighton University, Omaha, Nebraska 68131, USA*

Dr Michele C. LaBuda *Child Study Center, Yale University School of Medicine, 230 S. Frontage Road, PO Box 3333, New Haven, Connecticut 06510, USA*

Professor H. A. Lubs *Mailman Center for Child Development, University of Miami School of Medicine, Miami, Florida, USA*

Dr Erzsebet Marosi *Universidad National Autónoma de Mexico, Mexico, DF*

Dr Cecile E. Naylor *Section of Neuropsychology, Bowman Gray School of Medicine, Winston-Salem, North Carolina 27103, USA*

Dr Roberto Pascual *Central Nacional de Investigaciones Científicas de Cuba, La Habana, Cuba*

Professor George Th. Pavlidis *The Reading Center, George Washington University, 2021 K Street NW, Suite 720, Washington, D.C. 20006, USA*

Professor Bruce F. Pennington *University of Colorado Health Sciences Center, Denver, Colorado, USA*

Professor Leslie S. Prichep *Brain Research Laboratory, Department of Psychiatry, New York University Medical Center, 550 First Avenue, New York, New York 10016, USA*

Dr Alexis Ramos *Universidad Central de Venezuela, Caracas, Venezuela*

Dr P. M. Riddell *Royal Berkshire Hospital, Reading, Berkshire, UK*

Professor Peter B. Rosenberger *Learning Disorders Unit, Massachusetts General Hospital, Boston, Massachusetts 02114, USA*

Professor Byron P. Rourke *Department of Psychology, University of Windsor, Windsor, Ontario N9B 3P4, Canada*

Professor Paul Satz *Neuropsychology Department, Center for Health Sciences, UCLA School of Medicine, 760 Westwood Plaza, Los Angeles, California 90024, USA*

Dr Shelley D. Smith *Boys Town National Research Hospital and Creighton University, Omaha, Nebraska 68131, USA*

Dr John F. Stein *Department of Physiology, University of Oxford, Parks Road, Oxford OX1 3PT, UK*

Dr Pedro Valdes *Central Nacional de Investigaciones Científicas de Cuba, La Habana, Cuba*

Professor Frank B. Wood *Section of Neuropsychology, Bowman Gray School of Medicine, Winston-Salem, North Carolina 27103, USA*

Professor F. Yoshii *Department of Neurology, Tokai University, Bohseidai, Isehara 259-11, Japan*

Foreword

These two volumes on dyslexia are mainly the outcome of the stimulating and memorable Third World Congress on Dyslexia, chaired by Professor George Th. Pavlidis, that took place on the historic island of Crete, Greece. Dyslexia is a world-wide problem as individuals attempt to read or write. A word derived from the Greek, its modern meaning varies only slightly from language to language, i.e. difficulty with reading ability or skills. Dyslexia is rarely the complete absence of reading skills, but it is often an inability to deal adequately with specific phonemes or combinations of phonemes or an impairment especially of the power of the written language. It certainly impairs the rate of reading, which is markedly affected. In these two volumes experts from several disciplines and countries—individuals with world-class reputations—comprehensively present the theory and latest research results dealing with this complex problem.

From the point of view of etiology, dyslexia is generally seen as a problem involving the brain, and thus is a matter of central nervous system dysfunction. While the neurophysiological basis of the problem is accepted by the great majority of persons working in this field, there are those few who accredit this problem to psychoanalytic interpretation: mother–child deprivations and other environmental etiological factors. The latter suggestions do not hold up to rigorous analysis, while neuroradiological and technological developments of the past decades (particularly the most recent twenty years) are so sophisticated that positive diagnosis of cerebral dysfunction can be made, or in some instances at least a reasonable assumption that such exists is warranted.

Magnetic resonance imaging (MRI) and computed tomography (CT) provide remarkable pictures of the internal structures of the brain (and other organs as desired), while at the same time minimizing the danger of use of excessive amounts of X-rays. Positron emission tomography (PET) provides useful information about the functional aspects of the brain. Various chapters of this book provide extensive reviews and original data derived from such methods that help us to better understand dyslexia.

A second major development in understanding dyslexia and other forms of learning disabilities comes from the work of the neuropsychologist. Neuropsychology—the newest expansion of the general field of psychology—is rapidly taking precedence, particularly over 'school psychology', but also to a major degree over certain aspects of the work of clinical psychologists.

The neuropsychologist must function as a close associate of the neurologist and the neuroradiologist. This discipline is concerned not only with the quantitative assessment of the individual with whom the neuropsychologist works, but also with the qualitative assessments which result from a sound foundation in human anatomy, neurology, human physiology, and also a firm grasp of such qualitative psychological testing materials as the Goldstein–Scheerer tests, the Rorschach test, the Bender Gestalt, the Vigotsky technique and the Luria approach to intellectual assessment.

These two disciplines—neuroradiology and neuropsychology—working in close collaboration are able to provide an accurate evaluation of the presence or absence of cerebral pathology which may result in a diagnosis of dyslexia. The accuracy of their work makes it possible for the neuroeducator or other specialists to undertake appropriate programs of treatment and education. It is believed that in the near future their efforts will become even more accurate as instrumentation and technologies are perfected.

On the other side of the coin the remarkable work of Albert Galaburda, neuroanatomist at the Harvard Medical School and Beth Israel Hospital, Boston, must be recognized. Galaburda and his associates, with support from the Orton Society for Dyslexia, are, in an extremely detailed fashion, studying brains of individuals who in life were diagnosed as having had dyslexia. Posthumous findings do not affect diagnostic decisions needed during the life of an individual, but they do in large measure direct the diagnosticians in the right directions as the latter seek to understand the problem and subsequently to treat the individual whose life yet lies before him.

Dyslexia is a complicated form of central nervous system dysfunction, but it is not fatal—not fatal to occupational or to academic success. There are many examples of young men and women who in the universities greatly extend themselves and make tremendous efforts to succeed. Recently two young men (as examples of dozens), accurately defined and diagnosed as dyslexic, whom we had followed since high school and before, graduated from a first-rate university with accumulated grade point averages of 3.3 and 3.7 (out of 4.0). These are not exceptions to the rule but are young people whose lives have profited from several essential factors which together may make, or lacking may break, an individual's life.

There is an area of professional activity which is essential, but is most often overlooked, namely prognosis, early discovery, diagnosis and treatment. For the most part, the child later to be known as dyslexic is not 'discovered' until Grade 2 or Grade 4, as Pavlidis describes in Volume 2. This does not have to happen. Reading does not take place as it should during Grade 2, and the teacher may suspect a variety of causes. When by Grade 4 the child is definitely not reading he may be considered 'emotionally disturbed', 'mentally retarded', 'non-motivated', 'doesn't try', is oblivious to threats, or to a variety of other attempts by parents or teachers to teach him to read.

School people too often blame the child's failure on a lack of adequate diagnostic and assessment facilities for the young child. This is an excuse which if true at all, will not hold up for long, and indeed at the time of writing is outmoded in many places. In a longitudinal study of premature infants in Cuba, the EEG will be utilized routinely when the infant is as young as one hour of age. Ten thousand infants are anticipated to be included ultimately in this cohort. This obviously requires sophisticated electrophysiological techniques, but that is a detail which time will make right. In some few centers, the EEG with appropriate adaptations, according to Dr E. Roy John of the Brain Research Laboratories, New York University, is being utilized with fetuses at the prenatal level. We have argued for early discovery of learning disabilities for many years. A most encouraging study by Dr J. Jost in Czechoslovakia, using the 'Pavlidis Test' (eye movements), has shown that at the age of 6 years this test can predict with over 90% accuracy who would develop learning disabilities two years later. Soon the time will be on us when no excuse is valid for professional personnel not knowing with what they are dealing in a child (or indeed in an older individual).

Obviously, reading *per se* does not start prenatally or in early postnatal life. However, knowledge of the existence of a central nervous system dysfunction in a child prior to birth or during early postnatal life means that appropriate physical therapy, occupational therapy, speech supports, brain and infant stimulation as a whole and parent education can be started as and when needed. Reading or academic readiness then takes on new meanings. It does not happen spontaneously. The child is *made ready to learn*, and reading is one aspect of total learning. Early understanding of the infant on the part of parents and teachers is no substitute for other efforts which must be made. The child with dyslexia has a severe problem involving numerous perceptual deficits. Frequent neuropsychological assessments are in order so that the significance of perceptual pathology can be ascertained. At this point these are attacked by therapists and well-prepared neuroeducators. Treatment can be initiated as early as possible when the child demonstrates a readiness to respond to academic learning—reading, writing, spelling and arithmetical calculations.

It becomes obvious to those who have worked closely with children or adults who have dyslexia that the issue is not one for a single discipline. A multidisciplinary diagnostic team is essential, in which each team individual is *an equal among equals*. There is a basic membership of the team, namely the following (arranged alphabetically, not in terms of a historical perspective or traditional hierarchy):

(1) Electrophysiologist
(2) Neuroeducator
(3) Neuropsychologist
(4) Neuroradiologist or electrophysiologist
(5) Occupational therapist
(6) Pediatric neurologist
(7) Physical therapist
(8) Remedial teacher
(9) Speech therapist.

Quite obviously not all these disciplines are required at all times, but as the child matures developmentally each appears on the scene and assumes the role appropriate to ensure the child's even growth.

It must be obvious that dyslexia, accurately defined, is not the same as the remedial reading problems of many school-aged children who are in need of remedial assistance. The problems of these children are or may be the result of environmental factors of a widely diversified nature. As the pioneering work of Pavlidis has shown, the two groups, dyslexics and non-dyslexic retarded readers, are of entirely different genres and, from a research point of view, they are different cohorts. The failure to distinguish between these etiological factors is one of the reasons for the confusion too often observed among teachers who claim to be either specialists in dyslexia or remedial reading. The neuroeducator working with children who are dyslexic or who have learning disabilities will develop a highly individualized program which will counter the psychopathology isolated by the neuropsychologist. We have long felt and often demonstrated clinically that it is possible to offset every major characteristic of the child's psychopathology with a teaching technique which will minimize the former and enhance the achievement level of the pupil with dyslexia. The neuroeducator must know how to do this. It is not something taught in universities or colleges in the usual remedial reading classes. Specialized preparation is required.

In the secondary school, and later in college and university, students with dyslexia often face a problem not of their making. This issue pertains to the attitude of high-school faculty members towards the student who is not achieving to the maximum of his measured ability. Furthermore, faculty members at these levels are more concerned with content. They are content-oriented rather than student- or child-oriented. However, that can be changed, if only in the last resort, by administrative dictum. The student with dyslexia needs certain things to be able to maximize his efforts—all of which are not costly.

First, he needs a greater amount of time than others in order adequately to handle a reading assignment or to complete an examination. In universities in which this writer has been a professor, a student, for example, is referred to him for advice and counseling. The problem is, of course, in the student, but its solution is not necessarily his problem. Often the problem is exacerbated by those around him—in this case, the university faculty member(s). The counselor–professor makes an appointment with the colleagues in whose classes the dyslexic student is enrolled. With the student accompanying him, the two visit the instructor, explaining carefully from the outset that lowering of standards is not being requested, but that extensions of time are needed: two hours for an hour-long quiz; a half day for a two-hour midterm or final examination. These are simple adjustments which are usually accepted readily. In one university more than 400 professors willingly cooperated over a ten-year period. Only one refused!

Second, it is suggested to the student that he obtain, and to the faculty member that he provide, a list of major readings, textbooks and reading lists for the course to be taken the following semester. We try to accomplish this as early as six months ahead of the new semester. This leads to two other key elements, namely:

(1) An acquaintanceship by the student with materials which will be utilized later.
(2) Time to order the textbooks (via local and state libraries from the American Printing House for the Blind, Louisville, Kentucky, which are to be utilized. These come through a relatively recent modification in the US federal law, and are available to certified poor readers. (These materials are unfortunately available only to citizens of the USA.) The materials come to the student in the form of 'talking books' or cassettes for tape recorder use. They arrive and are returned postage-free. Now the student can 'hear' the textbook as well as read it as much as he successfully can. The program can become very effective.

Third, the typical high-school teacher or university faculty often assigns a reading on the spur of the moment. The dyslexic student cannot read the assignment quickly enough to be able to discuss it 'tomorrow', as the professor had stated. In our experience we seek to obtain approximately a dozen to 15 adults in the community who, on call, will read the assignment to the student, or read it onto a tape. We usually utilize retired men or women for this function, and once the need becomes known there is frequently an over-abundance of volunteers. The side effects developed from this relationship too are often significant and long-lasting, to say nothing of being very helpful.

Fourth, many dyslexic students have difficulties with short- and long-term memory. In a multiple-choice examination, for example, the dyslexic student often cannot hold all of the alternatives in mind, although he may be conversant with the topic and in reality knows the correct response. The professor gives permission to have a 'reader' accompany the student to the examination. The reader then *reads* (does not provide answers) the objective examination to the student item by item while the young person also visually reads the item to the best of his ability. He 'hears' the item as it is read aloud. The difference in the results is often extraordinary.

Finally, we request the faculty member to allow the student to bring to the class hand calculators and/or tape recorders. If the student understands the concept, the calculator merely speeds up action and assures accuracy. The dyslexic student whose memory hinders him in reading formulae for algebra, or theorems in geometry and whose recall of the multiplication tables or the appropriate sequence in long division is poor, is now able to compete with the class valedictorian! The tape recorder allows the student to listen and listen again to the teacher/professor's lecture or to the class discussion. Re-hearing reinforces recall in the young person whose memory is at fault.

Standards are not lowered by these five adjustments. The professor's time is not involved. The student succeeds, which brings satisfaction to everyone concerned. Success breeds success, and the student is motivated to continue trying. The professor often becomes more than a little interested in the student, is personally complimented by the student's successes, informs his colleagues, and the word spreads that it is possible to meet individual student needs without excessive time or fiscal costs to anyone.

Dyslexia is a severely inhibiting factor in the development of the young person. The effort which students make to succeed is often staggering. Studying all night in the library, not to cram for an examination but to read and read again an assignment for understanding or to write a theme with accuracy, is not unusual. There is more than one example of an interested professor cautioning a student that sleep can breed success too, and to stay out of the library and avoid as much as possible, through careful scheduling, these all-night sessions.

The dyslexic child and youth matures developmentally into a dyslexic adult. This process can either be a series of frustrations, failures and personal discouragements, or it can be a smooth progression of success experiences. Early discovery and an early attack on the perceptual processing deficits can ensure the latter, the results of which will be dyslexic adults who understand their problems and who can succeed socially and economically. This is the message of these two volumes.

William M. Cruickshank
University of Michigan

Preface

As dyslexia is a neurological condition, it affects people world wide. The international scope of the problem was reflected in the composition of the participants of the 3rd World Congress on Dyslexia. The Congress brought together prominent colleagues from 22 countries around the world. It took place in a beautiful seaside hotel on the historic island of Crete, Greece, between June 27 and July 2, 1987. It gave the opportunity to the participants to discuss a multitude of issues that are rarely described in publications. These discussions led to a better understanding of the work of colleagues with diverse views.

The scientific sessions were of high quality and were matched by most cordial social evenings that established new research cooperations, created new friendships, and reinforced old ones. Most importantly, the Congress exposed us to new views and approaches that lead to a more comprehensive appreciation of dyslexia. But it was not only hard science, as we celebrated Margaret Rawson's 88th birthday with special love. In addition the unforgettable Greek–International evening revealed the admirable artistic talents and human side of many colleagues.

Most chapters of this volume grew out of the invited authors' presentations at the Congress, although for the sake of completeness a few other colleagues were also asked to share their knowledge with the reader. The authors were asked to provide a review of their area, to freely discuss their theories, and to provide the data which support them.

It is difficult to keep abreast of the immense and diverse literature on dyslexia as it is published in hundreds of journals of many disciplines. Hence, a lot of important information frequently escapes most of us. The chapters were placed in two volumes which offer the reader the opportunity to appreciate the interdisciplinary flavor and diverse views of the many disciplines contributing to the field of dyslexia.

Volume 1 was organized to provide in easily understood language the conceptual, etiological, genetic, neuroanatomical, neurophysiological, electrophysiological, and visual electrophysiology aspects of dyslexia and of other related learning disabilities. This volume is particularly important because it can help the reader appreciate the significant gains that could be derived from this approach for its early objective diagnosis. Early diagnosis of dyslexia/learning disability is the key for more effective treatment and more balanced psycho-socio-educational adjustment. Volume 2 addresses the psycho-socio-educational perspectives, including cognitive, language, and treatment aspects of dyslexia/learning disability. These two complementary volumes cover almost the total spectrum of dyslexia/learning disability and provide the reader with a comprehensive understanding of it from childhood to adulthood.

Dr Cruickshank, who could be considered the father of the learning disability area, provides a thoughtful foreword that highlights the most promising advances in the field and emphasizes the significance of the genetic, neurological and electrophysiological aspects for a better understanding and a more effective treatment of dyslexia.

George Th. Pavlidis

Part I

Understanding Dyslexia
and its Subtypes

1

Developmental Dyslexia: An Etiological Reformulation

Paul Satz
University of California, Los Angeles

INTRODUCTION

In a review of the theory of learning disabilities—its current state and future prospects—Joseph Torgesen (1986) identified two broad assumptions for explaining these disabilities. One of the basic assumptions is that learning disabilities are caused by 'deficiencies in basic psychological processes that are not adequately measured by standard intelligence tests, but are required to successfully perform academic tasks' (p. 399). A second assumption is '. . . that these cognitive limitations are caused by naturally occurring variation in the neurological substrate that supports all intellectual activity, or by damage to this substrate caused by accident or disease' (p. 399). Torgesen then described three different scientific schools or orientations (i.e. paradigms) that have attempted to address these broad assumptions in the past fifty years. He defined these as the *neuropsychological*, the *information-processing* and the *applied behavior analysis* paradigms. According to Torgesen (1986), all three paradigms represent different viewpoints about learning disabilities in that they ask different kinds of questions, employ different types of explanatory constructs, use somewhat different methods, and emphasize different assumptions about their subject matter. For example, the neuropsychological paradigm conceptualizes intellectual/cognitive behavior in terms of the specific neural systems that presumably underlie it. The information-processing paradigm, on the other hand, views the mind as a limited-capacity symbol manipulator. Applied behavior analysis, in marked contrast to the preceding approaches, rejects the use of constructs that infer deficient neural or cognitive structures and attempts to explain behavior in terms of the environmental consequences that follow it or the stimulus conditions that precede it.

The author concluded that while each paradigm has potential contributions to make to our understanding and treatment of learning-disabled (LD) children, progress has been impeded not only by territorial rhetoric among approaches but also by failure to advance a theory that provides a better explanation for the underlying causes or differential treatment, at least for a subset of the LD population.

The present chapter, partly in response to Torgesen's (1986) recommendation, provides a neuropsychological analysis and explanation for one subset of the LD population, namely, the specific reading-disabled. Neuropsychological theory is important not only because it attempts to address one of the basic assumptions about learning disabilities—i.e. its putative neural substrate—but also because this substrate could provide the structural basis for the deficiency in psychological processes that Torgesen identified as the second basic assumption underlying these disabilities.

I shall focus my discussion on specific reading disability (i.e. developmental dyslexia), not only because it represents a smaller and presumably more homogeneous subset of the LD population (Waites, 1968), but also because of the historical interest that this disorder has evoked in terms of its putative brain substrate. Interestingly, if not surprisingly, the brain substrate presumed to underlie this disorder has changed little in the past century.

Since the seminal report of Dejerine (1892), which observed the onset of alexia with agraphia following an adult lesion of the left angular gyrus, investigators have long suspected that this neural substrate, in the posterior left cerebral hemisphere, may play a key role in the understanding of childhood developmental dyslexia. Later reports by Morgan (1896) and Hinshelwood (1900) postulated a similar locus for the first cases of congenital word blindness. Throughout the twentieth century this view was shared by those who conceptualized reading as a language or left hemisphere process. The strongest advocates of this view were those who observed the selected losses in reading, spelling and writing following acquired focal lesions in adults (Benson and Geschwind, 1969). In fact, some of the more formal theories of reading sprang from these reports (Coltheart *et al.*, 1980; Marshall and Newcombe, 1981; Vellutino, 1987; Liberman, 1982). With the advent of the neurolinguistic movement in the early 1970s, further attention focused on the role of the left hemisphere as a putative substrate for childhood dyslexia. Despite general agreement as to a possible locus, the mechanism presumed to underlie this 'congenital' form of the disorder remained unknown. It was not until 1968 that Drake reported a post-mortem analysis of the brain of a dyslexic which revealed abnormal subcortical neurons in *both* temporal lobes. These anomalous cellular migrations were later confirmed by Galaburda and Kemper (1979), who showed the first relatively convincing evidence of a _unilateral_ congenital abnormality of the left posterior temporal lobe. According to Geschwind (1985, p. 22) '. . . this patient was a 20 year old man still severely dyslexic at the time of death in an accident. The patient was left-handed, a highly skilled metalsmith and had two dyslexic brothers, as well as a mother with rheumatoid arthritis.'

It was not long after this initial report that Geschwind and his colleagues (Geschwind, 1985; Geschwind and Galaburda, 1985a,b; Geschwind and Behan, 1982) advanced the first formal neurobiological theory of childhood dyslexia. Briefly, the theory states that the disorder is due to an excess of testosterone during prenatal development which, in some males, slows the maturation of the left hemisphere, leading to structural anomalies of cell migration (heterotopias) and organization (dysplasias). It is further hypothesized that because of this anomalous cellular migration in the left hemisphere, certain compensatory functions in the right hemisphere are activated, leading to a shift in hand preference (left) and the development of superior visuospatial abilities. However, the substrate for speech and language remains in the left hemisphere, leading to later reading and writing disturbances. The theory also postulates that testosterone impacts on the thymus gland, leading to an increased risk for autoimmune disorder in later life. In sum, the theory predicts a triadic association involving handedness (left), cognition (reading/ language disability) and immunological status (autoimmune disorder) in males who are exposed prenatally to excessive amounts of testosterone.

The differential effect of testosterone on the left hemisphere is explained, in part, as a function of the right hemisphere's advantage in maturational rate, especially in males, which leaves the left hemisphere at greater risk during this early critical developmental period (Taylor and Ounsted, 1972). Additionally, the left hemisphere is invoked, probably because of its dominant role in language and reading processes.

The latter position represents an important theoretical advance that reaffirms traditional claims for a unilateral neural substrate in developmental dyslexia. Despite the obvious appeal and heuristic importance of this position, it does assume, implicitly or otherwise, that brain structures outside of the critical speech/language zones (both intra- and interhemispheric) lack the capacity to compensate for the putative left temporal/parietal insult in dyslexia (presumably congenital). This assumption, however, deserves closer scrutiny. Why, for example, should the _reading_ process be more vulnerable to a focal brain lesion (pre- or early postnatal) than other _related_ cognitive functions? With respect to _speech_ and _language_, it has long been reported that early left focal brain insult (pre- or postnatal) produces no long-term deficits in these functions. Rapid recovery from aphasia is the rule, although the status of other cognitive functions, including reading and writing, are less clear (Hecaen _et al._, 1984; Rasmussen and Milner, 1977; Kinsbourne and Hiscock, 1981; Woods and Teuber, 1978; Woods and Carey, 1978; Satz and

Bullard-Bates, 1981). Also, the mechanisms presumed to underlie the rapid recovery from aphasia in children with early left brain insult have not been critically reviewed to date.

For this reason, it might be helpful to review briefly those studies that report the status of speech and language functions in subjects with *known* left focal brain injury during infancy or childhood, and then to examine the mechanisms presumed to underlie instances of sparing or recovery on speech and, if possible, on reading and writing skills. To address this problem I will focus on three data sources: (1) infantile and childhood hemiplegia; (2) childhood and adolescent hemispherectomy; and (3) reports of childhood aphasia onset and course.

Paralysis of one side of the body result of lesion on contralateral cerebral hemisphere

INFANTILE AND CHILDHOOD HEMIPLEGIA

A comprehensive review of the effects of childhood hemiplegia on speech and language functions has previously been reported by Dennis and Whitaker (1977). Table 1 presents a summary of 14 studies that report the percentage of language impairment as a function of hemiplegic side. Inspection of this table reveals a significantly higher incidence of language impairment associated with right hemiplegia ($X\%$ right = 40.1, $X\%$ left = 18.3). Although these data were correctly interpreted as evidence of early left hemisphere specialization (as opposed to hemispheric equipotentiality), they also permit another interpretation—namely, that although the left hemisphere is at greater risk for language impairment when injured during childhood, the degree of this risk is relatively small in terms of *frequency* and *severity*.

Note that the majority of cases (60%) were asymptomatic for speech or language disturbance and, when present, such disturbance was confined largely to articulation or language delay. The incidence of aphasia was extremely rare despite the fact that in some cases the whole left hemisphere was atrophied.

One of the better-controlled studies (Ammett, 1973) also found that the incidence of speech disturbance was much lower in cases of *infantile* hemiplegia. Onset after age 1 year revealed a higher incidence of speech impairment, although this conclusion is weakened by a much smaller sample size in the childhood onset cases. It is worth noting that the mean overall percentage of language impairment after right hemiplegia in the childhood cases (40%; Dennis and Whitaker, 1977) is much lower than clinical reports of right hemiplegia in adults (approximately 80%), the vast majority of whom are aphasic (D. F. Benson, personal communication). Although the preceding results should be viewed with appropriate caution, especially with respect to the reliability of the different speech and language assessments, many of

Table 1. Language disorder as a function of laterality of childhood hemiplegia across studies[a]

	Language disorder	
Study	Proportion rt hemiplegia	Proportion lt hemiplegia
Cotard (1868)	8/13	1/10
Gaudard (1884)	25/55	8/25
Bernhardt (1885)	11/14	0/4
Lovett (1888)	3/13	4/13
Wallenberg (1886a)	45/94	17/66
Osler (1888)	12/68	1/52
Sachs and Peterson (1890)	10/52	7/53
Wulff (1890)	6/9	2/15
Freud and Rie (1891)	7/23	3/12
Dundson (1952)	31/34	8/30
Basser (1962)	16/48	18/54
Ingram (1964)	11/44	1/31
Bishop (1967)	5/7	1/8
Ammett (1973)	24/59	7/49
Total	211/533(40%)	78/422(18%)

[a]After Dennis and Whitaker (1977). For the above references, please see the original paper.

which were anecdotal, the expected bias of over-reporting cases of language disturbance after left-sided injury was not demonstrated. As such, the mean incidence of 40% may represent a reasonable upper level of occurrence.

removal of cortical structures of one cerebral hemiplegia

CHILDHOOD AND ADOLESCENT HEMISPHERECTOMY

According to St James-Roberts (1981):

> Hemispherectomy studies are important because of their relevance to organization of function in the cerebral hemispheres and because they provide a model for the study of brain damage recovery processes in humans. Isaacson (1975) has emphasized that they provide the only case analogous to animal lesion studies, in that both the tissue ablated and the substrate of remaining function are known. (p. 31)

Despite the importance of these claims, the review by St James-Roberts (1981) on the effects of hemispherectomy on language and intelligence was hindered by numerous methodological and assessment problems across studies. With respect to speech and language most of the studies provided only global reports on the presence or absence of aphasia and dysarthria. However, these reports revealed few cases of impaired speech production or comprehension and even fewer cases of aphasia after left-sided hemispherectomy. This finding is even more striking given the extreme age range across studies, including age at hemispherectomy, the high frequency of mental retardation, likelihood of residual damage in the remaining hemisphere in many of the cases (Smith and Sugar, 1975) and the tendency to over-report aphasia incidence with left brain injury or right hemiplegia. In fact, St James-Roberts (1981) stated that '. . . although infant left hemispherectomy cases have achieved apparently normal speech production and comprehension, together with verbal IQs in the normal range, only one adult case (Smith and Sugar, 1975) has been reported to have normal speech comprehension' (p. 36). While he interpreted these results as suggesting superior (left) hemisphere adaptation in infant cases, he felt that other etiological, recovery-period and experiential variables offered equally plausible alternative explanations.

As noted earlier, the purpose of the present chapter, in contrast to St James-Roberts (1981), is addressed primarily to whether sparing or recovery in speech and language occur after injury to the immature brain and not whether this sparing is qualitatively different in children and adults. A more objective assessment of language functions following early brain injury (infancy) and later hemispherectomy (childhood–adolescence) can be found in the seminal reports of Dennis and Kohn (1975), Dennis and Whitaker (1976, 1977) and Dennis (1980). These isolated brain studies have clearly demonstrated sparing in a wide range of speech and language skills after early left-sided brain injury and later resection of the left cerebral hemisphere. In fact, none of the case reports showed signs of aphasia. Subjects with only a remaining right hemisphere showed similar speech and language production to those with only a remaining left hemisphere. There was no global language breakdown nor a deficiency in verbal cognitive capacity in the former group. The only linguistic defect noted in the reports by Dennis and associates (1975–80) involved the capacity of the right brain half to understand auditory language, especially when meaning is conveyed by syntactic diversity. However, it should be noted that even this specific syntactical defect has been challenged as impressionistic by more recent investigators (Bishop, 1983). Similar claims of sparing or recovery in speech and language have been made by Smith (1981) and Smith and Sugar (1975). In their long-term follow-up of a left hemisperectomy case operated on at age 5 years, Smith and Sugar (1975) noted that '. . . his speech which earlier (pre-surgery) has been practically unintelligible, had rapidly become normal' (p. 814). At age 26 years, the patient continued to show improvement, particularly in language and verbal reasoning capacities where he performed in the superior range.

In sum, the hemispherectomy studies, while subject to innumerable methodological, procedural and assessment flaws, at least provide further evidence of relative sparing of speech and language functions after early brain injury and later left-sided hemispherectomy.

The preceding reports on the status of speech and language functions in childhood hemiplegia and after hemispherectomy are informative. Despite inconsistencies in the quality and type of assessment measure across studies, including differences in subject variables (age, sex, lesion onset and focus) and lesion onset to assessment intervals, the results were surprisingly consistent with respect to speech and language functions after early brain injury. Injury to the left cerebral hemisphere, if sustained early in life (probably before age 6 years) resulted in significant *sparing* or *recovery* of speech and language functions across studies. Although most of these follow-up studies provided little retrospective information regarding speech function during the early lesion-onset period, except for occasional anecdotal reports of mild and transitory aphasic symptoms in selected cases, the subjects at follow-up assessment were uniformly free of speech or aphasic disturbances. These null findings are rather dramatic given the severity and acute onset of many of the lesions. At the same time, it should be remembered that aphasic disturbances are often part of the early clinical picture, especially in cases of acute vascular etiology involving the left hemisphere (Hecaen, 1976; Woods and Teuber, 1978; Satz and Bullard-Bates, 1981). For this reason, it is necessary that a brief review of the reported cases of aphasia onset be made in order to determine more clearly the status and recovery of speech and language functions after early brain injury in man. This review is based in part on an earlier review on acquired aphasia in children (Satz and Bullard-Bates, 1981).

CHILDHOOD APHASIA ONSET AND COURSE

One of the most distinguishing features attributed to the childhood aphasias is the recovery course. It has long been reported that the symptoms are transient and rarely permanent. Recovery from childhood aphasia is much more dramatic in comparison to the adult aphasias. These observations date from the early reports by Clarus (1874), Bernhardt (1885) and Freud (1897) and have been accepted generally by most twentieth-century clinicians (Alajouanine and Lhermitte, 1965; Basser, 1962; Benson, 1972; Byers and McLean, 1962; Geschwind, 1974; Guttman, 1942; Hecaen, 1976; Lenneberg, 1967; Woods and Teuber, 1978).

The first major twentieth-century paper was by Guttman (1942). This study comprised 30 unilateral cases (trauma, abscess, thrombosis), only 10 of which were available at follow-up. Moderate to complete recovery in speech was observed for all but one of the cases (vascular). Basser (1962) reported follow-up data on 30 children who sustained an acute hemiplegia (left = 15, right = 15) after the onset of speech. An initial non-fluent aphasia was observed in most of the cases. At follow-up (3 months–2 years), Basser (1962) reported significant recovery in all cases. Despite the robust recovery in speech, the intellectual levels were in the retarded range for a majority of the sample, regardless of lesion side. Unfortunately, no additional information was available with respect to school placement or achievement.

Similar recovery results were reported in a subsequent paper by Lenneberg (1967). Age at insult ranged from 3 to 18 years. Etiology was mixed and included cases of trauma ($N = 4$), stroke ($N = 3$) and neoplasm ($N = 1$). All of the children were aphasic at the initial examination, but only two were aphasic at follow-up. These two were in adolescence when the lesion (one trauma, one neoplasm) occurred (ages 15 and 18 years, respectively). Recovery was complete for all children who were under age 11 years at the time of injury. Lenneberg (1967) provided no data on intellectual level or on school achievement.

Alajouanine and Lhermitte (1965) reported a 1-year follow-up of 32 children (ages 6–15 years), all of whom were aphasic at initial contact following injury to the left hemisphere (trauma, neoplasm, stroke). At follow-up 24 of the children had regained 'a normal or nearly normal language' (p. 659). No agrammatism was observed in these children. In contrast, the remaining eight children showed a more unfavorable course. Most of these children had large cerebral lesions. On the basis of these results, Alajouanine and Lhermitte concluded that recovery is an indisputable fact and one very particular to children. This conclusion, however, should be tempered by an additional finding concerning intellectual level and school achievement. The authors were the first to note that, despite a dramatic remission in aphasia, none of the children could follow a normal progress in school. Unfortunately, no data were available on reading status, although it was suggested that most of the academic difficulties were due to intellectual impairment.

Byers and McLean (1962) also observed persisting cognitive impairments, despite restitution of speech functions in their follow-up study of ten children with unilateral vascular lesions. Again, no information was provided on reading status.

Hecaen (1976) reported follow-up data on the language status of 17 children (ages 3–19 years) who became aphasic following unilateral left brain injury. Spontaneous recovery was noted in a majority of the cases. However, most of the patients were reported to show long-term difficulties in writing and naming, although no data were presented in support of this claim.

Woods and Teuber (1978) reported follow-up data on 25 aphasic patients who ranged in age from 2 to 15 years at onset. The cases were mostly of vascular origin but included trauma cases as well. At follow-up four years later, 21 of the cases showed spontaneous recovery of speech. In each of these cases, the lesion occurred before 8 years of age. The four cases who remained aphasic ranged in age from 8 to 13 years at the time of the lesion. No information was provided on school achievement.

In a later study of 27 children with predominant vascular injury to the left hemisphere, Woods and Carey (1978) reported nearly complete *sparing* of speech in those children whose lesion onset was before the first birthday ($N = 11$) and in approximately half of those children whose onset was later ($N = 7$). In those children who became aphasic post-insult, all ($N = 7$) recovered speech if their lesion was before age 8 years. With respect to linguistic functions, deficits were observed only in those children who were initially or later aphasic. No information was reported on academic skills.

A final study by Van Dongen and Loonen (1979) reported aphasia status three years after brain injury in 14 right-handed children who ranged in age from 4 to 14 years at onset. Nine of the cases were trauma. Spontaneous recovery was observed in half of the cases. Unfortunately, it is unclear whether recovery was more associated with lesion onset (i.e. early) or type (i.e. unilateral). Also, no information was provided on follow-up academic status.

The preceding studies, in summary, revealed spontaneous recovery in the vast majority of children who developed aphasia after early left hemisphere insult. Recovery from aphasia ranged from a low of 50% (Van Dongen and Loonen, 1979) to a high of 100% (Basser, 1962; Byers and McLean, 1962). Most of the studies reported spontaneous recovery in approximately 75% of the cases. Spontaneous recovery was also shown to be unrelated to the presence of severity of hemiparesis, which is compatible with results presented in Table 1. A majority of the cases improved despite the residual presence of hemiparesis (Alajouanine and Lhermitte, 1965; Basser, 1962; Byers and McLean, 1962; Woods and Teuber, 1978; Woods and Carey, 1978). No studies disconfirmed this finding. It was also shown that when the left lesion occurred before the first birthday, the child was usually *spared* any aphasia onset or subsequent linguistic impairment (Woods and Carey, 1978). Unfortunately, many of the studies failed to document the age of lesion onset which, if after age 8 years, may have accounted for some of the infrequent cases of residual aphasia. In fact, when age of lesion onset was documented, no reports of residual aphasia were observed before ages 6–8 years. Although the recovery from childhood aphasia seems both dramatic and consistent in these reports, the effects on subsequent cognitive and academic skills remain unknown, especially reading. While some of the studies reported instances of cognitive and/or academic difficulties in these children (Alajouanine and Lhermitte, 1965; Hecaen, 1976; Byers and McLean, 1962; Woods and Carey, 1978), the reports were largely qualitative or anecdotal in nature. No study provided any objective data on achievement variables, including word recognition, reading comprehension, spelling or mathematics. However, when academic difficulties were reported, they may have been associated with cases of later lesion onset (i.e. after 6–8 years). More on this point later.

MECHANISMS OF SPARING AND RECOVERY

What brain mechanism(s) might account for the preceding instances of sparing or recovery of speech after early injury to the left cerebral hemisphere? The strongest evidence comes from studies that have investigated the nature of hemispheric speech dominance in patients (children and adults) with verified focal lesions, predominantly epileptogenic. The studies, which have recently been reviewed for another purpose (Satz *et al.*, 1988) represent the few known sources that report parametric data on lesion focus, lesion type, age of onset of damage, handedness and hemispheric speech dominance using different assessment methods (amobarbital, temporal lobectomy, dichotic listening). Two of the studies, both seminal investigations, have already been published. Rasmussen and Milner (1977) used the sodium amytal technique (Wada and Rasmussen, 1960) on a large series of left brain-impaired patients ($N = 396$) where hemispheric dominance was based on the presence of *speech arrest* following unilateral carotid injection. Penfield and Roberts (1959) assessed the presence or absence of aphasia in patients ($N = 246$) after left temporal lobectomy; patients were classified (our tabulations) as left dominant for speech if aphasic and atypical (i.e. right) if not aphasic following surgery. Strauss *et al.* (in preparation) used the sodium amytal technique on 53 consecutive left brain-impaired cases in which age of onset of damage was estimated in months. Orsini (1984) used a test–retest dichotic verbal listening task (free recall) on 40 consecutive children and adolescents with verified left focal seizures in which age of onset of damage was also estimated in months. A ratio score, $(R - L)/(R + L)$, was used to determine the ear advantage which was then used to infer the probable contralateral side of hemispheric speech dominance.

The results are presented in the following tables. Table 2 shows the percentage of left versus atypical speech cases by age of lesion onset (Early <

Table 2. Percentage speech type by lesion onset across studies

Onset	Left	Atypical
Early	107/262 (41%)	155/262 (56%)
Late	377/473 (80%)	96/473 (20%)

Table 3. Percentage MLH by speech type by lesion onset across studies

Onset	Left	Atypical
Early	35/107	127/155
	(33%)	(82%)
Late	102/377	43/96
	(27%)	(45%)

6 years; Late > 6 years). The data from each of these studies (left lesions only) have been retabulated and pooled for abbreviation and ease of presentation. Cases of bilateral and right-sided speech have also been pooled into a single group labeled atypical.

The results were remarkably consistent across studies. Early left focal brain injury (before age 6 years) is associated with a dramatic shift from the expected pattern of left hemisphere speech dominance observed in normal populations (approximately 96%) versus the present series ($107/262 = 41\%$, $\overline{X}^2 (1) = 186.0$, $p < 0.001$). Within the present series, the incidence of left hemisphere speech dominance was also much lower in the early versus late onset groups (41% versus 80%, $\overline{X}^2 (1) = 150.0$, $p < 0.001$).* Inspection of Table 2 shows that this difference was due to a dramatic increase in the percentage of atypical speech dominance in the early left brain injury cases (Early = 59%; Late = 20%; $\overline{X}^2 (1) = 124.5$, $p < 0.0001$).

A similar association was noted for handedness (Table 3). Early left brain injury was associated with a dramatic increase in the incidence of manifest left-handedness (MLH) observed in non-brain-injured populations (approximately 10%) versus the present series ($162/262 = 62\%$, $\overline{X}^2 (1) = 122.0$, $p < 0.0001$). Also, the incidence of MLH, after early brain injury, was almost threefold higher in the atypical speech dominant group (left = 33%, atypical = 82%, $\overline{X}^2 (1) = 84.5$, $p < 0.0001$), suggesting that the interhemispheric shift in speech was associated with a corresponding shift or alteration in hand preference. However, the association is by no means invariant. There were cases of both unimodal (speech only) and bimodal (speech and hand) transfer. Table 4 presents data on the incidence and proportion of early onset cases for each type of *interhemispheric transfer*.

Interhemispheric Reorganization: Unimodal versus Bimodal Shift

Inspection of Table 4 shows that the incidence of bimodal transfer, while high across studies (68% versus 32%), was significantly more often associated with

*The percentage of left dominant speech (80%) in the late onset group is lower than the 96% estimate for normal populations because of the inclusion of left-handed subjects.

Table 4. Effects of age of onset on type and incidence of interhemispheric reorganization

Study	Speech only (unimodal)				Speech and hand (bimodal)			
	N	(%)	N Early	(%)	N	(%)	N Early	(%)
1	10	(50)	6	(60)	10	(50)	9	(90)
2	14	(14)	8	(57)	102	(88)	66	(65)
3	3	(23)	2	(67)	10	(77)	9	(90)
4	54	(53)	12	(22)	48	(47)	43	(90)
Total	81	(32)	28	(35)	170	(68)	127	(75)

early onset of damage (bimodal = 75% (127/170) versus unimodal = 35% (28/81), $\bar{X}^2$ (1) = 37.4, $p < 0.000$). In fact, the incidence of early onset of damage was higher in each of the four studies. When age of damage onset was reported in months (Strauss *et al.*, in preparation; Orsini, 1984), the bimodal group showed a much earlier onset (bimodal = 22.75 months versus unimodal = 59.54 months, t (31) = 1.99, $p < 0.05$) as well as a lower incident of bilateral speech (bimodal = 10% (1/10) versus unimodal = 60% (6/10), Fisher exact test, $p = 0.058$).

Inter- versus Intrahemispheric Organization

Table 5 presents the percentage of early onset of damage and MLH cases associated with each type of hemispheric speech organization (intra- and interhemispheric) across studies. Inspection of this table reveals a substantially higher incidence (in each study) of both early onset of damage and MLH in cases of interhemispheric speech reorganization (Early onset = 62% (170/ 251) versus 28% (137/484), X^2 (1) = 105.6, $p < 0.0001$). In fact, the rela-

Table 5. Lesion age and handedness (MLH) by type of hemispheric speech organization

Study	Intra					Inter				
	N	Early	(%)	MLH	(%)	N	Early	(%)	MLH	(%)
1	33	16	(49)	2	(0.06)	20	15	(75)	10	(50)
2	280	60	(21)	112	(40)	116	74	(64)	102	(88)
3	27	15	(56)	4	(15)	13	11	(85)	10	(77)
4	144	16	(13)	19	(13)	102	55	(54)	48	(47)
Total	484	107	(22)	137	(28)	251	155	(62)	170	(68)

tionship is robust in terms of frequency, magnitude and consistency across studies for both variables. When age of onset of damage was reported in months (Strauss *et al.*, in preparation; Orsini, 1984), the interhemispheric group showed a much earlier onset (37.2 months (3.1 years) versus 102.2 months (8.52 years), $t(1) = 3.25$, $p < 0.002$). Also, the incidence of MLH was substantially higher in cases of interhemispheric transfer (*intra* = 10% (6/60), *inter* = 61% (20/33), $X^2(1) = 27.1$, $p < 0.001$). In fact, the incidence of MLH was almost negligible in the intrahemispheric group.

What conclusions, if any, can be drawn from these results? The most striking finding is that the earlier the left hemisphere perturbation (i.e. before 12 months), the greater the likelihood of a bimodal interhemispheric reorganization including a shift in both speech and handedness. Lesions occurring between the ages of 12 and 72 months (6 years) are more likely to result in either a unimodal interhemispheric shift in speech, a bilateral or less complete form of hemispheric speech reorganization, or an intrahemispheric reorganization, primarily speech. In each of the latter three cases, the likelihood of a corresponding shift in handedness is lower than with lesions occurring before the first birthday, which are more likely to result in a bimodal hemispheric reorganization. It is hypothesized that this latter type of hemispheric reorganization probably accounts for instances of *sparing* following left hemisphere injury while the former modes of reorganization account for instances of *recovery* in speech. Unfortunately, it is unclear whether the rate and/or degree of recovery is related to the type of inter- or intrahemispheric reorganization. This question has yet to be tested empirically.

Although the sodium amytal studies provide the clearest evidence for an interhemispheric mode of speech reorganization, they provide only indirect evidence with respect to an intrahemispheric mode. It is primarily the data from Penfield and Roberts (1959) that address the latter issue. In fact, the seminal chapter by Roberts, which is seldom cited, provides the most direct evidence for an intrahemispheric mode of speech reorganization. The data (Table 6) have been retabulated by this author to illustrate the hypothesized effect. The table reports the presence or absence of an aphasia after left temporal lobectomy in an adult sample of non-aphasic patients with early ($<$ age 2 years) or later ($>$ age 2 years) occurring epileptogenic lesions of the left hemisphere. Inspection of this table shows that with later onset lesions ($>$ age 2 years) most of the patients (right- and left-handed) became aphasic after operation on the side of the lesion (approximately 75%). However, with early onset lesions, only 22% (16/71) of the adult patients became aphasic after surgical removal of brain tissue on the side of the old epileptogenic lesion (i.e. left). The onset of aphasia in these cases strongly suggests that speech reorganization had been mediated by adjacent structures in the same hemisphere that were activated after the initial brain perturbation. We have recently hypothesized (Satz and Strauss, in press) that these structures, i.e.

Table 6. Aphasia onset after left lobectomy by age of lesion and handedness

	Early (<age 2 years)				Late (>age 2 years)		
Hand	N	No. aphasic	%	Hand	N	No. aphasic	%
Right	22	10	0.46	Right	157	115	0.73
Left	49	6	0.12	Left	18	13	0.72

Penfield and Roberts (1959).

posterior association cortex, represent equipotential substrates that were not functionally committed at the time of the initial perturbation. Similar viewpoints have also been expressed by Hacaen *et al.* (1984).

Table 6 also presents data indirectly on the presence of an interhemispheric mode of reorganization. In contrast to the later occurring lesions, most of the early left-sided lesion cases (12 right-handers, 43 left-handed = 55/71 = 78%) had no aphasia whatsoever after resection of brain tissue on the side of the original lesion. This *sparing* was most probably mediated by a bimodal interhemispheric shift in speech (right) and handedness (left). Consistent with the amobarbital data, this more dramatic type of interhemispheric reorganization is associated with a much earlier focal perturbation.

READING AND WRITING STATUS

What continues to remain unclear, however, is the status of other cognitive functions—namely, reading and writing. As noted earlier, few studies have addressed this topic systematically or empirically. Also the few reports available are largely anecdotal in nature, leaving ambiguous the status of lesion onset or side (i.e. left or bilateral). The only study available—which meets most of the criteria necessary for addressing this issue—was reported recently by Aram and Ekelman (1988). The authors report scholastic aptitude and academic achievement data for 32 children with carefully documented focal vascular lesions (20 left, 12 right) ranging from prenatal to childhood onset. In addition, the authors employed an individually matched control child for each of the lesion cases. The majority of lesions consisted of cerebral vascular accidents usually sustained after cardiac catheterization or surgery (11 lefts; 10 rights); six children with prenatal insults (4 lefts; 2 rights); four children with arteriovenous malformations (all left); and one child with a subcortical lesion. Table 7 presents the adjusted percentiles (by full-scale IQ) on the *scholastic aptitude* measures (reading, mathematics, written language and knowledge) and *academic achievement* measures (reading, mathematics,

Table 7. Mean percentile aptitude and achievement scores[a] by lesion side and controls

Test	Scores	Left	Control	Right	Control
Apt.	Reading	61.9	66.9	59.7	59.3
	Maths	68.1[a]	82.5	60.5[a]	76.7
	W. lang.	70.9	79.0	60.7	73.2
	Knowledge	70.6	75.5	62.6	73.2
Ach.	Reading	55.3	58.7	52.9	57.1
	Maths	65.8	68.9	45.7	60.2
	W. lang.	62.6	72.5	53.3[a]	70.3

[a]Adjusted by full-scale IQ.

written language) for the two lesion and control groups. The aptitude and achievement clusters were assessed by subtest from the Woodcock and Johnson Psychoeducational Battery (1977). For brevity, the table excludes data on the cognitive cluster (verbal, reasoning, perceptual speed and memory).

Inspection of Table 7 reveals only three instances (3/14) in which the lesioned group was lower than the matched control. Two of the instances involved mathematical aptitude (one with left lesions, the other with right lesions) and the other involved written language on achievement (right lesion group). All other comparisons were non-significant. In fact, inspection of the percentile scores reveals relatively high scores for both lesion and control groups on the scholastic aptitude and academic achievement measures. These percentile levels clearly contradict any overall evidence of a major reading or learning disability in either lesioned group. However, Aram and Ekelman (1988) correctly noted that the relatively high performance scores tended to mask instances of academic difficulty in some of the unilateral cases. With respect to grade repetition, four of the left (20%) and four of the right lesion group (33%) had been held back. Also, with respect to special class placement, six of the left (30%) and four of the right lesion group (33%) were receiving remedial help. However, these difficulties, while infrequent, were not related to lesion side.

Although these findings are based on a single report, no matter how meritorious, they should be replicated. At the same time, it should be recognized that the lesions sustained by these children, while unilateral, were quite severe, and predominantly of vascular etiology. Yet, they failed to produce any striking evidence of reading or learning failure. Furthermore, as a group, neither the left- nor right-lesioned children showed formal signs of a developmental dyslexia. Why? The most reasonable explanation, and one consistent with the previous section on speech and language, is that the onset of the damage in most of Aram and Ekelman's cases (27/32 = 85%) was before age 8 years. In fact, the frequency of late onset of damage was slightly higher in their left lesioned group (25% versus 0%) which, if anything, would tend to bias the effect in favor of traditional views of developmental dyslexia—namely, a putative left hemisphere substrate.

Is there any clinical evidence that an acquired *early* left hemisphere lesion can produce a major reading or learning disability? A recent study by Levine *et al.* (1981) provides one of the few reports on this question. The authors described the case of a 33-year-old right-handed man who had no family history of reading, speech or spelling disorder and whose development was normal until age 5 years 8 months, when he had an abrupt onset of symptoms including nocturnal spells of screaming, pallor and stiffening of the arms. At age 6 years 1 month he had his first seizure followed by bilateral retinal hemorrhages and increasing confusion. Ventriculography revealed a mass in the left temporal lobe which, after frontotemporal craniotomy, disclosed a large hemorrhage which was then resected. He returned to school but was unable to learn to read or write and was referred to special classes. At age 7 years 8 months, EEG revealed an epileptogenic focus in the left temporal lobe anterior to the original cortical scar. Following left anterior lobectomy, the patient became *aphasic* but *recovered* within three months. However, he was never able to make any academic progress, primarily in reading, despite several years of remedial intervention. Interestingly, at age 17, while asymptomatic, an amobarbitol test of the right carotid artery was conducted. While producing a dense left hemiplegia, the test revealed no arrest of speech, suggesting that his recovery from aphasia was mediated by an intrahemispheric mode of reorganization, probably adjacent to the two original lesions. As noted earlier in this chapter, this mode of reorganization, primarily unimodal, is more often associated with a later childhood onset lesion (i.e. ages 4–6 years). In fact, the patient remained right-handed despite two lesions in the critical speech/hand zones of the left hemisphere. This finding further strengthens the importance of time of lesion onset (i.e. before age 1 year) in inducing a more complete and bimodal form of hemispheric reorganization.

Theoretical Clue

Although the later onset of lesions (ages 6/1 and 7/8) probably account for the occurrence of a less complete form of hemispheric reorganization, as well as speech recovery, one must ask why the patient never managed to learn to read or write. The report indicates that the patient's right hemisphere was intact and therefore capable of taking over speech and language functions. However, an intrahemispheric mode of reorganization occurred. The answer probably lies in the later onset of the initial lesion (approximately 6 years) followed relatively soon by the second lesion (age 7 years 8 months) which may have further compromised the degree of intrahemispheric reorganization, especially the acquisition of a new and later developing skill—namely, reading. Furthermore, the child's seizure disorder and multiple symptoms after the initial lesion probably interfered with or delayed the acquisition of reading prior to the onset of the second lesion which occurred perilously close to the *critical period* for recovery. As noted earlier, this period generally marks the onset of more permanent sequelae in speech and language functions following injury to the left cerebral hemisphere. It is also the period (approximately 8 years) during which the adult pattern of acquired aphasia—and alexia—are more likely to be observed (Benson and Geschwind, 1969).

If early focal insult to the left hemisphere (before age 6–8 years) leads to relative sparing and/or recovery of speech, language and reading processes, and that similar lesions after this critical period do not, then what neural substrate, if any, might account for the relatively severe and permanent form of developmental or congenital dyslexia? The answer most probably involves some insult to both cerebral hemispheres, either prenatally or during early postnatal life when the nervous system is still immature and undergoing major morphogenesis. Despite the plasticity of the nervous system during this period, the presence of a bilateral lesion or neurodevelopmental anomaly prevents the establishment of a hemispheric reorganization that would permit some form of sparing or recovery of speech, language or reading processes. It is now commonly accepted that developmental or congenital *aphasia* is caused by a bilateral lesion, primarily affecting the temporal lobes, either prenatally or during early postnatal life (Sarno, 1981; Kinsbourne and Hiscock, 1977; Dennis and Whitaker, 1977; Witelson, 1977). Unfortunately, the traditional claim, as well as appeal, for a left hemisphere substrate in developmental dyslexia has remained so dominant that it has probably dampened inquiry into alternative etiological explanations.*

Is there any evidence to support the presence of a bilateral hemispheric substrate in developmental dyslexia? Interestingly, the strongest support comes from the pioneering post-mortem cytoarchitectonic studies in Boston by Galaburda, Geschwind and associates (Galaburda, 1986; Galaburda and Edelberg, 1982; Galaburda and Kemper, 1979; Galaburda et al., 1985a,b). The particular data I wish to focus on concern the presence of structural anomalies of cell migration (heterotopias) and organization (dysplasias) in the cerebral hemispheres of the first four autopsied cases of adult dyslexics reported by Galaburda et al. (1985a). Although the frequency of anomalies clearly favored the left hemisphere (approximately 3:1), there were striking anomalies in the right hemisphere in each of the cases. In fact, the areas of

---

*History records numerous examples of document theories or diagnoses which during their time commanded such uncritical acceptance that they became hypostasized. Hypostasis derives from a deeply theological term implying the essence as opposed to what is attributed.

maximum involvement included the *bilateral* frontal cortex and the left temporal cortex. Note also that Drake (1968) reported the presence of bilateral temporal lobe anomalies in the first autopsied case of an adult dyslexic. It should also be mentioned that additional cases of bilateral asymmetric anomalies have been reported by Galaburda (1987). Although Galaburda's recent efforts (1987; Galaburda *et al.*, 1985a,b) have focused on the atypical presence of symmetry in the planum temporale of his autopsied dyslexic brains, the fact remains that heterotopias and dysplasias have been observed in both cerebral hemispheres. It is also worth noting that a recent positron emission tomography (PET) study examining rCMRGLu in dyslexics during reading revealed an active participation of the insular cortex bilaterally (Gross-Glenn *et al.*, 1986). Also, two recent regional cerebral blood flow (rCBF) studies by Hynd *et al.* (1987a,b) have revealed an active participation of the right central and posterior cortex (as well as the left) during the reading of narrative text. Some evidence of bilateral though asymmetric indices in event-related potentials has also been suggested in dyslexics with attention deficit disorders (Conners, 1987; Harter, 1987). Additional, though indirect, support for a putative bilateral substrate in dyslexia comes from the autopsied cases of Geschwind and colleagues. To date, only one left-handed subject (out of approximately 10) has been identified. As discussed earlier, the expression of left-handedness is far less frequent in cases of bilateral insult. A left-sided focus is the primary trigger for pathological left-handedness (Satz *et al.*, 1988). Also, epidemiological surveys have consistently failed to report an association between left-handedness and dyslexia (Ammett, 1985). Although clinic studies (which are often subject to subject ascertainment bias) have occasionally reported an association (Ammett, 1985), the strength of the relationship across studies is modest at best (Satz and Fletcher, 1987).

The preceding studies, in sum, provide strong evidence for a bilateral hemispheric substrate in at least a subset, if not the majority, of congenital dyslexics. Although the initial autopsied cases have revealed more extensive left hemisphere anomalies—which have been cited as evidence for the traditional unilateral brain substrate (Geschwind, 1984; Geschwind and Behan, 1982)—the fact remains that both cerebral hemispheres have been involved. The present reformulation provides a more heuristic framework for explaining much of the heterogeneity, if not diagnostic subtypes, that have been observed in reading-disabled children (Bakker, 1979; Satz and Morris, 1981; Rourke, 1985; Lyon, 1985). In cases of predominant left hemisphere anomaly one might expect to find the characteristic language disorder subtype that has been observed in at least 50–60% of dyslexic children (Satz and Morris, 1981; Rourke, 1985; Lyon and Watson, 1981; Doehring, 1978). This subtype is also compatible with Bakker's (1979, 1984) P-type which is characterized by over-reliance on perceptual strategies because of the delay or impairment in linguistic processing. In case of predominant right hemisphere anomaly, one might expect to find the characteristic visuo-spatial disorder subtype that has been observed in approximately 10–30% of dyslexic children (Satz and Morris, 1981; Lyon, 1985; Rourke, 1985). This subtype is compatible with Bakker's (1979, 1984) L-type which is characterized by over-reliance on left hemisphere strategies because of the delay or impairment in abstracting perceptual features from script. In cases of predominant bifrontal lobe anomaly, as reported in some of the Galaburda cases (Galaburda *et al.*, 1985a,b), one might expect to find some of the attentional and disinhibition difficulties observed in unknown subsets of dyslexic children with attention deficit disorder (ADD) (Conners, 1987; Harter, 1987).

What remains unknown is the etiological mechanism responsible for the neuropathological substrate. Are we talking about a structural brain lesion or some type of developmental brain anomaly that affects cell migration and/or organization early in prenatal life? In the former case, the lesion could occur prenatally or in early postnatal life as, for example, in some of Aram and Ekelman's (1988) cerebral vascular cases. In the latter case, the brain anomaly is most probably prenatal. Geschwind (1985) concluded that such cases (i.e. heterotopias and dysplasias), presumably unilateral in origin, produced more severe and long-term cognitive effects than did focal lesions occurring during early postnatal life. This conclusion, however, is at variance with the earlier reports of Taylor and Ounsted (1972), who reported similar unilateral anomalies (i.e. alien tissue) in the brains of epileptics, many of whom were free of major cognitive dysfunction. Also, much of the data on sparing or recovery of speech and language functions after early focal brain injury (prenatal and postnatal), which was discussed in this chapter, were based on patients with epilepsy. Finally, the dorsolateral prefrontal cortex lesions of *fetal* rhesus monkeys, by Goldman and Galkin (1978), revealed a dramatic *sparing* of the delayed response and alternation tasks that are known to be differentially affected by early postnatal or adult lesions. One of the fetuses, which was operated on between days 102 and 119 of embryonic life, was then replaced in the womb until delivered by Caesarian section at approximately 159 days of gestation. According to the authors, this monkey showed absolutely no behavioral deficits on any of the tasks and may even have performed somewhat better than normal subjects on some of them. Why? Post-mortem anatomical analyses revealed unusual (ectopic) growth of new gyri and sulci in the area adjacent to the lesion and also in regions of the cortex far removed from the initial site of injury. In reviewing this interesting case, Finger and Stein (1982) noted also that there was no retrograde degeneration in the mediodorsal nucleus of the thalamus, which is the primary projection area to the prefrontal cortex. Goldman and Galkin (1978) suggested that the behavioral sparing in learning was probably due to the proliferation of collateral branches that may have established synaptic contacts elsewhere in the cortex, apparently in association cortex which was able to subserve the acquisition and maintenance of these cognitive skills.

With respect to developmental dyslexia, it is likely that the disorder can spring from a structural lesion or brain anomaly that occurs either pre- or postnatally, as long as the neural substrate is bilateral. If bilateral asymmetric, the subtype of dyslexia may vary as noted above. Lesions occurring after the critical period for speech and language recovery—probably between ages 6 and 8 years—need not be bilateral. At such time, a unilateral lesion to the left hemisphere can produce the developmental equivalent—namely, an acquired alexia.

It is of course possible that the majority of cases of developmental dyslexia spring from prenatal microscopic cellular anomalies. This is the position advanced by Geschwind and associates (Geschwind and Behan, 1982; Geschwind and Galaburda, 1986; Galaburda et al., 1985a,b) and it is yet to be disconfirmed. The role of testosterone, which these authors cite as the trigger mechanism, is also an interesting and heuristic hypothesis that deserves further investigation. What remains unclear is the role of other putative trigger mechanisms (e.g. genetic) in the etiology of this baffling childhood disorder. It is hoped that the present reformulation helps to stimulate alternative hypotheses that can be integrated within the context of other theoretical positions.

ACKNOWLEDGEMENTS

Much of the content and scope of this chapter took shape while the author was on sabbatical at the University of Jyvaskyla, Finland, in 1986. Special gratitude is expressed to Professor Heikki Lyytinen (Finland) and to Professors David Galin and Marcel Kinsbourne (USA) for their helpful comments and critique. This chapter was an invited presentation at the Third World Congress of Dyslexia, Crete, Greece, June 1987.

REFERENCES

Alajouanine, T., and Lhermitte, F. (1965). Acquired aphasia in children. *Brain*, **88**, 653–662.

Ammett, M. (ed.) (1985). *Left, Right, Hand and Brain: The Right Shift Theory*. London: Lawrence Erlbaum.

Aram, D. M., and Ekelman, B. L. (1988). Scholastic aptitude and achievement among children with unilateral brain lesions. *Journal of Clinical and Experimental Neuropsychologia*, **26**, 903–916.

Bakker, D. (1979). Hemispheric differences and reading strategies: Two dyslexias? *Bulletin of the Orton Society*, **29**, 84–100.

Bakker, D. (1984). The brain as a dependent variable. *Journal of Clinical Neuropsychology*, **6**, 1–16.

Basser, L. S. (1962). Hemiplegia of early onset and the faculty of speech with special reference to the effects of hemispherectomy. *Brain*, **85**, 427–460.

Benson, D. F. (1972). Language disturbances of childhood. *Clinical Proceedings of the Children's Hospital of Washington*, **28**, 93–100.

Benson, D. F., and Geschwind, N. (1969). The alexias. In P. J. Vinken and G. W. Bruyn (eds), *Handbook of Clinical Neurology*, Vol. 4. Amsterdam: North-Holland.

Bernhardt M. (1885). Ueber die spastiche cerebral paralyse in Kindesalter. (Hemiplegia spastica infantilis), Nebst einem Excurse uber: 'Aphasie bei Kindern'. *Archiv für Pathologische Anatomie und Physiologie und für Klinische Medizin*, **102**, 26–80.

Byers, R. K., and McLean, W. (1962). Etiology and course of certain hemiplegias with aphasia in childhood. *Pediatrics*, **29**, 376–383.

Clarus, A. (1874). Uber Aphasie bei Kindern. *Jahresb. Kinderheilkd.*, **7**, 369–400.

Coltheart, M., Patterson, K., and Marshall, J. C. (eds) (1980). *Deep Dyslexia*. London: Routledge & Kegan Paul.

Conners, K. (1987). Dyslexia and the neurophysiology of attention. *Third World Congress on Dyslexia*, Crete, Greece.

Dejerine, J. (1892). Contribution à l'étude anatomopathologique et clinique des différentes variétés de céicité verbale. *Mem. Soc. Biol.*, **4**, 61.

Dennis, M. (1980). Strokes in childhood I: Communicative intent, expression, and comprehension after left hemisphere arteriopathy in a right-sided nine year old. In R. W. Reiber (ed.), *Language Development and Aphasia in Children*. New York: Academic Press.

Dennis, M., and Kohn, B. (1975). Comprehension of syntax in infantile hemiplegics after cerebral hemidecortication: Left hemisphere superiority. *Brain and Language*, **2**, 472–482.

Dennis, M., and Whitaker, H. (1976). Language acquisition following hemidecortication: Linguistic superiority of the left over the right hemisphere. *Brain and Language*, **3**, 404–433.

Dennis, M., and Whitaker, H. (1977). Hemispheric equipotentiality and language acquisition. In S. J. Segalowitz and F. A. Gruber (eds), *Language Development and Neurological Theory*. New York: Academic Press.

Doehring, D. G. (1978). The tangled web of behavioral research on developmental dyslexia. In A. L. Benton and D. Pearl (eds), *Dyslexia: An Appraisal of Current Knowledge*. New York: Oxford University Press.

Drake, W. E. (1968). Clinical and pathological findings in a child with a developmental learning disability. *Journal of Learning Disabilities*, **1**, 486–502.

Finger, S., and Stein, D. G. (1982). *Brain Damage and Recovery: Research and Clinical Perspectives*. New York: Academic Press.

Freud, S. (1968). *Infantile Cerebral Paralysis* (trans. L. A. Russin). Coral Gables: University of Miami Press (originally published 1897).

Galaburda, A. M. (1986, November). *Human Studies on the Anatomy of Dyslexia*. Paper presented at the Annual Conference of the Orton Dyslexia Society, Philadelphia.

Galaburda, A. M. (1987). Morphological advances in dyslexia. *Conference on Child's Learning Disabilities and Brain Function*. Stavanger, Norway.

Galaburda, A. M., and Eidelberg, P. (1982). Symmetry and asymmetry in the human posterior thalamus. II. Thalamic lesions in a case of developmental dyslexia. *Archives of Neurology*, **39**, 333–336.

Galaburda, A. M., and Kemper, T. L. (1979). Cytoarchitectonic abnormalities in developmental dyslexia: A case study. *Annals of Neurology*, **6**, 94–100.

Galaburda, A. M., Sherman, G. F., Rosen, G. D., Aboitiz, F., and Geschwind, N. (1985a). Developmental dyslexia: Four consecutive patients with cortical anomalies. *Annals of Neurology*, **18**, 222–233.

Galaburda, A. M., Signoret, J. C., and Ronthal, M. (1985b). Left posterior angiomatous anomaly and developmental dyslexia: Report of five cases. *Neurology*, **35** (suppl.), 198.

Geschwind, N. (1974). Disorders of higher cortical functions in children. In N. Geschwind (ed.), *Selected Papers on Language and the Brain*. Dordrecht: Reidel.

Geschwind, N. (1984). Cerebral dominance in biological perspective. *Neuropsychologia*, **22**, 675–683.

Geschwind, N. (1985). The biology of dyslexia: The unfinished manuscript. In D. G. Gray and J. F. Kavanagh (eds), *Biobehavioral Measures of Dyslexia*. Parkton, MD: York Press.

Geschwind, N., and Behan, P. O. (1982). Left handedness: Association with immune disease, migraine, and developmental learning disorders. *Proceedings of the National Academy of Sciences*, **79**, 5097–5100.

Geschwind, N., and Galaburda, A. M. (1985a). Cerebral lateralization: Biological mechanisms, associations, and pathology. I. A hypothesis and a program for research. *Archives of Neurology*, **42**, 428–459.

Geschwind, N., and Galaburda, A. M. (1985b). Cerebral lateralization: Biological mechanisms, associations and pathology. II. A hypothesis and a program for research. *Archives of Neurology*, **42**, 521–552.

Goldman, P., and Galkin, T. W. (1978). Prenatal removal of frontal association cortex in the fetal rhesus monkey: Anatomical and functional consequences in postnatal life. *Brain Research*, **152**, 451–485.

Gross-Glenn, K., Duara, R., Yoshii, F., Barker, W. W., Chang, J. Y., Apicella, A., Boothe, T., and Lubs, H. A. (1986). PET-scan studies during reading in dyslexic and non-dyslexic adults. *Neuroscience* (abstract).

Guttman, E. (1942). Aphasia in children. *Brain*, **65**, 205–219.

Harter, R. M. (1987). Distinct even-related potential indicants of reading disability and attention deficit disorder. *Third World Congress on Dyslexia*, Crete, Greece.

Hecaen, H. (1976). Acquired aphasia in children and the autogenesis of hemispheric functional specialization. *Brain and Language*, **3**, 114–134.

Hecaen, H., Perenin, M. T., and Jeannerod, M. (1984). The effects of cortical lesions in children: Language and visual functions. In C. R. Almli and S. Finger (eds), *Behavioral Biology of Early Brain Damage*, pp. 277–298. New York: Academic Press.

Hinshelwood, J. (1900). Congenital word-blindness. *Lancet*, **1**, 1506–1508.

Hynd, G. W., Hynd, C. R., Sullivan, H. G., and Kingsbury, T., Jr (1987a). Regional cerebral blood flow (rCBF) in developmental dyslexia: Activation during reading in a surface and deep dyslexic. *Journal of Learning Disabilities*, **20**, 294–300.

Hynd, G. W., Rosenthal, B. L., and Huettner, M. I. S. (1987b). *Regional Cerebral Blood Flow (rCBF) in Normal Readers: Bilateral Activation with Narrative Text*. Manuscript submitted for publication.

Isaacson, R. L. (1975). The myth of recovery from early brain damage. In N. E. Ellis (ed.), *Aberrant Development in Infancy*. London: Wiley.

Kinsbourne, M., and Hiscock, M. (1977). Does cerebral dominance develop? In S. W. Segalowitz and F. A. Gruber (eds), *Language Development and Neurological Theory*. New York: Academic Press.

Kinsbourne, M., and Hiscock, M. (1981). Cerebral lateralization and cognitive development: Conceptual and methodological issues. In G. W. Hynd and J. E.

Obrzut (eds), *Neuropsychological Assessment and the School-age Child: Issues and Procedures*, pp. 125–166. New York: Grune & Stratton.

Lenneberg, E. (1967). *Biological Foundations of Language*. New York: Wiley.

Levine, D. N., Hier, D. B., and Calvanio, R. (1981). Acquired learning disability for reading after left temporal lobe damage in childhood. *Neurology*, **31**, 257–264.

Liberman, I. (1982). A language-oriented view of reading and its disabilities. In H. Myklebust (ed.), *Progress in Learning Disabilities*, Vol. 5, pp. 81–101. New York: Grune & Stratton.

Lyon, R. (1985). Educational validation studies of learning disability subtypes. In B. P. Rourke (ed.), *Neuropsychology of Learning Disabilities*. New York: Guilford Press.

Lyon, R., and Watson, B. (1981). Empirically derived subgroups of learning disabled readers: Diagnostic considerations. *Journal of Learning Disabilities*, **14**, 256–261.

Marshall, J. C., and Newcombe, F. (1981). Lexical access: A perspective from pathology. *Cognition*, **10**, 209–214.

Morgan, W. P. (1896). A case of congenital word-blindness. *British Medical Journal*, **2**, 1378.

Orsini, D. (1984). Early Brain Injury and Lateral Development. Doctoral dissertation, State University of New York, Stony Brook.

Penfield, W., and Roberts, L. (1959). *Speech and Brain Mechanisms*. Princeton, NJ: Princeton University Press.

Rasmussen, T., and Milner, B. (1977). The role of early left brain injury in determining lateralization of cerebral speech functions. *New York Academy of Science*, **299**, 355–379.

Rourke, B. (1985). *Neuropsychology of Learning Disabilities*. New York: Guilford Press.

St James-Roberts, I. (1981). A reinterpretation of hemispherectomy data without functional plasticity of the brain (Vol. 1): Intellectual function. *Brain and Language*, **13**, 31–53.

Sarno, M. T. (1981). *Acquired Aphasia*. New York: Academic Press.

Satz, P., and Bullard-Bates, C. (1981). Acquired aphasia in children. In M. T. Sarno (ed.), *Acquired Aphasia*, pp. 399–426. New York: Academic Press.

Satz, P., and Fletcher, J. M. (1987). Left-handedness and dyslexia: An old myth revisited. *Journal of Pediatric Psychology*, **12**, 291–298.

Satz, P., and Morris, R. (1981). Learning disability subtypes: A review. In F. J. Pirozzolo and M. C. Wittrock (eds), *Neuropsychological and Cognitive Processes in Reading*, pp. 109–141. New York: Academic Press.

Satz, P., and Strauss, E. (in press). The ontogeny of hemispheric specialization: Some old hypotheses revisited. *Brain and Language*.

Satz, P., Strauss, E., Wada, J., and Orsini, D. (1988). Some correlates of intra- and interhemispheric speech organization after left focal brain injury. *Neuropsychologia*, **26**, 345–350.

Smith, A. (1981). Principles underlying human brain functions in neuropsychological sequelae of different neuropathological processes. In S. Filskov and T. Ball (eds), *Handbook of Clinical Neuropsychology*. New York: Wiley.

Smith, A., and Sugar, C. (1975). Development of above normal language and intelligence 21 years after left hemispherectomy. *Neurology*, **25**, 813–818.

Strauss, E., Wada, J., and Satz, P. (in preparation). Cerebral speech dominance and handedness after early focal and diffuse brain injury.

Taylor, D., and Ounsted, E. (1972). The nature of gender differences explored through ontogenetic analyses of sex ratios in disease. Unpublished manuscript.

Torgesen, J. K. (1986). Learning disabilities theory: Its current state and future prospects. *Journal of Learning Disabilities*, **19**, 399–407.

Van Dongen, H. R., and Loonen, M. C. (1979). Neurological factors related to prognosis of acquired aphasia in childhood. In Y. Lebrun and R. Hoops (eds), *Recovery in Aphasics*. Amsterdam: Swetz & Zeitlenger.

Vellutino, F. R. (1987). Dyslexia. *Scientific American*, **256**, 34–41.

Wada, J., and Rasmussen, T. (1960). Intracarotid injection of sodium amytal for the lateralization of cerebral speech dominance. *Journal of Neurosurgery*, **17**, 266–282.

Waites, L. (1968). World Federation of Neurology: Research group on developmental dyslexia and world illiteracy. *Report of Proceedings*, **22**.

Witelson, S. (1977). Early hemisphere specialization and interhemispheric plasticity: An empirical and theoretical review. In S. J. Segalowitz and F. A Gruber (eds), *Language Development and Neurological Theory*. New York: Academic Press.

Woods, B. T., and Carey, S. (1978). Language deficits after apparent recovery from childhood aphasia. *Annals of Neurology*, **5**, 405–409.

Woods, B. T., and Teuber, H. L. (1978). Changing patterns of childhood aphasia. *Annals of Neurology*, **3**, 273–280.

Woodcock, R. W., and Johnson, M. D. (1977). *Woodcock–Johnson Psycho-Educational Battery*. Hingham, MA: Teaching Resources.

Address for correspondence:

Professor Paul Satz; Center for Health Sciences, UCLA School of Medicine, 760 Westwood Plaza, Los Angeles, California 90024, USA

2

Learning Disability Subtypes:
A Neuropsychological Perspective[*]

Byron P. Rourke
University of Windsor, Ontario, Canada

INTRODUCTION

Scientific investigation of learning disability subtypes emerged primarily from careful clinical observations of children who were assessed because they were thought to be experiencing perceptual and/or learning disabilities. Astute observers of learning-disabled children, such as Johnson and Myklebust (1967), noted that there are very clear differences in patterns of abilities and deficits exhibited by such children, and that specific developmental problems (e.g. learning to read) appeared to stem from these very different patterns of abilities and deficits. In other words, equally impaired levels of learning appeared to result from quite different etiologies of relative perceptual and cognitive strengths and weaknesses.

The search for subtypes of learning disability took on added importance when it was inferred that these potentially isolatable patterns of perceptual and cognitive strengths and weaknesses (that were thought to be responsible for learning difficulties) might be more or less amenable to different modes of intervention. Indeed, the 'subtype by treatment interaction' hypothesis—i.e. the notion that the tailoring of specific forms of treatment to the underlying abilities and deficits of learning-disabled children would be advantageous— was alive and well very early in the history of the learning disabilities field (e.g. Kirk and McCarthy, 1961). This constituted a second clinical issue that

---

*Much of the material presented in this chapter has appeared in other publications (Rourke, 1987, 1988a, 1988b, 1989). The chapter was cast along the lines suggested by the editor: that is, it was designed as an illustration of the manner in which our group approaches issues relating to the reliability and validity of learning disability subtypes from a neuropsychological perspective.

---

encouraged researchers to seek a determination of subtypal differences among such children. Indeed, many researchers and professionals in the field virtually *assumed* that the matching of intervention/treatment to the underlying strengths and weaknesses of the child who is experiencing outstanding difficulties in learning would be the most efficient and effective therapeutic course to follow.

OVERVIEW

In the presentation that follows, no attempt is made to review in detail the research efforts that have transpired with increasing intensity over the past 10–15 years to determine the reliability and validity of learning-disability subtypes. (The interested reader is referred to extensive reviews of several such programs in Rourke, 1985.) Rather, the aim is to emphasize a general framework within which neuropsychological research efforts have arisen and taken shape, and to illustrate and discuss the conclusions arrived at on the basis of the approach that has been used extensively in our laboratory. It is hoped that this framework and the description of a particular neuropsychological approach to the determination of learning disability subtypes will serve to illustrate the importance of this research enterprise, both with respect to our understanding of learning disabilities and with respect to our attempts to intervene successfully with children so afflicted.

However, before beginning this discussion, it would be well to review the principal historical alternative—viz., an essentially piecemeal, atheoretical or narrow theoretical emphasis that is possibly best characterized as a 'comparative-populations' approach (described by Applebee, 1971)—to this particular research, model-building and clinical tack.

LEARNING DISABILITIES AS A HOMOGENEOUS ENTITY

As can be gleaned from any systematic review of the learning-disabilities literature prior to the late 1970s (e.g. Benton, 1975; Rourke, 1978a), the almost exclusive approach of North American and European researchers to this field was one that involved comparisons of supposedly learning-disabled youngsters with age- and otherwise-matched 'normal' controls. Researchers who used this approach were interested in determining *the* deficit(s) that characterize the neuropsychological ability structure of learning-disabled youngsters (Doehring, 1978). This approach to the determination of the neuropsychological abilities and deficits of learning-disabled children assumed, implicitly or explicitly, that such children formed a univocal diagnostic entity. This approach was also characterized by rather narrow samplings of areas of human performance that were thought to be related to the learning (primarily reading) disability. There are a host of other problems with such an approach to research in this field, some of which are addressed below.

Obvious exceptions to this research strategy were mirrored in the studies conducted by Johnson and Myklebust (1967) and later by Mattis *et al.* (1975). These investigators employed an essentially 'clinical' approach to the identification of learning-disability subtypes. This rather different thrust to research, involving as it did an emphasis on subtypal patterns, was accompanied in the late 1970s by that of investigators who sought to isolate reliable subtypes of learning-disabled children through the use of statistical algorithms such as Q-type factor analysis and cluster analysis (e.g. Doehring and Hoshko, 1977; Doehring *et al.*, 1979; Fisk and Rourke, 1979; Petrauskas and Rourke, 1979)—a mode of approach to this area of research that is well under way in this decade (e.g. Del Dotto and Rourke, 1985; Fisk and Rourke, 1983; Joschko and Rourke, 1985; Morris *et al.*, 1981). There are indications that this type of systematic search for reliable subtypes of learning-disabled children has begun to have a profoundly positive effect on investigative efforts in this area. Furthermore, systematic attempts at establishing the concurrent, predictive and construct validity of such subtypes have been proceeding apace (e.g. Fletcher, 1985; Lyon, 1985).

However, there are many who still persist in comparative-populations or contrasting-groups methodology, with all of the limitations that such methodology involves, not only with respect to research findings but also with respect to model-building and theory development. This mode of approach to research relating to the supposed cognitive and other correlates of children with learning disabilities has not been terribly contributory: for example, the results of many studies are trivial, contradictory to one another and not supported in replication attempts; there is little to suggest that the factors identified as 'characteristic' of learning-disabled children in these studies are related to one another in any meaningful fashion (Rourke, 1985). In sum, the evidence regarding cognitive, mnestic and other forms of functioning that emerges from the contrasting-groups approach to research is, at best, equivocal. A coherent and meaningful pattern of neuropsychological characteristics of children with learning disabilities does not emerge from this literature. I would maintain that this is the case because such a univocal pattern does not obtain (more on this point below).

In any event, there would appear to be at least three major reasons why the results of these studies have not been very contributory to the testing of important hypotheses relating to the neuropsychological integrity of learning-disabled youngsters. These, together with some brief comments on alternative approaches, are as follows.

Lack of a Conceptual Model

In the vast majority of studies that can be characterized in terms of the comparative-populations or contrasting-groups rubric, there is an obvious absence of a comprehensive conceptual model that could be employed to elucidate the skills involved in perception and learning and that are deficient in learning-disabled children. Most models that have been developed in this genre of research bear the marks of either *post hoc* theorizing about a very limited spectrum of skills or abilities or 'pet' theories derived from what are characterized as more 'general' models of learning, memory and cognition. Research that is cast in terms of these very limited, narrow-band models and, *a fortiori*, research that is essentially atheoretical in nature is virtually certain to yield a less than comprehensive explanation of learning disabilities.

As an example of an alternative to this conceptually limited approach, a componential analysis of academic and other types of learning should sensitize the researcher to the possibility that, whereas some subtypes of learning-disabled children may experience learning problems because of deficiencies in certain perceptual, cognitive or behavioral skills, others may manifest such problems as a more direct result of attitudinal/motivational or vastly different perceptual, cognitive or behavioral difficulties. It should also be clear that different patterns of perceptual, cognitive and behavioral skills and abilities may encourage different types or degrees of learning difficulties. Recently, theories that emphasize this type of comprehensive, componential approach to the design of developmental neuropsychological explanatory models in this area have emerged (e.g. Fletcher and Taylor, 1984; Rourke, 1982, 1987, 1988b, 1989).

Definition of Learning Disabilities

There has been no consistent formulation of the criteria for learning disabilities in the contrasting-groups genre of study. For example, most studies of this ilk employ vaguely defined or even undefined groups, and others use the ratings of teachers and other school personnel that remain otherwise unspecified. Some even employ the guidelines of a particular political jurisdiction to define learning disabilities! It is obvious that this lack of clarity and consistency has had a negative impact on the generalizability of such findings.

Clear, consensually validatable definitions are a crying need in this area of investigation. In this connection, it would seem patently obvious that the very definitions themselves should be a *result* of sophisticated subtype analysis rather than the starting point of such inquiry (Morris and Fletcher, 1988; Rourke, 1983a,b, 1985; Rourke and Gates, 1981).

Developmental Considerations

Part and parcel of the contrasting-groups approach to the study of learning-disabled youngsters is a gross insensitivity to age differences and developmental considerations. Several studies offer support for the notion that the nature and patterning of the skill and ability deficits of (some subtypes of) learning-disabled children vary with age (e.g. Fisk and Rourke, 1979; Fletcher and Satz, 1980; McKinney et al., 1985; Morris et al., 1986; Ozols and Rourke, 1988; Rourke et al., 1973). Since it would seem reasonable to infer that the neuropsychological functioning of (some subtypes of) learning-disabled children varies as a function of age (considered as one index of developmental change), the aforementioned inconsistencies in contrasting-groups research results could reflect differences in the ages of the subjects employed. Be that as it may, it is abundantly clear that more cross-sectional and longitudinal studies are necessary in order to clarify the nature of those developmental changes that appear to take place in some learning-disabled children. It is also clear that attention to the issues involved in the study of developmental changes in learning-disabled children is an almost direct function of the sophistication in subtype analysis exhibited by the neuropsychological investigators in this area. Unfortunately, those who pay little or no attention to subtype analysis also demonstrate little or no regard for the changes in the neuropsychological ability structures of learning-disabled children that may transpire during the course of development.

Examples of some of the research carried out in our laboratory that has attempted to grapple with these three sets of difficulties are presented below. However, before presenting these results, it is necessary to place this program of research within the context of a general approach to the neuropsychological investigation of central processing abilities and deficits in learning-disabled and frankly brain-damaged youngsters.

A SYSTEMATIC DEVELOPMENTAL NEUROPSYCHOLOGICAL APPROACH TO THE STUDY OF LEARNING DISABILITIES

It is unfortunate that the utilization of a neuropsychological framework for the investigation of learning disabilities in children has so often been misinterpreted as reflecting an emphasis on static, intractable (and, therefore, limited) notions of the effects of brain impairment on behavior. Indeed, although specific statements to the contrary have been made on many occasions (e.g.

Rourke, 1975, 1978b), many otherwise competent researchers and clinicians persist in the notion that such an approach *assumes* that brain damage, disorder or dysfunction lies at the basis of learning disabilities. Nothing could be further from the truth, since the thrust of much work in this area (see Benton, 1975; Rourke, 1978a; Taylor, 1983) has been to *demonstrate* whether and to what extent such might be the case.

Be that as it may, the emphasis that I and my colleagues have brought to this enterprise is one that attempts to integrate dimensions of individual and social development on the one hand with relevant central processing features on the other—all of this in order to fashion a useful model with which to study crucial aspects of perceptual, cognitive and other dimensions of development. That models and explanatory concepts developed with this aim in mind (e.g. Rourke, 1976, 1982, 1983b, 1987, 1988b, 1989) contain explanations that are thought to apply both to some types of frankly brain-damaged and learning-disabled children as well as to some aspects of normal human development should come as no surprise, since maximum generalizability is one goal of any scientific model or theory. Specifically, with respect to the learning-disabled child, the aspects of these concepts and models that are most relevant are those that have to do with proposed linkages between patterns of central processing abilities and deficits that may predispose a youngster to predictably different patterns of social as well as academic learning disabilities. In addition, these models are designed to encompass developmental change and outcome in patterns of learning and behavioral responsivity.

In the neuropsychology of learning disabilities, the important relationship to bear in mind is that between *patterns* of performance and a *model* of developmental brain–behavior relationships. This is not meant to imply something as trite as learning disabilities being the *result* of brain damage or dysfunction. Indeed, the illogical leap that such an implication (assumption) implies is only one of its shortcomings. More important is the fact that, even were such a cause–effect (brain damage/dysfunction–learning disabilities) relationship shown to be the case, it would carry few, if any, corollaries for (a) the understanding of developmental brain–behavior relationships or (b) their treatment.

This is not to say that brain–behavior relationships in the study of learning disabilities are not important. Rather, it is simply the case that we currently understand much more about developmental–neuro*psychological* performance interactions than we do about developmental–*neuro*psychological performance interactions. In other words, we are at much the same stage of theorizing about the latter interactions as was Donald Hebb at the time he composed his landmark monograph *The Organization of Behavior* (1949). Far from discouraging us from pursuing research and model-building in this area, the seminal heuristic influence of Hebb's work in general neuropsychology should serve to remind us that the patterns of interaction among brain, development and behavior, though sometimes exquisitely hypothesized, are still largely unexplored and must be the subject of rigorous scientific test (Taylor, 1983).

For these and other reasons, we chose to study developmental patterns of neuropsychological abilities and deficits within a context provided by the results of neuropsychological research relating to subtypes of learning-disabled children. One of the approaches that we have found to be particularly useful in this regard has involved the constitution of subtypes on the basis of patterns of reading (word-recognition), spelling and arithmetic skills (references below). Another rather heuristic approach has involved the study of the degree of phonetic accuracy of misspellings of learning-disabled youngsters (Sweeney and Rourke, 1978, 1985). The next section contains an example of what we think we have discovered as a result of the investigation of the neuropsychological implications of various patterns of academic achievement in learning-disabled youngsters.

PATTERNS OF READING, SPELLING AND ARITHMETIC ACHIEVEMENT

Since 1971, my colleagues and I have been investigating three subtypes of learning-disabled children. Children in Groups 1 and 2 are those who exhibit many relatively poor psycholinguistic (especially semantic–acoustic) skills in conjunction with very well-developed visual–spatial–organizational, tactile–perceptual, psychomotor and non-verbal problem-solving skills and abilities. Group 1 exhibits a pattern of uniformly deficient reading (word-recognition), spelling and mechanical/arithmetic skills; Group 2 exhibits very poor reading and spelling skills and significantly better, though still impaired, mechanical/arithmetic competence. The other group (Group 3) exhibits outstanding problems in visual–spatial–organizational, tactile–perceptual, psychomotor and non-verbal problem-solving skills, within a context of clear strengths in psycholinguistic skills such as rote verbal learning, regular phoneme–grapheme matching, amount of verbal output, and verbal classification. Group 3 children experience their major academic learning difficulties in mechanical arithmetic, while exhibiting advanced levels of word-recognition and spelling.

Group 1 is probably composed of several different subtypes of learning-disabled children (Petrauskas and Rourke, 1979), and will not be considered further in this presentation. Both of the other subtypes of learning-disabled children—especially the subtype (Group 3) that we have characterized as having a 'non-verbal learning disability' (Myklebust, 1975)—have been the subject of much scrutiny in our laboratory (for reviews see Rourke, 1975,

1978b, 1982, 1987, 1988b, 1989; Rourke and Strang, 1983; Strang and Rourke, 1985a,b).

The principal investigations that have involved Group 2 and Group 3 youngsters are as follows: Ozols and Rourke (1988), Rourke and Finlayson (1978), Rourke and Strang (1978, 1983), Strang and Rourke (1983, 1985a,b). The first investigations to illustrate the patterns of abilities and deficits confirmed in these later studies were the following: Rourke *et al.* (1973); Rourke and Telegdy (1971); Rourke *et al.* (1971). On the basis of the results of this program of research, the following conclusions appear warranted. (For the sake of clarity, Group 2 is referred to as the Reading–Spelling (R–S) Group; Group 3 as the Arithmetic (A) Group. 'Older' refers to 9- to 14-year-old children; 'younger' to 7- and 8-year-old children.)

(1) Older Group R–S children exhibit some deficiencies in the more rote aspects of psycholinguistic skills such as the recall of information and word definitions; Group A exhibits average to superior skills in these areas.

(2) Older Group R–S children perform at markedly impaired levels on tests involving the more complex semantic–acoustic aspects of psycholinguistic skill development, such as sentence memory and the auditory analysis of common words. Group A children exhibit less than normal performances on such tests, but their levels of performance are superior to those of Group R–S children. Group A children tend to perform least well on those tests of semantic–acoustic processing that place an emphasis upon the processing of novel and/or meaningful material.

(3) Older Group R–S children exhibit normal levels of performance on visual–spatial–organizational, psychomotor and tactile–perceptual tasks; Group A children have outstanding difficulties on such tasks. The deficiencies exhibited by Group A children on tactile–perceptual and psychomotor tasks are bilaterally evident; when there is evidence of lateralized impairment on such tasks for the Group A child, it is almost always a relative deficiency in performance on the left side of the body. In general, the more novel the visual–spatial, psychomotor and tactile–perceptual task, the greater the impairment, relative to age-based norms, that is evident in the Group A child's performance.

(4) Older Group R–S children perform normally on non-verbal problem-solving tasks. They have no difficulty in benefiting from experience with such tasks. They are particularly adept at utilizing non-verbal informational feedback in order to modify their performance to meet the demands of such tasks. Group A children exhibit profound problems on non-verbal problem-solving tasks. They give little or no evidence of benefiting from informational feedback and continued experience with such tasks, even when the information provided would be expected to be

well within estimates of their general level of abilities and learning capacities that are based upon aspects of their verbal functioning (e.g. Verbal IQ).

(5) The adaptive implications of the relative abilities and deficits of older Group R–S and Group A children extend well beyond the confines of the academic setting. For example, Group R–S children tend to fare far better in most complex social situations than do Group A children (see below for a more precise delineation of these extra-academic learning considerations).

(6) As compared to older children in these two groups, younger Group R–S and Group A children exhibit very similar inter- and intragroup patterns of relative abilities and deficits on automatic (rote) verbal, semantic–acoustic and visual–spatial–organizational tasks. The exception to this generalization is that the more rote aspects of verbal skills tend to be more deficient relative to age-based norms in younger than in older Group R–S children.

(7) Differentiations in terms of psychomotor and tactile–perceptual skills and abilities are far less marked in younger than in older children of these two groups.

(8) Although there is some evidence to suggest that younger Group A children have more difficulty in adapting to novel problem-solving situations than do their Group R–S counterparts, the precise measurement of such suspected difficulties has yet to be completed.

These conclusions and generalizations should be sufficient to make the desired point: viz., that learning-disabled children chosen solely on the basis of specific variations in patterns of academic performance (with adequate controls for age, Full-Scale IQ and other important attributes) can be shown to exhibit very different patterns of neuropsychological abilities and deficits. In this connection, it should be noted that both of the groups (subtypes) under consideration exhibited deficient mechanical arithmetic performance. Thus, members of each of these groups could have been included in the 'learning-disabled' sample of a contrasting-groups type of study that is designed to compare 'arithmetic-disabled' and 'normal' children. It should be clear, from the above conclusions and generalizations, that such an 'arithmetic-disabled' group could be made up of at least two very distinct arithmetic-disabled subtypes. It is also the case (a) that these subtypes of children share virtually nothing in common, from a neuropsychological standpoint, with each other, (b) that their similarly deficient levels of performance in mechanical arithmetic reflect these quite different 'etiologies', and (c) that their needs for academic habilitation/rehabilitation with respect to mechanical arithmetic differ markedly from one another (for a discussion of these issues, see Rourke and Strang, 1983; Strang and Rourke, 1985a,b).

In addition to the study of the differences in the neuropsychological skills and ability structures of Group R–S and Group A children, we have been intensely interested in attempting to determine if these subtypes are differentially predisposed toward different types or degrees of socio-emotional disturbance. Studies to determine such relationships have characteristically been carried out within a framework of hypothesis generation prompted by the expected differences in the social learning potential of these two subtypes of learning-disabled children. What follows is a summary of our findings regarding the issue. The conclusions cited are derived from an interrelated series of investigations (Del Dotto et al., 1987; Fuerst et al., 1989; Ozols and Rourke, 1985; Porter and Rourke, 1985; Rourke, 1988a; Rourke and Fisk, 1988; Rourke and Strang, 1983; Rourke et al., 1985; Rourke et al., 1989; Rourke et al., 1986b; Strang and Rourke, 1985a,b).

(1) Group R–S children appear to be much less prone to socio-emotional disturbance than are Group A children.
(2) When Group R–S children exhibit socio-emotional disturbance, it tends to be of the 'externalized' variety (i.e. characterized by acting-out, conduct disorder, and other forms of intrusive and aggressive behavior). This form of socio-emotional disorder is seen very infrequently in older Group A children.
(3) The manifestations of psychopathology in Group A youngsters tend to be of the 'internalized variety' (i.e. characterized by anxiety, withdrawal and depression).
(4) There is little evidence to suggest that Group R–S children become more disturbed, from a socio-emotional perspective, as they grow older.
(5) There is very much evidence to suggest that Group A youngsters tend to manifest an increasing amount of psychopathology as they grow older.

These generalizations, important as they may be in and of themselves, are of less importance than is the development of the theoretical model (Rourke, 1982) that was formulated in concert with them.

THEORETICAL IMPLICATIONS

The first model that we developed (Rourke, 1982) provides a context for the interpretation of these generalizations and for the specification of the interrelationships between socio-emotional disturbance and manifestations of academic learning difficulties. Many aspects of this model are reasonably well known and need not be elaborated upon here. It is sufficient to point out that the focus of this model was on developmental and task-related differences and interactions between right and left hemispheral systems.

In order to expand the generalizability and explanatory potential of aspects of the Rourke (1982) neuropsychological model to manifestations of neurological disease, disorder and dysfunction, it was felt necessary to formulate an extension of this model that would focus extensively on differences and interactions between white and grey matter in the brain. This extension of the model (Rourke, 1987, 1988, 1989) would appear to be particularly helpful in the explication of the development of abilities and deficits in at least one well-defined subtype of learning disability (i.e. Group A, above). This is one group of youngsters who are thought to exhibit the 'non-verbal learning disabilities' (NLD) syndrome. The following summary excerpt from the Rourke (1987) model illustrates some of the historical antecedents of this model, its application to children with neurological disease, disorder and/or dysfunction, and its specific relevance to learning-disabled children of the Group A subtype.

The NLD Syndrome

We first investigated children who exhibit the NLD syndrome within the context of our general approach to the neuropsychology of learning disabilities (Rourke, 1975, 1978b, 1981, 1983b; Rourke and Fisk, 1981; Rourke and Strang, 1983; Strang and Rourke, 1985a,b). Within this framework, we were particularly interested in studying children who presented with outstanding difficulties in mechanical arithmetic as compared to their performances in reading (word-recognition) and spelling. As a first approximation to a developmental neuropsychological explanation of this subtype of learning-disabled child, it was suggested that these youngsters may be particularly deficient in those abilities and skills ordinarily thought to be subserved primarily by systems within the right cerebral hemisphere (Rourke, 1982; Rourke and Fisk, 1988). Specifically, it was hypothesized that such children were either deficient in right hemispherical systems or that they experienced significant difficulty in accessing such systems.

Although we isolated the NLD syndrome in studies that were geared to the determination of the neuropsychological and socio-emotional capacities and deficits of children chosen solely on the basis of their presenting profile of academic learning skills, it became clear that children whom we had examined for other reasons also exhibited this syndrome. The groups of children who manifested this syndrome most exactly are as follows (citations of our own case studies and the research reports of some others appear in parentheses):

(1) Many children with moderate to severe head injuries who are able to undergo a comprehensive neuropsychological investigation (Ewing-Cobbs *et al.*, 1985; Fletcher and Levin, 1988).

(2) Most children with a hydrocephalic condition that was not treated promptly and/or with success (Rourke *et al.*, 1983, pp. 290–297, 1986a, pp. 59–68).

(3) Survivors of acute lymphocytic leukemia and other forms of childhood cancer who had received very large doses (treatments) of X-irradiation over a prolonged period of time (Copeland *et al.*, 1985; Fletcher and Copeland, 1988; Rourke *et al.*, 1986a, pp. 108–116; Taylor *et al.*, 1987).

(4) Children with congenital absence of the corpus callosum and who exhibit no other demonstrable neurological disease process (see case study in Rourke, 1987).

(5) Children with significant tissue removal from the right cerebral hemisphere (Rourke *et al.*, 1983, pp. 230–238).

Children and adolescents whose clinical pictures bear a striking resemblance to the social and behavioral characteristics of the NLD child include children with Turner's syndrome (Rourke *et al.*, 1986a, pp. 136–143) and Asperger's syndrome (Baron, 1987; Stevens and Moffit, 1988; Wing, 1981), Williams syndrome (MacDonald and Roy, 1988), fragile-X syndrome (Cicchetti *et al.*, in press), and the so-called 'inadequate–immature' delinquent prescribed by Quay (1972). Many children afflicted with cerebral palsy (CP) of perinatal, as opposed to postperinatal, etiology would also be expected to manifest the NLD syndrome. However, the large number of neurological abnormalities lumped under the rubric of CP necessitates the separate treatment of this group of disorders.

It should be pointed out that all of the above five types of cerebral lesions involve significant destruction or disturbance of function of white matter (long myelinated fibers) in the brain, although the mechanisms of destruction and/or disturbance differ significantly (e.g. *shearing* in the case of the head-injured child, *absence* in the case of children with congenital corpus callosum agenesis, and *removal of tissue* within the right hemisphere). With respect to lesions affecting large portions of the right cerebral hemisphere, it should be emphasized that much destruction of white matter is quite probable in such instances. This is so because the ratio of white matter to grey matter is much larger in the right cerebral hemisphere than in the left cerebral hemisphere (Goldberg and Costa, 1981)—i.e. there is considerably less grey matter relative to white matter in the right than in the left cerebral hemisphere.

It would take us too far afield to demonstrate the more wide-ranging implications of this model, many of which are contained in Rourke (1987, 1988b, 1989). What is important within the present context is the odyssey that can be seen to unfold throughout this investigative effort: it began in the early 1970s with investigations involving groups of learning-disabled children differentiated on the basis of verbal IQ–performance IQ discrepancies. It continued with validity studies aimed at determining the patterns of neuropsychological abilities and deficits of groups of learning-disabled children chosen on the basis of patterns of academic performance. Next, we studied the current and long-range socio-emotional/adaptive implications of the patterns of neuropsychological abilities and deficits isolated in these groups of children. Now we are focusing on the investigation of the manifestations of one subtype of learning disability in children suffering from various forms of neurological disease, disorder and/or dysfunction. In all of this, the clear aim was to develop and refine a comprehensive theoretical model of brain–behavior relationships that would be capable of encompassing the developmental/adaptive dimensions of learning disabilities in all of their complex manifestations.

CONCLUSIONS AND GENERALIZATIONS

In order to summarize the foregoing, the following conclusions and generalizations are offered:

(1) There is no single, unitary pattern of neuropsychological abilities and deficits displayed by learning-disabled children.

(2) Distinct subtypes of learning disabilities have been isolated in a reliable fashion in a number of studies.

(3) There is an emerging body of evidence attesting to the concurrent and predictive validity of some subtypes of learning-disabled youngsters.

(4) There is at least one pattern of central-processing abilities and deficits (non-verbal learning disabilities) that appears to lead both to a particular configuration of academic achievement (i.e. well-developed word-recognition and spelling as compared to significantly poorer mechanical arithmetic) and to a particular form of socio-emotional disturbance (i.e. internalized psychopathology). Other patterns of central-processing abilities and deficits (i.e. those marked by outstanding difficulties in psycholinguistic skills) appear to lead to particular patterns of academic achievement (i.e. outstanding problems in reading and spelling and varying levels of performance in mechanical arithmetic), with no correlative effect upon either the incidence of psychopathology or its particular manifestations.

(5) Developmental differences in the manifestations of learning disabilities appear to obtain for some subtypes of learning disabilities. For example, with advancing years, there appears to be a worsening of the manifestations of psychopathology and increasing discrepancies between abilities and deficits exhibited by children with non-verbal learning disabilities. This is the case in spite of the fact that their *pattern* of neuropsychological abilities and deficits and their specific manifestations of psychopathology (except for activity level) remain remarkably stable over time.

(6) Efforts to clarify the relationships between learning disabilities and patterns of neuropsychological abilities and deficits should eschew the 'contrasting-groups/unitary deficit' approach. Instead, research efforts should deal adequately with the heterogeneity of the learning-disabled population, both with respect to their patterns of abilities and deficits and with respect to their distinctive forms and manifestations of psychopathology.

(7) It would appear that at least one subtype of learning disability (i.e. non-verbal learning disability) is evident within groups of children who are suffering from various types of neurological disease, disorder and/or dysfunction. Among other things, this should encourage the search for reliable patterns of central-processing abilities and deficits among other groups that are typically excluded from such scrutiny (e.g. the mentally retarded).

(9) Model developments (e.g. Rourke, 1982, 1987, 1988b, 1989; Fletcher and Taylor, 1984) must be sufficiently complex and sophisticated to encompass and illuminate the heterogeneous patterns of central-processing abilities/disabilities among learning-disabled children (Adams, 1985). Continuing to carry out essentially atheoretical, univariate studies of matched groups of learning-disabled and normally achieving children to address the important theoretical and clinical issues in this area is counterproductive. The crucially important issues relating to definitions, reliable and valid classification, and theory development are simply not adequately addressed by such studies.

REFERENCES

Adams, K. M. (1985). Theoretical, methodological, and statistical issues. In B. P. Rourke (ed.), *Neuropsychology of Learning Disabilities: Essentials of Subtype Analysis*, pp. 17–39. New York: Guilford Press.

Applebee, A. N. (1971). Research in reading retardation: Two critical problems. *Journal of Child Psychology and Psychiatry*, **12**, 91–113.

Baron, I. S. (1987). The childhood presentation of social-emotional learning disabilities: On the continuum of Asperger's syndrome. *Journal of Clinical and Experimental Neuropsychology*, **9**, 30 (abstract).

Benton, A. L. (1975). Developmental dyslexia: Neurological aspects. In W. J. Friedlander (ed.), *Advances in Neurology*, Vol. 7, pp. 1–41. New York: Raven Press.

Cicchetti, D. V., Sparrow, S. S., and Rourke, B. P. (in press). Adaptive behavior profiles of psychologically disturbed and developmentally disabled children. In J. L. Matson and J. Mulich (eds.), *Handbook of Mental Retardation*. New York: Pergamon Press.

Copeland, D. R., Fletcher, J. M., Pfefferbaum-Levine, B., Jaffe, M., Ried, H., and Maor, M. (1985). Neuropsychological sequelae of childhood cancer in long-term survivors. *Pediatrics*, **75**, 745–753.

Del Dotto, J. E., and Rourke, B. P. (1985). Subtypes of left-handed learning-disabled children. In B. P. Rourke (ed.), *Neuropsychology of Learning Disabilities: Essentials of Subtype Analysis*, pp. 89–130. New York: Guilford Press.

Del Dotto, J. E., Rourke, B. P., McFadden, G. T., and Fisk, J. L. (1987). Developmental analysis of arithmetic-disabled children: Impact on personality adjustment and patterns of adaptive functioning. *Journal of Clinical and Experimental Neuropsychology*, **9**, 44 (abstract).

Doehring, D. G. (1978). The tangled web of behavioral research on developmental dyslexia. In A. L. Benton and D. Pearl (eds.), *Dyslexia: An Appraisal of Current Knowledge*, pp. 125–135. New York: Oxford University Press.

Doehring, D. G., and Hoshko, I. M. (1977). Classification of reading problems by the Q-technique of factor analysis. *Cortex*, **13**, 281–294.

Doehring, D. G., Hoshko, I. M., and Bryans, B. N. (1979). Statistical classification of children with reading problems. *Journal of Clinical Neuropsychology*, **1**, 5–16.

Ewing-Cobbs, L., Fletcher, J. M., and Levin, H. S. (1985). Neuropsychological sequelae following pediatric head injury. In M. Ylvisaker (ed.), *Closed Head Injury Rehabilitation: Children and Adolescents*, pp. 71–89. San Diego: College Hill.

Fisk, J. L., and Rourke, B. P. (1979). Identification of subtypes of learning-disabled children at three age levels: A neuropsychological, multivariate approach. *Journal of Clinical Neuropsychology*, **1**, 289–310.

Fisk, J. L., and Rourke, B. P. (1983). Neuropsychological subtyping of learning disabled children: History, methods, implications. *Journal of Learning Disabilities*, **16**, 529–531.

Fletcher, J. M. (1985). External validation of learning disability typologies. In B. P. Rourke (ed.), *Neuropsychology of Learning Disabilities: Essentials of Subtype Analysis*, pp. 187–211. New York: Guilford Press.

Fletcher, J. M., and Copeland, D. R. (1988). Neurobehavioral effects of central nervous system prophylactic treatment of cancer in children. *Journal of Clinical and Experimental Neuropsychology*, **10**, 495–537.

Fletcher, J. M., and Levin, H. S. (1988). Neurobehavioral effects of brain injury in children. In D. K. Routh (ed.), *Handbook of Pediatric Psychology*. New York: Guilford Press.

Fletcher, J. M., and Satz, P. (1980). Developmental changes in the neuropsychological correlates of reading achievement: A six-year longitudinal follow-up. *Journal of Clinical Neuropsychology*, **2**, 23–37.

Fletcher, J. M., and Taylor, H. G. (1984). Neuropsychological approaches to children: Towards a developmental neuropsychology. *Journal of Clinical Neuropsychology*, **6**, 39–56.

Fuerst, D., Fisk, J. L., and Rourke, B. P. (1989). Psychosocial functioning of learning-disabled children: Replicability of statistically derived subtypes. *Journal of Consulting and Clinical Psychology*, **57**, 275–280.

Goldberg, E., and Costa, L. D. (1981). Hemisphere differences in the acquisition and use of descriptive systems. *Brain and Language*, **14**, 144–173.

Hebb, D. O. (1949). *Organization of Behavior*. New York: Wiley.

Johnson, D. J., and Myklebust, H. R. (1967). *Learning Disabilities*. New York: Grune & Stratton.

Joschko, M., and Rourke, B. P. (1985). Neuropsychological subtypes of learning-disabled children who exhibit the ACID pattern on the WISC. In B. P. Rourke (ed.), *Neuropsychology of Learning Disabilities: Essentials of Subtype Analysis*, pp. 65–88. New York: Guilford Press.

Kirk, S. A., and McCarthy, J. J. (1961). The Illinois Test of Psycholinguistic Abilities: An approach to differential diagnosis. *American Journal of Mental Deficiency*, **66**, 399–412.

Lyon, R. (1985). Educational validation studies of learning disability subtypes. In B. P. Rourke (ed.), *Learning Disabilities in Children: Essentials of Subtype Analysis*, pp. 228–253. New York: Guilford Press.

MacDonald, G. W., and Roy, D. L. (1988). Williams syndrome: A neuropsychological profile. *Journal of Clinical and Experimental Neuropsychology*, **10**, 125–131.

McKinney, J. D., Short, E. J., and Feagans, L. (1985). Academic consequences of perceptual-linguistic subtypes of learning disabled children. *Learning Disabilities Research*, **1**, 6–17.

Mattis, S., French, J. H., and Rapin, I. (1975). Dyslexia in children and young adults: Three independent neuropsychological syndromes. *Developmental Medicine and Child Neurology*, **17**, 150–163.

Morris, R., and Fletcher, J. M. (1988). Classification in neuropsychology: A theoretical framework and research paradigm. *Journal of Clinical and Experimental Neuropsychology*, **10**, 640–658.

Morris, R., Blashfield, R., and Satz, P. (1981). Neuropsychology and cluster analysis: Potentials and problems. *Journal of Clinical Neuropsychology*, **3**, 79–99.

Morris, R., Blashfield, R., and Satz, P. (1986). Developmental classification of reading-disabled children. *Journal of Clinical and Experimental Neuropsychology*, **8**, 371–392.

Myklebust, H. R. (1975). Nonverbal learning disabilities: Assessment and intervention. In H. R. Myklebust (ed.), *Progress in Learning Disabilities*, Vol. III, pp. 85–121. New York: Grune & Stratton.

Ozols, E. J., and Rourke, B. P. (1985). Dimensions of social sensitivity in two types of learning-disabled children. In B. P. Rourke (ed.), *Neuropsychology of Learning Disabilities: Essentials of Subtype Analysis*, pp. 281–301. New York: Guilford Press.

Ozols, E. J., and Rourke, B. P. (1988). Characteristics of young learning-disabled children classified according to patterns of academic achievement: Auditory-perceptual and visual-perceptual abilities. *Journal of Clinical Child Psychology*, **17**, 44–52.

Petrauskas, R. J., and Rourke, B. P. (1979). Identification of subtypes of retarded readers: A neuropsychological, multivariate approach. *Journal of Clinical Neuropsychology*, **1**, 17–37.

Porter, J., and Rourke, B. P. (1985). Socio-emotional functioning of learning-disabled children: A subtypal analysis of personality patterns. In B. P. Rourke (ed.), *Neuropsychology of Learning Disabilities: Essentials of Subtype Analysis*, pp. 257–279. New York: Guilford Press.

Quay, H. C. (1972). Patterns of aggression, withdrawal, and immaturity. In H. C. Quay and J. S. Weiry (eds.), *Psychopathological Disorders of Childhood*, pp. 1–29. New York: Wiley.

Rourke. B. P. (1975). Brain–behavior relationships in children with learning disabilities: A research program. *American Psychologist*, **30**, 911–920.

Rourke, B. P. (1976). Reading retardation in children: Developmental lag or deficit? In R. M. Knights and D. J. Bakker (eds), *Neuropsychology of Learning Disorders: Theoretical Approaches*, pp. 125–137. Baltimore: University Park Press.

Rourke, B. P. (1978a). Neuropsychological research in reading retardation: A review. In A. L. Benton and D. Pearl (eds.), *Dyslexia: An Appraisal of Current Knowledge*, pp. 141–171. New York: Oxford University Press.

Rourke, B. P. (1978b). Reading, spelling, arithmetic disabilities: A neuropsychologic perspective. In H. R. Myklebust (ed.), *Progress in Learning Disabilities*, Vol. IV, pp. 97–120. New York: Grune & Stratton.

Rourke, B. P. (1981). Neuropsychological assessment of children with learning disabilities. In S. B. Filskov and T. J. Boll (eds), *Handbook of Clinical Neuro-psychology*, pp. 453–478. New York: Wiley–Interscience.

Rourke, B. P. (1982). Central processing deficiencies in children: Toward a developmental neuropsychological model. *Journal of Clinical Neuropsychology*, 4, 1–18.

Rourke, B. P. (1983a). Outstanding issues in research in learning disabilities. In M. Rutter (ed.), *Developmental Neuropsychiatry*, pp. 564–574. New York: Guilford Press.

Rourke, B. P. (1983b). Reading and spelling disabilities: A developmental neuropsychological perspective. In U. Kirk (ed.), *Neuropsychology of Language, Reading, and Spelling*, pp. 209–234. New York: Academic Press.

Rourke, B. P. (ed.) (1985). *Neuropsychology of Learning Disabilities: Essentials of Subtype Analysis*. New York: Guilford Press.

Rourke, B. P. (1987). Syndrome of nonverbal learning disabilities: The final common pathway of white matter disease/dysfunction? *The Clinical Neuropsychologist*, 1, 209–234.

Rourke, B. P. (1988a). Socio-emotional disturbances of learning-disabled children. *Journal of Consulting and Clinical Psychology*, 56, 801–810.

Rourke, B. P. (1988b). The syndrome of nonverbal learning disabilities: Developmental manifestations in neurological disease, disorder, and dysfunction. *The Clinical Neuropsychologist*, 2, 293–330.

Rourke, B. P. (1989). *Nonverbal Learning Disabilities: The Syndrome and the Model*. New York: Guilford Press.

Rourke, B. P., Bakker, D. J., Fisk, J. L., and Strang, J. D. (1983). *Child Neuropsychology: An Introduction to Theory, Research, and Clinical Practice*. New York: Guilford Press.

Rourke, B. P., Dietrich, D. M., and Young, G. C. (1973). Significance of WISC Verbal-Performance discrepancies for younger children with learning disabilities. *Perceptual and Motor Skills*, 36, 275–282.

Rourke, B. P., and Finlayson, M. A. J. (1978). Neuropsychological significance of variations in patterns of academic performance: Verbal and visual–spatial abilities. *Journal of Abnormal Child Psychology*, 6, 121–133.

Rourke, B. P., and Fisk, J. L. (1981). Socio-emotional disturbances of learning disabled children: The role of central processing deficits. *Bulletin of the Orton Society*, 31, 77–88.

Rourke, B. P., and Fisk, J. L. (1988). Subtypes of learning-disabled children: Implications for a neurodevelopmental model of differential hemispheric processing. In D. L. Molfese and S. J. Segalowitz (eds), *Developmental Implications of Brain Lateralization*, pp. 547–565. New York: Guilford Press.

Rourke, B. P., Fisk, J. L., and Strang, J. D. (1986a). *Neuropsychological Assessment of Children: A Treatment-oriented Approach*. New York: Guilford Press.

Rourke, B. P., and Gates, R. D. (1981). Neuropsychological research and school psychology. In G. W. Hynd and J. E. Obrzut (eds), *Neuropsychological Assessment and the School-aged Child: Issues and Procedures*, pp. 3–25. New York: Grune & Stratton.

Rourke, B. P., Pohlman, C. L., Fuerst, D. R., Porter, J. E., and Fisk, J. L. (1985). Personality subtypes of learning-disabled children: Two validation studies. *Journal of Clinical and Experimental Neuropsychology*, 7, 157 (abstract).

Rourke, B. P., and Strang, J. D. (1978). Neuropsychological significance of variations in patterns of academic performance: Motor, psychomotor, and tactile–perceptual abilities. *Journal of Pediatric Psychology*, 3, 62–66.

Rourke, B. P., and Strang, J. D. (1983). Subtypes of reading and arithmetical disabilities: A neuropsychological analysis. In M. Rutter (ed.), *Developmental Neuropsychiatry*, pp. 473–488. New York: Guilford Press.

Rourke, B. P., and Telegdy, G. A. (1971). Lateralizing significance of WISC Verbal-Performance discrepancies for older children with learning disabilities. *Perceptual and Motor Skills*, **33**, 875–883.

Rourke, B. P., Young, G. C., and Flewelling, R. W. (1971). The relationships between WISC Verbal-Performance discrepancies and selected verbal, auditory–perceptual, and problem-solving abilities in children with learning disabilities. *Journal of Clinical Psychology*, **27**, 475–479.

Rourke, B. P., Young, G. C., and Leenaars, A. A. (1989). A childhood learning disability that predisposes those afflicted to adolescent and adult depression and suicide risk. *Journal of Learning Disabilities*, **21**, 169–175.

Rourke, B. P., Young, G. C., Strang, J. D., and Russell, D. L. (1986b). Adult outcomes of central processing deficiencies in childhood. In I. Grant and K. M. Adams (eds.), *Neuropsychological Assessment in Neuropsychiatric Disorders: Clinical Methods and Empirical Findings*, pp. 244–267. New York: Oxford University Press.

Stevens, D. E., and Moffitt, T. E. (1988). Neuropsychological profile of an Asperger's syndrome case with exceptional calculating ability. *The Clinical Neuropsychologist*, **2**, 228–238.

Strang, J. D., and Rourke, B. P. (1983). Concept-formation/non-verbal reasoning abilities of children who exhibit specific academic problems with arithmetic. *Journal of Clinical Child Psychology*, **12**, 33–39.

Strang, J. D., and Rourke, B. P. (1985a). Adaptive behavior of children with specific arithmetic disabilities and associated neuropsychological abilities and deficits. In B. P. Rourke (ed.), *Neuropsychology of Learning Disabilities: Essentials of Subtype Analysis*, pp. 302–328. New York: Guilford Press.

Strang, J. D., and Rourke, B. P. (1985b). Arithmetic disability subtypes: The neuropsychological significance of specific arithmetic impairment in childhood. In B. P. Rourke (ed.), *Neuropsychology of Learning Disabilities: Essentials of Subtype Analysis*, pp. 167–183. New York: Guilford Press.

Sweeney, J. E., and Rourke, B. P. (1978). Neuropsychological significance of phonetically accurate and phonetically inaccurate spelling errors in younger and older retarded spellers. *Brain and Language*, **6**, 212–225.

Sweeney, J. E., and Rourke, B. P. (1985). Spelling disability subtypes. In B. P. Rourke (ed.), *Neuropsychology of Learning Disabilities: Essentials of Subtype Analysis*, pp. 147–166. New York: Guilford Press.

Taylor, H. G. (1983). MBD: Meanings and misconceptions. *Journal of Clinical Neuropsychology*, **5**, 271–288.

Taylor, H. G., Albo, V. C., Phebus, C. K., Sachs, D. R., and Bierl, P. G. (1987). Post-irradiation treatment outcomes for children with acute lymphocytic leukemia: Clarification of risks. *Journal of Pediatric Psychology*, **12**, 395–411.

Wing, L. (1981). Asperger's syndrome: A clinical account. *Psychological Medicine*, **11**, 115–129.

Address for correspondence:

Professor Byron P. Rourke; Department of Psychology, University of Windsor, Windsor, Ontario N9B 3P4, Canada

Part II

The Role of Genetics in Learning Disabilities

3

Genetic Etiology of Reading Disability: Evidence from a Twin Study

Michele C. LaBuda[1] and John C. DeFries[2]

[1]*Yale University School of Medicine and* [2]*University of Colorado*

INTRODUCTION

Conceptualizations of dyslexia and other learning disabilities typically assume an underlying biological or genetic etiology. For example, the World Federation of Neurology defined specific developmental dyslexia as 'a disorder manifested by difficulty in learning to read despite conventional instruction, adequate intelligence, and socio-cultural opportunity. It is dependent upon fundamental cognitive disabilities which are frequently of constitutional origin' (Critchley, 1970, p. 11).

More recently, the National Joint Committee on Learning Disabilities (NJCLD) issued a position paper that addressed problems resulting from the current definition of learning disabilities and urged the adoption of a new definition. One of four major issues discussed in the position paper concerned etiology:

> The etiology of learning disabilities is not stated clearly within the current definition but is implied by a listing of terms and disorders. The NJCLD urges that the disorders represented by the collective term 'learning disabilities' are understood as intrinsic to the individual and that the basis of the disorders is presumed to be due to central nervous system dysfunction. While the NJCLD supports the idea that failure to learn or to attain curricular expectations occurs for diverse reasons, learning disabilities have their bases in inherently altered processes of acquiring and using information. (National Joint Committee on Learning Disabilities, 1981)

The NJCLD also emphasized the central importance of an understanding of etiology to the field: 'An understanding of etiological mechanisms (a) facilitates a determination of prognosis, (b) provides information to individuals and their families that helps to clarify their understanding of the manifest disorder(s), and (c) provides direction for research studies that will influence educational practice.'

Although current conceptualizations of dyslexia and other learning disabilities assume a constitutional or heritable basis, definitive evidence has yet to be reported. Results of family studies, such as those reviewed by Finucci and Childs (1983) and DeFries *et al.* (1986), conclusively demonstrate the familial nature of reading disability. However, members of intact nuclear families share both genetic and environmental influences; thus, familial resemblance alone does not provide sufficient evidence for heritable variation.

More direct evidence for a genetic etiology has been reported by Smith *et al.* (1983), who discovered a possible linkage between a form of reading disability in families with apparent autosomal dominant transmission and a cytological marker on chromosome 15. The authors cautiously noted, however, that confirmation by a second study will be required before genetic linkage can be accepted with confidence.

Results of twin studies also suggest that reading disability may be due at least in part to heritable influences. The logical basis for an inference of genetic etiology from results of twin studies is self-evident. Identical (monozygotic, MZ) twins result from the division of one fertilized ovum and, thus, are genetically identical. Fraternal (dizygotic, DZ) twins, on the other hand, develop from two fertilized ova, thereby sharing 50% of heritable variation on the average. If the environmental influences shared by members of MZ twin pairs are similar to those shared by DZ twins, then a greater observed resemblance between members of MZ pairs is ascribed to their greater genetic similarity. The validity of this 'equal environments assumption' has been discussed in detail by Plomin *et al.* (1980).

Previous twin studies of reading disability have used a comparison of concordance rates as a test for genetic etiology. A pair is concordant if both members of the pair have been diagnosed as affected, but discordant if only one member of the pair is affected. Thus, a higher concordance rate for MZ pairs than for DZ pairs provides evidence for genetic influence. As indicated in the following section of this chapter, twin studies of reading disability consistently obtain higher MZ than DZ concordance rates. However, considerable variation in concordance rate exists among studies, somewhat diminishing the confidence to be placed in the individual reports.

Although previous twin studies of reading disability suggest the possibility of a genetic etiology, additional research is clearly warranted. Following a recent discussion of the contribution of twin research to the study of the etiology of reading disability, Harris (1986) concluded that 'Twin studies can and should play a larger role in etiological studies . . . a large and well ascertained sample of affected twins and their cotwins, whose affection status is documented and zygosity is determined by highly reliable methods, has not to my knowledge been described and would be a welcomed addition to research in this area' (Harris, 1986, pp. 15–16).

Since 1982, researchers at the University of Colorado (DeFries, 1985; Decker and Vandenberg, 1985) have been administering a test battery that includes measures of cognitive abilities and of reading and language processes to a sample of identical and fraternal twin pairs in which at least one twin is reading-disabled, and to twin pairs of normal reading ability. Moreover, during this period we have developed a new multiple regression analysis of twin data (DeFries and Fulker, 1985; LaBuda *et al.*, 1986). This regression analysis provides a direct statistical test for genetic etiology which is more flexible and powerful than conventional concordance comparisons. In the present chapter, we review previous twin studies of reading disability, discuss the multiple regression analysis of twin data, apply this methodology to analyze twin data collected in the Colorado Reading Project, and present the best evidence to date for a genetic etiology of reading disability.

TWIN STUDIES OF READING DISABILITY

The initial reports of reading-disabled twins each involved a single concordant pair of identical twins (Brander, 1935; Ley and Tordeur, 1936; Jenkins *et al.*, 1937; Schiller, 1937, as cited by Hallgren, 1950; von Harnack, 1962, as cited by Zerbin-Rüdin, 1967). In 1950, however, descriptions of six twin pairs in which at least one member of the pair was affected were included in Hallgren's classic family study of dyslexia. Five of the twin pairs were identified through school registers and records from the Stockholm Child Guidance Clinic as part of the larger family study. A sixth twin pair was referred to Hallgren by a colleague. In three cases, members of the pairs were of opposite sex and, thus, were classified as dizygotic. Members of the three same-sexed pairs had identical physical features and the same blood group combination (ABO, MNS, P and Rh systems); thus, they were classified as monozygotic.

Each of the three MZ twin pairs described by Hallgren was concordant for dyslexia, whereas only one of the three DZ pairs was concordant. Although these results are consistent with a hypothesis of genetic etiology, the sample size is very small. In addition, Hallgren's diagnostic methods have been criticized due to an apparent preoccupation with familial transmission (Finucci, 1978). Nevertheless, this was an important first study of differential MZ and DZ twin concordance for specific reading disability.

During the next several years, a series of publications originating from the Institute for Word-Blindness, Copenhagen, added significantly to the world literature on reading disabilities in twins. The twin series of Norrie (Norrie, 1954; Hermann and Norrie, 1958) included 9 MZ pairs and 10 of 30 DZ pairs

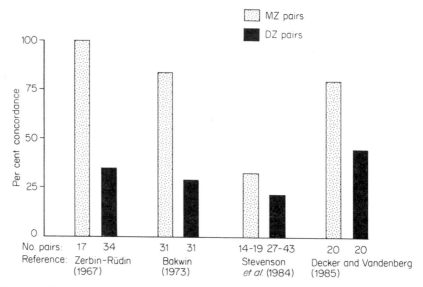

Figure 1. Pairwise concordance rates from published twin studies of reading disability. MZ, monozygotic; DZ, dizygotic

concordant for dyslexia. Zerbin-Rüdin (1967) subsequently reviewed the data from twins in the Norrie series, those reported by Hallgren and individual case studies. These combined data yield concordance rates of 100% and 35% for MZ and DZ twin pairs, respectively, and are plotted in Figure 1 as a summary of the early twin studies on reading disability.

In 1973, results from one of the largest twin studies of reading disability were reported by Bakwin. A sample of 338 like-sexed twin pairs was obtained through clubs for mothers of twins and screened via parental interviews, telephone calls and mail questionnaires for evidence of reading difficulties. Reading disability was defined as performance below that which was expected based upon the child's achievement in school subjects other than reading. The twins ranged in age from 8 to 18 years, attended public schools and came from middle-income families. Zygosity was reportedly determined clinically and, in cases not obviously dizygotic, by blood group testing. Ninety-seven of the 676 twin children screened had a history of reading disability, suggesting that the prevalence rate in twins (14.3%) may be somewhat higher than that typically found in singletons (5–10%). Although reading disability was more prevalent in boys (61/344 = 17.7%) than girls (36/332 = 10.8%) ($\chi^2(1)$ = 4.66, $0.01 < p < 0.05$), the ratio of disabled males to females is lower than the typically cited sex ratio of 3 or 4 to 1.

Bakwin's sample contained 31 pairs of MZ twins and 31 pairs of DZ twins in which at least one member of the pair was affected. Concordance rates in the MZ and DZ twin pairs were 84% and 29%, respectively. These rates are also plotted in Figure 1 in order to provide a comparison with results obtained in the earlier twin studies. Although the MZ concordance rate is high in Bakwin's study, discordant MZ twin pairs were reported for the first time, suggesting that the etiology of reading disability is due at least in part to environmental influences not shared by members of twin pairs.

Bakwin also reported concordance rates separately by zygosity and gender. Concordances among MZ males and MZ females were virtually identical (84% and 83%, respectively); however, the concordance rate in male DZ twins was considerably higher than that in female DZ twins (42% versus 8%). In addition, Bakwin examined the relationships of birth weight and birth order to reading disabilities. No significant difference in incidence of dyslexia was found between those twins weighing less than 2500 g at birth (13.0%) and those weighing more than 2500 g (13.8%). Similarly, no significant association between birth order and reading difficulty was found.

More recently, Stevenson et al. (1984, 1987) presented results from another large twin study of reading disability. Two hundred and eighty-five pairs of 13-year-old twins were obtained by screening hospital records at the time of birth in five London boroughs or through primary schools in the London area. Zygosity was determined by physical similarity and, when necessary, by dermatoglyphics and blood group testing. Schonell Reading and Spelling Age (Schonell and Schonell, 1960) and Neale Accuracy Reading Age (Neale, 1967) were used to identify twins who were reading- or spelling-'backward' (i.e. reading or spelling age more than 18 months behind the child's chronological age) and those twins who were reading- or spelling-'retarded' (i.e. 18 months or more below the expected reading or spelling age predicted by the child's IQ and chronological age). The rates of reading and spelling difficulties varied as a function of definition as well as zygosity group. For example, only 8.9% of the MZ twins were diagnosed as reading-retarded based upon Schonell Reading Age, whereas 25.5% of the DZ twins were classified as spelling-backward based upon Schonell Spelling Age. Overall, the incidence of reading and spelling disabilities in DZ twins was nearly twice that observed in MZ twins (average rates of 11.4% and 20.4% were found for MZ and DZ twins, respectively). Probandwise concordance rates (concordant pairs are counted twice) for reading and spelling difficulties ranged from 33% to 59% for MZ pairs and 29% to 54% for DZ pairs (Stevenson et al., 1987).

In the earlier report, Stevenson et al. (1984) used the Schonell tests to diagnose reading disability. In addition to the reading-backward, reading-retarded, spelling-backward and spelling-retarded groups defined above, a 'dyslexia' group that included children who were reading-backward but with an IQ score of at least 90 were also included. Pairwise concordance rates (every pair is counted only once) for the five groups of twins ranged from 21% to 42% for MZ twin pairs and 17% to 27% for DZ twin pairs. For comparability across studies, the average pairwise concordance rates for MZ and DZ twins reported in this study (32% and 21%, respectively) are also plotted in Figure 1. As the authors indicate, the lower concordance rates obtained in their study may be due to differences in ascertainment, definition or zygosity determination. They also suggest the interesting hypothesis that genetic factors may be less important as a cause of reading disability in children 13 years of age than in younger children.

Preliminary results from the Colorado Reading Project based upon analyses of data from 20 MZ and 20 DZ reading-disabled twin pairs were reported by Decker and Vandenberg (1985). Subjects were ascertained from school districts within a 150-mile radius of Denver, Colorado, and selection criteria included the following: age between 8.5 and 18 years, a score below the 41st percentile on the Reading Recognition subtest of the Peabody Individual Achievement Test (PIAT; Dunn and Markwardt, 1970), and a score of at least 90 on either the Verbal or Performance scales of the WISC-R (Wechsler, 1974) or WAIS-R (Wechsler, 1981). Exclusionary criteria included evidence of neurological, emotional or behavioral problems or uncorrected auditory or visual acuity deficits. Zygosity was determined by selected items from the zygosity questionnaire of Nichols and Bilbro (1966), which has a reported accuracy of 95%. Obtained concordance rates of 80% and 45% for MZ and DZ pairs, respectively, are also plotted in Figure 1.

In an alternative analysis, Decker and Vandenberg (1985) employed a discriminant function composite as a more comprehensive indication of reading difficulties in cotwins. The composite was based upon scores obtained from the Reading Recognition, Reading Comprehension and Spelling subtests of the PIAT, the Verbal and Performance IQ scales, and the mother's report of whether or not the child experienced difficulties in learning to read. In an independent sample of 80 non-twin subjects, the discriminant function score correctly classified 93% of the disabled and 97% of the control subjects. Although the composite was not used to ascertain the index cases, each index case could be classified as reading-disabled using the discriminant function criterion. With regard to the cotwins, more cases were diagnosed as being disabled using the discriminant score, yielding MZ and DZ concordance rates of 85% and 55%, respectively.

The higher MZ than DZ concordance rate for each study depicted in Figure 1 is consistent with the hypothesis of a genetic etiology for reading disability; however, substantial variation in concordance rates among studies is evident. Differences in diagnostic criteria, ascertainment methods, nature of the samples, etc., may account at least in part for this variability. Such variation among results of previous studies substantiates the need for a large, well-designed twin study of reading disability (Harris, 1986). Moreover, alternative analyses of twin data may yield more insight into the heritable nature of reading disability.

Although a comparison of concordance rates has been employed as a test of genetic etiology in previous twin studies, the concept of dyslexia is operationally defined (Wong, 1986) and diagnosis is based, at least in part, upon quantitative measures with arbitrary cut-off points (Stevenson *et al.*, 1987). Obviously, twin concordance rates will differ as a function of changing diagnostic criteria (Decker and Vandenberg, 1985; Stevenson *et al.*, 1987). Transformation of a continuous measure (e.g. reading performance) into a categorical variable (disabled or normal) also results in a loss of important information pertaining to individual differences. In contrast, multiple regression analysis of continuous measures obtained from probands and their cotwins provides a direct test of genetic etiology as well as an estimate of the magnitude of the contribution of heritable influences to the observed difference between normal and disabled readers. This simple but statistically powerful test of genetic etiology is outlined below.

Method

Multiple regression analyses of twin data

In order to facilitate a test of genetic etiology based upon an analysis of continuous measures, we recently formulated a multiple regression model for the analysis of twin data (DeFries and Fulker, 1985; LaBuda *et al.*, 1986). Specifically, we proposed that the differential regression of MZ and DZ cotwins' scores toward the mean of the unselected population provides a direct and powerful test of genetic etiology that is more appropriate than a comparison of MZ and DZ concordance rates. The logic of this methodology is outlined in this section, including descriptions of the basic model, possible extended models to test for differential genetic etiology in different groups, and an augmented model that can be used to assess the heritable nature of individual differences within the normal range of variation.

Figure 2 depicts the hypothetical distribution of reading performance from an unselected sample of twins (top) and from identical and fraternal cotwins of probands with a reading disability. When probands have been ascertained because of low test scores on a continuous measure, the distributions of scores from both the MZ and DZ cotwins are expected to regress toward the mean of the unselected population (μ). However, if the depressed performance of probands is due at least in part to heritable influences, the magnitude of this regression should differ for MZ and DZ cotwins. Because the coefficient of relationship for MZ twins is 1.0 (i.e. they are genetically identical), whereas that for DZ twins is 0.5 (i.e. they share half the genes, on the average), scores of DZ cotwins should regress more toward the mean of the unselected population than do those of MZ cotwins to the extent that the condition is heritable.

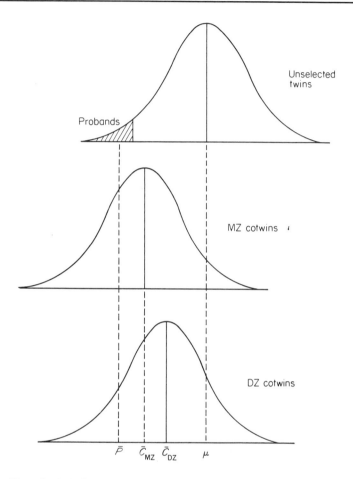

Figure 2. Hypothetical distributions for reading performance of an unselected sample of twins, and of the monozygotic (MZ) and dizygotic (DZ) cotwins of reading-disabled probands. (From DeFries *et al.*, 1987.)

Assuming that the MZ and DZ probands have similar scores on the average, the expected means of their cotwins are as follows:

$$\bar{C}_{MZ} = \mu + (h_g^2 + c_g^2)(\bar{P} - \mu) \tag{1}$$

$$\bar{C}_{DZ} = \mu + (0.5h_g^2 + c_g^2)(\bar{P} - \mu) \tag{2}$$

where $\bar{C}_{MZ}$ and $\bar{C}_{DZ}$ are the expected MZ and DZ cotwin means, μ is the mean of the unselected population, $\bar{P}$ is the observed proband mean, h_g^2 is a measure of the extent to which the deviation of the proband mean from the mean of the unselected population (i.e. $\bar{P} - \mu$) is heritable, and c_g^2 is a measure of the degree to which probands and their cotwins (both MZ and DZ) share environmental influences. Accordingly:

$$\bar{C}_{MZ} - \bar{C}_{DZ} = 0.5h_g^2(\bar{P} - \mu) \tag{3}$$

i.e. the difference between the means of MZ and DZ cotwins is a simple function of h_g^2 when the MZ and DZ proband means are equal. Consequently, when this condition is met, a simple t-test of the difference between the MZ and DZ cotwin means could be used as an index of genetic etiology. However, as shown below, fitting a multiple regression equation in which a cotwin's score is predicted from the proband's score and the coefficient of relationship to the data provides a more general and powerful test.

Basic model   The basic multiple regression model formulated by DeFries and Fulker (1985) is as follows:

$$C = B_1P + B_2R + A \tag{4}$$

where C is the cotwin's predicted score, P is the proband's observed score, R is the coefficient of relationship ($R = 1.0$ for MZ pairs and 0.5 for DZ pairs) and A is the regression constant. B_1 is the partial regression of cotwin's score on proband's score, a measure of average MZ and DZ twin resemblance. B_2 is the partial regression of cotwin's score on the coefficient of relationship and equals twice the difference between the means of MZ and DZ cotwins after covariance adjustment for any difference that may exist between the means of MZ and DZ probands. Therefore, B_2 provides a test for genetic etiology that is analogous to that of differential MZ and DZ twin concordance and more general than a t-test of the difference between the MZ and DZ cotwin means. Moreover, as discussed later, the test of significance for B_2 is more powerful than a concordance comparison or a comparison of MZ and DZ cotwin means.

From equation 3 it may be seen that when the means of MZ and DZ probands are equal, the ratio of twice the difference between the means of MZ and DZ cotwins to the deviation of the proband mean from that of the unselected population provides an estimate of h_g^2, i.e.

$$h_g^2 = \frac{2(\bar{C}_{MZ} - \bar{C}_{DZ})}{\bar{P} - \mu} \tag{5}$$

Because B_2 equals twice the difference between the means of MZ and DZ cotwins when the proband means are equal, the ratio of B_2 to $\bar{P} - \mu$ also provides an index of h_g^2. If the means of MZ and DZ probands differ, h_g^2 may be estimated as follows:

$$h_g^2 = 2\left[\left(\frac{\bar{C}_{MZ} - \mu}{\bar{P}_{MZ} - \mu}\right) - \left(\frac{\bar{C}_{DZ} - \mu}{\bar{P}_{DZ} - \mu}\right)\right] \tag{6}$$

However, the assumption that $\bar{P}_{MZ} = \bar{P}_{DZ}$ should usually be met, at least within sampling error.

An alternative approach is to express each proband's and cotwin's score as an inverse function of $\bar{P} - \mu$ prior to analysis, i.e.

$$P' = \frac{P}{\bar{P} - \mu} \tag{7}$$

and

$$C' = \frac{C}{\bar{P} - \mu} \tag{8}$$

where P' and C' are the transformed scores of probands and cotwins, respectively. By fitting the basic regression model (equation 4) to P' and C', $B_2 = h_g^2$ and its associated standard error are estimated directly. This approach also yields direct estimates of h_g^2 when the MZ and DZ proband means differ.

Extended model   The basic model of DeFries and Fulker (1985) can be extended in a number of different ways to accommodate more comprehensive genetic analyses. For example, age adjustment of data can easily be accomplished using this approach by including age of proband as another independent variable in the regression equation. Moreover, the model could be readily extended to include main effects and interactions (Cohen and Cohen, 1975) involving gender, ethnic group, socio-economic status, etc. Two obvious extensions of particular relevance to the genetics of reading disability are interactions involving gender and subtype classifications.

Harris (1986) recently suggested that twin analyses of reading disability should be conducted separately for males and females because of the possibility of differential genetic etiology. However, by fitting a model that includes gender (a dummy variable) and an interaction term between gender and the coefficient of relationship to data from males and females simultaneously, a hypothesis of differential genetic etiology in male and female probands can be tested directly. This extended multiple regression model is as follows:

$$C = B_1 P + B_2 R + B_3 S + B_4 PS + B_5 RS + A \tag{9}$$

where S is a dummy variable representing gender ($S = -0.5$ for males and $+0.5$ for females), PS is the product of proband's score and the dummy variable, and RS is the product of the coefficient of relationship and the dummy variable. B_4 provides a measure of differential twin resemblance in males and females, whereas B_5 yields a direct test of differential genetic etiology as a function of gender.

In a similar manner, data from probands of ostensibly different subtypes could be analyzed simultaneously to test for differential genetic etiology. For example, if one subtype of reading disability were due to a deficit in phonological processing and another were due to poor orthographic skills, one might be highly heritable, whereas the other might be due largely to inadequate instruction. If the regression model in equation 9 were fitted to such data, where S would now symbolize a dummy variable for subtype, a significant B_5 would indicate differential genetic etiology for the two subtypes. Such a finding would provide compelling evidence for subtype validity.

Augmented model   The basic model (equation 4) may also be extended by including an interaction term between proband's score and the coefficient of relationship (DeFries and Fulker, 1985). This augmented model facilitates estimates of heritability (h^2) and the proportion of variance due to environmental influences shared by members of twin pairs (c^2) potentially relevant to individual differences in the unselected population. Although this model may be fit to data from either selected or unselected samples, it is especially appropriate for the analysis of data from twins in which one member of each pair has been selected because of a deviant score. When analyzing such attenuated data, regression coefficients are more appropriate than correlations because regressions are less influenced by restriction of range of the independent variables (Cohen and Cohen, 1975).

The augmented regression model is as follows:

$$C = B_1P + B_2R + B_3PR \tag{10}$$

where PR is the product of the proband's score and the coefficient of relationship. B_3, the coefficient of the interaction term, equals twice the difference between the bivariate MZ and DZ regression coefficients. Thus, assuming an additive genetic model, little or no assortative mating and equal shared environmental influences for MZ and DZ twin pairs (i.e. the usual assumptions underlying genetic analyses of twin data), B_3 provides a direct estimate of population h^2. Recall that the expectation for B_1 in the basic model (equation 4) is average MZ and DZ resemblance. However, when the interaction term is added to the model as in equation 10, the expectation differs. When the augmented model (equation 10) is fitted to the data, B_1 is a measure of twin resemblance independent of genetic influence. Thus, when B_1 is estimated from the augmented model, its expectation is c^2. This augmented model can also be extended to test for differential h^2 and c^2 in different groups (LaBuda *et al.*, 1986). For example, the augmented model (equation 10) may be extended to test for differential h^2 and c^2 in males and females as follows:

$$C = B_1P + B_2R + B_3S + B_4PR + B_5PS + B_6RS + B_7PRS + A \tag{11}$$

where S is a dummy variable representing gender (as in equation 9) and PRS is the three-way interaction of proband's score, the coefficient of relationship and gender. B_5 and B_7 provide direct tests for differential c^2 and h^2, respectively, in males and females. In addition, B_1 estimates average c^2 in males and females and B_4 estimates average h^2. These estimates are valid when the tests of differential h^2 and c^2 are not significant.

It is important to note that h_g^2 (a measure of the extent to which the deviation of the proband mean from the mean of the unselected population is due to heritable influences) may differ from h^2 (a measure of the extent to which individual differences within the normal range are heritable). In a similar manner, c_g^2 and c^2 may differ. Obviously, the etiology of reading disability may differ from that of individual differences within the normal range. For example, deviant scores of probands could be due to major-gene effects, chromosomal anomalies or gross environmental insult. Variation among individuals within the normal range, however, could be due to polygenic influences and/or differences in teaching methods. Consequently, a comparison of h_g^2 and h^2 estimated from the same data set could be used to test the hypothesis that probands merely represent the lower tail of a normal distribution of individual differences in reading performance (Rodgers, 1983).

Subjects

Subjects were ascertained through participating school districts within a 150-mile radius of Denver, Colorado. Parents of twin pairs identified by school personnel were contacted for permission to review their children's school records. Records were screened for evidence of reading difficulties (e.g. low reading achievement scores, referral to resource rooms due to poor reading performance or reports by school psychologists) and same-sexed pairs in which at least one twin had evidenced reading problems were then invited to participate in an extensive testing session (see Decker and Vandenberg, 1985, for a list of the tests included in the psychometric test battery). Zygosity was determined by selected items from the Nichols and Bilbro (1966) zygosity questionnaire (reported accuracy 95%). However, in doubtful cases, blood samples were drawn and sent to the Minneapolis War Memorial Blood Bank for analysis.

Analyses in the present chapter are based upon data from 117 reading-disabled twin pairs (62 MZ and 55 DZ pairs) and a comparable sample of 107 control twin pairs (62 MZ and 45 DZ pairs). Control twin pairs were matched to reading-disabled pairs, whenever possible, on the basis of age, gender and zygosity. Diagnosis of reading disability was based in part upon a discriminant function composite created from scores on the psychometric test battery. In an independent sample of 140 reading-disabled and 140 control subjects, a discriminant score based upon the Reading Recognition, Reading Comprehension and Spelling subtests of the Peabody Individual Achievement Test (PIAT; Dunn and Markwardt, 1970), the Coding-B and Digit Span subtest of either the Wechsler Intelligence Scale for Children—Revised (WISC-R; Wechsler, 1974) or the Wechsler Adult Intelligence Scale—Revised (WAIS-R; Wechsler, 1981), and the Colorado Perceptual Speed Test (CPS; DeFries *et al.*, 1981) correctly reclassified 93.6% of the reading-disabled subjects and 92.9% of the controls. Diagnostic criteria included: (1) evidence of reading difficulties in school; (2) classification as affected using the discriminant score; (3) a score of 90 or above on either the Verbal or Performance subscales of the WISC-R or WAIS-R; (4) no evidence of neurological, emotional or behavioral problems; and (5) no uncorrected visual or auditory acuity deficits. If both twins met these criteria for reading disability, the more severely disabled member of the pair, as determined by the discriminant score, was designated as the index case or proband. The twins came from English-speaking, middle-class homes and ranged in age from 7.7 to 20.5 years of age.

School records of 909 same-sexed twin pairs yielded 365 individuals for which some evidence of low reading performance was obtained. Within a sample of 286 subjects with a positive history for reading difficulties who were subsequently tested, 205 were classified as affected using the discriminant score. Thus, an estimate of the prevalence rate in the twin sample could be obtained by multiplying the proportion of individuals screened whose school records indicated reading difficulties (365/1818) by the percentage of the individuals with a positive history who later were diagnosed as affected using the discriminant score (205/286). Assuming that participation in the study is independent of reading status (i.e. no volunteer bias), the prevalence rate for reading disability within the Colorado twin sample is approximately 14.4%. Although this estimate is higher than that typically reported for singletons, it is similar to prevalence rates for twins previously provided by Bakwin (1973), Johnston *et al.* (1984) and Stevenson *et al.* (1987).

In contrast to previous studies, the number of female probands ($N = 62$) exceeds the number of male probands ($N = 55$) in the present study. This is probably due at least in part to a differential volunteer rate of male and female twin pairs. Lykken *et al.* (1978) have noted that female and MZ twin pairs are often over-represented in twin studies. However, it is also possible that female twins, in comparison to singletons, may be at an elevated risk for reading disability. In singletons, the lower risk for reading disability in females may be due to their more strongly developed language skills (Masland, 1981). In the case of twins, however, delays may occur in the acquisition and development of linguistic abilities of both boys and girls (Johnston *et al.*, 1984). Of course, it is also possible that the excess of reading-disabled males reported in previous studies may be due at least in part to a referral bias (Finucci, 1978). Unfortunately, reports of the only other well-ascertained sample of reading-disabled twins potentially informative with regard to this

Table 1. Mean (±S.D.) Verbal and Performance IQ scores for male and female reading-disabled and control index cases

| | Reading-disabled | | | | Control | | | |
| | MZ | | DZ | | MZ | | DZ | |
IQ	Males	Females	Males	Females	Males	Females	Males	Females
Verbal	95.68 ± 7.32	92.78 ± 6.63	95.20 ± 8.94	92.52 ± 9.42	111.37 ± 12.39	108.91 ± 10.69	114.32 ± 10.58	110.26 ± 9.21
Performance	101.40 ± 10.05	99.89 ± 7.76	105.33 ± 8.89	100.49 ± 9.68	111.89 ± 11.48	111.14 ± 12.87	113.14 ± 11.31	111.70 ± 12.83
N	25	37	30	25	27	35	22	23

issue (Stevenson *et al.*, 1984, 1987) do not indicate the number of affected twins by gender.

As shown in Table 1, the average Verbal and Performance IQ scores of the reading-disabled probands are well within the normal range. For comparison, average scores of the MZ and DZ control index cases are also presented. As expected, the difference in Verbal IQ between the reading-disabled and control index cases is significant ($F(1,216) = 180.19, p < 0.001$), accounting for 44.8% of the variance in Verbal IQ scores. The difference in Verbal IQ between males and females is also significant ($F(1,216) = 5.17, p = 0.02$); however, it accounts for only 1.3% of the total variance. In contrast, the average scores of MZ and DZ probands do not differ significantly ($F(1,216) = 0.38, p = 0.54$). With regard to Performance IQ, a significant difference also exists between the reading-disabled and control index cases ($F(1,216) = 50.56, p < 0.001$), accounting for 18.7% of the observed variance; however, neither the gender difference nor the difference between zygosity groups is significant ($F(1,216) = 2.03, p = 0.16$, and $F(1,216) = 1.44, p = 0.23$, respectively). When Performance IQ is used as a covariate, the difference between the Verbal IQ scores of the reading-disabled and control index cases remains significant ($F(1,215) = 111.76$, $p = 0.001$) and accounts for 24.8% of the observed variance. However, the gender difference in Verbal IQ scores is no longer significant when Performance IQ is used as a covariate ($F(1,215) = 3.62, p = 0.06$), accounting for less than 1% of the total variance. When Verbal IQ is used as a covariate, the difference in Performance IQ scores of reading-disabled and control index cases is still significant ($F(1,215) = 4.49, p = 0.04$) but accounts for only 1.5% of the observed variance.

Analyses

Previous analyses of data from the Colorado Twin Study have focused on those tests which comprise the discriminant function composite (DeFries *et al.*, 1987). In contrast, data from the Rapid Automatic Naming of colors, numbers, letters and pictures (Denckla and Rudel, 1976) and the Detroit Tests of Learning Aptitude Auditory Attention Span for Unrelated Words and Related Syllables (Baker and Leland, 1959) will be featured in the present chapter. Because the discriminant score was employed as one of the diagnostic criteria in this study, analyses of this composite score will also be reported. A regression procedure was used to remove the linear and quadratic effects of age for all variables prior to analysis. Analyses undertaken in the present study include: (1) a comparison of MZ and DZ concordance rates for reading disability based upon school records and subsequent discriminant function classification; (2) an examination of the means and standard deviations for all variables separately by gender and zygosity for the reading-disabled and control groups; (3) fitting an extension of the basic model to twin data for each variable to test for differential genetic etiology in males and females (equation 9); and (4) application of equation 11 to test for differential heritability of test scores in males and females.

Results

Concordance rates

Concordance rates for reading disability are presented in Table 2. A subject was diagnosed as reading-disabled based upon evidence of reading difficulties in school as well as the discriminant function composite. In agreement with results from previous twin studies, a greater concordance is found for MZ twin pairs than for DZ twin pairs in the Colorado Reading Project. Consistent with a hypothesis of genetic etiology, the concordance rate for MZ pairs is significantly greater than that for DZ pairs ($\chi^2(1) = 4.25$, $p < 0.05$ (one-tailed)).

Descriptive statistics

Average, age-adjusted scores for the discriminant composite, the Rapid Automatic Naming tasks and the Detroit Tests of Learning Aptitude Attention for Related Syllables and Unrelated Words are presented separately for male and female twins in Tables 3 and 4. Results of a multivariate analysis of variance of data from reading-disabled and control index cases indicate that probands perform significantly lower than controls on all seven measures ($F(7,210) = 92.86$, $p < 0.001$). However, unlike the data obtained in the twin study of reading disability by Stevenson *et al.* (1987), no significant differences are found between MZ and DZ probands ($F(7,210) = 0.43$, $p = 0.88$). Although the main effect of gender is not significant ($F(7,210) = 1.53$, $p = 0.16$), a significant multivariate interaction is present between gender and group (i.e. reading disabled versus control) ($F(7,210) = 2.47$, $p = 0.02$). The difference between reading-disabled and

Table 2. Concordance rates for reading disability based upon school records and the discriminant function composite[a]

Zygosity	Number of concordant pairs	Number of discordant pairs	Pairwise concordance rate
MZ	32	30	52%
DZ	18	37	33%

[a]See text for explanation of discriminant function composite.

Table 3. Mean test scores (±S.D.) for male reading-disabled and control twin pairs

| | Reading-disabled | | | | Control | |
| | MZ | | DZ | | | |
	Proband	Cotwin	Proband	Cotwin	MZ	DZ
Discriminant score	-1.17 ± 0.84	-0.53 ± 0.94	-1.26 ± 0.82	-0.15 ± 1.03	1.39 ± 0.90	1.49 ± 0.99
Rapid Automatic Naming:						
Colors	20.83 ± 4.32	22.43 ± 4.60	20.76 ± 3.52	22.19 ± 3.72	24.73 ± 3.97	25.30 ± 3.90
Numbers	31.64 ± 5.92	34.16 ± 5.94	30.54 ± 4.19	34.97 ± 6.54	37.79 ± 6.32	38.87 ± 4.99
Letters	27.90 ± 5.15	29.26 ± 5.78	28.55 ± 5.91	31.41 ± 6.26	35.51 ± 5.45	37.58 ± 3.73
Pictures	19.99 ± 3.11	19.55 ± 2.98	19.56 ± 3.72	20.36 ± 3.65	21.09 ± 4.05	21.51 ± 2.35
Detroit Tests of Learning Aptitude:						
Related syllables	61.14 ± 8.74	60.26 ± 10.68	57.46 ± 12.89	63.03 ± 12.79	71.23 ± 13.67	71.71 ± 12.08
Unrelated words	43.13 ± 5.24	41.65 ± 5.79	41.54 ± 6.16	44.30 ± 6.68	46.36 ± 6.44	47.89 ± 6.35
Number of pairs	25		30		27	22

Table 4. Mean test scores (±S.D.) for female reading-disabled and control twin pairs

| | Reading-disabled | | | | Control | |
| | MZ | | DZ | | | |
	Proband	Cotwin	Proband	Cotwin	MZ	DZ
Discriminant score	−0.99 ± 0.53	−0.32 ± 0.65	−0.86 ± 0.54	−0.02 ± 0.72	1.33 ± 0.90	1.36 ± 0.72
Rapid Automatic Naming:						
Colors	22.51 ± 4.82	22.87 ± 3.76	22.40 ± 3.44	25.00 ± 5.82	27.04 ± 3.36	25.66 ± 3.99
Numbers	34.53 ± 4.21	34.96 ± 5.03	33.76 ± 5.77	35.92 ± 5.36	38.61 ± 5.70	37.10 ± 6.17
Letters	30.86 ± 4.61	31.78 ± 4.64	31.22 ± 6.91	32.38 ± 6.63	37.09 ± 5.53	35.74 ± 4.54
Pictures	19.82 ± 3.17	20.23 ± 3.15	20.15 ± 2.87	19.91 ± 3.05	22.73 ± 3.32	22.15 ± 2.96
Detroit Tests of Learning Aptitude:						
Related syllables	57.36 ± 13.06	59.33 ± 13.48	61.72 ± 8.26	67.21 ± 14.68	75.98 ± 12.34	75.31 ± 11.37
Unrelated words	42.60 ± 4.91	41.95 ± 6.10	41.61 ± 5.61	44.45 ± 7.34	47.57 ± 6.33	46.45 ± 5.48
Number of pairs	37		25		35	23

control male index cases is greater than the difference between reading-disabled and control female index cases for the Rapid Automatic Naming of Numbers and Letters and the discriminant score ($F(1,216) = 6.66, p = 0.01$, $F(1,216) = 3.95, p = 0.05$, and $F(1,216) = 6.88, p = 0.009$, respectively).

Genetic etiology

As previously discussed, MZ and DZ cotwins' scores should regress differentially toward the mean of the unselected population to the extent that reading disability is heritable. When the means of MZ and DZ probands are equal, a t-test of the difference between MZ and DZ cotwin means will suffice as a test of genetic etiology. For example, the MZ and DZ cotwin mean discriminant scores within the affected sample are -0.40 and -0.09, respectively, whereas the MZ and DZ proband means are almost identical. Consistent with the hypothesis of genetic etiology, a t-test of the difference between the MZ and DZ cotwin means is significant ($t(115) = -2.02$, $p = 0.02$ (one-tailed)). As indicated in an earlier section of this chapter, the multiple regression analysis of selected twin data provides a more powerful test of genetic etiology. More specifically, the B_2 coefficient from equation 4 estimates twice the difference between the means of MZ and DZ cotwins after covariance adjustment for any difference between MZ and DZ proband means. Thus, as expected, this coefficient is highly significant when estimated from the discriminant score data ($B_2 = -0.65 \pm 0.24$, $p = 0.004$ (one-tailed)).

For the present report, the basic model has been extended to test for differential genetic etiology in male and female probands (equation 9). Because the discriminant score was used as a criterion for the selection of probands, each twin's score was expressed as an inverse function of the deviation of the proband mean from that of the unselected population mean (equations 7 and 8) in order to facilitate direct estimates of h_g^2 for that measure. Partial regression coefficients resulting from the application of the extended basic model to data for each of the measures obtained from the reading-disabled probands and cotwins are presented in Table 5.

The partial regression of cotwin's scores on proband's score (P) provides a measure of average twin resemblance in the reading-disabled male and female twin pairs. Although the magnitude of this coefficient ranges from 0.21 to 0.74 for the various measures, each is highly significant. With regard to the discriminant score, the partial regression of cotwin's score on the coefficient of relationship (R) estimates average h_g^2 (the extent to which the deviation of the proband mean from the unselected population mean is heritable) in males and females. This coefficient is highly significant, thereby providing evidence of a genetic etiology for reading disability; however, the magnitude of the estimate indicates that only about 30% of the reading deficit

Table 5. Regression coefficients (±S.E.) estimated from an extension of the basic regression model[a]

	P	R	S	PS	RS
Discriminant score	0.74 ± 0.09**	0.28 ± 0.10**	0.28 ± 0.17	-0.27 ± 0.19	-0.19 ± 0.20
Rapid Automatic Naming:					
Colors	0.44 ± 0.09**	-1.97 ± 1.52	3.15 ± 2.60	-0.31 ± 0.19	-4.73 ± 3.06
Numbers	0.43 ± 0.10**	-2.63 ± 2.00	-2.48 ± 3.50	-0.29 ± 0.20	0.54 ± 3.99
Letters	0.21 ± 0.10*	-2.53 ± 2.14	-1.63 ± 3.63	-0.09 ± 0.19	2.89 ± 4.28
Pictures	0.23 ± 0.09**	-0.44 ± 1.18	-1.41 ± 1.94	0.22 ± 0.18	2.58 ± 2.37
Detroit Tests of Learning Aptitude:					
Related syllables	0.70 ± 0.09**	-9.58 ± 3.89**	5.18 ± 6.71	0.26 ± 0.17	0.34 ± 7.77
Unrelated words	0.38 ± 0.11**	-6.18 ± 2.33**	-1.43 ± 3.97	-0.17 ± 0.21	1.20 ± 4.65

[a]Partial regression of cotwin's score on proband's score (P), coefficient of relationship (R), gender (S) and their interactions.
*$p < 0.05$; **$p < 0.01$.

of probands may be attributed to heritable factors. Thus, environmental differences also contribute importantly to the observed difference between disabled and normal readers.

Estimates of h_g^2 were not obtained for the Rapid Automatic Naming tasks or the subtests of the Detroit Tests of Learning Aptitude because these measures, although correlated with reading performance, were not used for the selection of probands. The partial regression of cotwin's score on the coefficient of relationship for these six measures is a function of the genetic covariance between each test and the discriminant score (the variable of selection). As shown in Table 5, evidence for significant genetic covariance with the discriminant score was obtained for the Related Syllables and Unrelated Words subtests of the Detroit Tests of Learning Aptitude.

The partial regression of cotwin's score on gender (S) is a function of the difference between male and female cotwins' scores, whereas the partial regression of cotwin's score on the product of proband's score and gender (PS) indicates differential resemblance in male and female twin pairs. Neither of these coefficients is significant for any of the measures in Table 5.

Finally, the partial regression of cotwin's score on the product of the coefficient of relationship and gender (RS) provides a test of differential genetic etiology as a function of gender. None of the coefficients representing this interaction is significant in the present analysis, indicating that the null hypothesis of equivalent genetic etiology in male and female probands cannot be rejected. However, as discussed elsewhere in this chapter, the power to detect differential genetic etiology in two groups is relatively low; thus, larger samples may be required to test this hypothesis adequately.

Individual differences in reading ability

The etiology of individual differences (as opposed to the difference between the means of probands and controls) may be assessed by fitting the augmented model (equation 10) of DeFries and Fulker (1985) to twin data. As previously discussed, the partial regression of cotwin's score on the product of proband's score and the coefficient of relationship provides an estimate of the extent to which individual differences are due to heritable influences (h^2), whereas the partial regression of cotwin's score on proband's score yields an estimate of the proportion of variance due to environmental factors shared by members of twin pairs (c^2). This estimate of h^2 is equivalent to doubling the difference between the MZ and DZ bivariate regressions (the regression of cotwin's score on proband's score). Moreover, c^2 could be estimated from the difference between the simple MZ regression and the estimate of h^2. For example, the MZ and DZ bivariate regressions within the reading-disabled sample for the discriminant score are 0.91 and 0.65, respectively. Thus, $h^2 = 2\ (0.91 - 0.65) = 0.52$ and $c^2 = 0.91 - 0.52 = 0.39$. When the aug-

Table 6. Regression coefficients (±S.E.) estimated from an extension of the augmented model[a]

	P	PR	PS	PRS
Discriminant score	0.28 ± 0.31	0.60 ± 0.38	−0.63 ± 0.61	0.42 ± 0.75
Rapid Automatic Naming:				
Colors	0.43 ± 0.34	0.05 ± 0.40	0.71 ± 0.69	−1.23 ± 0.80
Numbers	0.55 ± 0.33*	−0.11 ± 0.41	−1.47 ± 0.66*	1.53 ± 0.81
Letters	0.25 ± 0.29	−0.06 ± 0.40	−0.14 ± 0.58	0.07 ± 0.79
Pictures	0.0003 ± 0.31	0.33 ± 0.38	0.52 ± 0.61	−0.47 ± 0.77
Detroit Tests of Learning Aptitude:				
Related syllables	0.29 ± 0.32	0.57 ± 0.40	0.47 ± 0.64	−0.47 ± 0.80
Unrelated words	−0.42 ± 0.32	1.08 ± 0.42**	−0.82 ± 0.65	0.78 ± 0.84

[a]Partial regression of cotwin's score on proband's score (P) and the interactions between proband's score and the coefficient of relationship (PR), proband's score and gender (PS), and proband's score, the coefficient of relationship, and gender (PRS).
*$p < 0.05$; **$p < 0.01$.

mented model (equation 10) is fitted to these data, the following estimates of h^2, c^2 and their associated standard errors are obtained: $h^2 = 0.52 \pm 0.34$ and $c^2 = 0.39 \pm 0.27$.

Just as the basic model was extended to test for differential genetic etiology in males and females, the augmented model can be extended to test for differential h^2 and c^2. However, because large samples are required to obtain reliable estimates of h^2 and c^2, even larger samples are necessary to detect differential h^2 or c^2. This is as true for the multiple regression analysis of selected twin data as for estimates obtained from other twin analyses. Nevertheless, the extended model (equation 11) was used to test null hypotheses of equal h^2 and equal c^2 in reading-disabled males and females. The coefficients that test for differential h^2 (PRS) and c^2 (PS) as a function of gender in the affected sample are presented in Table 6, as well as estimates of average h^2 (PR) and c^2 (P).

As indicated in the last column of Table 6, no evidence was obtained for differential h^2 in males and females for any of the measures. With regard to differential c^2, the partial regression of cotwin's score on proband's score and gender was significant only for the Rapid Automatic Naming of Numbers. As will be discussed later, however, the power to detect significant interactions is relatively low.

The average proportions of variance due to heritable influences (h^2) and environmental factors shared by members of twin pairs (c^2) estimated from males and females are meaningful when there is no evidence for differential

h^2 or c^2 as a function of gender. As may be seen in Table 6, the estimates of h^2 (the partial regression of cotwin's score on the product of proband's score and the coefficient of relationship) are substantial for the discriminant score and the Related Syllables and Unrelated Words subtests of the Detroit Tests of Learning Aptitude; thus, heritable influences contribute importantly to observed individual differences for these measures. The estimates of c^2 (the partial regression of cotwin's score on proband's score) indicate that shared environmental influences account for a significant proportion of variance only for the Rapid Automatic Naming of Numbers.

Discussion

Genetic etiology

The wealth of data collected in the Colorado Reading Project, its large sample size and the breadth of analyses facilitated by the multiple regression analysis of selected twin data yield additional insights into the etiology of reading disability. For example, with regard to the variable used for the selection of probands, fitting the basic model to data from MZ and DZ probands and cotwins provides a powerful test of genetic etiology. Moreover, when the data are suitably transformed prior to analysis, the extent to which performance deficits in probands are due to heritable influences (h_g^2) is directly estimated. For those measures correlated with the variable of selection, application of the basic model tests the influence of genetic factors upon the resulting difference between the reading-disabled probands and the unselected population.

Results from fitting the basic model to the transformed discriminant function score data indicated that approximately 30% of the observed difference between disabled and normal readers, on the average, may be attributable to genetic factors. Such a finding suggests that the performance deficits of reading-disabled children in the Colorado Reading Project could not be due solely to a fully penetrant major gene. If, however, the sample contains etiologically distinct subtypes, one or more of its forms may be inherited in a fairly simple Mendelian manner (e.g. Smith et al., 1983).

Evidence for significant genetic covariance between each of the two subtests of the Detroit Tests of Learning Aptitude and the discriminant score was obtained by fitting an extension of the basic model to the untransformed data. Thus, the deficits with regard to those correlated measures are also due at least in part to heritable influences. In addition, the extended model was used to test for differential genetic etiology in male and female probands. Although no evidence for differential genetic etiology was obtained, this may be due to the greater statistical power of the analysis to detect significant main effects than interactions.

Individual differences

The multiple regression analysis of twin data may also be employed to assess the etiology of individual differences. The augmented multiple regression model provides estimates of the extent to which differences among individuals are due to heritable factors (h^2) or to shared environmental influences (c^2). An extension of the augmented model that tests for differential h^2 and c^2 as a function of gender was also fitted to the proband and cotwin data. Only the Unrelated Words subtest of the Detroit Tests of Learning Aptitude yielded a significant h^2 estimate, and no evidence for differential h^2 in males and females was obtained. With regard to c^2, only the Rapid Automatic Naming of Numbers is significant. Although the standard error of its estimate is rather large, the regression coefficient that tests for differential c^2 is also significant for this measure.

Single versus double entry

The multiple regression analysis outlined in the present chapter provides a simple and highly flexible approach to the analysis of twin data that is analogous to the estimation of pairwise concordance rates (i.e. for each twin pair, the more severely affected twin is designated a proband). An alternative approach, analogous to the estimation of probandwise concordance rates, is to double enter each member of every concordant pair of affected twins, once as a proband and once as a cotwin. Although the multiple regression analyses previously described require little modification for use with the proband method, some simplicity is lost because the standard errors associated with the regression coefficients must be adjusted after the analysis in order to reflect the true sample size.

In order to compare the results from these two different approaches, the extended basic model was also fitted to the discriminant function score data of the MZ and DZ probands and cotwins using the double-entry procedure. The resulting h_g^2 estimate of 0.29 ± 0.13 was highly similar to that previously obtained (0.28 ± 0.10) using single entry. Thus, at least for the selected variable, the two approaches yield similar results.

Statistical power

As previously asserted, the multiple regression analysis of twin data provides a more powerful test of genetic etiology than do alternative analyses. Comparisons of MZ and DZ concordance rates, for example, are based upon a dichotomous classification with arbitrary cut-off points; thus, such comparisons may be expected to have relatively low power. The MZ and DZ pairwise concordance rates for reading disability within the Colorado Reading Project are 52% and 33%, respectively. Given these concordance rates in a sample of 50 MZ and 50 DZ pairs, the power to detect a significant difference at the 0.05 level (one-tailed test) would be 62% (Cohen, 1977). If 100 MZ and 100 DZ twin pairs were available for study, the power would increase to 86%.

As previously discussed, a differential regression of MZ and DZ cotwin means toward the mean of the unselected population is expected if the difference between the mean of probands and that of the unselected population is due at least in part to heritable influences. Thus, when the MZ and DZ proband means are equal, a t-test of the difference between the MZ and DZ cotwin means also provides a test for genetic etiology. In the Colorado Reading Project, the average MZ and DZ discriminant scores of cotwins were -0.40 and -0.09, respectively. If these means were population parameters, the power to establish a significant difference at the 0.05 level (one-tailed test) in a sample of 50 MZ and 50 DZ twin pairs is 57%. If the sample included 100 MZ and 100 DZ pairs, the statistical power of the analysis would increase to 82%.

In contrast to the simple comparison of cotwin means, the basic multiple regression analysis of twin data utilizes the proband scores as a covariate. Thus, when twin resemblance is substantial, the partial regression of cotwin's score on the coefficient of relationship provides a more powerful test of genetic etiology. Given the results of fitting the basic model to the discriminant score data in the Colorado Reading Project, the power to detect significant genetic etiology at the 0.05 level (one-tailed test) is 72% with a sample of 50 MZ and 50 DZ twin pairs, and would increase to 94% if 100 MZ and 100 DZ twin pairs were available. Thus, given the sample statistics estimated in the present study, the basic multiple regression model (equation 4) has more power than either a t-test between MZ and DZ cotwin means or a comparison of concordance rates to establish significant genetic etiology.

Although the basic multiple regression model provides a powerful test of genetic etiology, the power to detect differential genetic etiology is relatively low. For example, the estimates of h_g^2 for the discriminant scores of males and females in the present study are 0.37 and 0.18, respectively. The power to detect a significant interaction at the 0.05 level (two-tailed test) given this small difference is less than 16% if the analysis were based upon data from a sample of 100 MZ and 100 DZ twin pairs. Of course, with a larger difference in h_g^2, the statistical power will increase. If h_g^2 were 0.70 for males and 0.20 for females, for example, the power to detect differential genetic etiology as a function of gender in a sample of 50 MZ and 50 DZ twin pairs would be 40%. Moreover, with a sample of 100 MZ and 100 DZ twin pairs, the power would increase to 73%. Therefore, when the heritable nature of a disorder is sufficiently different in two groups, an adequate test of differential genetic etiology may be feasible.

Estimates of h^2, the extent to which genetic factors contribute to observed individual differences, are based upon the difference between estimates of MZ and DZ regression coefficients. For this reason, estimates of h^2, whether obtained from alternative analyses of twin data or the augmented multiple regression model (equation 10), require large samples for reliability. For example, given the estimate of $h^2 = 0.52$ obtained from an analysis of discriminant function score data from the present sample of 117 reading-disabled twin pairs, the power to detect significance at the 0.05 level (one-tailed test) is only 33%. The power would increase to 48% if 100 pairs of each zygosity were tested and to 77% if data from 200 MZ and 200 DZ pairs were available. Given this relatively low power to detect a significant h^2, a test of differential h^2 in different groups would require very large samples.

A comparison of h_g^2, the extent to which the deviation of the proband mean from the unselected population mean is due to genetic factors, and h^2, the extent to which individual differences in the normal range are heritable, could be used to test whether reading-disabled individuals merely represent the lower tail of a normal distribution of reading performance (Rodgers, 1983). Recently, DeFries and Fulker (1988) noted that the B_2 estimate in the augmented regression model (equation 10) provides a test of this difference when the data are expressed as deviations from the unselected population mean and divided by the deviation of the proband mean from that of the unselected population ($\bar{P} - \mu$). Although the power to detect a significant h_g^2 is substantial, the power associated with estimates of h^2 is relatively low; therefore, an adequate test of the difference between h_g^2 and h^2 would also require very large samples.

Prevalence rates

The Colorado Reading Project is the largest twin study of reading disability conducted to date. The sample is ascertained systematically through cooperating school districts, and both zygosity and diagnosis are determined using objective criteria. Because parents of twins with reading problems may be more willing to participate in research than parents of twins who are normal readers, some ascertainment bias may be present in our sample. Such a bias could explain, at least in part, the relatively high prevalence rate for reading disability (14.4%) observed in the present sample. Of course, it is also possible that twins may be at an increased risk for reading problems (Johnston *et al.*, 1984).

The large sample of twins studied in the Colorado Reading Project are also informative with regard to the differential prevalence of reading disability in males and females. Although the ratio of affected males to females is typically 3 or 4 to 1 in studies of reading-disabled singletons, the number of female twin probands actually exceeds the number of male twin probands in the Colorado

Reading Project (62 females versus 55 males). As previously discussed, this may be due to differential volunteer rates of male and female twin pairs (Lykken *et al.*, 1978) or to an elevated risk for reading disability in female twins. Alternatively, the differential prevalence rate in males and females reported in previous studies may be due in part to a referral bias (Finucci, 1978). A referral bias could occur, for example, if academic problems of boys were a greater concern than those of girls (Sladen, 1970).

Multiple Regression Analysis of Twin Data

The multiple regression analysis of twin data provides a powerful and highly flexible test of genetic etiology. The ready availability of multiple regression computer packages and the ease of most applications make the multiple regression analysis of twin data an appealing alternative for the analysis of twin data.

The basic and augmented models formulated in the present chapter may be readily extended to address issues of special relevance to the study of dyslexia. For example, the hypothesis of Stevenson *et al.* (1987) that genetic factors are less influential in the expression of reading disability at age 13 than at younger ages could be tested by incorporating a main effect for age and an interaction between the coefficient of relationship and age in the basic model (equation 4). Furthermore, covariates such as gender, socio-economic status, ethnic group, etc. may be included in the regression model and products of variables may be used to test for differential relationships.

This multiple regression analysis may also be applied to data from relatives other than twins and to data from more than two relationships simultaneously. For example, reading performance data from twins and siblings were recently subjected to multiple regression analysis to estimate h^2 and differential c^2 for twins and siblings (Zieleniewski *et al.*, 1987). In addition, although the multiple regression analyses described in the present chapter assume a simple additive genetic model, estimates of non-additive genetic variance could be obtained by incorporating dummy variates indicative of resemblance due to non-additive effects in the model and by including data from other genetic relationships such as adoptive and non-adoptive siblings (LaBuda *et al.*, 1986).

In conclusion, the multiple regression analysis of selected twin data from the Colorado Reading Project yields definitive evidence of a genetic etiology for reading disability. However, results of the present study suggest that environmental factors also contribute importantly to the difference between disabled and normal readers. Additional studies pertaining to the genetic and environmental etiologies of reading disability could yield improved risk estimates, facilitate early diagnosis and intervention, provide validity tests for alternative typologies and suggest the possibility of differential remediation.

ACKNOWLEDGEMENTS

This work was supported in part by a program project grant from the NICHD (HD-11681), and the report was prepared while M. C. LaBuda was supported by NICHD training grant HD-07289. We wish to acknowledge the invaluable contributions of staff members of the many Colorado school districts and of the families who participated in the study.

REFERENCES

Baker, H. J., and Leland, B. (1959). *Detroit Tests of Learning Aptitude*. Indianapolis: Test Division of Bobbs-Merrill.

Bakwin, H. (1973). Reading disability in twins. *Developmental Medicine and Child Neurology*, **15**, 184–187.

Brander, T. (1935). Bidrag till kannedomen om den kroppsliga och psykista utvecklingen hos tvillingar. *Läkaresällskapt Handlinger*, **77**, 195.

Cohen, J. (1977). *Statistical Power Analysis for the Behavioral Sciences*. New York: Academic Press.

Cohen, J., and Cohen, P. (1975). *Applied Multiple Regression/Correlation Analysis for the Behavioral Sciences*. New York: Halstead Press.

Critchley, M. (1970). *The Dyslexic Child*, 2nd edn. London: Heinemann.

Decker, S. N., and Vandenberg, S. G. (1985). Colorado twin study of reading disability. In D. B. Gray and J. F. Kavanagh (eds), *Biobehavioral Measures of Dyslexia*, pp. 123–135. Parkton, MD: York Press.

DeFries, J. C. (1985). Colorado reading project. In D. B. Gray and J. F. Kavanagh (eds), *Biobehavioral Measures of Dyslexia*, pp. 107–122. Parkton, MD: York Press.

DeFries, J. C., and Fulker, D. W. (1985). Multiple regression analysis of twin data. *Behavior Genetics*, **15**, 467–473.

DeFries, J. C., and Fulker, D. W. (1988). Multiple regression analysis of twin data: Etiology of deviant scores versus individual differences. *Acta Geneticae Medicae et Gemellologiae*, **37**, 205–216.

DeFries, J. C., Plomin, R., Vandenberg, S. G., and Kuse, A. R. (1981). Parent–offspring resemblance for cognitive abilities in the Colorado Adoption Project: Biological, adoptive, and control parents and one-year-old children. *Intelligence*, **5**, 245–277.

DeFries, J. C., Vogler, G. P., and LaBuda, M. C. (1986). Colorado Family Reading Study: An overview. In J. L. Fuller and E. C. Simmel (eds), *Behavior Genetics: Principles and Applications II*, pp. 29–56. Hillsdale, NJ: Lawrence Erlbaum.

DeFries, J. C., Fulker, D. W., and LaBuda, M. C. (1987). Evidence for a genetic aetiology in reading disability of twins. *Nature*, **329**, 537–539.

Denckla, M. B., and Rudel, R. G. (1976). Rapid 'automatized' naming (R.A.N.): Dyslexia differentiated from other learning disabilities. *Neuropsychologia*, **14**, 471–479.

Dunn, L. M., and Markwardt, F. C. (1970). *Examiner's Manual: Peabody Individual Achievement Test*. Circle Pines, MN: American Guidance Service.

Finucci, J. M. (1978). Genetic considerations in dyslexia. In H. R. Myklebust (ed.), *Progress in Learning Disabilities*, Vol. 4, pp. 41–63. New York: Grune & Stratton.

Finucci, J. M., and Childs, B. (1983). Dyslexia: Family studies. In C. L. Ludlow and J. A. Cooper (eds), *Genetic Aspects of Speech and Language Disorders*, pp. 157–167. New York: Academic Press.

Hallgren, B. (1950). Specific dyslexia: A clinical and genetic study. *Acta Psychiatrica et Neurologica Scandinavica* (Suppl.), **65**, 1–287.

Harris, E. L. (1986). The contribution of twin research to the study of the etiology of reading disability. In S. D. Smith (ed.), *Genetics and Learning Disabilities*, pp. 3–19. San Diego: College-Hill Press.

Hermann, K., and Norrie, E. (1958). Is congenital word-blindness a hereditary type of Gerstmann's syndrome? *Psychiatria et Neurologia*, **136**, 59–73.

Jenkins, R. L., Brown, A. W., and Elmerdorf, L. (1937). Mixed dominance and reading disability. *Zentralblatt für die Gesamte Neurologie und Psychiatrie*, **85**, 519.

Johnston, C., Prior, M., and Hay, D. (1984). Prediction of reading disability in twin boys. *Developmental Medicine and Child Neurology*, **26**, 588–595.

LaBuda, M. C., DeFries, J. C., and Fulker, D. W. (1986). Multiple regression analysis of twin data obtained from selected samples. *Genetic Epidemiology*, **3**, 425–433.

Ley, J., and Tordeur, G. W. (1936). Alexie et agraphie d'évolution chez des jumeaux monozygotiques. *Journal Belge de Neurologie et Psychiatrie*, **36**, 102.

Lykken, D. T., Tellegen, A., and DeRubeis, R. (1978). Volunteer bias in twin research: The rule of two-thirds. *Social Biology*, **25**, 1–9.

Masland, R. L. (1981). Summary of the conference proceedings. In A. Ansara, N. Geschwind, A. Galaburda, M. Albert and N. Gartrell (eds), *Sex Differences in Dyslexia*, pp. ix–xii. Towson, MD: Orton Dyslexia Society.

National Joint Committee on Learning Disabilities (1981). Learning disabilities: Issues on definition (a position paper of the National Joint Committee on Learning Disabilities, 30 January, 1981). Reprinted in *Journal of Learning Disabilities*, 1987, **20**, 107–108.

Neale, M. D. (1967). *Neale Analysis of Reading Ability*. London: Macmillan.

Nichols, R. C., and Bilbro, W. C. (1966). The diagnosis of twin zygosity. *Acta Geneticae Medicae et Gemellologiae*, **16**, 265–275.

Norrie, E. (1954). Ordblindhedens (dyslexiens) arvegang. *Laesepaedagogen*, **2**, 61.

Plomin, R., DeFries, J. C., and McClearn, G. E. (1980). *Behavioral Genetics: A Primer*. San Francisco: Freeman.

Rodgers, B. (1983). The identification and prevalence of specific reading retardation. *British Journal of Educational Psychology*, **53**, 369–373.

Schiller, M. (1937). Zwillingsprobleme, dargestellt auf Grund von Untersuchungen an Stuttgarter Zwillingen. *Zeitschrift für Menschliche Vererbungs und Konstitutionslehre*, **20**, 284.

Schonell, F. J., and Schonell, P. E. (1960). *Diagnostic and Attainment Testing*. Edinburgh: Oliver & Boyd.

Sladen, B. K. (1970). Inheritance of dyslexia. *Bulletin of the Orton Society*, **20**, 30–40.

Smith, S. D., Kimberling, W. J., Pennington, B. J., and Lubs, M. A. (1983). Specific reading disability: Identification of an inherited form through linkage analysis. *Science*, **219**, 1345–1347.

Stevenson, J., Graham, P., Fredman, G., and McLoughlin, V. (1984). The genetics of reading disability. In C. J. Turner and H. B. Miles (eds), *The Biology of Human Intelligence*, pp. 85–97. Nafferton, UK: Nafferton Books Unlimited.

Stevenson, J., Graham, P., Fredman, G., and McLoughlin, V. (1987). A twin study of genetic influences on reading and spelling ability and disability. *Journal of Child Psychology and Psychiatry*, **28**, 229–247.

von Harnack, G. A. (1962). Das Schulversagen als arztliches Problem. *Zeitschrift für Psychotherapie und Medizinische Psychologie*, **12**, 102–111.

Wechsler, D. I. (1974). *Examiner's Manual: Wechsler Intelligence Scale for Children—Revised*. New York: Psychological Corporation.

Wechsler, D. I. (1981). *Examiner's Manual: Wechsler Adult Intelligence Scale—Revised*. New York: Psychological Corporation.

Wong, B. Y. L. (1986). Problems and issues in the definition of learning disabilities. In J. K. Torgesen and B. Y. L. Wong (eds), *Psychological and Educational Perspectives on Learning Disabilities*, pp. 3–26. Orlando, FL: Academic Press.

Zerbin-Rüdin, E. (1967). Congenital word-blindness. *Bulletin of the Orton Society*, **17**, 47–54.

Zieleniewski, A. M., Fulker, D. W., DeFries, J. C., and LaBuda, M. C. (1987). Multiple regression analysis of twin and sibling data. *Personality and Individual Differences*, **8**, 787–791.

Addresses for correspondence:

Dr Michele C. LaBuda; Child Study Center, Yale University School of Medicine, 230 S. Frontage Road, PO Box 3333, New Haven, Connecticut 06510, USA

Professor John C. DeFries; Institute for Behavioral Genetics, University of Colorado, Campus Box 447, Boulder, Colorado 80309, USA

4

Genetic Linkage Analysis with Specific Dyslexia: Use of Multiple Markers to Include and Exclude Possible Loci

Shelley D. Smith,[1] Bruce F. Pennington,[2] William J. Kimberling,[1] and P. S. Ing[1]

[1]*Boys Town National Research Hospital, Omaha;* [2]*University of Colorado Health Sciences Center, Denver*

INTRODUCTION

The familial nature of dyslexia has been noted since the early 1900s, and there is strong evidence that this is due to genetic influences (Herschel, 1978; DeFries and Decker, 1981; DeFries *et al.*, 1987). Several studies have attempted to define the mode of inheritance. The earlier studies (Hallgren, 1950; Zahalkova *et al.*, 1972) suggested that the mode of inheritance was autosomal dominant, but these were later recognized to have methodological problems (Finucci, 1978; Smith and Goldgar, 1986). More recent studies of the segregation of dyslexia in families have indicated that there probably is genetic heterogeneity (Finucci *et al.*, 1976; Omenn and Weber, 1978; Lewitter *et al.*, 1980); the inheritance may be polygenic (a combination of many genes) in some families, but in others the inheritance may be due to alleles at a single locus. In still other families, of course, non-genetic transmission may occur. Our current results suggest that there may be an autosomal dominant form of dyslexia, and that there is genetic heterogeneity even within this subtype, in that there may be more than one such gene.

The technique we used to identify a single gene is called linkage analysis, which is used to map the location of genes on the chromosomes. Knowledge of the position of a gene and of the genes around it has unique advantages. By studying the inheritance of the surrounding genes in a family, the presence of a gene in a child can be inferred even before its effects can be measured. That is, the presence of a gene influencing reading disability could be predicted (with a certain probability) in a child before reading problems would become evident. The presence of more than one dominant gene may also be detected, since different genes would have different positions on the chromosomes. Ultimately, gene localization can be used to isolate a gene. Decoding this gene could provide important insight into the underlying biological mechanisms causing reading disability and aid in understanding what functions must be present for normal reading to occur.

LINKAGE ANALYSIS

The principles of linkage analysis and the application to reading disability have been reviewed elsewhere (Houseman *et al.*, 1985) and will be only briefly discussed here. Each chromosome consists of a linear strand of DNA that carries the code for a specific set of genes. All chromosomes, and thus all genes, come in pairs: one inherited from the mother and one from the father. In turn, one member of each pair is selected at random for transmission to a child. A gene may have different forms, termed alleles; e.g., a gene for a blood type may have an 'A' allele or a 'B' allele. Since genes are inherited as part of chromosomes, alleles for genes that are close together on the same chromosome—or linked—tend to be transmitted together to the offspring. The alleles for linked genes may be separated, however, if crossing-over and recombination occur between them during the formation of gametes. During this process, chromosomal material is exchanged between the two chromosomes in a pair. The probability that a crossover will occur between two genes is proportional to the distance between them. This probability is termed theta (θ), the recombination fraction. Unlinked genes, either on different chromosomes or far apart on the same chromosome, would show a recombination fraction of 0.50, indicating that the alleles are transmitted independently of each other. Linkage can be detected in family studies by finding that the recombination fraction between two genes is less than 0.50.

In order to see if a decreased recombination fraction is actually statistically significant, the odds of the likelihood of linkage versus no linkage is computed for each pedigree at different levels of recombination; 5%, 10%, 20% and so on to 50%. The log of the odds, termed the LOD score, can be added together from different families across all of the levels of recombination. The recombination level that gives the maximum LOD score is taken as the best estimate of the distance between the genes. By convention, a maximum LOD score of at least 3, or odds of 1000 to 1 favoring linkage, is required to accept the hypothesis of linkage, and a score of -2, or odds of 100 to 1 against linkage, rejects linkage at that level of recombination. An intermediate LOD score, between -2 and $+3$, indicates that more data are necessary (Morton, 1955).

Gene localization studies are typically done by comparing the transmission of a disorder (the 'test' gene) to that of a battery of 'marker' genes scattered throughout the chromosomes, to see if any one of the markers happens to be close to the test gene. Two properties of a good marker gene are that the genotype is readily detectable, as with a blood type, and that the locus is highly polymorphic, i.e. that there are at least two frequent alleles so that the probability is high that an individual is heterozygous (has two different alleles) for both the marker and test genes. The finding of a linkage is optimized if there are many such markers evenly distributed throughout the genome. A major factor in the recent explosion of localizations is the discovery of a new class of markers that fulfill these requirements, called restriction fragment length polymorphisms (RFLPs) (Botstein *et al.*, 1980; Housman *et al.*, 1985).

Restriction enzymes cleave DNA into small fragments at specific sites determined by the base sequence. A variation in the DNA code which adds or eliminates a restriction site, or a variation in the amount of DNA between two sites, will be reflected by variation in the size of a given fragment. The fragments are separated by size with electrophoresis, and the position of a given fragment is detected with a complementary radioactive DNA probe which anneals to the fragment in the gel. RFLPs are quite numerous, making them ideal markers for linkage analysis. Since these have been developed, several genes that previously eluded localization, simply because there were no markers nearby, have been localized.

For accurate linkage analysis, one must be able to determine who in the family carries the gene for the disorder and who does not. Diagnosis is easier if it can be made on the basis of a biochemical test. However, many dominant genetic disorders are recognized only by clinical evaluation, and problems of variable expression and decreased penetrance can make the diagnosis very difficult.

Variable expression refers to the different manifestations that a disorder may have; neurofibromatosis, for example, may be expressed as only a few café au lait spots, with a continuum of severity to numerous tumors of the skin and organs. For reading disability, there could be variation in severity or in manifestation at different ages. Penetrance refers to the percentage of individuals with a given genotype that actually express the disorder phenotypically. A non-penetrant person is one who carries the gene for a disorder but does not detectably express it, at least in the ways it is being measured. Ascertainment and diagnostic procedures must be designed to try to minimize these problems.

PREVIOUS STUDIES

Nine families were included in the initial study. The methodology has been reported by Pennington *et al.* (1984), and Smith *et al.* (1986b). When this study was done, RFLPs were not available. Classical genotyping markers were used along with chromosomal heteromorphisms. The latter are heritable, normal variations in staining characteristics that can be used to trace the transmission of a chromosomal region. Linkage analysis with these markers in the initial families showed evidence for linkage only for the heteromorphic area (the short arm and centromere) of chromosome 15 (Smith *et al.*, 1983b). Eight of the nine families were informative for this marker (i.e. the affected parent was also heterozygous for the heteromorphisms). The maximum LOD score was 3.2 at about 13% recombination. One family's LOD scores looked quite negative, which suggested that they might not be linked, but statistical testing did not show that the LOD scores were heterogeneous.

THE CURRENT STUDY

Methods

Families were ascertained through special schools for teaching disabled children, through tutors, through advocacy groups, or from Dr Pennington's neuropsychological clinic. Three families were ascertained through the Colorado Family Reading Study of the Institute for Behavioral Genetics (DeFries and Decker, 1981). In an effort to reduce what might be confounding influences, all families were native English-speaking and of middle-class background, and all family members in the study had to have a Verbal or Performance IQ of at least 90 as measured by the WISC-R (Wechsler, 1974) or WAIS-R (Wechsler, 1981). In a few families, the IQ was measured using Raven's Progressive Matrices as adapted by the Institute for Behavioral Genetics. Both biological parents and at least two children over 7 years of age had to be available for the study.

Families were interviewed and a detailed family history was taken. School and medical history were reviewed and appropriate records requested when necessary. If the history and pedigree were consistent with an autosomal dominant form of specific reading disability through several generations on one side of the family, each family member was asked to take a battery of tests to be sure that the reading disability was specific, and to confirm who was actually affected. These tests included the Peabody Individual Achievement Tests (Dunn and Markwardt, 1970) the Gray Oral Reading Test (Gray, 1963) and the WRAT Spelling Test (Jastak and Jastak, 1984).

The diagnosis of reading disability was based on three factors: (1) a Reading Quotient (RQ); (2) the Specific Dyslexia Algorithm (SDA); and (3) an early history of significant and persistent problems with learning to read, without known etiology. This history had to be corroborated by school records or, in the case of adults, by parents or siblings.

Following the method suggested by Finucci (1978), the RQ was computed as the ratio of reading and spelling ability to expected ability based on age, education and intelligence. For children, the RQ formula was

$$\frac{(\text{Gray Oral age equivalent} + \text{WRAT Spelling age equivalent})/2}{(\text{Chronological age} + \text{age for grade} + \text{IQ age})/3}$$

Age for grade equivalents were taken from a table provided by Dr Finucci. IQ age was calculated as the chronological age $\times$ (Full-Scale IQ/100). For adults, the PIAT Spelling test was substituted for the WRAT Spelling test because of ceiling effects in the latter. Chronological age and IQ age could not be used for adults since they would continue to increase while the academic ages would tend to plateau, so the age equivalents for the Mathematic and General Information tests were substituted. Age for grade was figured as the age equivalent for the last grade completed. Thus, the RQ for adults was figured as:

$$\frac{(\text{Gray Oral age equivalent} + \text{PIAT Spelling age equivalent})/2}{(\text{Age for grade} + \text{Math. age equivalent} + \text{General Info. age equivalent})/3}$$

A quotient less than 0.80 was considered indicative of RD, from 0.80 to 0.89 was borderline, and 0.90 and above indicated normal reading ability.

The Specific Dyslexia Algorithm was developed by Dr Pennington and reflected the pattern of scoring on the PIAT tests seen in the affected individuals in the initial study (Pennington et al., 1984). Essentially, scoring was lowest on spelling and reading recognition, with better achievement on reading comprehension, and best performance on General Information or Mathematics. The algorithm consists of specific criteria based on the z-scores for these tests.

A child or adult was considered to be affected if he or she was positive on either the RQ or SDA and had a positive history. It was recognized, however, that an additional category was necessary for adults, since adults can learn to compensate for earlier reading disability and score in the non-disabled range on the RQ and SDA, but still have a history (corroborated by relatives) of reading disability. Since what we are trying to detect is the presence of a putative gene, rather than current reading ability, classification of such an individual as unaffected would result in misdiagnosis for the linkage analysis. This is similar to a study of the genetic influences on stuttering, in which the important phenotype was 'ever stuttered' rather than whether an adult currently stuttered (Kidd, 1977). We also included the category of obligate carrier. Dominant genes may not be completely penetrant, and we had to allow for this by assuming that an unaffected individual with an affected child and an affected parent or sibling was actually a gene carrier. Of course, our pedigrees were selected to minimize non-penetrance, and the initial study and current study each had only one such individual.

From these criteria, five different categories were defined: Affected (positive RQ or SDA and positive history); Unaffected (negative RQ, SDA and history); Compensated (negative RQ and SDA, positive history); Obligate carrier (negative RQ, SDA and history, but an affected child and affected sibling or parent); and Questionable (anything other than the above; e.g. positive RQ but negative history). For the linkage analysis, compensated individuals and obligate carriers were considered affected, and questionable individuals were omitted.

These criteria represent a change from the initial study, in which the RQ and SDA were not used. Instead, a two-grade level discrepancy between the Gray Oral Reading Test and the mean of the PIAT Mathematics and General Information Tests was required. The change to the current criteria was made to make our study comparable to other studies and to facilitate replication, and represent refinement rather than real change. In practice, when the criteria from the current study were applied to the initial study, there were no changes in classification.

Results

Nineteen new families were screened for the study and 14 were accepted. Two families were from Miami, and the rest were ascertained by Dr Pennington either through his clinical practice or by review of family histories in the Colorado Family Reading Study. In addition, Dr Pennington expanded 5 of the original 8 pedigrees. It was particularly notable that the segregation and the phenotype remained consistent as new branches of these families were studied. Table 1 gives the numbers of individuals in each diagnostic category.

Because of the positive linkage with chromosome 15 found in the initial study, chromosome 15 heteromorphisms were examined first in the continuation study. Twelve of the new families were informative. The results of the new linkage analysis with the chromosomal heteromorphisms are shown in Table 2. This combines data from all of the families that have been studied. Ten of the 20 informative families show crossovers, and 5 clearly look unlinked (i.e. 372, 484, 491, 100 and 8001). Of the 8 positive families, 2 are large enough to have fairly good LOD scores, and one clearly looks linked (432). The overall LOD score has gone down, with θ now estimated at 34%

Table 1. Diagnostic categories

Affected	118
Unaffected	111
Compensated	23
Obligate carrier	2
Questionable	10
Total	264

instead of 13%, but a test for homogeneity of the recombination fraction between families is significant (Smith *et al.*, 1986a).

The test of homogeneity is designed to evaluate whether the population could be made up of two types of families, some showing linkage of RD to chromosome 15 (low recombination fraction) and some rejecting linkage (recombination fraction = 0.50). Significant heterogeneity would imply that in the linked families the dyslexia is due to a gene on chromosome 15. For the unlinked families, the dyslexia could be due to another gene or genes at a

Table 2. Linkage analysis: reading disability versus chromosome 15 heteromorphisms

Family no.	Recombination fraction				
	0.00	0.10	0.20	0.30	0.40
371	0.602	0.465	0.318	0.170	0.049
372	$-\infty$	−1.963	−0.765	−0.232	−0.009
375	0.220	0.354	0.248	0.117	0.022
432	2.961	2.441	1.901	1.333	0.714
484	$-\infty$	−2.312	−0.779	−0.156	0.056
491	$-\infty$	−1.331	−0.581	−0.227	−0.053
576	0.189	0.055	0.002	−0.005	−0.002
1002	0.292	0.208	0.129	0.062	0.016
1000	$-\infty$	−1.586	−0.786	−0.373	−0.132
1001	0.292	0.208	0.129	0.062	0.016
8001	$-\infty$	−1.553	−0.756	−0.371	−0.145
8002	$-\infty$	−0.889	−0.298	−0.084	−0.014
8005	−1.411	−0.304	−0.108	−0.031	−0.005
8006	$-\infty$	0.013	0.121	0.109	0.059
8007	0.301	0.255	0.204	0.146	0.079
8008	0.898	0.722	0.539	0.355	0.175
8010	$-\infty$	−0.258	−0.100	−0.042	−0.012
9007	$-\infty$	−0.181	0.076	0.079	0.014
9008	$-\infty$	−0.267	−0.110	−0.049	−0.014
9102	−2.131	−1.005	−0.457	−0.180	−0.042
Total	$-\infty$	−6.673	−0.869	0.829	0.799

different location, or to a non-genetic effect. For the test of homogeneity, the program HOMOG by Ott was used (Ott, 1985). This program uses a maximum likelihood method to estimate two parameters: α, the proportion of linked families; and θ, the recombination fraction in linked families. Three hypotheses were formulated and tested. The null hypothesis was that none of the families showed linkage to chromosome 15. Alpha was set at 0 and θ at 0.50, which is non-linkage. The first alternative hypothesis was that all families showed linkage. Alpha was set at 1 (all families linked) and the program estimated the maximum value of θ over all families. It obtained a value of 0.30. The second alternative hypothesis was that there was heterogeneity, with a proportion of families showing linkage. Both α and θ are estimated from the data. These maximized at an α of 0.18 and a θ of 0.00. The likelihood of each hypothesis was computed, and the hypotheses were compared by calculating twice the difference in log likelihoods for competing hypotheses. This statistic is distributed as a χ^2 so that a traditional χ^2 test was used to compare these hypotheses. When the first alternative hypothesis of all families linked is compared to the null hypothesis (no linkage), a significance level of $p = 0.0297$ is obtained. Similarly, a value of $p = 0.0047$ is obtained when the second alternative hypothesis, linkage with heterogeneity, is compared to the null hypothesis. Finally, when the hypothesis of heterogeneity is used as the alternative hypothesis, compared to a null hypothesis of homogeneity (all families linked), a value of $p = 0.0081$ is obtained.

Thus the hypothesis that there is heterogeneity, with 18% of the population showing linkage, provides the best fit to the LOD score data if it is assumed that there is linkage between chromosome 15 heteromorphisms and specific reading disability. It is important to emphasize that, although the p value obtained in the comparison of the hypothesis of homogeneity versus no linkage ($p = 0.0297$) would be considered significant by most standards, this does not meet the stringent levels required for the acceptance of linkage, i.e. $p < 0.001$. If an LOD score from a single family was greater than 3.000, the hypothesis of linkage in at least one family could be considered proven. The score of 2.961 in family 432 almost reaches that criterion. Thus, at this point, we cannot assert that linkage is proven, but we can say that, if there is linkage of reading disability to chromosome 15, it is present in about 15–20% of families.

Our current work has two aims: to confirm the linkage on chromosome 15 through heteromorphisms and by demonstrating linkage to an RFLP, and to define an alternative linkage or linkages for the families not showing linkage to chromosome 15. To date, two RFLP probes, pDP151 and pMS1-14, have been examined for chromsome 15. LOD scores for both of them were low for linkage with dyslexia (Kimberling *et al.*, 1985). However, these probes were not detectably linked to the centromeric area of chromosome 15, whereas our results indicate tight linkage of dyslexia to the centromere. Thus, these probes may be too far down the long arm of chromosome 15 to detect linkage. Also, the scores were too low for detection of heterogeneity. Studies are under way with two different probes which should be closer to the heteromorphic region.

Since the majority of the families studied did not show linkage to chromosome 15, we feel it is important to try to detect any other gene or genes that may be present. This will be done with a battery of classical markers, heteromorphisms and RFLPs. This results in considerable improvement in the coverage of the genome and improves the chances of finding a linkage, if one exists. Exclusion of linkage from a region is also valuable information. Using a method of interval analysis, which combines information from several markers in a region, we can effectively identify the most likely areas for study. We have already begun testing with several of these markers. For example, on chromosome 1 we have very negative LOD scores for Rh, PGM1 and NGFB, with fairly negative LODs for the surrounding markers H3H2 and Fy. DR78 is thought to be farther down on the long arm, and the LOD score is also negative for it. Taking all of the markers together, we can state that it is unlikely that there is another major gene influencing reading disability on chromosome 1. The numbers are too small to rule out heterogeneity, but the data appear to be homogeneous.

Similarly, on chromosome 13 we have looked at p7F12, p9D11 and p9A7, which are fairly evenly spaced. All three had negative LOD scores, but none less than -2.0. Other markers have been tested on chromosomes 2, 6 and 16, but the results to date are also equivocal.

DISCUSSION

The results of this study indicate that, if there is a gene influencing reading disability on chromosome 15, it is not the only cause of familial reading disability. All of the families studied had histories consistent with autosomal dominant transmission of reading disability, often in several branches of the family, so it is reasonable to hypothesize that the cause is genetic in all of the families, and to examine them for other possible linkages.

In addition to confirming the finding of genetic heterogeneity for specific reading disability by identifying an additional gene, detection of an alternative linkage would facilitate the classification of families into etiologically distinct subtypes. For example, the probability that a family shows linkage to a given gene can be computed, but the family has to be fairly large to reach a high enough probability of linkage to be reliable for classification purposes. With identification of an additional gene, the probability of linkage to one gene and not the other can be computed, giving much more information for classification of an individual family.

A complementary approach to the confirmation of genetic heterogeneity through linkage analysis would be to look for clinical differences between families with a high probability of linkage to chromosome 15 and those which are clearly unlinked. We have examined the phenotype in these families at several levels, including spelling error patterns (Pennington *et al.*, 1984, 1986, 1987a,b), neuropsychological measures (Smith *et al.*, 1983a, 1986b), and immune function and handedness (Pennington *et al.*, 1987), and we have not been able to detect any clear evidence of clinical heterogeneity. While this could suggest that this is an etiologically homogeneous population, there is evidence that the genetic influence on reading disability is restricted to a portion of the overall reading process. The work of Pennington *et al.* (as cited above) indicates that the deficits in these families is in phonemic processing. In a study of the genetics of dyslexia utilizing twins, Olson and Wise (1986) found significant heritability for a phonological task but not for an orthographic task. As Pennington *et al.* (1987) summarize, 'a deficit in the process that acquires rule-like knowledge of sound–spelling correspondences in spelling and spelling–sound correspondences in reading appears to be a final, common pathway in etiologically disparate forms of dyslexia. Therefore, this phenotype is not only genetically mediated, it can be produced by different genetic influences' (p. 86). Indeed, it appears that deficits in phonemic processing may be a primary problem in well-defined dyslexics regardless of etiology, as reviewed by several of the authors in this volume.

This situation of multiple causes for one phenotype is not unusual. A gene has its effect on a given process within a pathway. Another type of interference with that process or even elsewhere in the pathway could produce the same end result. The interference could be produced by another gene, in which the resulting phenotype is called a 'genocopy', or by a non-genetic insult, resulting in a 'phenocopy'. Profound deafness is one example of genocopies and phenocopies that produce an identical phenotype, in that there are several different autosomal recessive forms of isolated deafness, as well as environmental agents such as antibiotics or infections.

Linkage analysis can be valuable in detecting genocopies or phenocopies. In 1956, linkage analysis showed that elliptocytosis, a disorder of the red blood cells, had at least two causes. Some families showed tight linkage of elliptocytosis to the Rh blood group genes on chromosome 1, but other families clearly rejected that linkage (Morton, 1956). Similarly, some families with olivo-pontocerebellar atrophy, an adult-onset progressive neurological disorder, show linkage of the disorder to the HLA region of chromosome 6, but other families do not (Morton *et al.*, 1980). In a third example, affective disorder has been found to be related to at least two different genes, one on chromosome 11 (Egeland *et al.*, 1987) and one on the X chromosome (Baron *et al.*, 1987). Evidence for further heterogeneity is reported by Hodgkinson *et al.* (1987), who studied three families with apparent autosomal dominant transmission of affective disorder who did not show linkage to chromosome 11. With all of these disorders, as in specific reading disability, further studies will be very important in discovering alternative linkages and defining phenotypic differences between families in different linkage groups.

ACKNOWLEDGEMENT

This work was supported by National Institutes of Health grants HD19423, HD11681, MH00419, and MH38820.

REFERENCES

Baron, M., Risch, N., Hamburger, R., Mandel, B., Kushner, S., Newman, M., Drumer, D., and Belmaker, R. H. (1987). Genetic linkage between X-chromosome markers and bipolar affective illness. *Nature*, **326**, 289–292.

Botstein, D., White, R. L., Skolnick, M., and David, R. W. (1980). Construction of a genetic linkage map in man using restriction fragment length polymorphisms. *American Journal of Human Genetics*, **32**, 314–331.

DeFries, J. C., and Decker, S. N. (1981). Genetic aspects of reading disability: The Colorado Family Reading Study. In P. G. Aaron and M. Malatesha (eds), *Neuropsychological and Neuropsycholinguistic Aspects of Reading Disability*. New York: Academic Press.

DeFries, J. C., Fulker, D. W., and LaBuda, M. C. (1987). Evidence for a genetic aetiology in reading disability of twins. *Nature*, **329**, 537–539.

Dunn, L. M., and Markwardt, F. C. (1970). *Peabody Individual Achievement Test*. Circle Pines, MN: American Guidance Service.

Egeland, J. A., Gerhard, D. S., Pauls, D. L., Sussex, J. N., Kidd, K. K., Allen, C. R., Hostetter, A., and Houseman, D. E. (1987). Bipolar affective disorders linked to DNA markers on chromosome 11. *Nature*, **325**, 783–787.

Finucci, J. M. (1978). Genetic considerations in dyslexia. In H. R. Myklebust (ed.), *Progress in Learning Disabilities*, Vol. IV, pp. 41–63. New York: Grune & Stratton.

Finucci, J. M., Guthrie, J. T., Childs, A. L., Abbey, H., and Childs, B. (1976). The genetics of specific reading disability. *Annals of Human Genetics (London)*, **40**, 1–23.

Gray, W. S. (1963). In H. M. Robinson (ed.), *The Gray Oral Reading Test*. Indianapolis: Bobbs-Merrill.

Hallgren, B. (1950). Specific dyslexia ('congenital word-blindness'): A clinical and genetic study. *Acta Psychiatrica et Neurologica Scandinavia*, Suppl. 65.

Herschel, M. (1978). Dyslexia revisited: A review. *Human Genetics*, **40**, 115–134.

Hodgkinson, S., Sherrington, R., Gurling, H., Marchbanks, R., Reeders, S., Mallet, J., McInnis, M., Petursson, H., and Brynjolfsson, J. (1987). Molecular genetic evidence for heterogeneity in manic depression. *Nature*, **325**, 805–806.

Housman, D., Smith, S. D., and Pauls, D. (1985). Applications of recombinant DNA to neurogenetic disorders. In D. B. Gray and J. F. Kavanagh (eds), *Biobehavioral Measures of Dyslexia*, pp. 155–162. Parkton, MD: York Press.

Jastak, J. F., and Jastak, S. R. (1984). *Wide Range Achievement Test—Revised.* Wilmington, DE: Jastak Association.

Kidd, K. (1977). A genetic perspective on stuttering. *Journal of Fluency Disorders*, 2, 259–269.

Kimberling, W. J., Fain, P. R., Ing, P. S., Smith, S. D., and Pennington P. F. (1985). Linkage analysis of reading disability with chromosome 15. *Behavior Genetics*, 15, 597. Presentation to the Behavior Genetics Association, University Park, PA, June 1985.

Lewitter, F. I., DeFries, J. C., and Elston, R. C. (1980). Genetic models of reading disability. *Behavior Genetics*, 10, 9–30.

Morton, N. E. (1955). Sequential tests for the detection of linkage. *American Journal of Human Genetics*, 7, 277–318.

Morton, N. E. (1956). The detection and estimation of linkage between genes for elliptocytosis and the Rh blood type. *American Journal of Human Genetics*, 8, 80–96.

Morton, N. E., Lalouel, J. M., Jackson, J. F., Currier, R. D., and Yee, S. (1980). Linkage studies in spinocerebellar ataxia (SCA). *American Journal of Medical Genetics*, 6, 251–257.

Olson, R. K., and Wise, B. (1986). Heritability of phonetic and orthographic word decoding skills in dyslexia. Paper presented at the meetings of the Psychonomics Society, New Orleans.

Omenn, G. S., and Weber, B. A. (1978). Dyslexia: Search for phenotypic and genetic heterogeneity. *American Journal of Medical Genetics*, 1, 333–342.

Ott, J. (1985). *Analysis of Human Genetic Linkage.* Baltimore: Johns Hopkins University Press.

Pennington, B. F., Smith, S. D., McCabe, L. L., Kimberling, W. J., and Lubs, H. A. (1984). Developmental continuities and discontinuities in a form of familial dyslexia. In R. Emde and R. Harman (eds), *Continuities and Discontinuities in Development*, pp. 123–151. New York: Plenum.

Pennington, B. F., McCabe, L. L., Smith, S. D., Lefly, D. L., and Bookman, M. O. Errors in adults with a form of familial dyslexia. *Child Development*, 57, 1001–1013.

Pennington, B. F., Smith, S. D., Kimberling, W. J., Green, P., Haith, M. M. (1987a). Left handedness and immune disorders in familial dyslexics: A test of Geschwind's hypothesis. *Archives of Neurology*, 44, 634–639.

Pennington, B. F., Lefly, D. L., Van Orden, G. C., Bookman, M. O., and Smith, S. (1987b). Is phonology bypassed in normal or dyslexic development? *Annals of Dyslexia*, 37, 62–89.

Smith, S. D., and Goldgar, D. E. (1986). Single gene analyses and learning disabilities. In S. D. Smith (ed.), *Genetics and Learning Disabilities*, pp. 47–65. San Diego: College-Hill Press.

Smith, S. D., Pennington, B. F., Kimberling, W. J., and Lubs. H. A. (1983a). A genetic analysis of specific reading disability. In C. Ludlow and J. Cooper (eds), *The Genetic Aspects of Speech and Language*. New York: Academic Press.

Smith, S. D., Kimberling, W. J., Pennington, B. F., and Lubs, H. A. (1983b). Specific reading disability: Identification of an inherited form through linkage analysis. *Science*, 219, 1345–1347.

Smith, S. D., Pennington, B. F., Kimberling, W. J., Fain, P. R., Ing, P. S., and Lubs, H. A. (1986a). Genetic heterogeneity in specific reading disability. *American Journal of Human Genetics*, 39, 169A.

Smith, S. D., Goldgar, D. E., Pennington, B. F., Kimberling, W. J., and Lubs, H. A. (1986b). Analysis of subtypes of specific reading disability: Genetic and cluster analytic approaches. In G. Th. Pavlidis and D. F. Fisher (eds), *Dyslexia: Its Neuropsychology and Treatment*, pp. 181–202. Chichester: Wiley.

Wechsler, D. (1974). *Wechsler Intelligence Scale for Children—Revised*. New York: The Psychological Corporation.

Wechsler, D. (1981). *Wechsler Adult Intelligence Scale—Revised*. New York: The Psychological Corporation.

Zahalkova, M., Vrzal, V., and Klobovkova, E. (1972). Genetical investigations in dyslexia. *Journal of Medical Genetics*, **9**, 48–52.

Addresses for correspondence:

Professor Shelley D. Smith, Professor William J. Kimberling and Professor P. S. Ing; Boys Town National Research Hospital, Omaha, Nebraska 68131, USA

Professor Bruce F. Pennington; University of Colorado Health Sciences Center, Denver, Colorado, USA

Part III

Neuroanatomical and Neurophysiological Aspects of Dyslexia

5

Morphological Cerebral Asymmetries and Dyslexia

Peter B. Rosenberger
Massachusetts General Hospital, Boston

INTRODUCTION

One may safely bank on widespread agreement, at least among contemporary students of the topic, that developmental dyslexia is in some way related to altered function of the central nervous system. Although the precise nature of the functional disturbance is a subject of much dispute, the consensus is that failure of the otherwise normally intelligent schoolchild to acquire written language skills at the expected rate is frequently due to a deficit of some basic *aptitude* for those skills, rather than simply lack of motivation and/or opportunity to learn.

The current state of thinking about the nature of the functional deficit in dyslexia is the topic of much of the remainder of the present volume. This chapter will review recent studies that have excited much interest in the question of possible *structural* alteration in the dyslectic's brain. We shall present data from our own laboratories, then suggest a basis for synthesis with varied and apparently disparate findings of others.

To jump ahead a bit: assuming the brain of the dyslectic person *is* structurally abnormal, how did it get that way? Is the deficit the result of a lesion occurring in a previously normal brain at some point in its development, or was it programmed into the brain's development from the start? To put the question another way: is the abnormality best described as a *deficit* in the true sense, or rather as an atypicality of development, in the same sense as if one extremity were larger than the other, or the two eyes of different colors? It will become apparent that our discussion of morphological asymmetries favors the latter assumption: that what is clinically identified as a 'learning disorder' usually represents the low end of a spectrum of talent or

Perspectives on Dyslexia Vol. 1
Edited by G. Th. Pavlidis   © 1990 John Wiley & Sons Ltd

aptitude, having very much to do with brain function and/or structure, but not properly considered a 'disease' except in the broadest sense. We are mindful, however, that as understanding of brain pathophysiology progresses, disorders previously considered 'developmental' are often seen to result from acquired lesions in early stages of development. The schizencephalies, previously thought to represent a developmental failure in formation of the telencephalon during embryonic life, but recently shown to result from occlusions of the middle cerebral arteries in fetal stages, are a case in point.

The reader should be aware of a serious methodological problem confronting the student of the developmental anatomy or physiology of any higher cortical function of the brain. Much of what is known about the neuroanatomy of language disorders was learned from adults who suffered strokes that incapacitated some specific language function but left the remainder of the intellect intact, who improved sufficiently to be tested, and who then died within a few years of heart attacks or other non-neurological catastrophes. This sequence of events does not usually pertain to children's language. Children who suffer isolated deficits of language function, whether congenital or acquired, usually live a normal life span, until long after the students of their deficits have themselves passed away. Those who succumb to the diseases that caused their language deficits usually show such widespread brain disease at the time of their demise that anatomical localization at autopsy is impossible. This probably explains why substantive progress in anatomy of children's language disorders had to await introduction of non-invasive study techniques such as the CT scan and magnetic resonance imaging, much as the study of functional hemispheric dominance in the child has depended upon such techniques as dichotic listening and tachistoscopic presentation to visual hemi-fields.

FUNCTIONAL ASYMMETRY

This chapter will assume as a matter of general agreement that the two cerebral hemispheres do not participate symmetrically in the functions relevant to reading; and will not attempt to review the voluminous recent literature supporting that assumption. By way of explanation of the ontogeny of hemispheric asymmetry, we have nothing to add to the suggestion of Kinsbourne (1974a) that those functions are represented asymmetrically that do not relate directly to the organism's response to its environment. We also subscribe to Kinsbourne's further formulation (1974b) that to say that one hemisphere is 'dominant' for a particular function does not necessarily imply that the other hemisphere does not participate at all, but more likely that its input is temporarily 'overridden', in much the same way as when activity from one hemisphere drives the organism's attention to the opposite half of external space.

Despite considerable evidence that hemispheric specialization in at least some of its manifestations is inborn, there is reason to believe that its expression in language function undergoes some development in early years. Three important clinical facts about acquired language disorders in children are consistent with this hypothesis. First, the child under pubertal age who loses language skills already acquired because of a lesion in one hemisphere typically shows considerable recovery, usually within a year. There is evidence (Basser, 1962) that reacquired language in this case resides in the opposite, formerly non-dominant hemisphere. There is further reason to believe that this reacquisition is accomplished at the expense of non-verbal skills (Woods and Teuber, 1973). Second, children are more likely to show at least transient language deficit with lesions of either hemisphere—in which respect they resemble left-handers. Third, the so-called 'fluent' dysphasias are extremely uncommon in children, except occasionally in the first few hours after the ictus.

It may not be immediately apparent how this last fact speaks in favor of a developmental character of cerebral dominance. In adults with receptive dysphasias (with the exception of conduction aphasia), jargon and paraphasic errors tend to disappear as comprehension improves. We suggest that children, having relatively bilateral hemispheric representation of language, may have enough residual comprehension following acute lesions of one hemisphere to preclude protracted output of nonsensical speech. Indeed, the child with profound receptive language deficit, as for example in verbal auditory agnosia, may appear more emotionally disturbed than language-deficient.

Is there a single function, asymmetrically represented in the hemispheres, developmental in character, that is so essential to acquisition of reading skills that lack of aptitude for it constitutes dyslexia? This question has been addressed since the days of Samuel Orton (1937), who first called attention to the various clinical correlates of disordered language function in the dyslectic child. Numerous studies in recent years (reviewed by Satz, 1976; Rosenberger, 1980) have solidified the case for specific deficits in language processing in these children. The studies of A. Liberman and colleagues, reviewed elsewhere in this volume, have established for the major temporal lobe the unique function of interpretation of the *speech code*, which they have defined as the construction of phonemes from rapid alterations in frequency of the auditory signal over small units of time. Together with more recent studies of I. Liberman, Shankweiler and co-workers on reading disorder (Liberman *et al.*, 1977; Shankweiler and Liberman, 1978), they make a persuasive argument that phonological analysis of sounds represented by combinations of written letters, with subsequent re-synthesis into spoken words, is essential to any reading skill that goes beyond simple association of ideographs with spoken words.

Numerous recent studies by Tallal and co-workers (Tallal and Piercy, 1975; Tallal and Newcombe, 1978; Tallal *et al.*, 1981; Tallal and Stark, 1981, 1982; Tallal, 1983; Tallal *et al.*, 1985a,b) have further specified what is presumably the same function described in Liberman's researches. As recently reviewed by Tallal (1987), they show that language-impaired children are deficient in discrimination of the temporal order of sounds of different frequencies presented at intervals less than 500 ms, and in discrimination of speech sounds that differ from one another in the *sequence* of frequencies over these brief epochs. Furthermore, the severity of this perceptual deficit correlates with the severity of the language delay, and efficiency of rapid acoustic analysis correlates with phonological awareness in general. Applying these studies to reading-disabled children, Tallal has found deficits in rapid acoustic analysis among dyslectics who show auditory-processing deficits on the usual clinical measures, but not among those who do not. In longitudinal studies, she has shown that failure in non-verbal auditory processing at age 4 years predicts 70% of children who show language impairment at age 8 years, also 80% of children with reading disorder. She has also found that adult dyslectics maintain inability to process these non-verbal acoustic stimuli even after they have learned to read.

If the above formulations of the functional deficit in dyslexia are correct, then in seeking an anatomical substrate it would make sense to turn attention upon (a) the 'language areas', as classically understood, and (b) asymmetries between the two hemispheres. Such will be the focus of the remainder of this review.

ANATOMICAL ASYMMETRY IN THE NORMAL BRAIN

There has long been considerable interest among anatomists in the question of what about the human brain enables language and other functions apparently unique to the species. It is clearly not either the size or weight alone. Humans have neither the largest brains in the animal kingdom nor the greatest ratio of brain to body weight (von Bonin, 1941). Among humans, brain weight is only partially related to language development; Yakovlev (1959) has pointed out that although the severely retarded tend to have small brains, brain weight does not otherwise correlate with intelligence.

If language is asymmetrically represented in the hemispheres, what is different anatomically about the language-dominant hemisphere? Not its total mass, according to von Bonin (1962). Different patterns of cytoar-chitecture have long been known to exist in different areas of the brain, but with the exception of those described recently by Galaburda *et al.* (1978b) none clearly characterizes those areas known to be relevant to language function.

Autopsy Studies

Although there is mention of previous reports, current understanding of the anatomy of language function got its start with the report of Geschwind and Levitsky (1968) that when the adult brain at autopsy is sliced horizontally so as to expose the superior surface of the temporal lobes, the planum temporale—a triangular area defined anteriorly by Heschl's gyrus and posteriorly by the posterior margin of the Sylvian fissure—describes a wider arc on the left than the right in 65 of 100 cases, with relative symmetry in an additional 24. This finding was later confirmed by Witelson and Pallie (1973) as well as by Wada *et al.* (1975), who found that a similar asymmetry applies to the frontal operculum as well. Falzi *et al.* (1982) defined as the 'anterior speech region' the area including both the triangular and opercular portions of the inferior frontal gyrus, and reported this region to be larger on the left in 9 of 12 brains of right-handed adults.

The studies of Witelson and Paillie and of Wada *et al.* included neonates, and Wada *et al.* reported the asymmetry in fetuses as young as 29 weeks. Chi *et al.* (1977) examined 207 fetal brains ranging in age from 10 to 44 weeks, and reported that the asymmetry is recognizable by 31 weeks gestation. LeMay (1976) reported that asymmetries of frontal and occipital petalia seen on contrast studies in humans (see below) can be found on direct examination in the brains of non-human primates, and suggested that asymmetries in skulls of fossil man reflect these findings.

Asymmetries in the decussation (crossing) of the pyramidal tracts in the brain stem were reported in the brains of adult humans at autopsy by Kertesz and Geschwind (1971). Of 158 such specimens, crossing from left to right (left brain to right extremities) began at a higher level in 73%, with right to left higher in 17% and no asymmetry in 10%. Weinberger *et al.* (1982) reported that the right frontal and left occipital lobes were larger than their counterparts in 32 of 40 brains examined in serial section, and that this asymmetry could be seen as early as 32 weeks gestation. More recently, Kooistra and Heilman (1988), also applying planimetric analysis to serial sections from normal brains in the Yakovlev collection, have reported a significant asymmetry in the volume of the globus pallidus, the left side being larger in 16 of 18 brains.

Early Contrast Studies

At about the time of the initial report of Geschwind and Levitsky, McRae *et al.* (1968) measured the occipital horns in 100 consecutive pneumoencephalograms from unselected neurological patients. They found asymmetrical lengths in 70 cases, with the left being longer in 57 and the right in 13. LeMay and Culebras (1972) reported a number of measures on carotid arteriography showing greater development of the parietal operculum on the left than on the right in 38 of 44 cases.

CT Scan Studies

Demonstration of hemispheric asymmetry by the radiological technique of computed tomography (CT) scanning represented a considerable advance, since for the first time it allowed correlative studies in living human brains not damaged by diseases of sufficient severity to justify more invasive contrast procedures. This technique was pioneered by LeMay in a number of studies (LeMay, 1976, 1977; Galaburda et al., 1978a; LeMay and Kido, 1978). She reported greater width and/or protuberance (petalia) in the right frontal and/or left occipital areas in a majority of unselected scans from adult neurological patients, between 60 and 70% depending upon whether left-handers are included (see below). Figure 1 depicts a comparison between two such scans, showing the 'typical' and 'atypical' asymmetries, respectively.

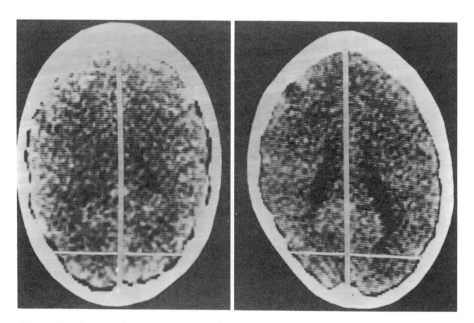

Figure 1. Computed tomography (CT) scans from two dyslexic young adults. The heavy white stripe lies along the interhemispheric fissure. The thin white stripe has been drawn perpendicular to the other, through the parieto-occipital region. The scan on the left shows the typical asymmetry, that on the right the atypical

Confirmation of LeMay's findings has been complicated by methodological problems, including standardization of measurement techniques as well as differences in tomographic angle by successive generations of CT scanners. However, Deuel and Moran (1980) found 50% 'typical' and 32% 'atypical' asymmetries, respectively, among 94 children referred for CT scan for miscellaneous neurological reasons. Pieniadz and Naeser (1984), using improved measurement methods, have shown greater occipital length on the left in the CT scans of 12 of 15 adult males. They have made the further valuable contribution of post-mortem examination of the same 15 brains, showing a significant correlation between occipital length on the CT scan and length of the planum temporale on the autopsied brain. This finding provides the first assurance that the CT scan measurements are telling us something about language-relevant areas of the brain. Finally, a recent letter (Bear *et al.*, 1988) has reported a preliminary study showing reversal of the usual right frontal width predominance in the CT scans of 9 out of 16 men with diagnosis of acquired immunodeficiency syndrome, evidence relating to the finding by Geschwind and Behan (1982) of a relation between dyslexia and immune disorders.

CORRELATION OF ANATOMICAL AND FUNCTIONAL ASYMMETRY

It was to be anticipated that, as soon as the anatomical asymmetries reviewed above were discovered, the search would begin for evidence that they are related to the functional asymmetries that characterize language. The search has been complex, and the results not entirely straightforward. However, as it is hoped the following review will demonstrate, there is to date too much positive evidence to discount.

Handedness

Motor laterality preference was the first functional correlation attempted by the earliest studies. McRae *et al.* (1968), in their PEG study, showed a significantly higher prevalence of their 'atypical' asymmetry (longer right occipital horn) among their left-handers, although the sample size was small. LeMay and Culebras (1972), using arteriograms, measured the arches formed by the arteries leaving the posterior ends of the Sylvian fissures, and found significantly greater symmetry in the brains of their left-handers. LeMay (1977), in her measurements of torque of the skull on plain X-ray, found both less asymmetry and more 'atypical' (left frontal–right occipital) prominence among the left-handers. Her initial CT scan measurements (LeMay and Kido, 1978), employing a large group of left-handers (85 in all), showed that approximately equal numbers had the 'typical' and 'atypical' asymmetries, significantly different from the right-handers. Chui and Damasio (1980) found a significant difference between right-handers and non-right-handers in occipital length but not width. On the negative side, Kertesz and Geschwind (1971) found no correlation between handedness and pattern of pyramidal decussation, but again the number of left-handers in their sample was small (four). Finally, Deuel and Moran (1980), working with children, failed to show a significant correlation between their CT scan asymmetry and either observed or stated hand preference.

Language Laterality

The more relevant functional correlation for anatomical asymmetry of the hemispheres is of course with language rather than motor laterality. As is usually the case in such studies, it has been necessary to infer language laterality through aphasic response to unilateral hemisphere disease. The question has been most thoroughly researched in recent years by Naeser and co-workers at the Boston Veterans' Administration Hospital. Among studies by this group, Pieniadz et al. (1983) showed an association between atypical asymmetry on CT scan and improved recovery of one-word language functions in patients with global aphasia following stroke; and Schenkman et al. (1983), using an overlapping patient population, reported a similar relation to improved recovery from hemiplegia. Naeser (1984) reviews these and other data, including some from 'crossed aphasias' (those following lesions of the hemisphere ipsilateral to the preferred hand), and proposes a model suggesting that concordance between occipital CT scan asymmetry and dominance for speech output is a risk factor for poor recovery from aphasia. However, studies from the same group (Henderson et al., 1984), using right-handed subjects aphasic following lesions of both right and left hemispheres, showed that CT scan asymmetry does not in itself correlate with language laterality as inferred from side of lesion.

Developmental Language Disorders

While the relevance of hemispheric language specialization to developmental language disorders is still a subject for debate, CT scan studies of asymmetry have been informative in these children. Our own laboratory has approached the question from a number of perspectives. First, Hier et al. (1978), using LeMay's measurements, identified a subgroup of young adult dyslectic patients with an increased prevalence of reversed or atypical asymmetry on CT scan. Rosenberger and Hier (1980) confirmed this finding among 22 of 53 patients from a learning disorders clinic, selected partly for large differences between verbal and non-verbal IQ scores (see below). Next, Hier et al. (1979)

Table 1. Cerebral asymmetry in developmental language disorders

	N	L > R	R > L
		P–O widths (%)	
Language disorders	24	58	42
Dyslexia	16	44	56
Autism	22	45	55
Delayed speech			
Comparison groups			
Mentally retarded	44	77	23
Other neurological	100	75	25

showed a similar increase in a group of autistic mentally retarded adults, whose scans were measured blindly along with those of a similarly retarded but non-autistic control group. Finally, Rosenberger et al. (1978) showed atypical asymmetry in a group of otherwise intelligent children who were late to develop spoken language. Table 1 summarizes the numbers of cases in each comparison.

These results have been only partially confirmed by other investigators. Haslam et al. (1981) showed more frequent symmetry of occipital width in dyslexic boys as compared to controls, but could not confirm the relation to onset of spoken language. Voeller et al. (1983), measuring CT scans by the method of Chui and Damasio (1980), found the typical asymmetry in only 10 of 28 severely dyslectic children of normal intelligence. Four of their subjects, three of whom were girls, showed unequivocal atypical asymmetry. Damasio et al. (1980) found no significant petalia (i.e. relative symmetry) in approximately half of a group of 16 autustic children.

Verbal Intellect

As a functional correlate of difference in anatomical asymmetry of the hemispheres, a direct measure of specific aptitudes would be even more relevant than a diagnosis of language deficit or learning disability, which is usually predicated on achievement or skills. In our initial study (Hier et al., 1978) we compared Verbal and Performance IQs by the Wechsler Scale for the dyslectic subjects with typical and atypical asymmetry, and found a relative verbal intellectual deficit in the atypical asymmetry group (mean VIQ 87, PIQ 96) as compared to the others (VIQ 99, PIQ 103). In a further study (Rosenberger and Hier, 1980) we sought such a correlation in a learning disorders clinic population of 53 children. We compared the subgroups of 31 showing typical asymmetry and 22 with atypical asymmetry on these measures. Although the two subgroups were highly comparable in full-scale IQ

(97.0 versus 98.2), the atypical asymmetry group showed a much wider distribution of verbal and non-verbal aptitudes (mean VIQ 91.0, PIQ 107.3) than did the typical asymmetry group (mean VIQ 97.0, PIQ 97.8). The difference remained significant when the 'Verbal Comprehension' and 'Perceptual Organization' factors of Kaufman (1975) were computed in place of Verbal and Performance IQ.

Since a history of delayed onset of speech is known to predict verbal intellectual deficits in later life (Warrington, 1967), we hypothesized that age of speech acquisition would be a significant interacting variable in our correlations. Indeed, of our 53 learning disabled subjects, 23 had a history of delayed onset of speech (first phrases age 36 months or later). Furthermore, of those 23, a majority (12) showed atypical asymmetry on CT scan, a significantly higher incidence than among those with normal speech development (10 out of 30). However, although the subjects with delayed speech showed a significantly lower mean full-scale IQ than the others (90.5 versus 107.5), the Verbal − Performance IQ difference was nearly identical for the two groups (−16.7 versus −16.6).

We next attempted a more quantitative correlation between degree of cerebral asymmetry and difference between VIQ and PIQ. Figure 2 shows this correlation. Plotted on the abscissa is the asymmetry index (L − R/ L + R) from parieto-occipital widths. On the ordinate is the VIQ − PIQ

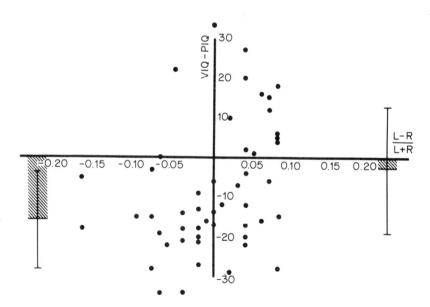

Figure 2. Correlation of asymmetry index measure from CT scan (abscissa) with VIQ − PIQ difference on Wechsler Scale ordinate for 53 learning-disabled children

difference. What was found was a 'curvilinear fit' rather than straight correlation. Those subjects showing typical asymmetry (to the right of the midline)
showed an essentially even IQ distribution. Of the 22 subjects with atypical
asymmetry, only one showed a higher verbal than performance IQ.

Related findings were reported by Yeo et al. (1987) in adult subjects *not*
selected for learning disability. Using sophisticated computer-assisted
measurements of cerebral volume from the CT scan, they showed a significant
correlation between degree of difference in volume between the hemispheres
and VIQ − PIQ difference on the Wechsler Scale.

An additional finding of our 1980 study deserves comment at this point. Of
our 53 learning-disabled subjects, eight were left-handed. While the left-
handers showed a significantly different VIQ–PIQ distribution (102.6 versus
97.1) than the right-handers (93.1 versus 102.6), in fact seven of the eight
left-handers showed the *typical* asymmetry on CT scan. Combining this
finding with that of LeMay that up to half of left-handers show the atypical
asymmetry, we infer that some discordance between the anatomical expression of hemispheric asymmetry and the functional expression of handedness
constitutes the risk factor for dyslexia. We note that this does not coincide
with the experience of Naeser (1984), for whom a comparison of motor
dominance and CT scan asymmetry did not predict recovery from aphasia in
adults.

COMMENT

We have made clear at the outset our bias on the question of the nature of the
functional deficit in dyslexia. To our clinical appraisal, dyslexia is a lack of
aptitude for one or more specific skills necessary for making sense out of
(deriving meaning from) the printed word. Although it makes perfectly good
sense to select cases for studies of dyslexia from among poor readers, we view
definitions of dyslexia based upon reading underachievement (including the
'official' NIH definition) as essentially mistaken. Dyslexia is an *aptitude*
deficit. It is entirely possible for a dyslectic youngster, by virtue of proper
tutorial assistance, to read at grade level; and selection criteria that require an
achievement deficit of one or two grade equivalents, even those that take IQ
into account, will miss this important subgroup. By the same token, dyslexia,
being a lack of aptitude for learning, is an intellectual deficit, however
restricted. Dyslectic youngsters of normal IQ should be referred to as
otherwise normally intelligent, despite the fact that in the majority of cases
standard intelligence tests have failed to specify the deficit.

What then is the nature of the physiological deficit? Is the 'lesion' acquired,
or programmed into the brain's original development? We have noted above
that, as the techniques for investigation of developmental malformations

improve, lesions previously considered developmental are frequently recognized on second glance as acquired.

The initial report of Galaburda and Kemper (1979) focused attention upon cytoarchitectonic abnormalities in the major temporal lobe in dyslectic brain. However, as Kinsbourne and Satz both note elsewhere in this volume, there are problems with attribution of developmental language deficits to unilateral brain lesions since, as noted above, the opposite hemisphere has considerable ability to assume the lost function (Basser, 1962), and in the case of language usually at the expense of non-verbal skills (Woods and Teuber, 1973). Language deficits attributable to brain damage, such as verbal auditory agnosia, can usually be correlated with bilateral lesions, as was noted in early descriptions (Landau and Kleffner, 1957) and has recently been confirmed by studies employing magnetic resonance imaging (Filipek *et al.*, 1987).

Galaburda's recent studies (1987) are more readily reconciled with these considerations. He reports that all seven of the brains of dyslectic individuals examined so far in his laboratory have shown relative *symmetry* of the temporal planes of the two hemispheres. He shows from studies of normal brains that relative symmetry of these areas is more likely to be explained by larger size on the right than by smaller size on the left; and reasons from studies involving actual neuronal counts in rat cortex that the larger size on the right is more likely accounted for by greater number of neurons than by larger size of neurons or by non-neuronal structures. He then alludes to recent studies in developmental neuropathology suggesting that cell death is an important event in normal development of the cerebral cortex, and hypothesizes that the pathogenesis of disorders of hemispheric dominance may be related to factors influencing cell death in corticogenesis.

Relating these findings to those of our own studies and others regarding 'atypical asymmetry' in language-delayed and learning-disabled subjects, one must then ask whether it is 'reversed' asymmetry or *lack* of asymmetry that is the important finding. This is certainly reminiscent of the old question as to whether sinistrality or ambidexterity is the more significant motor preference finding in dyslexia. Given the likelihood that any of these findings, if at all relevant, represents more of a risk factor than a direct cause of the disorder, the question may be unimportant. It may be that just as all forms of non-right-handedness seem to share the same physiological correlates, so all 'non-typical' hemispheric asymmetry, including symmetry, has the same implication for language development.

REFERENCES

Basser, L. (1962). Hemiplegia of early onset and the faculty of speech with special reference to the effects of hemispherectomy. *Brain*, **85**, 427–460.

Bear, D., Agostini, M., and Saporta, J. (1988). Anomalous cerebral asymmetries in acquired immunodeficiency syndrome. *Archives of Neurology*, **45**, 248.

Bonin, G. von (1941). Sidelights on cerebral evolution: Brain size of lower vertebrates and degrees of cortical folding. *Journal of General Psychology*, **25**, 273–282.

Bonin, G. von (1962). Anatomical asymmetries of the cerebral hemispheres. In V. Mountcastle (ed.), *Interhemispheric Relations and Cerebral Dominance*. Baltimore: Johns Hopkins University Press.

Chi, J., Dooling, E., and Gilles, F. (1977). Left–right asymmetries of the temporal speech areas of the human fetus. *Archives of Neurology*, **34**, 346–348.

Chui, H., and Damasio, A. (1980). Human cerebral asymmetries evaluated by computerized tomography. *Journal of Neurology, Neurosurgery and Psychiatry*, **43**, 873–878.

Damasio, H., Maurer, R., Damasio, A., and Chui, H. (1980). Computerized tomographic scan findings in patients with autistic behavior. *Archives of Neurology*, **37**, 504–510.

Deuel, R., and Moran, C. (1980). Cerebral dominance and cerebral asymmetries on computed tomogram in childhood. *Neurology*, **30**, 934–938.

Falzi, G., Perrone, P., and Vignolo, L. (1982). Right–left asymmetry in anterior speech region. *Archives of Neurology*, **39**, 239–240.

Filipek, P., Kennedy, D., Caviness, V., Klein, S., and Rapin, I. (1987). In vivo magnetic resonance imaging-based volumetric brain analysis in subjects with verbal auditory agnosia. *Annals of Neurology*, **22**, 410.

Galaburda, A. (1987). The pathogenesis of childhood dyslexia. In F. Plum (ed.), *Language, Communication, and the Brain*. New York: Raven Press.

Galaburda, A., and Kemper, T. (1979). Cytoarchitectonic abnormalities in developmental dyslexia: A case study. *Annals of Neurology*, **6**, 94–100.

Galaburda, A., LeMay, M., Kemper, T., and Geschwind, N. (1978a). Right–left asymmetries in the brain. *Science*, **199**, 852–856.

Galaburda, A., Sanides, F., and Geschwind, N. (1978b). Human brain: Cytoarchitectonic left–right asymmetries in the temporal speech region. *Archives of Neurology*, **35**, 812.

Geschwind, N., and Behan, P. (1982). Left handedness: Association with immune disease, migraine, and developmental learning disorders. *Proceedings of the National Academy of Science*, **79**, 5097–5100.

Geschwind, N., and Levitsky, W. (1968). Human brain: Right–left asymmetries in temporal speech region. *Science*, **161**, 186–187.

Haslam, R., Dalby, T., Johns, R., and Rademaker, A. (1981). Cerebral asymmetry in developmental dyslexia. *Archives of Neurology*, **38**, 679–682.

Henderson, V., Naeser, M., Weiner, J., Pienadz, J., and Chui, H. (1984). CT criteria of hemisphere asymmetry fail to predict language laterality. *Neurology*, **34**, 1086–1089.

Hier, D., LeMay, M., Rosenberger, P., and Perlo, V. (1978). Developmental dyslexia: Evidence for a subgroup with a reversal of cerebral asymmetry. *Archives of Neurology*, **35**, 90–92.

Hier, D., LeMay, M., and Rosenberger, P. (1979). Autism and unfavorable left–right asymmetries of the brain. *Journal of Autism and Developmental Disorders*, **9**, 153–159.

Kaufman, A. (1975). Factor analysis of the WISC-R at 11 age levels between 6½ and 16½ years. *Journal of Consulting and Clinical Psychology*, **43**, 135.

Kertesz, A., and Geschwind, N. (1971). Patterns of pyramidal decussation and their relationship to handedness. *Archives of Neurology*, **24**, 326–332.

Kinsbourne, M. (1974a). Mechanisms of hemispheric interaction in man. In M. Kinsbourne and W. Smith (eds), *Hemispheric Disconnection and Cerebral Function*. Springfield, CT: Thomas.

Kinsbourne, M. (1974b). Lateral interaction in the brain. In M. Kinsbourne and W. Smith (: .), *Hemispheric Disconnection and Cerebral Function*. Springfield, CT: Thomas.

Kooistra, C., and Heilman, K. (1988). Motor dominance and lateral asymmetry of the globus pallidus. *Neurology*, **38**, 388–390.

Landau, W., and Kleffner, F. (1957). Syndrome of acquired aphasia with convulsive disorder in children. *Neurology*, **7**, 523–530.

LeMay, M. (1976). Morphological cerebral asymmetries of modern man, fossil man, and nonhuman primate. *Annals of the New York Academy of Sciences*, **280**, 349–366.

LeMay, M. (1977). Asymmetries of the skull and handedness. *Journal of Neurological Science*, **32**, 243–253.

LeMay, M., and Culebras, A. (1972). Human brain: Morphologic differences in the hemispheres demonstrable by carotid arteriography. *New England Journal of Medicine*, **287**, 168–170.

LeMay, M., and Kido, D. (1978). Asymmetries of the cerebral hemispheres on computed tomograms. *Journal of Computer Assisted Tomography*, **2**, 471–476.

Liberman, I. Shankweiler, D., Liberman, A., Fowler, C., and Fischer, F. (1977). Phonetic segmentation and recoding in the beginning reader. In A. Reber and D. Scarborough (eds), *Toward a Psychology of Reading*. Hillsdale, NJ: Erlbaum.

McRae, D., Branch, C., and Milner, B. (1968). The occipital horns and cerebral dominance. *Neurology*, **18**, 95–98.

Naeser, M. (1984). Relationship between hemispheric asymmetries on computed tomography scan and recovery from aphasia. *Seminars in Neurology*, **4**, 136–150.

Orton, S. (1937). *Reading, Writing, and Speech Problems in Children*. New York: Norton.

Pieniadz, J., and Naeser, M. (1984). Computed tomographic scan cerebral asymmetries and morphologic brain asymmetries. *Archives of Neurology*, **41**, 403–409.

Pieniadz, J., Naeser, M., Koff, E., and Levine, H. (1983). CT scan cerebral hemispheric asymmetry measurements in stroke cases with global aphasia: Atypical asymmetries associated with improved recovery. *Cortex*, **19**, 371–391.

Rosenberger, P. (1980). Neurological processes. In R. Schiefelbusch (ed.), *Bases of Language Intervention*. Baltimore: University Park Press.

Rosenberger, P., and Hier, D. (1980). Cerebral asymmetry and verbal intellectual deficits. *Annals of Neurology*, **8**, 300–304.

Rosenberger, P., Hier, D., and Epstein, A. (1978). Cerebral asymmetry in children with delayed speech. Read by title at Child Neurology Society annual meeting.

Satz, P. (1976). Cerebral dominance and reading disability. In R. Knights and D. Bakker (eds), *The Neuropsychology of Learning Disorders*. Baltimore: University Park Press.

Schenkman, M., Butler, R., Naeser, M., and Kleefield, J. (1983). Cerebral hemisphere asymmetry in CT and functional recovery from hemiplegia. *Neurology*, **33**, 473–477.

Shankweiler, D., and Liberman, I. (1978). Reading behavior in dyslexia: Is there a distinctive pattern? *Bulletin of the Orton Society*, **28**, 114–122.

Tallal, P. (1983). Neuropsychological foundations of specific developmental disorders of speech and language: Implications for theories of hemispheric specialization. In J. Cavenar (ed.), *Psychiatry*. Philadelphia: Lippincott.

Tallal, P. (1987). Auditory perceptual deficits and language impairment. Paper delivered at the International Association for Research in Learning Disabilities, Los Angeles.

Tallal, P., and Newcombe, F. (1978). Impairment of auditory perception and language comprehension in dysphasia. *Brain and Language*, **5**, 13–24.

Tallal, P., and Piercy, M. (1975). Developmental aphasia: The perception of brief vowels and extended stop consonants. *Neuropsychologia*, **13**, 69–74.

Tallal, P., and Stark, R. (1981). Speech discrimination abilities of normally developing and language-impaired children: Acoustic analysis. *Journal of the Acoustical Society of America*, **69**, 568–574.

Tallal, P., and Stark, R. (1982). Perceptual-motor profiles of reading-impaired children with or without concomitant oral language deficits. *Annals of Dyslexia*, **32**, 163–175.

Tallal, P., Stark, R., Kallman, C., and Mellits, D. (1981). A reexamination of some nonverbal perceptual abilities of language-impaired and normal children as a function of age and sensory modality. *Journal of Speech and Hearing Research*, **24**, 351–357.

Tallal, P., Stark, R., and Mellits, D. (1985a). Identification of language-impaired children on the basis of rapid perception and productions skills. *Brain and Language*, **25**, 314–322.

Tallal, P., Stark, R., and Mellits, D. (1985b). The relationship between auditory temporal analysis and receptive language development: Evidence from studies of developmental language disorder. *Neuropsychologia*, **23**, 527–534.

Voeller, K., Armus, J., and Alhambra, M. (1983). Atypical computed tomographic scans and cerebral asymmetries in dyslexic children and adolescents. *Annals of Neurology*, **14**, 362–363.

Wada, J., Clarke, R., and Hamm, A. (1975). Cerebral hemispheric asymmetry in humans. *Archives of Neurology*, **32**, 239–246.

Warrington, E. (1967). The incidence of verbal disability associated with reading retardation. *Neuropsychologia*, **5**, 175–179.

Weinberger, D., Luchins, D., Morihisa, J., and Wyatt, R. (1982). Asymmetrical volumes of the right and left frontal and occipital regions of the human brain. *Annals of Neurology*, **11**, 97–100.

Witelson, S., and Pallie, W. (1973). Left hemisphere specialization for language in the newborn. *Brain*, **96**, 641–646.

Woods, B., and Teuber, H. (1973). Early onset of complementary specialization of the cerebral hemispheres in man. *Transactions of the American Neurological Association*, **98**, 113–117.

Yakovlev, P. (1959). Anatomy of the human brain and the problem of mental retardation. In P. Bowman and H. Mautner (eds), *Mental Retardation*. New York: Grune & Stratton.

Yeo, R., Turkheimer, E., Raz, N., and Bigler, E. (1987). Volumetric asymmetries of the human brain: Intellectual correlates. *Brain and Cognition*, **6**, 15–23.

Address for correspondence:

Professor Peter B. Rosenberger; Learning Disorders Unit, Massachusetts General Hospital, Boston, Massachusetts 02114, USA

6

PET Scan Reading Studies: Familial Dyslexics

[1]Karen Gross-Glenn, [1]R. Duara, [3]F. Yoshii, [2]W. W. Barker,
[2]J. Y. Chang, [2]A. Apicella, [1]T. Boothe and [1]H. A. Lubs
[1]*University of Miami School of Medicine, Miami, Florida,* [2]*Mount Sinai Medical Center, Miami Beach, Florida, and* [3]*Tokai University, Japan*

INTRODUCTION

There is at least one subtype of developmental dyslexia that is of hereditary origin, with recent work demonstrating a genetic linkage to a marker on chromosome 15 (Smith *et al.*, 1983). Therefore, there is likely to be a specific neural basis for this cognitive difficulty in learning to read and spell.

Earlier studies have used EEG-derived measures to localize differences in brain functioning between dyslexic and normal readers (Duffy, 1980; Preston *et al.*, 1974; Sobotka and May, 1984; Weber and Omenn, 1977). These studies have yielded rather contradictory results. Divergent findings may be attributed, at least in part, to the now generally recognized heterogeneous nature of this disorder. To reduce the likelihood of obtaining very variable results, we restricted our dyslexic sample to individuals with a known family history of dyslexia among first-degree relatives. Although there may be heterogeneity even among the familial forms of dyslexia, nevertheless we expected this sample restriction to somewhat reduce the inter-subject variability among dyslexics.

A second source of difficulty in localizing differences in brain functioning between dyslexics and non-dyslexics stems from the nature of the methods that have heretofore been available for studying brain functioning in awake humans. Although EEG-derived measures can accurately monitor variations in brain activity on a moment-to-moment basis, they are rather less adequate if the goal is to localize differences in neural activity between groups to

Perspectives on Dyslexia Vol. 1
Edited by G. Th. Pavlidis   © 1990 John Wiley & Sons Ltd

particular regions of the brain. Because the brain is a three-dimensional structure of enormous variety and complexity, a tomographic method that can differentiate functioning of brain regions located both on the surface and within the depths of the brain is needed.

Positron emission tomography (PET) is a recently developed method that can be used for studying biochemical reactions in all brain regions in an awake alert human as he or she performs a specific cognitive task (Phelps and Mazziotta, 1985). This is accomplished by scanning the brain following an injection of an analog of glucose (2-deoxyglucose) that has been labeled with a short-lived positron-emitting isotope. The PET camera produces images representing radioactivity concentration in slices of the brain. The distribution of radioactivity in different brain regions is a quantitative representation of glucose metabolism in those regions. Radioactivity concentrations are transformed into glucose metabolic rates by the application of tracer kinetic models that mathematically describe the transport and biochemical reactions of the injected labeled glucose analog, in combination with data on plasma levels of glucose and radioactivity from samples obtained over the course of the experiment.

Clinical and behavioral studies of adult familial dyslexics have suggested that they use different cognitive strategies during reading than do adults who have not had difficulty in learning to read as children (Gross-Glenn *et al.*, 1985). To derive meaning from the printed word, reading requires the coordination of visual input and eye movements with language processes and memory. This activity requires the collaboration of many different brain regions, and it is likely that the apparently different reading strategies of dyslexics and non-dyslexics would show different patterns of cerebral metabolic activity as observed by PET scanning.

SUBJECTS

Criteria for subject selection for both groups were the following: males, age between 18 and 45 years, right-handed (according to Edinburgh Questionnaire), normal or corrected-to-normal vision, no gross sensory, neurological or psychiatric disorders, and educational level of at least high school, and good physical health.

Dyslexic subjects were those who reported a childhood history of reading and spelling problems severe enough to require treatment and/or disrupt their education, a similar history in at least one first-degree relative, and normal intelligence.

Control subjects had a negative childhood history of reading and spelling problems, and were without such history in their first-degree relatives.

METHOD

Psychometric data were obtained on dyslexic subjects. They showed normal intelligence (mean WAIS full-scale IQ = 112 ± 13.2), spelling deficits (Wide-Range Achievement Test, Level-II spelling, mean grade equivalent +6.1 ± 3.0); and a considerable range of oral reading abilities (Gray Oral Reading Test, mean grade equivalent = 8.5, ±4.5).

Several days before participating in the study, each subject visited the PET scan laboratory to become familiar with the equipment and procedures involved in a PET scan study. Informed consents were signed following this familiarization, and prior to participating on the day of the study.

Subjects abstained from alcohol, cigarettes, caffeine and all medication for 24 hours prior to the scan. To ensure a stable blood glucose level during the uptake period of the isotope, subjects were required to fast for a period of at least 3 hours before scanning.

For most subjects, an injection of ^{18}F-labeled 2-deoxyglucose (FDG) was administered through a catheter placed in the dorsal vein of one hand. (For the earliest subjects, the isotope used was [^{11}C]2-deoxyglucose.) The following cognitive task began 2 minutes prior to injection. Subjects were instructed to fixate binocularly on a small cross in the central field of view, and to pronounce each word as it was presented by an experimenter. Words appeared in random order at a presentation rate of one every 5 seconds, and a viewing distance of approximately 18 inches. They were printed in lower-case letters of high contrast, that subtended a visual angle of $0.6° \times 0.4°$. High-frequency three- to six-letter nouns (A or AA, based on the Thorndike–Lorge count), such as 'cake', 'boat', were selected so that neither dyslexics nor normal readers would experience any difficulty in reading them.

Word reading continued uninterrupted for 30 minutes. Immediately following this period, the subject's head was positioned in the scanner. PET scanning began, and lasted for a period of 20 minutes. During both phases of the study, the ambient light level was low and the room was quiet.

RESULTS

Absolute Metabolic Rates

Based on $N = 14$ (6 dyslexics, 8 age-matched control subjects), preliminary data have shown significant differences between the two groups. Absolute cerebral metabolic rates for glucose (CMR$_{glc}$) were calculated using an operational equation (Huang et al., 1980). Average gray matter CMR$_{glc}$ was not significantly different between groups (6.87 ± 0.60 mg 100 g^{-1} min^{-1}, controls; 8.14 ± 0.99 mg 100 g^{-1} min $^{-1}$, dyslexics).

Normalized Metabolic Activity

When regional metabolic values were normalized, relative to overall gray matter metabolism (rCMR$_{glc}$/overall gray matter CMR$_{glc}$) it was possible to assess the 'landscape' of metabolic activity across the whole brain, and in this case the two groups were observed to differ.

Before considering these differences, however, we shall describe the pattern of metabolic activity observed in normal readers in order to provide a baseline against which to compare dyslexics. Table 1 presents normalized metabolic data for a number of brain regions in both hemispheres for each group.

To obtain a general idea of the landscape of metabolic activity during reading across these brain regions, we have classified rCMR$_{glc}$ as 'high' if it was equal to or exceeded an rCMR$_{glc}$/overall gray matter ratio of 1.12, and 'low' if it was equal to or less than a ratio of 0.88. Values falling between these numbers are thus approximately equal to overall gray matter CMR$_{glc}$. Figure 1 shows the distribution of brain region showing either high or low normalized rCMR$_{glc}$ for both hemispheres for normal readers. Regions in which normals show relatively high rCMR$_{glc}$ include: pre-striate visual cortex, inferior frontal lobe, peri-insular cortex and median paracentral cortex. Regions

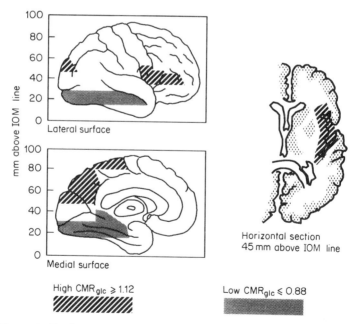

Figure 1. Regions showing relatively high and low normalized CMR$_{glc}$

Table 1. rCMR/overall gray matter CMR

Region		Normals (N = 8)		Dyslexics (N = 6)	
		Mean	SE	Mean	SE
Frontal lobe					
Superior	R	0.95 ± 0.06		0.92 ± 0.06	
	L	0.90 ± 0.07		0.93 ± 0.06	
Middle	R	1.16 ± 0.03		1.14 ± 0.05	
	L	1.08 ± 0.04		1.12 ± 0.04	
Inferior	R	1.22 ± 0.04		1.20 ± 0.03	
	L	1.17 ± 0.03		1.16 ± 0.03	
Parietal lobe					
Superior	R	1.01 ± 0.04		0.95 ± 0.03	
	L	1.01 ± 0.04		0.96 ± 0.04	
Inferior	R	1.09 ± 0.02		1.01 ± 0.02	
	L	1.07 ± 0.01		1.00 ± 0.03	
Occipital lobe					
Precuneus	R	1.25 ± 0.04		1.23 ± 0.11	
	L	1.24 ± 0.04		1.18 ± 0.09	
Cuneus	R	1.17 ± 0.07		1.21 ± 0.08	
	L	1.24 ± 0.06		1.20 ± 0.07	
Calcarine	R	1.04 ± 0.06		1.03 ± 0.03	
	L	1.04 ± 0.06		1.04 ± 0.04	
Lingual	**R	0.83 ± 0.05		1.06 ± 0.06	
	*L	0.87 ± 0.06		1.05 ± 0.05	
Temporal lobe					
Superior	R	0.96 ± 0.03		0.94 ± 0.06	
	L	0.93 ± 0.03		0.91 ± 0.02	
Middle	*R	0.83 ± 0.08		0.96 ± 0.01	
	**L	0.79 ± 0.07		0.96 ± 0.01	
Post. medial	*R	0.87 ± 0.04		1.00 ± 0.04	
	*L	0.88 ± 0.03		1.01 ± 0.04	
Insula	*R	1.14 ± 0.02		1.09 ± 0.02	
	***L	1.13 ± 0.02		1.05 ± 0.02	
Subcortical	R	1.04 ± 0.02		1.02 ± 0.04	
	L	1.03 ± 0.03		1.01 ± 0.03	
Cerebellum	R	0.82 ± 0.09		0.94 ± 0.05	
	L	0.78 ± 0.09		0.97 ± 0.05	
Median paracentral		1.17 ± 0.05		1.10 ± 0.05	
Average gray matter CMR		6.87 ± 0.60		8.14 ± 0.99	

***$p < 0.005$; **$p = 0.01$; *$p \leq 0.05$.

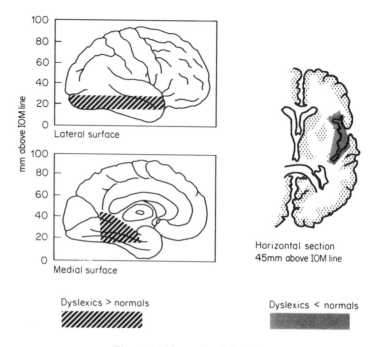

Figure 2. Normalized CMR$_{glc}$

observed to have relatively low rCMR$_{glc}$ include: lingual gyrus of the occipital lobe, middle gyrus and posterior medial region of the temporal lobe, and the cerebellum.

Data in Table 1 indicate that the dyslexic pattern of normalized rCMR$_{glc}$ is both the same as, and different from, that observed in normal readers, depending on the brain region involved. *t*-Tests were used to compare regional activity across groups. Both groups showed relatively high levels of metabolic activity bilaterally in inferior frontal and pre-striate occipital cortex, ranging from 15 to 25% above overall gray matter CMR$_{glc}$.

There are several regions in which groups differed significantly with respect to normalized rCMR$_{glc}$. These differences are depicted in Figure 2. The relatively low level of metabolic activity shown by normal readers in lingual, mid-temporal and posterior medial temporal cortex was not observed in dyslexics. The converse situation was obtained in the region of the peri-insular cortex. In this case, normal readers' relatively high rCMR$_{glc}$ was not observed in dyslexics. Although metabolic activity in both left and right peri-insular cortex was higher for normal readers than for dyslexics, the difference was more striking in the left hemisphere.

Hemispheric Symmetry of Metabolic Activity

Symmetry of $rCMR_{glc}$ was assessed by an unsigned laterality index: $100 \times |Right - Left|/(Right + Left)/2$. This measure reflects only the magnitude of the difference in metabolic activity for homologous regions in the two hemispheres, but not the direction of asymmetry.

Table 2 shows the distribution of these laterality indices across regions for both groups of subjects. t-Tests were used to evaluate these differences statistically.

For the normal readers, the pattern is generally a 'symmetrical' one, i.e. left and right $rCMR_{glc}$ values for homologous regions differ by less than 10%. The only exceptions to this rule are in the regions of superior and mid-frontal cortex, where values of 10% or slightly higher are found.

The dyslexic pattern is also generally a symmetrical one, but differs from that observed in normal readers in several respects. The regions in which

Table 2. Unsigned laterality index

Region	Normals (N = 8) Mean SE	Dyslexics (N = 6) Mean SE	p^{**}
Frontal lobe			
Superior	9.6 ± 1.1	2.8 ± 0.9	0.001
Middle	10.9 ± 2.8	4.1 ± 1.2	0.051
Inferior	5.0 ± 1.6	3.2 ± 2.5	
Parietal lobe			
Superior	3.1 ± 1.0	4.4 ± 0.8	
Inferior (ant.)	4.6 ± 0.8	5.8 ± 1.5	
Inferior (post.)	4.6 ± 1.3	6.4 ± 1.1	
Occipital lobe			
Precuneus	5.5 ± 1.2	8.1 ± 0.8	
Cuneus	7.4 ± 2.7	4.5 ± 1.5	
Calcarine	2.1 ± 0.5	3.6 ± 0.9	
Lingual	4.3 ± 1.3	2.4 ± 0.8	
Temporal lobe			
Superior (ant.)	6.1 ± 1.6	12.4 ± 2.1	0.038
Superior (post.)	4.2 ± 1.0	8.0 ± 1.4	0.039
Middle (ant.)	8.6 ± 2.7	3.9 ± 0.8	
Middle (post.)	9.3 ± 2.1	8.5 ± 1.8	
Posterior medial	6.4 ± 2.8	2.2 ± 0.7	
Insula	3.8 ± 0.8	4.3 ± 1.6	
Subcortical	4.9 ± 0.9	2.2 ± 0.5	0.028
Cerebellum	7.7 ± 3.0	3.8 ± 0.7	

*$100 \times |Right - Left|/(Right + Left)/2$.
**p values shown where $\leqslant 0.05$ (two-tailed test).

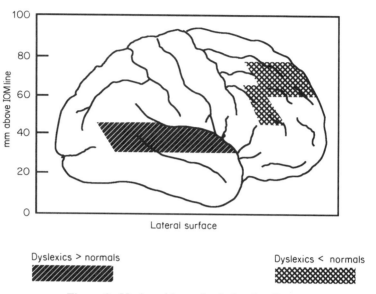

Figure 3. Unsigned laterality index for CMR_{glc}

laterality indices were significantly different for the two groups are shown in Figure 3. First, dyslexics do not show even the modest frontal lobe asymmetry observed in normals. Second, dyslexics do show a temporal lobe symmetry in both anterior and posterior regions, that is approximately twice as great as that observed in normal readers. Finally, a small degree of asymmetry (about 5%) noted in subcortical regions for normals was not observed in dyslexic subjects.

DISCUSSION

An attempt at detailed interpretation of these data would be premature, as the sample size is small, and the problem of the neural bases for dyslexia is a complex one. What these data do suggest, however, is that a number of different brain regions seem to be involved in the normal reading process. Regions that may subserve early visual discrimination processes (such as pre-striate cortex) and comprehension of meaning (such the inferior frontal cortices) were observed to show relatively higher than overall gray matter metabolism for both groups of subjects. The peri-insular cortex, a region that lies between the frontal and temporal lobe language regions, was significantly lower in relative metabolic activity for dyslexics than for normals. Lesions in this region, at least in the left hemisphere, are known to produce profound language disturbance (LeCours and Kaplan, 1984).

Other regions in which the two groups differed included mid-temporal and lingual gyri. These regions are part of the visual pathway and are included as the ventral outflow from the visual cortex. In monkeys, mid-temporal cortex has been shown to be essential for complex visual discrimination (Mishkin *et al.*, 1983). In these regions, dyslexics did not show the relatively low level of metabolic activity shown by normal readers, but rather demonstrated above-average metabolism. It is possible that visual discrimination of written words requires greater metabolic activity than average in the ventral outflow pathway from the visual cortex in dyslexics, because they find this task more difficult than do normal readers.

The asymmetry shown in frontal cortex by normal readers was less pronounced in dyslexic subjects. Activity in mid-frontal cortex may relate to oculomotor control by frontal eye field regions. This is an area that deserves further study, in view of the importance of eye movements for reading.

The lower-than-expected metabolic activity in peri-insular cortex may reflect either a relative disconnection of this important language area from the visual association area or an intrinsic dysfunction of the peri-insular cortex itself. Although we have no definite means of assessing the functional significance of relatively high or low metabolic activity in a brain region, most obvious brain lesions do produce hypometabolism both at the site of the lesions and in remote brain regions to which they have strong connections. However, our understanding of the relationships between regional metabolic activation and cognitive processes is as yet very incomplete. Our limited experience with other cognitive tasks indicates that poor performance may be correlated, in some circumstances, with higher metabolic activity (Parks *et al.*, 1988). As more PET scan studies are done in which patterns of metabolic activity are correlated with specific behavioral activation tasks, a very useful body of knowledge will develop. Until this has been done, interpretation of data such as those collected in this study will have to remain speculative.

SUMMARY

Positron-emission tomography (PET) was used to study cerebral metabolic activity during a simple word-reading task. PET-scans for a group of right-handed males with a childhood and family history of dyslexia were compared with scans for another age- and handedness-matched group without such a history. When regional metabolic values were normalized to overall gray-matter metabolism, the resulting patterns of activity across various brain regions differed for the two groups. Normal readers showed greater activation of peri-insular cortex, less activation of mid-temporal cortex, and more bilaterally symmetrical activation of regions within the superior temporal cortex than did dyslexic subjects. The functional significance of these regional differences is as yet unclear. However, it is interesting to note that these differences occur in regions that are thought to subserve speech, language, complex visual discriminations, and eye movements.

REFERENCES

Duffy, F. H. (1980). Regional differences in brain electrical activity by topographic mapping. *Annals of Neurology*, **7**, 412–420.

Gross-Glenn, K., Lewis, D. C., Smith, S. D., and Lubs, H. A. (1985). Phenotype of adult familial dyslexia: Reading of visually transformed texts and nonsense passages. *International Journal of Neuroscience*, **28**, 49–59.

Huang, S. C., Phelps, M. E., Hoffman, E. J., Sideris, K., Selin, C. J., and Kuhl, D. E. (1980). Noninvasive determination of local cerebral metabolic rate of glucose in man. *American Journal of Physiology*, **238**, E69–E82.

LeCours, A. R., and Kaplan, D. (1984). Augusta Dejerine-Klumpke or 'The Lesson in Anatomy'. *Brain and Cognition*, **3**, 166–197.

Mishkin, M., Ungerleider, L., and Macko, K. (1983). Object vision and spatial vision. Two cortical pathways. *Trends in Neuroscience*, **6**, 414–417.

Parks, R. W., Loewenstein, D. A., Dodrill, K. A., Barker, W. W., Yoshii, F., Chang, J. Y., Emron, A., Apicella, A., Sheremata, W. A., and Duara, R. (1988). Cerebral metabolic effects of a verbal fluency test: A PET scan study. *Journal of Clinical and Experimental Neuropsychology*, **10**, 565–575.

Phelps, M. E., and Mazziotta, J. C. (1985). Positron emission tomography: Human brain function and biochemistry. *Science*, **228**, 799–809.

Preston, M. S., Guthrie, J. T., and Childs, B. (1974). Visual evoked responses in normal and disabled readers. *Psychophysiology*, **11**, 452–457.

Smith, S. D., Kimberling, W. J., Pennington, B. F., and Lubs, H. A. (1983). Specific reading disability: Identification of an inherited form through linkage analysis. *Science*, **219**, 1345–1347.

Sobotka, K. R., and May, J. G. (1974). Visual evoked potentials and reaction time in normal and dyslexic children. *Psychophysiology*, **14**, 18–24.

Weber, B. A., and Omenn, G. S. (1977). Auditory and visual evoked responses in children with familial reading disabilities. *Journal of Learning Disabilities*, **10**, 153–158.

Addresses for correspondence:

Dr Karen Gross-Glen, Dr R. Duara, Dr T. Boothe, and Professor H. A. Lubs; Mailman Center for Child Development, University of Miami School of Medicine, Miami, Florida, USA

Mr W. W. Barker, Dr J. Y. Chang, and Dr A. Apicella; Mount Sinai Medical Center, Miami Beach, Florida, USA

Professor F. Yoshii; Department of Neurology, Tokai University, Bohseidai, Isehara 259-11, Japan

7

Neurometric and Behavioral Studies

I. Neurometric and Behavioral Studies of Normal and At-risk Children in Several Different Countries

E. Roy John,[1,2] Leslie S. Prichep,[1,2] Thalia Harmony,[3] Alfredo Alvarez,[4] Roberto Pascual,[4] Alexis Ramos,[5] Erzsebet Marosi,[3] Ana E. Diaz de Leon,[6] Pedro Valdes,[4] and Jacqueline Becker[3]

II. Neurometric Studies of Methylphenidate Responders and Non-responders

Leslie S. Prichep[1,2] and E. Roy John[1,2]

[1]New York University Medical Center; [2]Nathan S Kline Institute for Psychiatric Research; [3]Universidad Nacional Autónoma de Mexico; [4]Central Nacional de Investigaciones Científicas de Cuba; [5]Universidad Central de Venezuela; [6]Universidad Autónoma del Estado de Mexico

I. Neurometric and Behavioral Studies of Normal and At-risk Children in Several Different Countries

Learning disabilities and other cognitive dysfunctions may arise for a wide variety of reasons. Some of these causes are physiological in nature and relate to processes specifically involved in the registration, encoding, storage and retrieval of information in the nervous system: poor visual acuity, hearing loss, attentional deficits due to inadequate inhibition of orientation reflexes, interference with consolidation of memory due to epileptiform activity in the

Perspectives on Dyslexia Vol. 1
Edited by G. Th. Pavlidis   © 1990 John Wiley & Sons Ltd

limbic system or altered protein synthesis, or deficient synthesis of certain neurotransmitters involved in the retrieval process. Some of these causes are more social or psychological in nature or reflect more general biological factors: lack of interest in what is to be learned, alienation from values reflected in the formal educational process, preoccupation with family stresses or economic instability, or a low energy level due to improper nutrition or systemic disease. The basic justification for the attempt to develop new neurophysiological adjuncts to the evaluation and diagnosis of the child with learning difficulties is the insensitivity of the classical neurological examination to subtle cognitive dysfunctions and the inability of behavioral or neuropsychological tests to identify differential underlying patterns of pathophysiology. Even though the latter methods may reveal unequivocal inability of an individual to perform certain tasks, most of the behavioral products assessed depend upon multiple processes. The process responsible for a dysfunction can often not be uniquely inferred from demonstration that the dysfunction exists, and valuable adjuncts to differential diagnosis and the planning of individualized prescriptive remediation may be available from neurophysiological examinations.

One way to validate the accuracy of inferences about the causes underlying a demonstrated learning disability is to formulate successful individualized prescriptive remediation. While some skillful clinicians achieve impressive levels of success in such endeavors, most remedial procedures target a group whose members display similar behavioral symptoms as if the underlying causes were homogeneous. Predictably, the outcome is unreliable. Some members of the group benefit and some do not, and neither the reasons for success nor failure become explicitly evident.

Another approach to inference of the causes underlying learning disability is to seek comprehensively for objective evidence of brain dysfunction in children with demonstrable behavioral deficits, to fractionate groups which display a homogeneously shared deficit into heterogeneous subgroups which display different patterns of apparent pathophysiology and to validate the clinical significance of this physiological subtyping by demonstrating differential response to various clinical interventions.

This second approach immediately confronts a major problem: no external criteria exist to validate any subtyping which might be achieved. If subgroups are identified, no individual prescriptive remediations exist ready for use after identification of the appropriate targets. Those who choose this approach encounter a paradox: the reference for any physiologically based system of differential diagnosis is the pre-existing set of clinical neurological and neuropsychological diagnostic methods which we suspect are neither accurate nor adequate.

For 15 years, we have been trying to develop a solution to this problem. Numerous studies, reviewed elsewhere (John, 1977; John *et al.*, 1983;

Hughes, 1985; John *et al.*, 1988), have reported a high incidence of abnormal electroencephalographic (EEG), evoked potential (EP) and event-related potential (ERP) findings in children with learning disabilities. Most of these reports have been based upon qualitative evaluation of such data using visual inspection. Although subjective evaluations of this sort are prone to various sources of error, there exists a widespread consensus that learning disabilities are often associated with unusual brain electrical activity.

We elected to address the criterion problem by focusing first on the 'normal' child. We asked whether the evolution of brain electrical activity in healthy, normally functioning children proceeded in a way which could be described quantitatively and objectively, i.e. whether reliable *norms* could be established which encompassed the set of measurements derived from normal children. If such homogeneous developmental rules could be identified for normal children, possible deviations from such rules would then be explored for groups of children with cognitive dysfunctions. If such deviations occurred significantly more often in learning-disabled children, it would become possible to search for subgroups sharing different pathophysiological profiles, thus revealing the heterogeneous substrate underlying similar behavioral deficits.

Our findings can be summarized by a few major conclusions, which will be documented in the remainder of this chapter:

(1) A large number of parameters of brain electrical activity can be described which change in an orderly way with the maturation of healthy, normally functioning children. These are referred to as *normative* neurometric features.

(2) These developmental rules accurately describe the changes observed in the brain electrical activity of normal children in a variety of different cultures.

(3) Although the distribution of these electrophysiological features in normal children remains within usual statistical confidence intervals, subgroups with different profiles exist within the normal population.

(4) A high proportion of children with learning disabilities, neurological disorders or a variety of antecedent risk factors display significant deviations from the normal distribution of these electrophysiological features.

(5) Heterogeneous subgroups with different pathophysiological profiles can be identified within the population of children with learning disabilities.

(6) Some of these subgroups have identifiable behavioral concomitants or respond differentially to various treatments, as will be described later. Clinical correlates of other subgroups have not yet been identified, but are assumed to exist on a purely *a priori* basis.

(7) Abnormal neurometric features are a *necessary but not sufficient* concomitant of behavioral dysfunctions. To some extent, it appears that cultural

factors such as stimulation may enable a child to compensate for neurological damage sustained as a result of antecedent risk factors. Alternatively, cognitive limitations not evinced in a school environment requiring a low level of intellectual performance might become more evident in a more demanding environment. The enormous diversity of criteria for cognitive competence across cultures poses a severe problem for the identification of the normal child as well as the learning-disabled child.

Methods

The method which we have developed, called 'neurometrics', is based upon the analysis of quantitative features of brain electrical activity objectively extracted by automatic computer assessment of the EEG and EPs, evaluated statistically relative to a normative database. Many important diagnostic features can be reliably detected by computer programs with high precision and replicability. The extraction of reliable numerical indices reflecting different aspects of brain electrical activity permits powerful multivariate statistical methods to be applied to these data. Relationships between different brain regions can thereby be revealed which have been inaccessible by previous methods. Potentially, such relationships may provide sensitive indicators of subtle dysfunctions (John *et al.*, 1988).

Neurometric analysis of the EEG, to which this chapter will be limited, is based upon a 60-second-long artifact-free EEG sample. This is sufficient data to provide excellent reliability of quantitative features, with individual signatures stable over 1–3 years (John *et al.*, 1980; Fein *et al.*, 1983, 1984). Recordings are made from 19 electrodes positioned according to the International 10/20 System (Jasper, 1958), relative to linked ears. From each electrode, a large number of quantitative features are extracted, reflecting the absolute and relative power in four bands of the frequency spectrum: delta (1.5–3.5 Hz), theta (3.5–7.5 Hz), alpha (7.5–12.5 Hz) and beta (12.5–25.0 Hz). Additional features are then computed which reflect the synchronization and symmetry in each of these four frequency bands between all pairs of electrodes located symmetrically on the head. The same set of features is also computed for eight bipolar derivations which reflect the voltage gradients in fronto-temporal, temporal, central and parieto-occipital regions of each hemisphere.

In order to construct norms, the distribution of each such feature in the healthy population must be described. If these distributions are bell-shaped, or Gaussian, parametric statistical procedures such as the Z-transformation can be used to evaluate the probability that an individual measurement is outside the normal distribution. In the neurometric method, *abnormal findings are identified in terms of their statistical probability*. Inspection of the distributions of neurometric features in normal populations shows that they

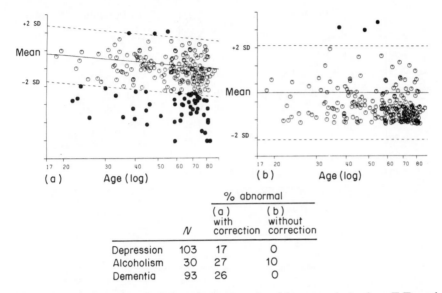

Figure 1. Scatterplots for coherence in the beta band between derivations T_3T_5 and T_4T_6, shown with both age regression and log transformation to approximate a Gaussian distribution (a) and without either (b). Dotted lines represent ± 2 SD from mean of the normative reference group (solid line). Solid circles indicate cases displaying significantly abnormal values. Note the far greater sensitivity achieved when features are corrected for biases

are usually skewed or kurtotic. We developed various transformations which corrected these biases to obtain Gaussian distributions, which have since been confirmed by others (John *et al.*, 1983; Gasser *et al.*, 1982). We also found that many of these features showed high correlations with age. Accordingly, we derived age regression equations which described the changes in mean values and standard deviations of each of these features as polynomial functions. Failure to take biases of distributions and age-related changes into consideration result in high incidence of false-positive findings and decreased sensitivity to abnormal function, as illustrated in Figure 1, an example from adult patients (John *et al.*, 1988).

Certain aspects of the electrical activity in different brain regions are highly correlated, reflecting normal interactions between them. On one hand, treating such correlated features as independent can yield misleading statistical findings. On the other hand, many brain dysfunctions uncouple these relationships. For this reason, we have derived a large number of multivariate features which define the normal interrelationships among sets of univariate features in terms of their covariances. Deviations from the multidimensional norm are referred to as 'Mahalanobis distances'. Incorporation of covariance

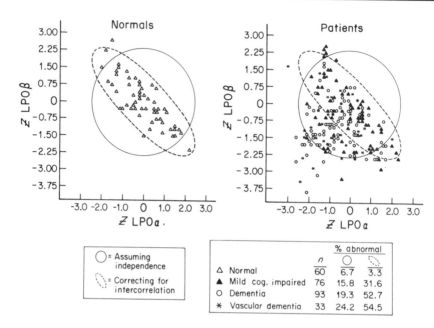

Figure 2. Scatterplot for Z values of relative power (percentage) in alpha and beta bands in derivation P_3O_1 for 60 normal subjects (a) and for 202 patients in three categories (b). In each graph, the 95% confidence region is represented within the circle, if the multivariate compression is computed as the square root of the sum of the squared Z values of these two features (for which one assumes independence), and within the ellipse, if the multivariate compression is computed as the Mahalanobis distance (which corrects for intercorrelation between the two features). Note the far superior sensitivity achieved by taking the intercorrelations among features into account. The percentage abnormal for points outside the circle and outside the ellipse, respectively, were as follows: normal subjects ($\triangle$, $n = 60$) 6.7 and 3.3; subjects with mild cognitive impairment ($\triangle$, $n = 76$) 15.8 and 31.6; patients with dementia ($\bigcirc$, $n = 93$) 19.3 and 52.7; patients with vascular dementia ($*$, $n = 33$) 24.2 and 54.5

data into neurometric assessments leads to a marked reduction in false positives and increased sensitivity to pathology, as illustrated in Figure 2, an example from adult patients (John *et al.*, 1988).

An especially interesting application of these multivariate descriptors is the distinction between 'maturational lag' and 'functional deviation'. A maturational lag is defined as abnormal Mahalanobis distance across some set of features which can be restored to the normal range by substituting an age different from the chronological age of the patient in the normative age-regression equations (see Figure 3). In other words, the apparent physiological age of the patient is not the same as his actual age.

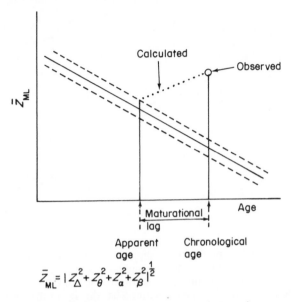

$$\bar{Z}_{ML} = |Z_{\Delta}^2 + Z_{\theta}^2 + Z_{\alpha}^2 + Z_{\beta}^2|^{\frac{1}{2}}$$

Figure 3. This idealized graph depicts the multivariate trajectory of normal brain development as the solid line, bracketed by dotted lines which represent the limits of normal variability of these neurometric features at any age. The circle represents the Mahalanobis distance of the observed set of values from the normal region. If the features in the set were independent of each other (uncorrelated), this distance would be the square root of the sum of the squares of their Z scores, which is the 'Euclidean distance'. The Mahalanobis distance corrects for intercorrelations among the features. *Maturational lag* exists when the observed set of values would fall within the normal range at some age different from the actual chronological age of the patient, which is the 'apparent (neurometric) age'. Maturational lag is defined by the discrepancy between the apparent age and the actual age

In contrast, a functional deviation is defined as an abnormal Mahalanobis distance which remains abnormal no matter what age is entered into the age regression equations (see Figure 4). The observed profile would not be normal at any age.

Normative age-regression equations for the mean values and standard deviations of over 1000 monopolar and over 200 bipolar univariate and multivariate neurometric features have now been constructed by us across the age range from 6 to 90. Complete computational details and tables for all of these features have just been published (John *et al.*, 1987). The result of neurometric feature extraction and transformation is a matrix of standard scores, in which each column represents a brain region or set of regions and each row represents a univariate feature or set of features. This matrix is illustrated in Figure 5 for the 208 bipolar features.

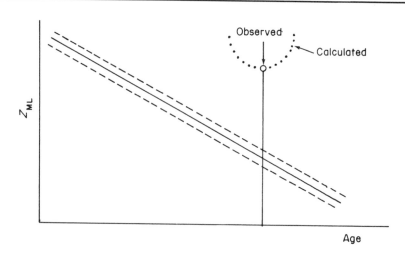

Figure 4. This idealized graph illustrates the concept of a 'developmental deviation'. In contrast to a maturational lag, a developmental deviation exists when an observed set of abnormal neurometric features, deviant from the normal region, would not fall within the normal range no matter what the age of the patient

Subjects

These methods have been used to evaluate samples of children in five different countries: Barbados, Cuba, Mexico, USA and Venezuela.*

Group 1: Normal US children ($n = 306$), ages 6–16.

Group 2: Normal Barbados children ($n = 129$), ages 7–12.

Group 3: Normal Cuban children ($n = 256$), ages 5–12.

Group 4: Normal Mexican children, middle class ($n = 28$), ages 7–12.

Group 5: Normal Venezuelan children, middle class ($n = 26$), ages 7–12.

Group 6: SLD US children, IQ above 85, WRAT below 90 in arithmetic, language skills or both ($n = 159$), ages 7–16.

Group 7: LD US children, IQ between 65 and 84, WRAT below 90 in arithmetic, language or both ($n = 143$), ages 7–16.

Group 8: Neurologically 'at-risk' US children ($n = 533$), ages 6–16.

Group 9: Mildly retarded Cuban children, IQ between 50 and 70 ($n = 127$), ages 5–12.

*Group 1 was studied under grants DAR 78-18772 and APR 76-24662 from the National Science Foundation. Group 2 was studied at the National Nutrition Center of Barbados, in collaboration with F. Ramsey, J. Galler and G. Solimano, under grant 770-0471 from the Ford Foundation. Groups 3, 4, 5, 9, 10, 11 and 12 were studied in an international collaborative project funded in part by a Regional Project of the United Nations Developmental Program. Groups 6 and 7 were studied under grant G008704516 from the US Office of Education, Bureau of the Educationally Handicapped. Group 8 was studied in collaboration with Dr Henry Baird at St Christopher's Hospital for Children, Philadelphia, funded in part by NIH General CRC Grant RR-75.

	Regions												
	Fronto-temporal		Temporal		Central		Parieto-occipital						
Electrophysiological features	L(1)	R(2)	L(3)	R(4)	L(5)	R(6)	L(7)	R(8)	$\bar{Z}_L$	$\bar{Z}_R$	$\bar{Z}_A$	$\bar{Z}_P^+$	$\bar{Z}_{ROW}^+$
Relative power													
1 % delta	Z_{11}	Z_{12}	Z_{13}	Z_{14}	Z_{15}	Z_{16}	Z_{17}	Z_{18}	$\bar{Z}_{1L}$	$\bar{Z}_{1R}$	$\bar{Z}_{1A}$	$\bar{Z}_{1P}$	$\bar{Z}_{1ROW}$
2 % theta	Z_{21}	Z_{22}		Z_{24}									
3 % alpha	Z_{31}												
4 % beta	Z_{41}												
5 % delta + theta	Z_{51}												
Frequency composites													
6 Z_F	Z_{61}												
7 $Z_{\text{BEST FIT}}$													
8 Maturational lag													
9 Develop. Dev.													
Absolute power													
10 Absolute power													
11 Power asymmetry													
Coherence													
12 delta													
13 theta													
14 alpha													
15 beta													
Coherence composite													
16 Z_{COH}													
Power asymmetry													
17 delta													
18 theta													
19 alpha													
20 beta													
Asymmetry composite													
21 Z_{ASYMM}													
22 $Z_R^{\P}$	$\dot{Z}_{RI}$												$\bar{Z}_{\text{HEAD}}$

Z MATRIX

REGIONAL (COLUMNS) × FEATURE (ROWS)

* Composite of fronto-temporal and temporal regions (anterior)
† Composite of central and parieto-occipital regions (posterior)
‡ Overall abnormality for feature across regions
§ Overall abnormality for region across feature
¶ Overall abnormality across features across regions

Figure 5. The neurometric examination yields a matrix of Z scores. The columns in the Z matrix represent different anatomical regions or sets of regions. The rows represent different neurometric features. Rows 6–9, 16, 21 and 22 represent Mahalanobis distances across sets of features. The matrix of bipolar deviations depicted here contains over 200 features. Rows 6–9, 16, 21 and 22 represent Mahalanobis distances across sets of features *within* regions. Columns $\bar{Z}_L$, $\bar{Z}_R$, $\bar{Z}_A$, $\bar{Z}_P$ and $\bar{Z}_{ROW}$ represent Mahalanobis distances of a given feature across sets of regions, respectively for the left hemisphere (L), right hemisphere (R), anterior half (ANT), posterior half (POST) and all derivations (ROW). The Mahalanobis distance $\bar{Z}_{\text{HEAD}}$ represents the total abnormality of all neurometric features in all derivations, taking their intercorrelations into account. Normative developmental equations have been derived for all of these features and for over 700 monopolar features not illustrated in this matrix (John *et al.*, 1987)

Group 10: 'At-risk' Mexican children, antecedent events, cultural/SES disadvantaged, IQ 90 or above (*n* = 28), ages 7–12.

Group 11: 'At-risk' Mexican children, antecedent events, low SES, IQ 90 or above (*n* = 30), ages 7–12.

Group 12: 'At-risk' Venezuelan children, antecedent events, low SES, IQ 90 or above (*n* = 55), ages 4–12.

The criteria for normality, learning disability or risk were basically similar in all of these studies and included medical history, academic records, WISC or WPPSI and WRAT or similar achievement tests, and a neurological examination except for Group 1.

Results

US–Swedish developmental equations

In 1980, we published data showing that the age-regression equations which we derived from 306 normal US children in Group 1 closely corresponded to those which we extracted from data published in 1973 for a group of 342 normal Swedish children, by Matoušek and Petersén (1973). The slopes of the equations describing normal black and white US children were identical with those for the Swedish children.

Sensitivity of neurometric developmental equations

Using the means and standard deviations of these neurometric equations, Ahn *et al.* (1980) compared the incidence of positive findings in US normals, Barbados normals, and US SLD, LD and neurologically at-risk groups. False positives in the Barbados normals were below the chance level, while the incidence of positive findings in single features among the 32 univariate features studied were as high as 35% for the SLDs, 39% for LDs and 47% for neurologically at-risk patients. The most common finding in the SLD and LD groups was an increase in delta and theta and a decrease in alpha activity in posterior regions. This finding is in agreement with a large number of similar reports using both conventional and computerized EEG evaluation (John, 1977; John *et al.*, 1983; Hughes, 1985).

Independent replications of neurometric norms

Since 1980, the accuracy of our neurometric developmental norms has been evaluated in studies published by US (Yingling *et al.*, 1986), Cuban (Alvarez *et al.*, 1987), Mexican (Harmony *et al.*, 1987) and Venezuelan (Harmony *et al.*, 1987) research teams. In each study, the conclusion was: 'the normative values published by John *et al.* (1980) are an appropriate benchmark against which to assess learning disabled or other patient groups . . .' (Yingling *et al.*, 1986). The successful replication of our norms in Sweden, Barbados, Cuba, Mexico and Venezuela indicates that these developmental rules describe the evolution of brain electrical activity in a way which is characteristic of healthy children from any ethnic background (Harmony *et al.*, 1987).* We believe all healthy human brains develop according to the same rules. Racial differences do not exist.

Independent replications of sensitivity

Since 1980, the sensitivity of our neurometric equations has been evaluated in six independent studies (Harmony *et al.*, 1987; Alvarez *et al.*, 1987; Yingling *et al.*, 1986; Gasser *et al.*, 1983). In five of these six studies, a high incidence of positive findings had been obtained in samples of learning-disabled or 'at-risk' children. In all of the five confirmatory studies, increased posterior slow waves were a common finding. The sole exception is the 'neurologically pure' group of dyslexics studied by Yingling *et al.* (1986). The reasons for this contradiction are not clear.

Sensitivity of maturational lag

Alvarez *et al.* (1987) used the single multivariate neurometric feature 'maturational lag' to classify normal versus mild mentally retarded Cuban children. They achieved accuracy on independent replication of 2.5% false positives and 87% correct positive findings.

Interaction of cultural with risk factors

A particularly interesting study on the contribution of cultural factors to brain compensatory mechanisms has been reported by Harmony and Diaz de Leon (in press). Intrigued by the low incidence of school failure among members of Groups 10 and 11, in spite of numerous neurometric abnormalities, these authors commented that schools in marginal areas serving families with low cultural and SES levels placed low demands on children and invalidated conclusions about learning disabilities drawn from schools with diverse criteria.

Accordingly, these workers studied the maturation of the EEG in 228 children in a small rural community called Tlaltizipan, about 50 km outside Mexico City in the state of Morelos. These children were members of a cohort

*Grants DAR 78-18772 and APR 76-24662 NSF, and a collaboration with Ramsey and colleagues, Grant 770-0471, Ford Foundation.

which has been evaluated at regular intervals from birth until present, by Dr Joaquin Cravioto of the Mexican Institute of Family Development (DIF). Their age range was from 6.5 to 15.5 years. All children attended the same school. The community under study is characterized by extensive poverty and extremely high levels of environmental pollution. In all of these children, risk factors were evaluated by examining personal and family medical histories, anthropometric curves, incidence of head injuries or loss of consciousness, perinatal hypoxia, birth order, and behavioral milestones relating to language comprehension or expression.

Using these criteria for risk, the sample was divided into four groups: (I) children at grade level; (II) children one grade below level appropriate for their age; (III) children who were regularly left back in school; (IV) children who were illiterate. Each group was subdivided into those with and without antecedent risk factors.

Neurometric abnormalities relative to our norms were more marked in posterior head regions, especially for slow activity in the delta and theta bands. The most important finding in this study was the relative incidence of maturational lag in the eight different subgroups.

Examination of Table 1 shows that the incidence of significant maturational lag was far higher in children at risk due to antecedent factors than those who were not, as would be expected. However, it was quite unexpected to find that in Group I maturational lag was 6% more frequent in children with antecedents than those without; in Group II the difference was 10%, in Group III it was 26%, and in Group IV it was 33%. The total incidence of abnormalities was similarly graded.

Since all of these children attend the same school and live in similar circumstances of pervasive high risk due to poverty and pollution, the striking differences in the high-risk members of each group in the incidence of

Table 1. Influence of cultural factors on neurometric results; incidence of abnormal neurometric results

Group	Category	Risk	n	% Abnormal	% Mat. lag
I	Grade level	Absent	51	15	12
		Present	55	18	18
II	One year below grade level	Absent	38	11	13
		Present	44	25	23
III	Consistent failure	Absent	7	0	0
		Present	19	21	26
IV	Illiterate	Absent	6	50	17
		Present	8	75	50

neurometric abnormalities, summarized by the multivariate index of maturational lag, is reasonably attributable to family environment and stimulation. Since the economic circumstances in this community are quite homogeneous, children who fail regularly in school or remain illiterate are likely to come from uncaring parents. These findings raise the intriguing possibility that neither antecedent risk nor neurometric abnormality are necessary and sufficient for learning disabilities, but can be compensated for by stimulation.

REFERENCES

Ahn, H., Prichep, L., John, E. R., Baird, H., Trepetin, M., and Kaye, H. (1980). Developmental equations reflect brain dysfunctions. *Science*, **210**, 1259–1262.

Alvarez, A., Pascual, R., and Valdes, P. (1987). U.S. EEG developmental equations confirmed for Cuban schoolchildren. *Electroencephalography and Clinical Neurophysiology*, **67**, 330–332.

Fein, G., Galin, D., Johnstone, J., Yingling, C. D., Marcus, M., and Kiersch, M. E. (1983). EEG power spectra in normal and dyslexic children. I. Reliability during passive conditions. *Electroencephalography and Clinical Neurophysiology*, **55**, 399–405.

Fein, G., Galin, D., Yingling, C. D., Johnstone, J., and Nelson, M. A. (1984). EEG spectra in 9–13 year old boys are stable over 1–3 years. *Electroencephalography and Clinical Neurophysiology*, **58**, 517–518.

Gasser, T., Bacher, P., and Mocks, J. (1982). Transformations toward the normal distributions of broad band spectral parameters of the EEG. *Electroencephalography and Clinical Neurophysiology*, **53**, 119–124.

Gasser, T., Mocks, J., Lenard, H. G., Bacher, P., and Verleger, R. (1983). The EEG of mildly retarded children: Developmental classification and topographic aspects. *Electroencephalography and Clinical Neurophysiology*, **55**, 131–144.

Harmony, T., and Diaz de Leon, A. (in press). Analisis Neurométrico del EEG en una poblacion rural. Coloquia de Investigacion. Enep-Istacala.

Harmony, T., Alvarez, A., Pascual, R., Ramos, A., Marosi, E., Diaz de Leon, A., Valdes, P., and Becker, J. (1987). EEG maturation of children with different economic and psychosocial characteristics. *International Journal of Neuroscience*, **31**, 103–113.

Hughes, J. R. (1985). Evaluation of electrophysiological studies on dyslexia. In P. B. Gray and J. F. Kavanagh (eds), *Biobehavioral Measures*. Maryland: York Press.

Jasper, H. H. (1958). The ten–twenty system of the International Federation, *Electroencephalography and Clinical Neurophysiology*, **10**, 371–375.

John, E. R. (1977). *Functional Neuroscience, Vol. II. Neurometrics: Clinical Applications of Quantitative Electrophysiology*. Hillsdale, NJ: Erlbaum.

John, E. R., Ahn, H., Prichep, L., Trepetin, M., Brown, D., and Kaye, H. (1980). Developmental equations for the electroencephalogram. *Science*, **210**, 1255–1258.

John, E. R., Prichep, L., Ahn, H., Easton, P., Fridman, J., and Kaye, H. (1983). Neurometric evaluation of cognitive dysfunctions and neurological disorders in children. *Progress in Neurobiology*, **21**, 239–290.

John, E. R., Prichep, L., and Easton, P. (1987). Normative data banks and neurometrics: Basic concepts, current status and clinical applications. In A. Remond and A. Gevins (eds), *Computer Analysis of EEG and Other Neurophysiological Variables: Clinical Applications*. EEG Handbook, Vol. III, pp. 449–495. Amsterdam: Elsevier.

John, E. R., Prichep, L. S., Fridman, J., and Easton, P. (1988). Neurometrics: Computer assisted differential diagnosis of brain dysfunctions. *Science*, **239**, 162–169.

Matoušek, M., and Petersén, I. (1973). Frequency analysis of the EEG in normal children and adolescents. In P. Kellaway and I. Petersén (eds), *Automation of Clinical Electroencephalography*. New York: Raven Press.

Yingling, C. D., Galin, D., Fein, G., Peltzman, D., and Davenport, L. (1986). Neurometrics does not detect 'pure' dyslexic. *Electroencephalography and Clinical Neurophysiology*, **63**, 426–430.

II. Neurometric Studies of Methylphenidate Responders and Non-responders

For some time, stimulants have been considered the drugs of choice for the treatment of hyperactivity/attention deficit disorder. Over the past decade there has been a change from the widespread use of the 1970s, leading to suggested regulations intended to decrease indiscriminate use in the late 1980s. However, although it has been reported that approximately two-thirds to three-quarters of the children thus treated respond favorably (see review by Barkley, 1977), there are still no clear criteria for selecting response candidates.

Several studies have attempted to identify electrophysiological characteristics of those children who are most likely to respond to such treatment (Shetty, 1971; Satterfield *et al.*, 1972, 1973, 1974; Swanson *et al.*, 1972; Saletu *et al.*, 1975; Halliday *et al.*, 1976, 1983; Prichep *et al.*, 1976; Steinhausen *et al.*, 1984). Using a wide variety of methods and measures, the findings of these studies suggest that electrophysiological features may be a useful way to select response candidates. In this preliminary study we evaluated a group of children who were receiving methylphenidate and compared the neurometric EEG profiles of responders and non-responders to see if we could discriminate between them.

Methods

Neurometrics

The neurometric methodology is described in detail in Part I of this chapter. Each subject received two neurometric examinations, one while on methylphenidate and one on placebo (or off drug). The order of the exams was randomized. On the day of the on-drug evaluation, the patients were given the medication when they arrived at the test site, and testing began approximately 1 hour later. This controlled for compliance and maximum drug effect as related to test time. Methylphenidate dosages were at levels used in standard treatment practice (varying from 10 to 60 mg/day). One minute of eyes closed 'artifact-free' monopolar EEG was collected from the 19 electrodes of the International 10/20 electrode system. Eight bipolar derivations were constructed by computer. For the analyses reported here, only bipolar data were studied. Several auditory (AEP) and visual (VEP) evoked potentials were also collected during each evaluation. The results of these tests will be reported elsewhere.

EEG data analysis

The neurometric data were analyzed using the methods described in detail in Part I above. Also as described above, measures of maturational lag and developmental deviation were calculated. These measures allow one to evaluate whether the neurometric abnormalities seen in the patient would fall within the normal limits for a person of a different age (maturational lag), or whether there is no age for which the observed neurometric values would fall within normal limits (developmental deviation). Although these measures can be calculated for each of the neurometric extracted features, in this case we used only the maturational lag and developmental deviation for the composite feature of overall frequency abnormality.

Discriminant functions

The main purpose in this study was to construct a 'classifier' function which could distinguish between methylphenidate responders and non-responders at pre-drug baseline. The statistical procedure used was multiple stepwise discriminant analysis,* a procedure which defines a mathematical classifier function, the value of which should be different for members of different *a priori* defined groups. This function is a weighted combination of some subset of variables, each of which makes some independent contribution to the overall discrimination. Because our groups were too small to split half, we used jack-knife replications. (In our past experience we have found this to be a conservative approach.) In order to reduce the number of variables entered into the initial discriminants:

(1) *t*-Tests for the significance of differences in the distribution of each variable in the different populations were examined. Variables for which these tests were highly significant were selected. The efficacy of such an approach has been previously reported (Weiner and Dunn, 1966).
(2) Variables reported in the literature as having been sensitive to differences between our groups were also included.

Clinical outcome measures

Since these children were evaluated as part of different studies, the criteria for 'response' varied slightly depending upon which group the patient was in. To be called a 'responder', the child had to show one or more of the following: (1) improvement on the hyperactivity factor on the Conners

---

Biomedical Computer Programs, P series, P7M, University of California Press.

Teachers and Parents Rating Scale (Conners, 1973); (2) 'improved' ratings on the Global Improvement Scale (Gittleman-Klein *et al.*, 1976); (3) improvement on paired associate performance; and/or (4) improvement in academic performance.

Subjects

'Normal' children

These were 160 normally functioning children. The details of the criteria used in subject selection are published elsewhere (see John *et al.*, 1980, 1983; Prichep and John, 1986). All of these children were born after an uneventful full-term pregnancy with no peri- or postnatal complications, had never suffered high febrile illness or head injury resulting in loss of consciousness, had no history of convulsions or neurological disease, were not on any prescriptive medication, were of normal intelligence, and were currently at age-appropriate grade level in school with no history of failure at any prior level, as confirmed by school report cards.

Methylphenidate recipients

It is important to note that this investigation was a clinical study in that children were not selected by us for participation, but rather were referred for neurometric evaluation after having already been selected to receive methylphenidate. This group included 28 male children between the ages of 6 and 12 (mean age of 9.5 years). The subjects were from the following sources:

(1) Thirteen children referred from a Special Education Facility.* These children were a subgroup of the learning-disabled and specifically learning-disabled (Groups 6 and 7) populations described in Part I, above. Most of these children were learning-disabled and hyperkinetic.
(2) Fifteen children referred by parents and/or teachers to an out-patient evaluation program.† These children were either hyperkinetic or had learning disabilities without hyperkinesis.

All children had IQs greater than 80 and were: (1) attending school; (2) non-psychotic; (3) had no diagnosed neurological disorders. (Informed consents were obtained from the parents of all children.)

---

*Board of Cooperative Educational Services (BOCES) District III, James E. Allen Learning Center, Dix Hills, NY. Supported in part by grant G007604516, Office of Education, Bureau of Education for the Handicapped.
†In collaboration with R. Gittleman-Klein and J. Mattes, Long Island Jewish Hillside Medical Center.

Results

Discrimination between methylphenidate responders and non-responders at pre-drug baseline

As can be seen in Table 1, discriminant accuracy of 82% was achieved in separation of methylphenidate responders and non-responders. In the jack-knife replications no accuracy was lost, suggesting the robustness of the discriminant. The neurometric variables which accounted for the majority of the variance in this analysis were a multivariate composite of fronto-temporal frequency deviation, anterior coherence in the theta band, posterior coherence in the alpha and beta bands, and fronto-temporal relative power in the delta band. (The subject to variable ratio in this analysis was approximately 5 : 1.)

Table 1. Discriminant classification of methylphenidate responders versus non-responders at baseline

		Classification (%) as	
Actual group	n	*I*	*II*
I Responders	16	*81* (81)	19 (19)
II Non-responders	12	17 (17)	*83* (83)
(jack-knifed replication)			

Maturational lag and developmental deviation in responders and non-responders

Table 2 shows the incidence of abnormal values of another variable, the multivariate Mahalanobis distance 'overall, all frequencies' (OAF) in different groups, and the percentage of this abnormality accounted for by maturational lag and developmental deviation. These measures are shown for normal children, responders and non-responders at baseline (BL) and both groups when medicated (ON).

The normal children displayed only the chance level of OAF abnormalities. In the pre-drug baseline (BL), a large proportion of the responders (50%) had abnormal OAF values, almost two-thirds of which were developmental deviations. On medication (ON), abnormal OAF values in the responders were reduced to almost one-half (28.6%), all of which were developmental deviations. This change was largely due to diminution of the pre-drug delta excess, which contributed heavily to the discrimination. These results are compatible with the previous reports of arousal-like effects in methylphenidate responders (Satterfield *et al.*, 1973, 1974).

Table 2. Incidence of significant overall frequency, developmental deviation and maturational lag in normal children, methylphenidate responders and non-responders at baseline (BL) and on medication (ON)

Group	Overall frequency (%)	Developmental deviation (%)	Maturational lag (%)
Normal	7.5	4.3	3.2
Responders BL	50.0	31.3	18.7
Responders ON	28.6	28.6	0.0
Non-responders BL	25.0	8.3	16.7
Non-responders ON	36.4	36.4	0.0

In the pre-drug baseline, only 25% of the non-responders had abnormal OAF values, two-thirds of which were maturational lags. On medication, abnormal OAF values in the non-responders increased to 36.4%, all of which were now developmental deviations. This change was largely due to an increase in delta activity after medication in the non-responders.

Thus, the maturational lags in both groups were reduced to zero. However, the effect of the drug on the responders was to produce more normal neurometric frequency profiles, while the effect on the non-responders was to increase brain deviance from normal profiles. Examination of individual data further indicated that those whose OAF scores decreased most on medication were those with high OAF scores at baseline.

Methylphenidate caused no change in anterior theta coherence in either group. Central coherence of alpha was slightly decreased in both groups. Parietal coherence of beta was markedly increased in the responders but slightly decreased in the non-responders.

Discussion

Although previous studies have suggested that methylphenidate 'responders' show significant electrophysiological differences compared to 'non-responders', only Steinhausen et al. (1984) using similar quantification (although not age regression) actually report discrimination between the two groups. They obtained a mean accuracy of 73.3% in the non-drug state.

The discriminant results reported herein achieved a mean discriminant accuracy of 82%. Our findings suggest that responders can be differentiated from non-responders by having greater frequency deviation abnormalities and excesses of relative power (%) in the delta band, in anterior regions and by incoherence in the beta frequency band in posterior regions. Non-responders displayed more incoherence in the theta frequency band in anterior regions, hypercoherence in the alpha band in central regions and more normal delta activity.

It is noted that using only the discriminating variables reported by Steinhausen *et al.*, we were only able to achieve a mean discriminant accuracy of 53% (jack-knife replicated). In the past (Prichep, 1987), we have reported that the use of multivariate composite neurometric features in addition to univariate features has led to increased discriminant accuracy. This may explain the discrepancy between the accuracy obtained by Steinhausen *et al.* and the present results.

Further, these preliminary results, which we are currently trying to confirm by independent replication, suggest that appropriate medication decreases or removes neurometric abnormalities, while inappropriate medication increases pre-existing abnormalities or causes new abnormalities to appear. The results also suggest that a neurometric examination before medicating a child may help to identify promising candidates for this treatment. Since methylphenidate causes clear electrophysiological changes within a very short period of time (approximately 60 minutes), a follow-up neurometric examination shortly after medication might serve as further assurance that the treatment might be beneficial.

REFERENCES

Barkley, R. A. (1977). A review of stimulant drug research with hyperactive children. *Journal of Child Psychology and Psychiatry*, **18**, 137–163.

Conners, C. K. (1973). Rating scales for use in drug studies with children. *Psychopharmacology Bulletin* (special issue).

Gittleman-Klein, R., Klein, D. F., Katz, S., Saraf, K., and Pollack, E. (1976). Comparative effects of methylphenidate and thioridazine in hyperkinetic children. *Archives of General Psychiatry*, **33**, 1217–1231.

Halliday, R., Rosenthal, J. H., Naylor, H., and Callaway, E. (1976). Averaged evoked potential predictors of clinical improvement in hyperactive children treated with methylphenidate: An initial study replication. *Psychophysiology*, **13**, 5.

Halliday, R., Callaway, E., and Naylor, H. (1983). Visual evoked potential changes induced by methylphenidate in hyperactive children: Dose/response effects. *Electroencephalography and Clinical Neurophysiology*, **55**, 258–267.

John, E. R., Ahn, H., Prichep, L., Trepetin, M., Brown, D., and Kaye, H. (1980). Developmental equations for the electroencephalogram. *Science*, **210**, 1255–1258.

John, E. R., Prichep, L., Ahn, H., Easton, P., Fridman, J., and Kaye, H. (1983). Neurometric evaluation of cognitive dysfunctions and neurological disorders in children. *Progress in Neurobiology*, **21**, 239–290.

McIntyre, H. B., Finemark, H. M., Cho, A. K., Bodner, L., and Gomer, M. (1981). Computer analyzed EEG in amphetamine-responsive hyperactive children. *Psychiatry Research*, **4**, 189–197.

Prichep, L. S. (1987). Neurometric quantitative EEG features of depressive disorders. In R. Takahashi, P. Flor-Henry, J. Gruzelier and S. Niwa (eds), *Cerebral Dynamics, Laterality and Psychopathology*, pp. 55–69. Amsterdam: Elsevier.

Prichep, L. S., and John, E. R. (1986). Neurometrics: Clinical applications. In F. H. Lopes da Silva, W. Storm van Leuwen and A. Rémond (eds), *Handbook of Electroencephalography and Clinical Neurophysiology, Vol. 2: Clinical Applications of Computer Analysis of EEG and other Neurophysiological Signals*, pp. 153–170. Amsterdam: Elsevier.

Prichep, L. S., Sutton, S., and Hakarem, G. (1976). Evoked potentials in hyperkinetic and normal children under certainty and uncertainty: A placebo and methylphenidate study. *Psychophysiology*, **13**, 419–428.

Saletu, B., Saletu, M., Simeon, J., Viamontes, G., and Itil, T. M. (1975). Comparative symptomatological and evoked potential studies with *l*-emphetamine, thioridazine, and placebo in hyperkinetic children. *Biological Psychiatry*, **10**, 253.

Satterfield, J. H., Cantwell, D. P., Lesser, L. I., and Posdin, R. L. (1972). Physiological studies of the hyperkinetic child: I. *American Journal of Psychiatry*, **128**, 1418.

Satterfield, J. H., Lesser, L. I., Saul, R. E., and Cantwell, D. P. (1973). EEG aspects in the diagnosis and treatment of minimal brain dysfunction. *Annals of the New York Academy of Sciences*, **205**, 274.

Satterfield, J. H., Cantwell, D. P., and Satterfield, B. T. (1974). Pathophysiology of the hyperactive child syndrome. *Archives of General Psychiatry*, **31**, 839–844.

Shetty, T. (1971). Alpha rhythms in the hyperkinetic child. *Nature*, **234**, 476.

Steinhausen, H. C., Romahn, G., and Gobel, D. (1984). Computer analyzed EEG in methylphenidate responsive hyperactive children. *Neuropediatrics*, **15**, 28–32.

Swanson, J., Kinsbourne, M., Roberts, W., and Zucker, K. (1972). Time–response analysis of the effect of stimulant medication on the learning ability of children referred for hyperactivity. *Pediatrics*, **61**, 709.

Weiner, J., and Dunn, D. (1966). Elimination of variates in linear discrimination. *Biometrics*, 268–275.

Addresses for correspondence:

Professor E. Roy John and Professor Leslie S. Prichep; Department of Psychiatry, New York University Medical Center, 550 First Avenue, New York, New York 10016, USA

Professor Thalia Harmony, Professor Erzsebet Marosi and Dr Jacqueline Becker; Universidad National Autónoma de Mexico, Mexico, DF

Professor Alfredo Alvarez, Professor Roberto Pascual and Professor Pedro Valdes; Central Nacional de Investigaciones Cientificas de cuba, La Habana, Cuba

Professor Alexis Ramos; Universidad Central de Venezuela, Caracas, Venezuela

Professor Ana E. Diaz de Leon; Universidad Autónoma del Estado de Mexico, Mexico, DF

8

Physiological Correlates of Reading Disability

Cecile E. Naylor, Frank B. Wood and D. Lynn Flowers
Bowman Gray School of Medicine, Winston-Salem

INTRODUCTION

The search for underlying anatomical and physiological mechanisms of dyslexia proceeds historically from the classical nineteenth-century efforts at clinico-pathological correlation in nervous system disease. This method initially focused on basic sensory and motor disorders (Charcot, 1889), but was soon applied as well to disorders of higher cortical function (Liepmann, 1920; Wernicke, 1874) and even to acquired reading disorder (Dejerine, 1892, 1914). This approach leads naturally to an initial consideration of what lesion might cause developmental dyslexia.

ANATOMICAL CONSIDERATIONS

The Dejerine model of acquired alexia, with its correlation to left angular gyrus lesions (Brodmann's area 39), has led to the expectation of a similar locus of disease or dysfunction in developmental dyslexia (Benton and Pearl, 1978). Many considerations, however, make this an obviously simplistic explanation, even if it has some heuristic value. In general, the developmental outcome of a congenital lesion cannot be expected routinely to resemble the outcome of an acutely acquired lesion in adulthood: the former might prevent learning in the affected brain areas; the latter clearly prevents the expression of skills already learned.

For the above reason, it is no surprise that the empirical data show a general lack of clinically obvious language impairment in cases of focal early left hemisphere lesions (Kimura, 1983; Rasmussen and Milner, 1977; Satz *et*

Perspectives on Dyslexia Vol. 1
Edited by G. Th. Pavlidis   © 1990 John Wiley & Sons Ltd

al., 1985); indeed, even full left hemispherectomies at birth do not induce gross or disproportionately severe language disorder (Dennis and Whitaker, 1976). The usual explanation involves the capability of non-damaged areas in either hemisphere to assume the learning of language functions, if forced to do so by a lesion that impairs the area that would normally assume such functions. By this line of reasoning, then, an early lesion sufficient to cause permanent disability would have to impair both the primary target area for the localization of the impaired function and any secondary areas to which that function could be displaced.

As a general matter, any redistribution of functional localization necessarily includes positive development of capabilities in areas which would not normally have them. This implies a degree of heightened function in those areas. Such enhanced function would not necessarily be related to the hypothesis of unusual talents in dyslexia as suggested by Geschwind and Galaburda (1985), however, since all that is being assumed is that an area not usually destined to carry out some function is now being required to do so.

A significant complication results from the relatively delayed onset of reading. Unlike spoken language, the absence of which would force the above relocation of language functions soon after birth, reading will not be 'missed' by the developing brain until perhaps at 5 or 6 years of age. If these neural processes on which reading depends are themselves not called upon in daily life until about this age, then pressure to relocate them will not yet have occurred by the time of beginning reading.

It should also be noted that any mechanism that presupposes an anatomically localized lesion would necessarily involve variability in the sites of lesions: no one expects lesions to be uniform in size or location. Lesions of greatly variable extent and location could overlap whatever target areas are implicated in dyslexia. To be sure, if such a lesion were quite widespread, it might induce a relatively generalized retardation of intellectual development that would not be confused with focal dyslexia. Less extensive lesions, however, would still contain many and variable sites of dysfunction in addition to the focal site implicated in dyslexia itself.

Individuals with a developmental history of reading problems do not show consistent deficits on neurological examination (Golden, 1982; Ludlam, 1981). That indicates clearly that the dysfunctional sites in dyslexia are anatomically distinct from the basic sensory and motor systems that are tested in the neurological examination. It further indicates that the correlated sites of dysfunction, arising from the variations in the putative lesion, also do not normally involve these classical sensory and motor systems.

Brain-imaging studies are also routinely negative for gross lesions (Hier *et al.*, 1978; Rumsey *et al.*, 1986). Some dyslexics do fail to show the typical left-greater-than-right hemispheric asymmetry in the width of the parieto-occipital region (Haslam *et al.*, 1981; Hier *et al.*, 1978). This has been taken as an indirect index of the size of the temporal planum. The left temporal planum was found to be longer in 65 out of 100 normal brains studied (Geschwind and Levitsky, 1968). However, this typical asymmetry was found in only 10–45% of dyslexics in the studies mentioned above. Classical (Geschwind, 1970) or revised (Ojemann, 1983) models assign this region of the left hemisphere a major role in primary linguistic or secondary semantic language processing.

Neuropathological studies of dyslexics at autopsy have found consistent cortical anomalies involving ectopias and architectonic dysplasias (Galaburda *et al.*, 1985). The anomalies were concentrated in the left temporal planum and related language areas, but in every case there was some bilateral involvement. Galaburda and colleagues described larger and more symmetrical temporal regions in four consecutive cases of male dyslexia. The observed symmetries seen in dyslexics typically involve right hemisphere differences, i.e. a longer than usual Sylvian fissure in the right hemisphere instead of a shorter than usual one in the left hemisphere, and a wider or symmetrical parieto-occipital region in the right hemisphere. Thus, it is heightened or excess endowment on the right (instead of diminished endowment on the left) that correlates with clinical deficit. By the above logic on heightened function, then, it would be possible to infer that the right hemisphere is compensating—in this case, anatomically—for a subtle lesion in the left hemisphere that has somewhat compromised the ability of the left hemisphere to carry out its usual functions, but which has not reduced the size of the relevant areas in the left hemisphere.

Alternatively, a larger right temporal planum may be a consequence of the disorder rather than reflective of some form of compensation. Marx (1983) and Galaburda and Kemper (1979) proposed that the left operculum and planum temporale areas mature at a slower rate than other cortical regions and, therefore, have extended vulnerability to pathological insult. If this region is slower to mature, then insult to the dominant left hemisphere could result in less inter-regional competition and, consequently, a reduction in normal cell death. In turn, that could result in a failure to develop the normal asymmetry, as described above. The relationship of reduced cell death in right hemisphere areas to compensation via heightened activation remains a question for further investigation.

PHYSIOLOGICAL DYSFUNCTION

Since the structural anomalies underlying dyslexia are relatively subtle, and since they imply a relatively complex profile of altered function across brain regions, then direct physiological measures of brain function would naturally be expected to show correspondingly complex differences between dyslexics and normals.

Early electrophysiological studies have yielded conflicting results, though many have supported a component of left hemisphere deficit in dyslexia. Several researchers (Conners, 1970; Preston et al., 1974, 1977; Symann-Louett et al., 1977) have shown reduced amplitude event-related potentials (ERPs) in reading-disabled subjects over left parietal regions. Although the majority of studies have reported a neural deficit associated with reading disability, Sobotka and May (1977) and Weber and Omenn (1977) found either no differences or greater amplitude ERPs to light flashes in dyslexics.

Sobotka and May found increased neural response to irrelevant stimuli and concluded that the findings could be attributed to attentional factors alone. They interpreted enhanced ERPs as a failure to show a deficit related to RD. However, an enhanced response to irrelevant stimuli could be interpreted as a failure to suppress the cortical response to ignored stimuli, which is itself an inefficiency or deficit in processing, i.e. a failure to show the typical relative enhancement to relevant stimuli. Another major problem with this as well as some other early studies was the failure to control for or exclude attention deficit disorder (ADD). That could well explain the apparent inconsistencies in the data, as described in the next section on ADD confounding.

Weber and Omenn (1977) found no differences in the amplitude of the auditory and visual evoked responses to white noise bursts and light flashes. Subjects were randomly assigned to attend conditions (noise versus flash), and the data were then combined across subjects. The design is poorly counterbalanced since all subjects did not participate in all conditions, and selective attention effects could not be interpreted. They also failed to control for ADD and/or emotional problems. However, of particular significance was the combination of data from three generations of subjects. This chapter will provide evidence that there are sufficient differences between the ERPs of adults and children to cloud the picture if age is not at least statistically controlled. Also, there are inherent problems in using 'non-affected' family members as the only control group. The previous chapter discussed the problems in assessing the presence or absence of childhood reading disability based on adult test scores no less on self-report measures alone. Thus, many of the 'unaffected' family members may not have been truly unaffected.

Attention Deficit Disorder as a Confound

As alluded to above, a major issue in many of the early physiological studies has been the confounding presence or absence of attention deficit disorder (ADD). Independent effects of ADD, distinct from those of dyslexia, have been reported (Dykman et al., 1982; Holcomb et al., 1985). Of particular interest is the demonstration of the separability of the ADD deficit from the dyslexic deficit when both are crossed in a factorial design (Harter *et al.*, 1988a,b). ADD had effects over different cortical regions (primarily bilaterally symmetrical frontal and occipital deficits) and at different latencies from those of RD.

In terms of the basic methodological issues identified above, the abnormally high incidence of ADD in a dyslexic sample (see Felton *et al.*, 1987) suggests that it is one of the most common additional deficits in dyslexic individuals. The clear implication is that unless the co-morbidity from ADD is controlled in the statistical design of dyslexia research, the physiological dysfunction found in a dyslexic sample may be due to the ADD component rather than the truly dyslexic component of the abnormality. In some instances, the ADD effect could conceivably mask the RD effect by contributing error variance if not statistically excluded.

Independent Physiological Deficit for RD in Children

The Harter studies examined a total of 52 children in the factorial design (presence versus absence of ADD and presence versus absence of RD), using a single flash attention paradigm. The stimuli were black and white letters and non-letters, with two attend conditions: letter and color. RD but not ADD was associated with reduced left central positivity at 240 ms. The authors interpreted this asymmetry as representing a left temporal or parietal deficit, and it is noteworthy that the effect was not limited to 'reading' stimuli (such as letters) but was also found for color stimuli. The finding suggests an interesting anatomical situation: deficit in auditory or multimodal association areas of the temporal and parietal lobe, even when the stimuli are purely visual. It is as though this region of association cortex will have at least some level of diminished function—whatever the instructions or the nature of the visual stimulus that could be 'associated' in that region.

On the other hand, some other effects were more specific to relevant stimuli, with a tendency toward greater deficit in orthographic processing, and in one case the deficit was clearly bilateral. This suggests that although there is a certain degree of deficit in the 'handling' of any stimulus in the left temporo-parietal area, it is selective attention to letter stimuli that most burdens this area of cortex—a burden that may in some cases extend to the right hemisphere as well. Thus, there was a hemispherically symmetrical reduction in central positivity around 320–340 ms in response to relevant stimuli, and it tended to be slightly greater for tasks demanding orthographic rather than color processing. Another difference was evident over left central and posterior regions at 400–440 ms; it was characterized by reduced positivity following relevant stimuli in children with RD, the reduction being greater over the left hemisphere.

Yet another finding illustrates the possibility that compensation can also be part of the physiological difference between normals and dyslexics. There was a symmetrical increase in the amplitude of a late positive component over frontal regions in children with RD. This effect was slightly greater for the more complex letter task which was believed to demand a greater processing load. Since the RD and non-RD groups performed the task equally well, the authors proposed that this late enhanced positivity over frontal regions may represent a compensatory mechanism in children with RD.

Using more complex verbal stimuli, Fried *et al.* (1981) reported that dyslexics with auditory–verbal processing deficits failed to show the typical asymmetry of greater amplitude ERPs to words versus musical chord stimuli over the left hemisphere. Duffy *et al.* (1980a,b) found an increase in alpha and beta activity in dyslexics primarily over left posterior regions which they interpreted as an indication of local cortical underactivation. This was found for a variety of activation states but was most evident for the more complex tasks such as reading. Interestingly, these authors also found evidence of more widespread deficit, including bilateral frontal regions.

Thus, well-controlled studies do point to a left central–posterior deficit in neural function in childhood dyslexia. This may include many types of stimuli but will apparently be most salient when the stimuli are verbally demanding. In some cases, more global frontal and/or right hemisphere deficit may also be observed—as would be expected from the analysis that suggests that dyslexia could include a bilateral failure (whereby the right hemisphere is itself marginally impaired and so unable fully to compensate for the left hemisphere deficit).

Adult Dyslexia

A study by Preston and colleagues (1977) is particularly relevant in that it is one of the few ERP studies to date on adult dyslexics. They found reduced amplitude ERPs for subjects with RD over left parietal regions in the negative component at 180 ms, a positive component at 200 ms and in a late positive component which was a composite of amplitudes from several latencies. The normal group showed a larger difference in the ERP waveform to words versus flashes than did the group with RD.

Adult studies are uniquely important for establishing the necessary and sufficient conditions for permanent disability: child studies always leave open the question of later remission or at least improvement. The obvious difficulty in adult studies is the converse—that of establishing the degree of childhood deficit which preceded it. However, if documentation of childhood deficit is available, then physiological studies of adults can provide indispensable information about the nature of the enduring deficit.

The remainder of this chapter will be devoted to a progress report of our current studies of the physiological indices of dyslexia in a well-defined population of adults who were evaluated an average of 21 years ago by June Lyday Orton. In each case, a subgroup of the population presented in the previous chapter served as subjects.

STUDY 1: ERP FINDINGS AT ADULT FOLLOW-UP

This study was the doctoral dissertation of one of the authors (Naylor, 1987). The subjects in this initial study were 38 males, 24 of whom were found to have reading problems in childhood, and 8 who scored within normal limits in childhood. The remaining 6 subjects were volunteers with no history of academic difficulty. Subjects with a history of ADD or emotional problems and those evidencing current major psychopathology were excluded from this study. The subjects seen by Orton were classified as reading disabled if childhood scores were at least two grade levels below expectation on the Gray Oral Reading Test (GORT) and/or the Wide Range Achievement (WRAT) reading subtest. (Although an either/or method of establishing groups was employed in this study, the results were quite similar to the more stringent criteria described in the previous chapter. Eighteen of 24 subjects classified as RD were deficient on both measures, with only 6 falling in the borderline range due to better performance on one or the other of the achievement measures.) Subjects also had to have achieved a verbal or performance IQ of at least 85 on the Wechsler Intelligence Scale for Children (WISC).

Table 1 presents the intelligence and achievement results of the childhood evaluation for those with reading disability (RD) and those without (NRD). Subjects with RD were well within normal limits on all IQ measures, and NRD tended to be in the high average to superior range of intellectual ability. Subjects with RD were on the average two to three grade levels behind in reading, while NRD were at or above grade level. Subjects with RD were also three years below grade level in spelling achievement, and over one and one half years behind in arithmetic. NRD performed well on all measures of achievement.

All subjects scored in the normal range on the Wechsler Adult Intelligence Scale—Revised version (Table 2). Subjects classified as RD remained relatively impaired in terms of reading achievement, although many of the subjects with a history of RD scored in the borderline or normal range in adulthood. The degree of residual reading deficit in adulthood was determined via two methods. First, the procedure used by Finucci et al. (1984) based on a regression equation which compared an individual's reading score to the level expected given IQ, sex and education was employed. The second method determined a reading quotient based on the age-corrected standard

Table 1. Intelligence and achievement variables for RD and NRD samples at Orton childhood evaluation

	RD			NRD		
	x̄ age = 13.8	x̄ GD. Level = 7.8		x̄ age = 14.1	x̄ GD. Level = 9.0	
Intelligence[a]	x̄	SD	Range	x̄	SD	Range
VIQ	106.92	(11.47)	91–134	121.13	(5.08)	115–131
PIQ	107.46	(11.47)	84–127	111.87	(6.58)	103–120
FSIQ	107.29	(9.56)	93–125	118.75	(4.10)	115–128
Achievement[b]	x̄		Range	x̄		Range
Gray oral	4.8		1.0– 9.3	9.8		5.1–12.0
WRAT reading	5.8		2.4–10.3	10.3		4.7–13.0
WRAT spelling	4.7		1.9– 7.4	9.3		3.8–12.8
WRAT arithmetic	6.0		3.6– 9.3	10.9		4.5–17.4

[a]Scores reported are from the WISC or WAIS.
[b]Scores reported are grade equivalents expressed in years and months.

Table 2. Means and standard deviations of predictor variables and achievement for Orton RD and NRD, NRD control and Finucci's regression samples

	Orton RD (n = 24)		Orton NRD (n = 8)		Control NRD (n = 6)		Regression (n = 46)	
	x̄	(SD)	x̄	(SD)	x̄	(SD)	x̄	(SD)
Predictor variables								
Age	33.9	(5.7)	36.0	(3.7)	33.9	(4.4)	37.9	(11.3)
Education	15.5	(2.0)	17.8	(1.5)	15.0	(2.2)	16.1	(2.5)
Verbal IQ	101.0	(10.3)	115.9	(8.5)	103.0	(4.7)	122.7	(10.6)
Performance IQ	100.8	(9.3)	112.3	(11.6)	105.8	(9.8)	117.0	(11.8)
Full-scale IQ	100.6	(9.6)	115.8	(8.4)	104.3	(7.4)	not given	
Achievement skill level								
GORT dev. score[a]	−1.12	(1.5)	1.55	(0.79)	1.66	(0.87)		
WRAT-R spelling dev. score[a]	−1.46	(1.2)	1.29	(1.4)	1.38	(1.9)		
WRAT-R reading quotient[b]	84.5	(9.5)	98.2	(8.1)	93.4	(13.1)		

[a]Normal reader > −1.0.   [b]Normal reader > 90.
Borderline reader > −2.0 but ≤ −1.0.   Borderline reader > 80 and ≤ 90.
Reading-deficient ≤ −2.0.   Reading-deficient ≤ 80.

score on the WRAT-R reading subtest divided by the full-scale WAIS-R score.

Event-related Potential Findings

The procedure used to collect event-related potential (ERP) data was identical to that of Harter *et al.* (1988a,b) using a single-stimulus presentation paradigm. In the letter game, the subject was to respond to black or white letters, ignoring non-letters. In the color game, black was relevant, and all white stimuli were ignored. ERP recordings were made from the left and right occipital (O1 and O2), central (C3 and C4) and frontal (F3 and F4) leads referenced to linked ears. A rejection system excluded data that were contaminated by body or eye movement as well as any trial involving a behavioral error.

There were no differences found in the overall accuracy, reaction time or total score between the groups, and therefore any differences in the ERPs cannot be attributed to behavioral performance. Since the two normal reading groups did not differ in terms of electrophysiological response, their results were combined for analysis comparing RD ($n = 24$) to NRD ($n = 14$).

The most prominent finding of this study was a generalized prolonged reduction in positivity for RD compared to NRD on both tasks (Figures 1 and 2). This difference started as early as 150 ms, well before the initiation of the behavioral response. Not only was this reduction in positivity bilateral, but it extended across time rather than being limited to a given latency (240 ms) as it was for children (Harter *et al.*, 1988a,b).

Similar to the findings for children, the amplitude of left central P240 was significantly correlated with current reading level (Figures 3 and 4; $r = 0.44$, $p < 0.03$); indicating that the better one reads orally in adulthood, the greater the amplitude of this component in left central regions. This is consistent with the Harter *et al.* study and supports the hypothesis of left central P240 as a marker of reading disability in both children and adults.

Adult reading deficit was highly correlated with childhood reading deficit. In other words, those who remained most impaired tended to be those that were the most severely affected in childhood. In addition, the physiological results of this study suggest that those who remained impaired showed more bilateral deficits in neural function, particularly in comparison to the unilateral deficit found for children. In childhood, a unilateral left hemisphere deficit alone may be sufficient to result in impaired reading on behavioral tests. Thus, subject selection for RD would include individuals with both unilateral and bilateral deficits. By adulthood, those with unilateral impairment alone may have compensated for their reading problems, so that adult subjects meeting the same behavioral criteria of RD may include only or primarily

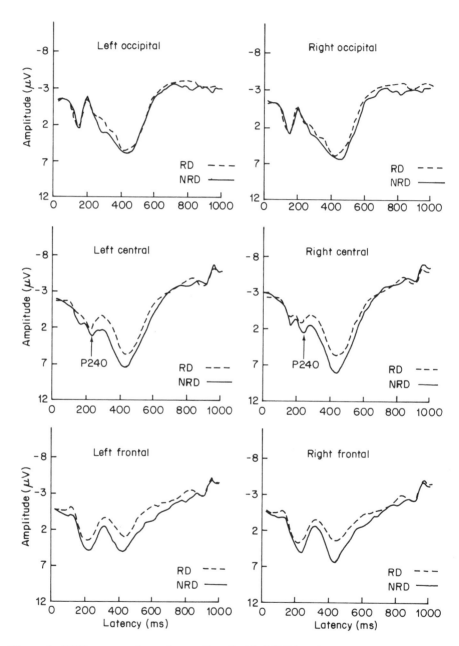

Figure 1. ERP raw waveforms for reading-disabled (RD) and normal readers (NRD): relevance independent effects in the letter game

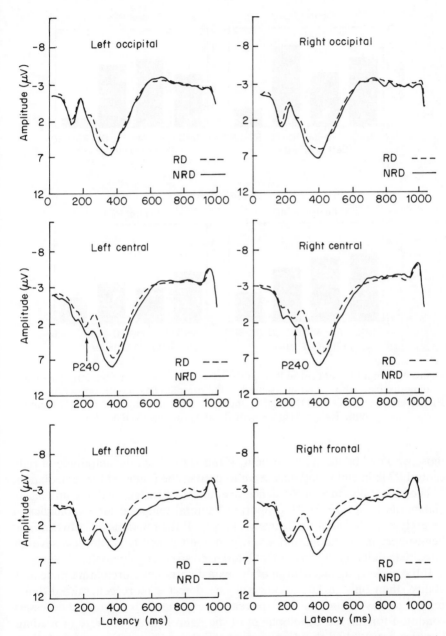

Figure 2. ERP raw waveforms for reading-disabled (RD) and normal readers (NRD): relevance independent effects in the color game

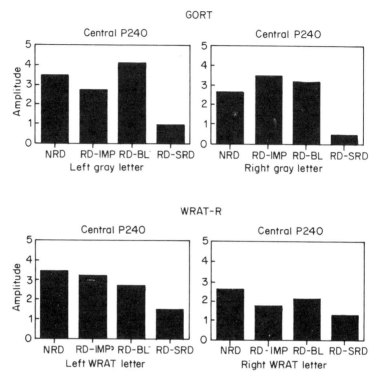

Figure 3. Amplitude of central P240 in the letter game for normal readers (NRD) and reading-disabled who, as adults, scored in the normal (RD–IMP), borderline (RD–BL) or impaired (RD–SRD) range on the Gray Oral Reading Test (GORT) and the Wide Range Achievement Reading Subtest (WRAT-R)

those who had bilateral impairment. If this is the case, the amplitude of right central P240 in childhood may serve to predict the potential for remediation.

The bilateral nature of the deficit in adults is consistent with the findings of Galaburda *et al.* (1985) who reported bilateral temporal lobe anomalies in severely impaired adult dyslexics at autopsy. If the relationship between right hemisphere involvement and severity of adult deficit is viable, less severely impaired adults should have more lateralized structural anomalies at autopsy.

If the underlying mechanism of dyslexia determines a premature plateau of ability, then only in later years will one detect a more generalized deficit related to this limitation. Perhaps reading experience is not only a necessary condition for the full development of the neurological substrate of reading, but also essential to the development of other high-level cognitive skills as well. Experience may serve to provide the cellular competition required for normal cell death which results in the adaptive 'pruning' required for normal

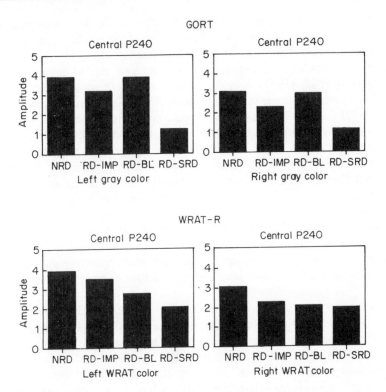

Figure 4. Amplitude of central P240 in the color game for normal readers (NRD) and reading-disabled who, as adults, scored in the normal (RD–IMP), borderline (RD–BL) or impaired (RD–SRD) range on the Gray Oral Reading Test (GORT) and the Wide Range Achievement Reading Subtest (WRAT-R)

brain function. If individuals with RD suffer from neural deficit which disrupts this process, the behavioral endpoint of development would be lower than that of normal readers. By adulthood, therefore, subjects who remain RD would look impaired on a wider variety of behavioral tests relative to their normal controls than would children. Thus, when individuals with a history of reading disability are evaluated in adulthood, the behavioral and physiological phenotype may look very different, i.e. more generally impaired, from that of children with a similar degree of reading deficit.

REGIONAL CEREBRAL BLOOD FLOW STUDIES

Regional blood flow is highly correlated with local cerebral metabolism (Raichle *et al.*, 1976) and can be successfully used to measure the functional metabolic activation that is induced by cognitive tasks. See Risberg (1980, 1986) for illustrative reviews; also Wood (1983, 1987) for methodological reviews related respectively to laterality and memory.

Several studies have investigated rCBF measures during reading-related tasks. Jacquy et al. (1977) demonstrated greater activation in the left pre-central and temporal areas in normal adults during silent reading; and Larsen et al. (1979) showed activation along the Sylvian fissure, including inferior parietal regions, during reading aloud. In a study in our own laboratory of reading aloud by two stutterers on and off haloperidol (Wood et al., 1980), successful reading with minimal stuttering was accompanied by greater left than right Broca's area flow, whereas reading with stuttering was accompanied by greater right than left Broca's area flow. Similarly, when normal right-handed males analyzed the plural endings of words presented monaurally, Maximilian (1982) found left flow was greater than right in the temporo-parietal regions. Thus, there is evidence in rCBF studies for a functional asymmetry in language processing in normal adults whereby classically relevant areas of the left hemisphere are more activated during reading-related tasks.

There are only two studies to date which have investigated rCBF in dyslexic adults. The first was reported by Hynd et al. (1987). They compared two males who were severely impaired in reading to two normal males, recording metabolic changes as they read a prose story silently. A resting baseline was used for comparison to the activation condition. Normal subjects showed an increase in temporal flow bilaterally while reading, greater over the right than left hemisphere. One dyslexic had normal left hemisphere flow, but right hemisphere flow was lower than that of his normal control. The other disabled reader had overall lower flow in both hemispheres as compared to his normal control with right hemisphere activation actually lower during reading than at rest. The authors concluded that 'both developmental dyslexics evidenced less significant degrees of metabolic change in rCBF during the activation study than the normals' (p. 298). Second, they emphasized the occurrence of significant right hemisphere activation in normal fluent readers while reading. Although of interest, this study must be viewed as a case study with limited generalizability.

A larger study by Rumsey et al. (1987) examined 14 men with severe developmental dyslexia and a matched control group. The dyslexic group in this study showed more hemispheric asymmetry, left greater than right, on a semantic classification task. However, there was a trend toward increased right-greater-than-left asymmetry on another task of a visual perceptual nature (judgment of line orientation). They concluded that 'adults with severe developmental dyslexia, characterized by deficits in phonological processing, may show more asymmetric hemispheric activation in either direction, depending on the nature of the task. This may indicate a tendency toward inadequate bihemispheric integration or inefficient simultaneous allocation of resources' (p. 1149).

The alternative explanation for the greater asymmetry is simply that it indicates bilaterally lower levels of function (since the dyslexic flows were generally lower than those of the normals). In that context, the greater asymmetry might simply mean a limitation of activation to those areas required for task performance—as though the subjects were unable or perhaps indisposed to generate a more comprehensive, bilateral cerebral effort.

The principal limitation of the Rumsey *et al.* study is that it looked only at cortical quadrants (left versus right; anterior versus posterior) instead of anatomically more specific sites. Thus, any more focal type of dysfunction would not have been evident in their analysis.

STUDY 2: REGIONAL CEREBRAL BLOOD FLOW FINDINGS AT ADULT FOLLOW-UP

To date, we have done regional cerebral blood flow studies on approximately 60 individuals who were tested by June Orton in childhood. As a progress report, we present here a sample of 40 individuals, all males with no history of attention deficit disorder, no major psychopathology in childhood or adulthood, and no neurological trauma.

These 40 individuals have been divided into three groups based on childhood scores using the same criteria as described in the preceding chapter of this volume. The reading-disabled (RD) group consisted of those who scored two standard deviations below the mean on both reading quotient measures based on the Gray Oral Reading Test (GORT) and the Wide Range Achievement Reading Subtest (WRAT). The non-reading-disabled (NRD) group included those who scored no worse than one standard deviation below the mean on both reading quotients in childhood. Finally, the borderline (BL) group was composed of those who did not meet criteria either for RD or NRD.

The behavioral data on these subjects were quite similar (Table 3) to those of the whole sample. The reader is referred to Volume 2 for an overview of the overall differences related to RD on behavioral measures and possible interpretations. As in the larger population, many subjects within the RD subgroup continued to have oral 'reading and spelling problems in adulthood, although both BL and NRD scored within normal limits on all measures of achievement.

Regional cerebral blood flow was measured using a xenon-133 inhalation technique while the subjects were engaged in a series of tasks involving cognitive activation. Only on task requiring orthographic analysis of

Table 3. Intelligence and achievement variables for reading-disabled (RD), borderline (BL) and normal reading (NRD) rCBF subjects

	RD N = 17		BL N = 13		NRD N = 10	
	Childhood	*Adult*	*Childhood*	*Adult*	*Childhood*	*Adult*
Age at testing	13.7	35.5	12.6	32.4	12.6	34.9
Educ. level	7.4	15.5	7.1	16.5	7.5	16.7
Intelligence						
VIQ	103.3	99.4	106.1	102.4	118.5	113.9
PIQ	111.7	105.4	105.4	100.6	111.0	104.2
FSIQ	106.9	101.5	105.6	101.4	116.7	110.8
Achievement						
Gray Oral	64.9	−2.04	83.0	0.22	98.2	1.04
WRAT reading	69.9	80.9	89.6	91.3	101.3	99.9
WRAT spelling[a]	64.6	−1.84	80.1	0.02	96.0	1.35
WRAT arithmetic[a]	77.5	90.9	85.7	90.7	102.7	96.6

[a]Missing values in all groups.

auditorily presented words is reported here. Subjects listened to 88 common
nouns on earphones, presented every 2.5 seconds. They were to respond with
a bilateral finger lift response only if the words contained exactly four letters,
which occurred at random half of the time. This was a fairly simple task which
individuals with no history of reading disability had little difficulty completing. However, this task proved to be quite difficult for many of the subjects in
this study, particularly those who remained significantly impaired in reading
in adulthood.

A sample of 22 normal male subjects with no history of reading problems is
shown for reference in Figure 5. Of particular interest is the relative peak of
activation in Wernicke's area in the left hemisphere. Not only is Wernicke's
area flow greater than at the immediately superior (post-central) and posterior (angular gyrus and inferior temporo-occipital) sites, but flow at the
Wernicke's area site was significantly correlated with task accuracy.

The blood flow patterns of both NRD and BL resembled the reference
group in showing the left temporal peak (Figure 6). However, the RD group
showed a conspicuous absence of the peak in left temporal regions with a
general flattening of the profile over the left hemisphere. Thus, across the
three groups, the amplitude of the Wernicke's area peak was predicted by
group membership ($p < 0.01$) after covarying for Wechsler Adult Full-Scale
IQ, education, childhood socio-economic status, and state anxiety rating scale
(Spielberger *et al.*, 1983) administered immediately before and after the
blood flow task. This relationship was not found over the right hemisphere.

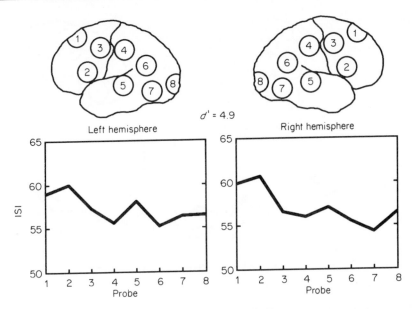

Figure 5. Regional cerebral blood flow activation profiles as measured by the initial slope index (ISI) for normal adult males ($n = 22$) during an orthographic analysis task

An interesting difference between the individuals originally seen by Orton and those in the reference group can be found in the right hemisphere. In Orton subjects, accuracy on the orthographic task was not only correlated with activation in core language areas of the left hemisphere but also with the peak of activation in the angular gyrus of the right hemisphere ($p < 0.05$); and this peak was significantly enhanced in all Orton subjects compared to the normal reference sample ($p < 0.05$). All comparisons were statistically independent of covariance with IQ, education and anxiety.

Reading ability in adulthood for Orton subjects was correlated with activation in the left temporal, Wernicke's area. It is possible that better readers, i.e. those whose reading skills are now within normal limits, had more intact primary language areas in the left hemisphere to start with. Thus, in adulthood, these subjects showed greater activation in left temporal regions as did normals with no history of reading problems. On the other hand, those who were still severely deficient in their reading skills failed to show activation in the primary language areas of the left hemisphere, showing instead only the peak of activation in the right angular gyrus.

At least two possible mechanisms could explain this right hemisphere component as a compensatory strategy. First, it could represent a non-language strategy, such as the use of visual imagery as in visualizing the word rather than decoding it phonetically. Another possibility was that this activa-

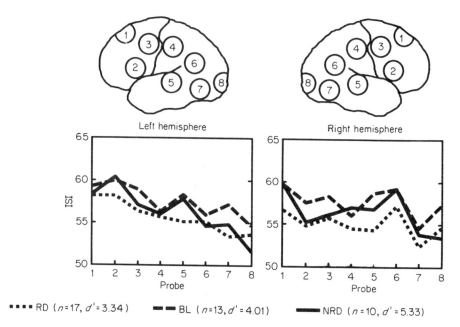

Figure 6. Regional cerebral blood flow activation profiles as measured by the initial slope index (ISI) for adults diagnosed as reading-disabled (RD), borderline reading-disabled (BL) and non-reading-disabled (NRD) in childhood during an orthographic analysis task

tion represented a relocation of language or related functions in individuals who suffered early damage to basic language areas in the left hemisphere.

However, the peak right angular gyrus activation was seen for borderline RD as well as those who had no documentable reading disability in childhood (Figure 6). Thus, this was not dependent on the level of reading disability in childhood, at least not as operationally defined in this study.

If these findings do reflect right hemisphere compensation, then its threshold is much lower than the threshold for focal left temporal flow reduction: it is as though right hemisphere strategies will 'kick in' at the subtlest or mildest level of reading impairment. It should be noted in this context that, even though some of the NRD subjects scored within normal limits in childhood, subjectively several of them described a past history or self-perception of reading problems. In fact, some of them underwent tutoring due to their own or their teachers' dissatisfaction with their performance even though their test scores were not below average. Note also that NRD were above average in intelligence, so scores in the average range, while technically falling within normal limits, may have seemed relatively weak in relation to other academic achievements. It is also quite possible that some in this group, being above average in intellectual ability, were already compensating to some extent at the time of Orton's evaluation for an actual deficit in reading.

The NRD group needs to be expanded and further subclassified to rule out these possibilities. Certainly, the group of subjects classified as BL may have indeed had significant reading problems, and the right hemisphere activation was representative of some form of compensation. The interpretation of this unusual pattern of right hemisphere activation will be aided by: (1) the addition of another group of non-referred, normal subjects who would undergo complete intellectual, neuropsychological and achievement evaluations; and (2) expanding the Orton NRD group.

CONCLUSIONS

The results of our physiological studies to date provide strong evidence of an underlying physiological deficit in left hemisphere functioning in core language areas, primarily the left temporal region. However, there is also strong evidence to suggest that the underlying physiological deficit, at least for those individuals who fail to improve their reading skills by adulthood, has a bilateral component as well. In comparison to the research findings we have available on children, the altered physiology associated with adult dyslexia appears more generalized than has usually been described in children. This is quite evident in the electrophysiological results and suggested by the blood flow data in the form of a trend toward lower mean flows for RD over both hemispheres.

Dynamic studies of brain activity during challenging cognitive tasks further provide information as to possible compensatory strategies in disabled populations. When subjects are equated in behavioral performance, enhanced activity (as found in frontal regions in the Harter *et al.* studies with children) could provide evidence of displaced function or the use of alternate strategies. If subjects vary in their ability to perform a task (as in the blood flow studies with adults), correlations between behavioral performance and indices of brain function can provide the same information. The extent to which this compensation involves the use of alternative strategies can then be investigated by comparing brain activation during a number of different tasks, some of which limit the usefulness of such strategies (e.g. visual imagery).

The results of these studies with both adults and children would suggest that physiological compensation begins at an early age, long before the permanence of the behavioral deficit becomes evident. However, the compensatory strategies operating in childhood may not be the same as those seen in adulthood. It is conceivable that alternate strategies, and therefore different brain regions, may be engaged in the performance of a language-related task until language functions can be relocated for more efficient processing. If relocation is impossible (as in cases of bilateral impairment), then one's performance will rely solely on the extent to which these other less efficient strategies serve as viable alternatives.

ACKNOWLEDGEMENTS

This work was supported by USPHS grant PO1 HD21887 to Bowman Gray School of Medicine and RO1 NS19413 to the University of North Carolina at Greensboro.

REFERENCES

Benton, A. L., and Pearl, D. (1978). *Dyslexia: An Appraisal of Current Knowledge.* New York: Oxford University Press.

Charcot, J.-M. (1889). *Clinical Lectures on Diseases of the Nervous System.* London: New Sydenham Society.

Conners, C. K. (1970). Cortical visual evoked response in children with learning disorders. *Psychophysiology*, **7**, 418–428.

Dejerine, J. (1892). Contribution à l'étude anatomo-pathologique et clinique des differentes variétés de cécité verbale. *Comptes Rendus des Seances de la Société de Biologie*, **9**, 61–90.

Dejerine, J. (1914). *Semiologie des Affections du Système Nerveux.* Paris: Masson et Cie.

Dennis, M., and Whitaker, H. (1976). Language acquisition following hemidecortication: Linguistic superiority of the left over the right hemisphere. *Brain and Language*, **3**, 404–433.

Duffy, F. H., Denckla, M. B., Bartels, P. H., and Sandini, B. (1980a). Dyslexia: Regional differences in brain electrical activity by topographical mapping. *Annals of Neurology*, **7**, 412–420.

Duffy, F. H., Denckla, M. B., Bartels, P. H., Sandini, G., and Kiessling, L. S. (1980b). Dyslexia: Automated diagnosis by computerized classification of brain electrical activity. *Annals of Neurology*, **7**, 421–428.

Dykman, R. A., Holcomb, P. J., Oglesby, D. M., and Ackerman, P. T. (1982). Electrocortical frequencies in hyperactive, learning-disabled, mixed, and normal children. *Biological Psychiatry*, **17**, 675–685.

Felton, R. H., Wood, F. B., Brown, I. S., Campbell, S. K., and Harter, M. R. (1987). Separate verbal memory and naming deficits in attention deficit disorder and reading disability. *Brain and Language*, **31**, 171–184.

Finucci, J. M., Whitehouse, C. C., Isaacs, S. D., and Childs, B. (1984). Derivation and validation of a quantitative definition of specific reading disability for adults. *Developmental Medicine and Child Neurology*, **26**, 143–153.

Fried, I., Tanguay, P. E., Boder, E., Doubleday, C., and Greensite, M. (1981). Developmental dyslexia: Electrophysiological evidence of clinical subgroups. *Brain and Language*, **12**, 14–22.

Galaburda, A. M., and Kemper, T. L. (1979). Cytoarchitectonic abnormalities in developmental dyslexia: A case study. *Annals of Neurology*, **6**, 94–100.

Galaburda, A. M., Sherman, G. F., Rosen, G. D., Aboitiz, F., and Geschwind, N. (1985). Developmental dyslexia: Four consecutive patients with cortical anomalies. *Annals of Neurology*, **18**, 222–233.

Geschwind, N. (1970). The organization of language and the brain. *Science*, **170**, 940–944.

Geschwind, N., and Galaburda, A. M. (1985). Cerebral lateralization. Biological mechanisms, association, and pathology: I. A hypothesis and a program for research. *Archives of Neurology*, **42**, 428–459.

Geschwind, N., and Levitsky, W. (1968). Human brain: Left–right asymmetries in temporal speech region. *Science*, **161**, 186–187.

Golden, G. S. (1982). Neurobiological correlates of learning disabilities. *Annals of Neurology*, **12**, 409–418.

Harter, M. R., Diering, S., and Wood, F. B. (1988a). Separate brain potential characteristics in children with reading disability and attention deficit disorder: Relevance—independent effects. *Brain and Cognition*, **7**, 54–86.

Harter, M. R., Arillo-Vento, L., Wood, F. B., and Schroeder, M. M. (1988b). Separate brain potential characteristics in children with reading disability and attention deficit disorder: Color and letter relevance effects. *Brain and Cognition*, **7**, 115–140.

Haslam, R. H. A., Dalby, J. T., Johns, R. D., and Rademaker, A. W. (1981). Cerebral asymmetry in developmental dyslexia. *Archives of Neurology*, **38**, 679–682.

Hier, D. B., LeMay, M., Rosenberger, P. B., and Perlo, V. P. (1978). Developmental dyslexia: Evidence for a subgroup with a reversal of cerebral asymmetry. *Archives of Neurology*, **35**, 90–92.

Holcomb, P. J., Ackerman, P. T., and Dykman, R. A. (1985). Cognitive event-related brain potentials in children with attention and reading deficits. *Psychophysiology*, **22**, 656–667.

Hynd, G. W., Hynd, C. R., Sulivan, H. G., and Kingsbury, T. B. (1987). Regional cerebral blood flow in developmental dyslexia: Activation during reading in surface and deep dyslexia. *Journal of Reading Disabilities*, **20**, 294–300.

Jacquy, J., Piraux, A., and Noel, G. (1977). Hemispheric pattern at rest and while reading in the normal adult, the normal child and the blind. *Archives of Neurology Scandinavia*, **56** (Suppl. 64), 528–529.

Kimura, D. (1983). Speech representation in an unbiased sample of left-handers. *Human Neurobiology*, **2**, 147–154.

Larsen, B., Skinhoj, E., and Lassen, N. A. (1979). Cortical activity of left and right hemispheres provoked by reading and visual naming: A rCBF study. *Acta Neurologica Scandinavia*, **59** (Suppl. 72), 6–7.

Liepmann, H. (1920). *Apraxic. Ergbn. der ges. Med.*, **1**, 516–543.

Ludlam, W. M. (1981). Visual electrophysiology and reading/learning difficulties. *Journal of Learning Disabilities*, **14**, 587–590.

Marx, J. L. (1983). The two sides of the brain. *Science*, **220**, 488–490.

Maximilian, V. A. (1982). Cortical blood flow asymmetry during monaural verbal stimulation. *Brain and Language*, **15**, 1–11.

Naylor, C. E. (1987). Event-related potentials and behavioral assessment: A 20 year follow-up of adults who were diagnosed as reading disabled in childhood (Doctoral dissertation, University of North Carolina–Greensboro, 1987). *Dissertation Abstracts International*.

Ojemann, G. A. (1983). Brain organization for language from the perspective of electrical stimulation mapping. *The Behavioral and Brain Sciences*, **6**, 189–230.

Preston, M. S., Guthrie, J. T., and Childs, B. (1974). Visual evoked responses (VERs) in normal and disabled readers. *Psychophysiology*, **11**, 452–457.

Preston, M. S., Guthrie, J. T., Kirsch, I., Gertman, D., and Childs, B. (1977). VERs in normal and disabled adult readers. *Psychophysiology*, **14**, 8–14.

Raichle, M. E., Grubb, R. L., Gado, M. H., Eichling, J. O., and Ter-Pogossian, M. M. (1976). Correlation between regional cerebral blood flow and oxidative metabolism. *Archives of Neurology*, **33**, 523–526.

Rasmussen, T., and Milner, B. (1977). The role of early left-brain injury in determining lateralization of cerebral speech functions. *Annals of New York Academy of Sciences*, **299**, 355–369.

Risberg, J. (1980). Regional cerebral blood flow measurements by 133 Xe-inhalation: Methodology and applications in neuropsychology and psychiatry. *Brain and Language*, **9**, 9–34.

Risberg, J. (1986). Regional cerebral blood flow in neuropsychology. *Neuropsychologia*, **24**, 135–140.

Rumsey, J. M., Berman, K. F., Denckla, M. B., Hamburger, S. D., Kruesi, M. J., and Weinberger, D. R. (1987). Regional cerebral blood flow in severe developmental dyslexia. *Archives of Neurology*, **44**, 1144–1150.

Rumsey, J. M., Dorwart, R., Vermess, M., Denckla, M. B., Kruesi, M. J., and Rapoport, J. L. (1986). Magnetic resonance imaging of brain anatomy in severe developmental dyslexia. *Archives of Neurology*, **43**, 1045–1046.

Satz, P., Orsini, D. L., Saslow, E., and Henry, R. (1985). The pathological left-handedness syndrome. *Brain and Cognition*, **4**, 27–46.

Sobotka, K. R., and May, J. G. (1977). Visual evoked potentials and reaction time in normal and dyslexic children. *Psychophysiology*, **14**, 18–24.

Spielberger, C. D., Gorsuch, R. L., Luchene, R., Vagg, P. R., and Jacobs, G. A. (1983). *Manual for the State-Trait Anxiety Inventory (STAI)—Form 4*. Palo Alto: Consulting Psychol. Press.

Symann-Louett, N., Gascon, G. G., Matsumiya, Y., and Lombroso, C. T. (1977). Wave form differences in visual evoked responses between normal and reading disabled children, *Neurology*, **27**, 156–159.

Weber, B. A., and Omenn, G. S. (1977). Auditory and visual evoked responses in children with familial reading disabilities. *Journal of Learning Disabilities*, **10**, 153–158.

Wernicke, C. (1874). *Der Aphasische Symptomencomplex*. Breslau: Franck & Weigert.

Wood, F. B. (1983). Laterality of cerebral function: Its investigation by measurement of localized brain activity. In J. B. Hellige (ed.), *Cerebral Hemisphere Asymmetry: Method, Theory and Application*. New York: Praeger.

Wood, F. B. (1987). Focal and diffuse memory activation assessed by localized indicators of CNS metabolism: The semantic–episodic memory distinction. *Human Neurobiology*, **6**, 141–151.

Wood, F. B., Stump, D., McKeehan, A., Sheldon, S., and Proctor, J. (1980). Patterns of regional cerebral blood flow during attempted reading aloud by stutterers both on and off haloperidol medication: Evidence for inadequate left frontal activation during stuttering. *Brain and Language*, **9**, 141–144.

Address for correspondence (all authors):

Section of Neuropsychology, Bowman Gray School of Medicine, Winston-Salem, North Carolina 27103, USA

9

Dyslexia and the Neurophysiology of Attention

C. Keith Conners
Duke University Medical Center, Durham, North Carolina

INTRODUCTION

It is estimated that 10–50% of children referred for attention-deficit and/or hyperactivity (ADHD) also have a concomitant learning disorder (Cantwell and Satterfield, 1978; Lambert and Sandoval, 1980; Safer and Allen, 1976), and it is quite common for parents and teachers to note attentional problems in children whose primary complaint is poor learning (Ackerman *et al.*, 1983; Aman, 1979). This common clinical observation of overlap among attentional and learning problems has led to speculation that selective attention deficits underlie both sets of problems (Ross, 1976). At the same time, the frequent observation of ADHD with normal reading, and poor readers without hyperactivity, has prompted others to insist that the two disorders represent fundamentally different states which can be properly understood only by defining purified samples; e.g. dyslexia-pure versus ADHD-pure (Denckla, 1978).

The consequences of selecting for ADHD when studying dyslexic samples is illustrated in a study by Denckla *et al.* (1985). They showed that a reading disorder group with ADHD screened out performed significantly better on tests of motor proficiency than equally poor readers who had not been screened for attention deficit. Thus, whether dyslexics have motor delays as part of their syndrome is merely a function of the selection criteria for the syndrome. The relationship of ADHD to reading disorder is implied to be adventitious, not intrinsic.

While such a strategy may be reasonable in pursuit of the unique features characterizing either disorder, it cannot address the question as to what the disorders have in common nor why they so frequently occur together.

Perspectives on Dyslexia Vol. 1
Edited by G. Th. Pavlidis   © 1990 John Wiley & Sons Ltd

Although it seems quite obvious that attentional dysfunction itself cannot account for reading disorder, since many children with quite severe attention-deficit disorders do not have a reading problem, it may be heuristically useful to regard the clinical overlap in these conditions as indicative of some important shared processes, along with the corollary that the non-overlap reveals important aspects of difference in the etiology of the conditions.

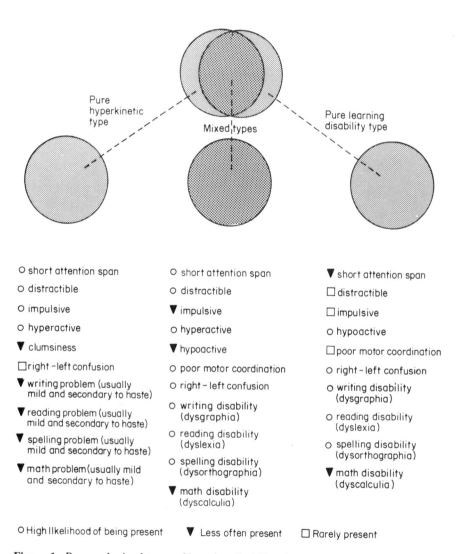

Figure 1. Pure and mixed types of learning disability. (Reproduced from Peters *et al.*, 1973, by permission of the authors.)

CLINICAL DESCRIPTION OF ATTENTION DEFICIT AND READING

Probably most clinicians who do careful, individualized assessments of children with behavior and learning problems would agree that such children manifest a wide range of subtle impairments, shading into pure types only in extreme cases; with most children representing some mixture of inattention, impulsivity, disorganization and learning deficits. 'Diagnosis' with such a spectrum often means a somewhat arbitrary focus upon the most salient symptom, such as hyperactivity. Pure cases or extreme types are in fact extremely rare.

Nevertheless, it is difficult to escape the impression that there are important qualitative differences between those reading, arithmetic or writing failures which appear to be secondary to a hasty and impulsive style; and those which occur without marked impulsivity, and which are often associated with a history of speech or language delay. It is not performances on particular tasks so much as the *pattern* of performances which suggests that there are 'pure types' among the array of behavior and learning disorders. Such a clinical approach suggests a typology in which behavioral and learning disorders share similar features but with different weighted combinations of those features, as in Figure 1 (Peters *et al.*, 1973).

If one accepts such a schema as a reasonably adequate description of the phenomenology of behavioral and learning disorders in children, it is tempting to look for some unifying concept or dimension along which they are varying. 'Attention' is such a concept, despite evidence that attention itself is a multidimensional notion in need of considerable explication. It is instructive to examine the way attention has been operationalized in behavioral studies of dyslexia and ADHD, and then to examine ways in which recent developments in the neurobiology of attention may offer clarification of attentional concepts.

BEHAVIORAL STUDIES OF ATTENTION DEFICIT AND READING

Reaction Time

Performance on warned versus unwarned reaction time (RT) has frequently been used as one behavioral index of attention. Dykman and colleagues (1971) were among the first to suggest that reading disability (RD) children have an attentional deficit in common with ADHD. Studies of RD children showed a notable increase in response latencies for visual RT stimuli compared with normals.

But these subjects were quite heterogeneous with respect to behavioral characteristics. When this mixed bag of 'MBD' subjects was subdivided into hyperactive, normoactive and hypoactive types, RT latencies were much slower for hypoactive than hyperactive children. In their earlier thinking these investigators regarded attention as a unitary trait with four interrelated components (alertness, stimulus selection, focusing and vigilance). Though the findings suggest some form of slower processing in the hypoactive RD subjects, the data do not indicate whether the delays are in an early perceptual or input stage, a processing stage, or at the level of response output. Clearly, RT by itself is inadequate to discriminate among these 'components' of attention.

Sustained versus Selective Attention

In subsequent studies (Dykman *et al.*, 1985) the concept of deficits in *selective* attention for RD children and *sustained* attention for ADHD children was applied in a number of different ways. For example, in the Pribram task a subject has to scan a visual field, discover a target symbol on the basis of reward, stay with it for five trials until it is no longer rewarded, learn to search for a new target, etc. Difficulty is manipulated by increasing the number of search items. Search trials are considered to require selective attention, and after-search trials sustained attention. This task has been successful in differentiating temporal lobe from frontal lobe lesions in monkeys. Contrary to prediction, however, there were no differences between the ADHD and RD groups, though both were inferior to controls (Dykman *et al.*, 1979, 1980).

Using the continuous performance test (CPT), these investigators did find some evidence that ADHD subjects had worse performance on later trials than RD subjects, thus implicating sustained attentional deficits in ADHD. The most discriminating task between the groups, however, was in an effortful task involving acoustic–semantic memory in a task described by Weingartner *et al.* (1980).

Other findings from this group include better performance on the Sternberg memory task for RDs under low memory load (suggesting that memory retrieval is adequate under low information demand), and a highly significant tendency for RDs to have faster visual RT relative to auditory RT compared to controls. This last finding is suggestive that RDs have more difficulty with sequential than parallel information processing.

Summarizing a number of their studies, Dykman *et al.* state that:

> . . . we are inclined to believe that [hyperactive] children's inability to sustain attention, their lack of will (effort) to think and remember, their inability to suppress extraneous responses and distracting stimuli, their aggressive or impulsive behavior indicate frontal–limbic dysfunction, most likely subtle defects in the 'wiring' of inhibitory connections . . . When information becomes excessive or

uninteresting, even normally attentive people exhibit attentional problems similar to those of [hyperactive] children . . . RD children exhibit attentional problems very similar to those of ADD children but the problems are less noticeable or severe until they are put into effortful information processing situations. (Dykman *et al.*, 1985: p. 60)

Thus, these authors tend to regard ADHD as having problems in effortful, sustained attention; while RD have such problems secondary to primary processing difficulties involving selective attention for linguistic stimuli. Our own impression, however, is that careful review of the data shows that in most measures and experimental paradigms the similarity between ADHD and RD are greater than their differences, with both performing poorly compared to normals on most measures conventionally described as attentional in nature. The theorizing regarding the neuro-anatomical and neurophysiological bases of these disorders, while reasonable, seems very loosely tied to the experimental data which fails to give direct support for the sustained–selective attention dichotomy. Part of the difficulty is in using tasks like Pribram's search task to operationalize attentional constructs without adequate validation at the human level.

Central versus Incidental Learning

A quite different paradigm for operationalizing attention is the incidental learning paradigm. A number of early studies purported to show that poor readers are more impaired by distraction than normal readers (Santostefano *et al.*, 1965; Denney, 1974; Hallahan, 1975). These studies led Ross (1976), like Dykman's group, to theorize that selective attention is related to reading disabilities. Pelham and Ross (1977) decided to employ an incidental learning paradigm, on the assumption that poor selective attention among the disabled readers would lead to inferior performance on a central task, but superior performance on the incidental task. This prediction was partly confirmed in a study of 37 poor readers and age/grade-matched controls. The poor readers were inferior on the incidental task but no different on the central task. There were no interactions with age.

These findings contrast with the earlier study by Hallahan *et al.* (1973), who found poorer performance of poor readers on the *central* task but no differences on the incidental task. But a subsequent study by Pelham (1979) failed to replicate the central–incidental task results, nor were there group differences on a speeded classification task involving completing information.

Pelham (1979) did find lower performance for poor readers on *auditory* versions of the incidental learning tasks. Word lists were presented binaurally, with the relevant word (an animal name) followed immediately by the distracting word (food names). Lists of varying length were recalled, with the incidental score being the recall of the irrelevant words. Controls were significantly better on the central task but there were no differences between poor readers and controls on the incidental recall.

A later study by Copeland and Wisniewski (1981) found no differences on either central or incidental visual learning by themselves, but a significant difference on a derived measure reflecting the relative advantage of central over incidental performance. Normal children had significantly better central relative to incidental performance (as in Pelham *et al.*'s earlier (1977) study), with the effect more apparent for younger than older children, though interactions with age were not statistically significant. They also reported a significant advantage of normals over poor readers in the speeded classification task, an advantage that was significantly greater among the younger children.

In another study, distraction and no-distraction were manipulated in an auditory short-term memory task by inserting distracting words into the word list to be recalled (Ford *et al.*, 1984). But performance of poor readers was impaired under both conditions, and training in rehearsal did not eliminate the differences, ruling out a rehearsal explanation as the source of the difficulty. The authors suggested that some deficit prior to rehearsal, such as verbal encoding or semantic retrieval must be involved.

Thus, overall, there is somewhat conflicting evidence regarding deficits in visual attention involving central versus incidental stimulus selection. One wonders whether the fact that the visual stimuli are typically presented together on cards without control over the inspection time allotted to relevant and competing information has something to do with the mixed results.

Dichotic Listening Tasks

Pelham (1979) had good and poor readers shadow (i.e. repeat immediately) a list of digits presented in one ear, with and without distractors presented simultaneously in the other ear. The results suggested that younger poor readers under conditions of distraction were significantly poorer at this task than normal readers. However, Pelham chose not to interpret the results in terms of selective attention, feeling that the pattern of results could be more parsimoniously explained by differential rehearsal in the two groups. Moreover, the putative tests of selective attention showed very low intercorrelations with one another, casting some doubt that a cognitive construct of selective attention could encompass the various measures.

However, very similar dichotic results were reported by Milberg *et al.* (1981), who also used a dichotic digit task with varying rates of presentation. Just as in Pelham *et al.*'s (1979) study, they found that poor readers performed more poorly than good readers at the faster presentation rates, and under conditions of distraction. In both sets of studies there appeared not to be a general distractibility, but only one which became apparent at faster processing rates.

In addition to replicating Pelham's findings, the Milberg *et al.* study reported two additional important facts. First, poor readers made more *channel confusion errors*, suggesting a specific problem in keeping attention switched to one channel, not merely a problem in the effortfulness of the task. Second, similar results were obtained when the channel was defined by a physical characteristic (voice quality), not just by the spatial location channel defined by reported ear. This latter finding is important because it suggests that the selective attention problem is not merely an issue of *hemispheric* channel selection or lateralization difference between good and poor readers, but extends to selection based upon other parameters.

Hebben and colleagues (1981) compared the dichotic performance of poor readers, good readers, and normal readers with behavior problems. They used spoken passages which subjects had to shadow in each ear separately and in a combined (distraction) condition. They also varied the level of difficulty of the passages. The poor readers were not only sensitive to the varying levels of difficulty, making more errors at the higher levels; but they made significantly more errors in the double message condition than the single condition, unlike the behavior problem and normal readers who were insensitive to difficulty of the passages and did not differ in performance under the distraction and non-distraction conditions. They concluded that poor readers show a specific attentional difficulty related to the syntactic–semantic nature of the information being processed. Once again, the data indicate that poor readers may have an attentional problem in which the task demand in terms of rate of information flow is crucial, and which may be somewhat specific to the type of material being processed.

When poor readers are not required to shadow a message in one ear, but are merely asked to detect a word which appears in either ear, they are not different from controls (Prior *et al.*, 1983). This further supports the notion that it is the process of switching to a channel, or selectively focusing, that characterizes the poor readers. (However, this study presented words at one word per second, which is slower than the rate at which Pelham *et al.* (1979) found interactions with reading group (i.e. 1 word per 0.67 s); and this sample was also somewhat older than the other study samples. Therefore one cannot be sure that the failure to find effects is not due to floor or ceiling effects.)

Literal Dyslexia

The condition of 'literal dyslexia', in which a subject cannot read letters within a word which itself can be read, is a rare, acquired dyslexia that provided Shallice and Warrington (1977) with an interesting opportunity to examine the role of selective attention in this unique disorder. From analyses of the types of visual confusions made by their patients, both with words and non-word stimuli such as numbers and pictorial stimuli, they concluded that the deficit consisted of the inability to selectively extract visual perceptual information when spatial or sequencing information in the visual field is such as to increase confusability. This in turn prevents the subjects from passing along the selected information to the stage of semantic processing. The neuropathological information from these patients indicated a left posterior parietal disturbance in both cases, confirmed by EMI scans and surgical exploration. The notion that there is a visual selective attention process prior to semantic–syntactic encoding is an interesting suggestion which we will consider further momentarily.

SUMMARY OF BEHAVIORAL STUDIES OF ATTENTION

The evidence for an attentional dysfunction in poor readers is stronger for tasks in which precise timing of the stimuli prevents the subjects from momentarily switching attention to the distractors without penalizing performance on the central task. The exceptions to this finding occur under conditions in which there is high confusability of the competing stimuli. Moreover, there is rather consistent indication that the effects are more pronounced when phonologic–syntactic information is involved, though this is by no means exclusively so. Finally, information-processing rate and the effects of information load seem to have a greater impact upon poor readers than normal readers, particularly at younger ages. ADHD subjects, in contrast, generally appear to perform more poorly than controls across the board, to make more impulsive errors, and to be less affected by the processing load or rate demands than poor readers without ADHD. Perhaps by considering some neuroanatomical and neurophysiological correlates of dyslexia, it may be possible to further refine the issues surrounding attention in these two conditions.

FUNCTIONAL NEUROANATOMY OF SENSORY PATHWAYS

Classical View

Hypotheses regarding the general pathways for information flow in the brain as it relates to language processing and reading have been available for some time. Since the early contributions of Broca and Wernicke, and their modern expositions by Geschwind, it has been widely accepted that pathways conveying visual information about written language converge on the primary visual cortex and are relayed to the temporal cortex, where eventually phonological information is integrated with its orthographic counterparts (Figure 2).

As stated by Geschwind:

We can now deduce from the model what happens in the brain during the production of language. When a word is heard, the output from the primary auditory areas of the cortex is received by Wernicke's area. If the word is to be spoken, the pattern is transmitted from Wernicke's area to Broca's area, where the articulatory form is aroused and passed on to the motor area that controls the movement of the muscles of speech. If the spoken word is to be spelled, the auditory pattern is passed to the angular gyrus, where it elicits the visual pattern. When a word is read, the output from the primary visual areas passes to the angular gyrus, which in turn arouses the corresponding auditory form of the word in Wernicke's area. (Geschwind, 1972: p. 79)

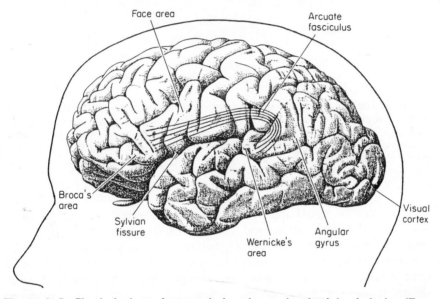

Figures 2–5. Classical view of anatomical pathways involved in dyslexia. (From Language and the brain, by N. Geschwind. Copyright © 1972 by Scientific American, Inc. All rights reserved.)

Figure 2. Primary language areas of the human brain are thought to be located in the left hemisphere, because only rarely does damage to the right hemisphere cause language disorders. Broca's area, which is adjacent to the region of the motor cortex that controls the movement of the muscles of the lips, the jaw, the tongue, the soft palate and the vocal cords, apparently incorporates programs for the coordination of these muscles in speech. Damage to Broca's area results in slow and labored speech, but comprehension of language remains intact. Wernicke's area lies between Heschl's gyrus, which is the primary-receiver of auditory stimuli, and the angular gyrus, which acts as a way station between the auditory and the visual regions. When Wernicke's area is damaged, speech is fluent but has little content and comprehension is usually lost. Wernicke and Broca areas are joined by a nerve bundle called the arcuate fasciculus. When it is damaged, speech is fluent but abnormal, and patient can comprehend words but cannot repeat them.

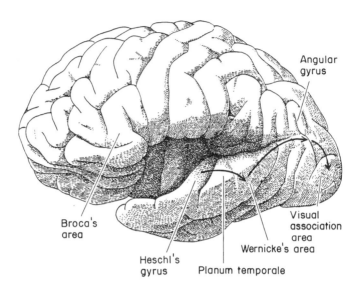

Angular
gyrus

Broca's
area

Visual
association
area

Wernicke's area

Heschl's
gyrus

Planum temporale

Figure 3. Understanding the spoken name of an object involves the transfer of the auditory stimuli from Heschl's gyrus (the primary auditory cortex) to Wernicke's area and then to the angular gyrus, which arouses the comparable visual pattern in the visual association cortex. Here the Sylvian fissure has been spread apart to show the pathway more clearly.

The transfer of visual information from hemi-retinal projections in the contralateral visual cortex, and the role of the splenium of the corpus callosum, have also been a familiar notion since the publication in 1892 of Dejerine's classic case of a man who could no longer read though he had normal visual acuity and could copy written words. The pattern of deficits shown at autopsy prompted the notion that the right visual cortex was receiving information from the left visual field, but that information could not cross over to the left hemisphere because of the damage to the splenium.

The Geniculostriate System

The classical model of information processing, as serviceable as it has been for generating hypotheses regarding dyslexia, is vastly oversimplified. In the first place, the pathway from ganglion cells in the retina, through the lateral geniculate body, to the visual cortex and inferior temporal lobe (the 'geniculostriate system') is only one of two major pathways in which visual information is processed.

As illustrated in this schematic (Figure 6) of the two pathways, one branch proceeds via the lateral geniculate to the primary visual cortex and the

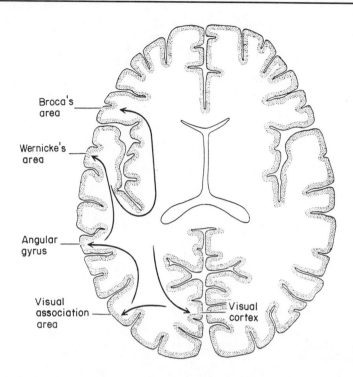

Figure 4. Saying the name of a seen object, according to Wernicke's model, involves the transfer of the visual pattern to the angular gyrus, which contains the 'rules' for arousing the auditory form of the pattern in Wernicke's area. From here the auditory form is transmitted by way of the arcuate fasciculus to Broca's area. There the articulatory form is aroused, is passed on to the face area of the motor cortex and the word then is spoken.

inferior temporal lobe for the precise visualization of object shape, size and color; while the other system largely conveys information regarding spatial relationships of objects with respect to their foveal position.

The contralateral projections of the visual fields are retinoptically organized at the level of the lateral geniculate; that is, a point-for-point image from the retina is maintained in the nuclei of the mini-retina called the lateral geniculate bodies. Within each of the two major systems there are further specializations related to feature extraction—a fact partly evident from the different types of neurons which are predominant in each system (Figure 7).

Within the geniculostriate system itself, there are two subsystems, as may be discerned from the two types of ganglion cells, X and Y, which convey different types of information: the faster-conducting Y-cells give only transient response to local illumination of center or surround, and are more

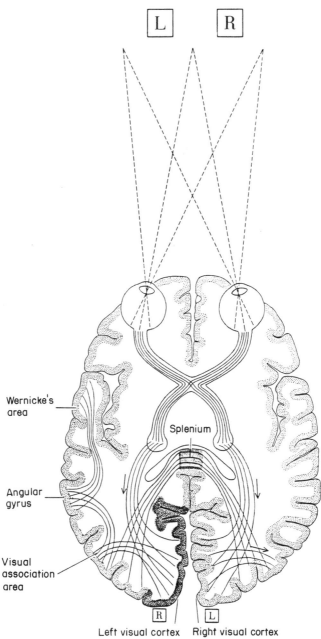

Left visual cortex   Right visual cortex

frequent in the peripheral visual fields and prefer faster velocities of stimulus movement. The slower-conducting X-cells show more prolonged sustained responses to local illumination, are more common in the central retina and prefer slower stimulus velocities.

The very slow-conducting W-cells, found only in the tecto-pulvinar system, give gross responses to flashing spots and are excited by dark or light objects crossing the receptive field, 'rather like the edge detectors of rabbit, pigeon, and frog' (Blakemore, 1975: p. 252); and in addition certain of these cells are inhibited by contrast, maintaining discharge in the presence of unpatterned illumination but being turned off by any patterned visual stimulus. Thus, we may not only wonder what specialized functions are performed by the two different major anatomical pathways—geniculostriate and tecto-pulvinar— but also what it means that within a pathway there are separate specialized mechanisms for central and peripheral vision and for patterned and unpatterned stimuli.

The architectural arrangement within the visual cortex is one which suggests that each neuron is a '*multichannel* coding device that contributes to the specification of information about many properties of the stimulus' (Blakemore, 1975: p. 264). Within the visual cortex one finds an arrangement that favors gradual generalization or abstraction of the stimulus and the possibility of independent parallel hierarchies, 'each generalizing for most stimulus attributes while retaining precise information about a single quality' (Blakemore, 1975: p. 265), such as color or movement. (The extent to which parallel and hierarchical models of the visual system adequately explain available data is still somewhat a matter of controversy—Stone *et al.*, 1979.)

At the terminus of the geniculostriate system—the infero-temporal cortex—sophisticated neuronal systems recognize fine details of objects, independent of location in space, and are sensitive to their task relevance. There is still debate as to the exact functions of the infero-temporal cortex, but considerable evidence suggests that in addition to its functions as the highest level of a feature abstraction process capable of detecting invariances across a wide range of changing retinal inputs, it also contributes to a selective

---

Figure 5. Classic case of a man who lost the ability to read even though he had normal visual acuity and could copy written words was described in 1892 by Joseph Jules Dejerine. Post-mortem analysis of the man's brain showed that the left visual cortex and the splenium (dark colored areas) were destroyed as a result of an occlusion of the left posterior cerebral artery. The splenium is the section of the corpus callosum that transfers visual information between the two hemispheres. The man's left visual cortex was inoperative, making him blind in his right visual field. Words in his left visual field were properly received by the right visual cortex, but could not cross over to the language areas in the left hemisphere because of the damaged splenium. Thus words seen by the man remained as meaningless patterns.

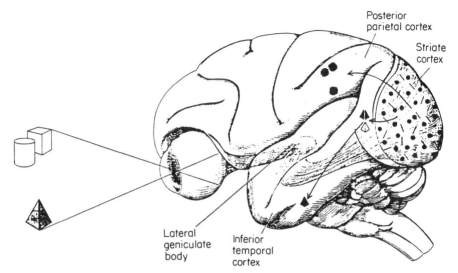

Figure 6. Schematic drawing showing two visual pathways for processing information. (From *The Anatomy of Memory*, by M. Mishkin and T. Appenzeller. Copyright © 1987 by Scientific American, Inc. All rights reserved.)

Visual system processes information along two pathways in the cortex, the outer layer of the brain. Initial processing of the information (which arrives from the retina by way of the lateral geniculate body) takes place at the beginning of the pathways, in the striate cortex. Individual neurons there respond to simple, spatially limited elements in the visual field, such as edges and spots of color. Along the lower pathway (which in fact consists of a number of diverging and reconverging channels) neurons analyze broader properties of an object, such as overall shape or color. At the far end of this 'object' pathway, in the inferior temporal cortex, individual neurons are sensitive to a variety of properties and a broad expanse of the visual world, which suggests that fully processed information about an object converges there. Along the upper cortical pathway, which has not been studied in the same detail, the spatial relations of a scene are analyzed. A perception of an object's position with respect to other landmarks in the visual field, for example, would take shape in the 'spatial' pathway's final station, which is situated in the posterior parietal cortex.

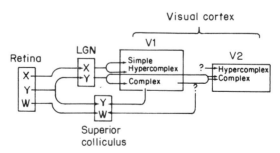

Figure 7. Schematic drawing of geniculostriate and tecto-pulvinar visual pathway cell types and organization. (Reproduced from Blakemore, 1975, by permission of Academic Press.)

attention effect, and thus like the parietal cortex and the tecto-pulvinar system has an important role in pre-selecting information of special interest to the organism (Rothblat and Pribram, 1972). The fact that the visual information at this level of the cortex is abstracted to a level of feature invariance and is related to higher-order memory codes (Mishkin and Appenzeller, 1987) makes it particularly appropriate for selections based upon abstract linguistic codes.

The Tecto-pulvinar System

The other major visual pathway involves fibers which bifurcate on the way to the lateral geniculate, passing through the superior colliculus of the thalamus, through the pulvinar, the lateral posterior thalamic nuclei, to the parietal cortex (area 7) and prestriate areas (18 and 19). This system also receives corticofugal input back from the primary visual cortex and has important mutual influences with the mesencephalic reticular system.

The targets of this system are two cortical surfaces: the posterior parietal cortex and the frontal eye fields. The superior colliculus is a relatively unsophisticated visual system. Most of the neurons in the superficial layers of this system are activated by small spots of light in particular small areas (receptive fields) in the contralateral visual fields. Stimulus orientation, direction of movement or color are essentially irrelevant to activation of this system.

However, there is a crucial behavioral feature of these collicular neurons that makes them highly significant: *these cells fire only when the organism will make a target eye-movement toward the stimulus*, not just any eye movement. And if the stimulus is not present, the same eye movement (say in the dark), will not activate these neurons (Goldberg, 1982). Thus, it is the relevance of the stimulus that is important in the issuing of a command from these neurons. It appears to be a system for selectively attending to visual space; perhaps, as has been suggested to help bring stimuli into foveal vision. A similar system exists in the frontal eye fields. If either the frontal eye fields or the superior colliculus is damaged there is a slight impairment of visual tracking, but if both are destroyed there is severe impairment of the ability to track visual targets.

In contrast to the frontal eye fields and the superior colliculus, in which enhancement of activity occurs only when the animal actually makes the eye movement, the neuronal receptive fields of the posterior parietal cortex are activated whenever the animal attends to the stimulus, *regardless of the way in which he will respond to it*. The enhancement of activity in the parietal cortex occurs not because of the eye movement, but because of the attention to the stimulus.

Damage to the posterior parietal cortex is well known from human clinical data to lead to visual and somatosensory neglect and to subtle impairment of movements or form perception in complicated environments. As in 'literal dyslexia', such impairments may become apparent only when competing visual information is such as to require selective attention to some parts of the visual field in preference to others. Thus, in the tecto-pulvinar system, there are separate mechanisms for attending to visual space, both when a target eye movement will occur, and when the eye movement does not occur but a stimulus in the periphery is nevertheless of interest.

Arousal and Attention Systems

There is an indisputable relationship between general level of arousal and attention, but behavioral concepts of arousal and attention have often proved difficult to operationalize. Moreover, it has not been clear from behavioral studies just how general arousal, either tonic or phasic in nature, relates to processes of selective attention.

The reticular activating system (RAS) acts both as gain control and modulator of sensory information, exerting a profound role both in tonic and phasic control over consciousness and general arousal, as well as the selective processing of information. In doing so, this system acts together with cortical systems, including both sensory and frontal cortices, to select and modulate the flow of information.

There are three major neurophysiological indicators of increased arousal and selective attention: desynchronization of the EEG, slow negative potentials related to task activity, and enhanced sensory evoked potentials. Using these indicators in higher animals, it has been possible to piece together a picture of how information flow through the sensory systems is selectively regulated by the RAS (Figure 8).

In this model (Skinner, 1978) the frontal cortex (FC) has phasic excitatory input on specific pathways within the thalamic reticular nucleus. In contrast, the mesencephalic reticular system (MRF) has tonic inhibitory (It) control over these specific reticular nuclei via diffuse or non-specific connections. The reticular nuclei project to specific thalamic relay nuclei (Th relay) such as the lateral geniculate or superior colliculus, which as we have seen receive retinoptically organized projections from the periphery. This relay forms a parallel series of inhibitory gates that control the transmission of afferent activity.

Figure 9 illustrates how selective attention to auditory stimuli might be attained. The tonic inhibitory control over the auditory pathway is released by *selective suppression of irrelevant stimuli* by excitation from the frontal cortex. Thus, excitation in these pathways accomplishes an inhibitory function.

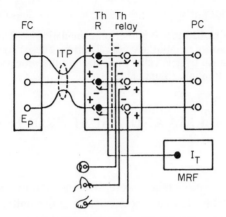

Figure 8. Model of frontal–reticular gating of sensory information. (Reproduced from Skinner and Yingling, 1977, by permission of S. Karger AG, Basel.)

Neurophysiological model for the regulation of sensory input to cerebral cortex. FC = frontal cortex; ITP = inferior thalamic peduncle; Th R = thalamic reticular nucleus; Th relay = thalamic relay nuclei for visual, auditory, and somatic afferent channels; PC = primary projection cortex; MRF = mesencephalic reticular formation. White neurons are excitatory and black ones inhibitory. FC neurons produce phasic excitation (E_P) of R cells via specific projections. MRF cells produce tonic inhibition (I_T) of R cells and have non-specific, widely distributed projections.

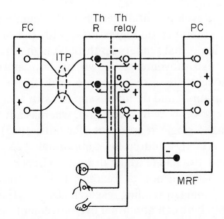

Figure 9. Selection of sensory information by combined frontal–reticular activation. (Reproduced from Skinner and Yingling, 1977, by permission of S. Karger AG, Basel.)

Example in which the neurophysiological model selects auditory input to the cerebral cortex because of a particular pattern of activity in FC and MRF. + = synaptic excitation of cell; − = synaptic inhibition of cell; 0 = no excitation or inhibition.

As stated by Skinner:

> It is important to realize that it is the joint regulation of R by FC and MRF that gives rise to the pattern of input to cerebral cortex. These two systems appear to vie constantly for control over R cells, thus titrating the processes of general arousal against selective attention. (Skinner, 1978: p. 623)

DYSLEXIA AND VISUAL PROCESSES

Eye Movements*

Dyslexics' erratic eye movements were first reported by Freeman in 1920 and attributed by Gray (1921) to a tendency to read in small units without proper attention to meaning. However, a peculiar defect in the return sweep of dyslexics' eye movements, appearing highly segmented, was noted by Moose and Daniels (1959), who named the condition 'linear dyslexia' and considered it responsible for difficulties in comprehension. Similar cases reported by Pirrozolo and Rayner (1978) were attributed to a congenital parietal lobe dysfunction. Lesevre (1968) tested 22 dyslexics and an equal number of normal controls in reading and non-reading tasks, finding that the dyslexics exhibited more ocular instability, greater number of short and long fixations and irregular eye movement patterns compared to controls. She concluded that these patterns could not be attributed to reading habits, poor teaching or environmental factors.

There are strong developmental trends in the number and duration of fixations, and in the number of regressions, with the latter measure continuing to decrease in normal readers up through high school (Taylor, 1965). In contrast to the eye movements shown by both normal and retarded readers, the eye movements of dyslexics are erratic, show unusual patterns and variability of duration, and do not disappear with age. Regressions often occur in clusters of two or more in succession, whereas advanced, normal and retarded readers make single regressions (Pavlidis, 1985). Similarly, it has been reported that ADHD children have abnormal eye movements, though most of those studied also had learning disorders (Bala et al., 1981).

The relationship between normal reading and eye movements has been known since the beginning of reading research (Dodge, 1907), but although a powerful relationship between abnormal eye movements and dyslexia is well accepted, there is strong disagreement about the nature of the causal relationship, many considering eye movements to be consequence rather than cause. Almost from the beginning it was suggested that the eye movements

---

*Written in collaboration with Professor G. Th. Pavlidis.

are merely a reflection of the greater difficulty dyslexics have in decoding the meaning of the text (Rayner, 1978).

Pavlidis has provided several lines of evidence *against* this point of view (Pavlidis, 1985):

(1) When dyslexics are matched for reading level with retarded readers or younger children of the same reading age, they still have more abnormal eye movements.

(2) When dyslexics read only one year below their reading age, or 'for fun' with easy text, their eye movements are still abnormal.

(3) When reading more difficult text than their reading age, normals show some increase in duration of fixation and number of regressions, but seldom with the same qualitative abnormalities nor to the same extent as dyslexics.

(4) Finally, and most significantly, dyslexics show abnormal pursuit eye movements for non-text visual moving targets.

These arguments notwithstanding, however, it could still be argued that a long history of struggling with the meaning of text has *conditioned* the eye movements of dyslexics into abnormal patterns which prevail even with easier text or non-reading tasks (Rayner, 1978).

From the previous discussions of neural mechanisms for selective visual attention, it is now possible to state an alternative hypothesis to the two most common explanations of the dyslexia/eye movement relationship: abnormal eye movements do not cause dyslexia; nor does dyslexia necessarily cause the abnormal eye movements. Rather, *abnormalities in central parietal mechanisms for visual selective attention cause both symptoms of dyslexia as well as the accompanying abnormal eye movements.*

Studies of foveal and peripheral vision, as well as recent electrophysiological studies in dyslexia, will be considered as evidence for this hypothesis.

Foveal and Peripheral Vision

In a provocative recent experiment, Geiger and Lettvin (1987) showed that dyslexics apparently identify letters better than normals when letters are presented to peripheral rather than foveal vision; and conversely, that normals do better than dyslexics in foveal vision. Additionally, it was shown that the phenomenon of lateral masking of embedded letters presented in peripheral vision was markedly attenuated in dyslexics compared to normal readers.

Although this experiment suffers from a number of flaws (stimuli presented peripherally only to the right visual field; poor subject sample description; no current measures of reading level; use of older subjects who were tutored for many years; no control over eye movements during stimulation), it is consistent with a number of well-controlled experiments which implicate differences between normals and dyslexics in foveal compared with parafoveal and peripheral vision (Babcock and Lovegrove, 1981; Hatae and Hatta, 1982; Lovegrove and Brown, 1978; Lovegrove et al., 1980, 1981, 1982; Slaghuis and Lovegrove, 1985; Stanley and Hall, 1973).

Considerable evidence exists that phenomena of forward and backward masking are attributable to the effects of two different classes of neurons in the visual pathway: sustained firing versus transient fibers (Blakemore, 1975; Breitmeyer and Ganz, 1976). As noted earlier, these X- and Y-cells, respectively, are differentially responsive to spatial frequency, movement and orientation, with the X-cells sensitive to higher spatial frequencies while the Y-cells are more sensitive to general spatial location and sudden movement. The Y-cells are more predominant in peripheral and the X-cells in foveal vision.

One of the properties of the interaction between sustained and transient fibers is that they mutually inhibit one another. Because there are relatively more Y-fibers in the periphery, responding mainly to gross rather than fine detail, they tend to inhibit the perception of fine detail in the periphery, thus accentuating refined analysis within the central visual field. Conversely, the larger number of slow-firing X-cells near the fovea allows stimuli with high spatial frequencies or complexity to receive preferential processing when foveated.

During an eye movement there is a loss of foveal acuity just prior to and after a saccade. It is the termination of sustained foveal X-cell activity by inhibitory activity of fast-acting Y-cells that permits sharp resolution and the prevention of forward masking; that is, the blurring of vision that would occur if foveal stimuli persisted after an eye movement to a new target (Breitmeyer and Ganz, 1976).

In an elegant series of studies (Badcock and Lovegrove, 1981; Bowling et al., 1979; Bowling and Lovegrove, 1980; Lovegrove and Brown, 1978; Lovegrove and Heddle, 1980; Lovegrove et al., 1980, 1981, 1982; Slaghuis and Lovegrove, 1985) it has been demonstrated that dyslexics have increased persistence of patterned stimulu compared with normals, *but only at low spatial frequencies* (2 cycles/degree), implicating Y-cell activity. At 12 cycles/ degree dyslexics do not differ from normals in the duration of visible persistence at any contrast level or stimulus duration above 100 ms. The relatively long duration of stimulus presentation time suggests type II (cortical) rather than type I (retinal) origin of this effect. These data, in conjunction with the well-known fact that Y-cells are differentially represented in the periphery and X-cells in the foveal region, strongly suggest an abnormality of the tecto-pulvinar pathway in dyslexics.

That is, the increased visible persistence of complex (high spatial frequency) visual information suggests that the normal inhibitory functioning of the peripheral Y-cells is impaired. This is exactly what would happen if the parietal cortical attention system failed to utilize peripheral information in order to guide the eyes to the next fixation point. The appropriate Y-cell activity would not occur; there would be a persistence of foveated information, which in turn would lead to visual confusion among stimuli in the central visual field.

But if dyslexics have a defect in the tecto-pulvinar pathway, as evidenced, for example, by increased visible persistence phenomena, what then is the explanation for the previously described results of Geiger and Lettvin in which there was superior *peripheral* vision in dyslexics? One explanation might be that dyslexics develop a bias to the peripheral field because they have a higher *ratio* of X- to Y-cell activity in the periphery, and consequently superior resolution within the sustained X-cell pathways mediating high spatial frequency (i.e. detailed pattern vision). There are fewer X-cells in the periphery, so that a bias to peripheral vision would have the effect of diminishing the masking interference from previously attended material. This explanation accounts for Geiger and Lettvin's finding of lower peripheral masking among dyslexics.

The abnormal eye movements of dyslexics may be viewed as one consequence of limited visual attention prior to initiation and termination of saccadic activity. The fact that parietal activity occurs by as much as 50 ms *prior to the actual eye movement* suggests that parietal activity could account for the 'priming' effects for letter recognition described by Posner (1980) and others. The loss of this priming effect is related to the visual–spatial, not the phonemic or semantic properties of the peripheral stimuli (Inhoff and Rayner, 1980; Rayner *et al.*, 1980). Loss of peripheral priming effects would be likely to increase the amount of attentional resource allocation to decoding of text and to contribute to slow letter recognition irrespective of semantic aspects of the orthography.

Behavioral studies using the duration of visible persistence at different spatial frequencies (Badcock and Lovegrove, 1981) suggest that as many as 75% of dyslexics have abnormalities in response to low spatial frequency information, and that subtypes identified with this method do not fit simply into previous subtyping methods (Boder, 1971; Mattis *et al.*, 1975; Pirozzolo, 1979). Contrary evidence exists (e.g. Arnett and DiLollo, 1979); but the findings relate to methods involving very short stimulus durations and thus probably reflect retinal rather than cortical processes (Slaghuis and Lovegrove, 1985). These other subtyping methods are based upon reading behavior or psychometric performance and not upon psychophysical or neurophysiological criteria, and it has yet to be determined whether these latter methods may turn out to be superior predictors of treatment response and developmental course.

EVENT-RELATED POTENTIALS, DYSLEXIA AND ADHD

Early Levels of Selection

In humans, it has been possible to study the neurophysiological phenomena of selective attention (ERPs, slow waves, EEG desynchronization) when subjects are attending or not attending to particular 'channels' of information. Subtracting the non-attending from the attending waves defines the magnitude of the selection effect. These 'Nd' or negative difference potentials may occur as early as 50 or 60 ms in the visual system, suggesting extremely early selective attention effects on the coding of visual information at the retinal level. There are increased Nd waves at both the retina and the occipital cortex when subjects are required to respond to stimuli presented at various locations in the visual field while attempting to ignore stimuli presented at other locations (Eason *et al.*, 1983). Thus, selective attentional control over visual inputs, including their spatial location on the retina, is demonstrated at the very earliest stage of sensory transmission.

Piracetam and ERPS in Dyslexia

We recently carried out two studies of dyslexics ($N = 34, 20$) rigorously selected to eliminate any other behavioral or emotional problems (Conners and Conry, 1987; Conners *et al.*, 1987). Although the purpose of these studies was to test the effects of the nootropic drug piracetam on dyslexic functioning, an important feature of these studies was the development of a stimulus paradigm for eliciting differential response to letters and non-letters in the two cerebral hemispheres. Block letters or forms equated for area and brightness (visual angle of 0.10° at 1.3 m) were presented for 50 ms at the center of a screen (ISI = 1.5 s). Eye movements were monitored and trials rejected based upon pre-set criteria and visual inspection. Subjects (Ss) were asked to press a reaction time key whenever two letters occurred in sequence or when two forms appeared in sequence. About 30% of 500 trials were letter–letter and form–form pairs.

Principal components analysis of the time-locked EEG obtained at Cz, P3 and P4 (vertex, left and right parietal areas), identified seven ERP factors in each study, having almost identical latency characteristics across the two studies. In both studies there were significant drug effects on a very early component beginning just prior to stimulus onset and extending up to 50 ms after stimulus occurrence. Figure 10 shows the plots of factor loadings (basis waves) obtained in two separate studies with this paradigm.

The drug effect on this early component occurred mainly for *letter-hits*; i.e. only when the stimulus target was a letter preceded by another letter. Since

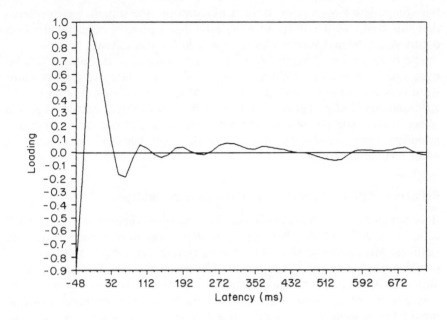

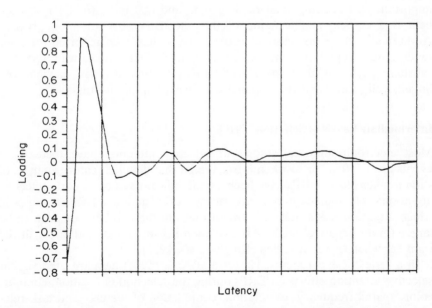

Figure 10. Plot of factor loadings (basis waves) for early component of event-related potentials found in two studies of dyslexics. This early component was found to change significantly under the influence of piracetam compared with placebo

this component begins prior to the actual onset of the stimuli, we concluded that this component reflects an early attentional priming adjustment which occurs when the first stimulus signals that a letter may follow.

The drug produced highly significant gains in reading in children treated over one academic year (Wilsher *et al.*, 1987). In addition to reading there were very few other neurocognitive drug effects, with the exception of rapid letter naming (Helfgott *et al.*, 1983). It seems reasonable to conclude that one effect of the drug piracetam has been a facilitation of the parietal cortical attention system, resulting in improved ocular control and increased facility in letter recognition.

Relation of ERP Findings to Linguistic Processing Subtypes

It is not possible to ascertain from these studies whether this early ERP component differentiates dyslexics from other types of poor readers or from normals. Most previous studies have used stimulus paradigms and tasks that would not reveal such a component. However, the fact that our subjects improved in reading with drug treatment; that this early component was the only one to change under both chronic and acute drug influence; and that rapid letter-naming was virtually the only non-reading task to also improve with piracetam (Helfgott *et al.*, 1983), suggests that letter recognition plays an important part in component reading skill, and that this early ERP component is a cortical manifestation of the selective visual attention process. Additionally, it seems reasonable that, just as has been reported for poor reading based upon abnormal vergence control (Stein and Fowler, 1982), a substantial portion of the poor readers may be 'mixed types', having both linguistically based and visuo-spatial selective attention disorders.

Intermediate Levels of Selection ('N100')

Most electrophysiological studies of selective attention have focused on events after 100 ms or so when it is assumed that detailed feature analysis of stimuli takes place. ERPs have been useful indicators of these early selective attentional phenomena in humans. In Figure 11, auditory ERPs to tones in which attention was switched between tones in the two ears are seen to be larger (more negative) in the left ear when it is attended, and larger in the right ear when that is attended (Knight *et al.*, 1981).

In a series of experiments, Harter and Aine (1984) demonstrated similar selective attention effects on ERPs during the selection of location, contour, color, spatial frequency, orientation, conjunction of features and task relevance. In accord with our earlier description of the properties of the visual pathways, attention to visual space in the peripheral visual field led to faster responses that were more prominent in extra-striate cortex. There was an

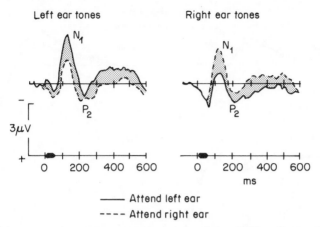

Figure 11. Example of selective attention on auditory ERPs. (Reproduced from Knight *et al.*, 1981, by permission of Elsevier Scientific Publishers Ltd.)

additional enhancement of the ERP when the type of stimulus was relevant and when the stimuli were foveal; and this effect was slower (as expected from the slower X-fibers in the fovea), and more prominent in striate cortex.

A particularly salient demonstration of the selective attention effect was provided when the same stimulus provided either color or semantic information. As in the familiar Stroop test, the word 'red' was printed in the color blue, while the word 'blu' (shortened to be equivalent in length) was printed in red. Attention was directed either toward a particular color or word by making it relevant in a reaction time task when the stimuli were presented foveally (Figure 12). As predicted, response to the color when it was relevant produced earlier Nd (difference waves) than words (beginning at about 150 ms compared to 273 ms for words); and the selection of words as relevant produced larger Nd effects over the left than the right hemisphere. Thus, the amplitude, latency and topographical features of the ERP are greatly altered, depending upon what aspect of the stimulus the subject is asked to attend to. As in this example, the same foveally presented pattern of light engages entirely different neural pathways, depending upon the attentional focus.

The selective attention paradigm has been used with ADHD boys across a wide age range, and found to clearly distinguish them from normal controls (Loiselle *et al.*, 1980; Zambelli *et al.*, 1977). In these studies, negative-going middle and long-latency components are reduced in amplitude among the ADHD compared with controls. In contrast, RD children (without ADHD) show no impairment in this stage of processing, but show impairments related to long-latency positive components (Lovrich and Stamm, 1983). These latter results were obtained with poor readers of a particular subtype (children who have difficulties with finger localization, sequencing and linguistic processing

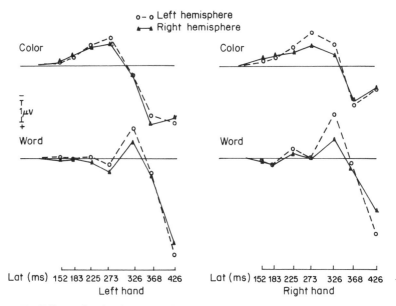

Figure 12. Effect of selective attention to color or meaning. (Reproduced from Harter and Aine, 1984, by permission of Academic Press.)

(type 2 of Petrauskas and Rourke, 1979)); but others have also found P300 deficits in poor readers (Dainer *et al.*, 1981). This deficit, however, could be non-specific since it shows up with other psychopathological conditions, including autism and hyperactivity.

Later Levels of Selection (P300)

More relevant are the recent findings of Holcomb *et al.* (1985, 1986), who reported that reading-disabled children show a deficit in P300 and later positive components *which is specific to words* (contrasted with non-alphabetic characters). The complexity of the stimuli and the late onset of these waves is suggestive of difficulties in selecting specifically linguistically related stimuli for higher-order processing.

Possibly this same selective attention effect for relevant compared with non-relevant verbal stimuli is an additional mechanism whereby target letter recognition is enhanced by piracetam. As noted above, in addition to the very early component effects, there were drug effects on later components. ERPs were obtained to relevant and irrelevant alphabetic characters. The amplitude of response to *relevant* letters was increased following the drug, while the amplitude of response to *irrelevant* letters was decreased after drug treatment. The result suggests an increased selectivity for the target stimulus letter compared to the non-target letter. This is apparently a different effect than early attention deployment, involving as it does a selection on the basis of the assigned meaning of the stimuli.

HYPOTHESES REGARDING ATTENTION DEFICITS AND DYSLEXIA

Selective attention effects have been shown to occur at a very early stage of information processing and may be particularly important for smooth sequential scanning of text. This may be considered a form of pre-semantic processing whose priming effects may be important in reducing the amount of effort allocated to the task of sequentially scanning material *prior to extracting its meaning*.

Deficits at this early stage would tend to show up as poor perceptual analysis, particularly at the level of the letter or grapheme. Difficulty in attaining foveation of written material and erratic eye movement control would be other characteristics of this type of dyslexia. Damage or delay of development of the posterior parietal cortices (which, along with the frontal cortex, is among the latest structures to myelinate), would tend to create more parafoveal noise and inadequate guidance of eye movements. One might therefore expect this type of reading disorder to have a developmental course and for normal children to show a gradual decrease in the distracting effects of patterned parafoveal noise. Such an effect has been demonstrated in normal Japanese children (Hatae and Hatta, 1982).

No studies of the abnormal eye movements associated with defects at this stage have been done in ADHD who do not also have reading disorders, so it is not possible to say whether this early stage of perceptual visual processing is crucial only to dyslexics. A comparison of pure ADHD and dyslexics in pursuit eye movements and in saccadic control during reading would seem to be indicated for further research.

ADHD children almost certainly suffer from a more generalized type of attention deficit in that they show evidence of decreased processing negativities (Nd waves) in the middle latency range, whereas pure dyslexics do not. We may speculate that this represents a deficit in the frontal cortical inputs in the attentional system. It is consistent with neuropsychological data (Hicks and Gualtieri, unpublished ms.) and cerebral blood flow data (Lou *et al.*, 1984) which implicate frontal lobe deficiencies in the hyperactive child. It is this aspect of attention that is probably related to impulsivity as well as the more generalized attentional deficits. Because these electrocortical events begin about the time the physical features of the stimuli are decoded, and continue over several hundred milliseconds, they may represent both a sustaining of attention to the task and further processing of the information.

Both children with ADHD and dyslexia share difficulties in P300 or its later variants (such as P3b or Pc). Thus, they share in common a difficulty in higher levels of feature extraction within a modality, being unable to distinguish the relevant from the irrelevant or target from non-target dimensions of the stimulus. In this respect, P300 appears to be a non-specific indicator of poorer processing in these two groups of children. However, those P300 deficiencies *specific* to dyslexics appear to be limited to selections involving linguistic stimuli. The implication, therefore, that stored linguistic codes must be involved in the categorization of the stimuli suggests that such dyslexics will show involvement of the geniculostriate system where it is more likely that higher-order perceptual or memory codes are involved in selection (Rothblat and Pribram, 1972).

There is some evidence that ADHD children also have abnormalities linked to the posterior parietal cortices (Satterfield *et al.*, 1988), and thus they may overlap in this regard with some dyslexics in having scanning and saccadic control problems. Because of additional difficulties at the level of the frontal lobe, these hyperactives may have a double attentional dysfunction: one involving suppression of distracting peripheral visual inputs as well as one involving the frontal regulation of impulsivity and sensory gating. These might then be the 'mixed types' seen most frequently in clinical practice.

It seems reasonable to suppose that selective attentional processes mediated by the geniculostriate-inferior temporal lobe pathway involve linguistic codes and selection on the basis of semantic content or lexical structure; whereas selective attentional processes mediated by the tecto-pulivinar-posterior parietal area involve spatial attention and eye movements. With appropriate experimental analysis it should be possible to identify both types from the same psychophysical and neurophysiological tests.

ACKNOWLEDGEMENTS

Work on this chapter was partially supported by grant no. 5-RO1-MH37320 from the National Institute of Mental Health. The author wishes to acknowledge the assistance of Dr G. Th. Pavlidis in the writing of the sections on eye movements in dyslexia.

REFERENCES

Ackerman, P. T., Dykman, R. A., and Oglesby, D. M. (1983). Sex and group differences in reading and attention disordered children, with and without hyperkinesis. *Journal of Learning Disabilities*, **16**, 407–415.

Aman, M. G. (1979). Cognitive, social, and other correlates of specific reading retardation. *Journal of Abnormal Child Psychology*, **7**, 153–168.

Arnett, J. L., and DiLollo, V. (1979). Visual information in relation to age and reading disability. *Journal of Experimental Child Psychology*, **27**, 143–152.

Badcock, D., and Lovegrove, W. (1981). The effects of contrast, stimulus duration, and spatial frequency on visible persistence in normal and specifically disabled readers. *Journal of Experimental Psychology*, **7**, 495–505.

Bala, S. P., Morris, A. G., Atkin, A., Gittelman, R., and Kates, W. (1981). Saccades of hyperactive and normal boys during ocular pursuit. *Developmental Medicine and Child Neurology*, **23**, 323–336.

Blakemore, C. (1975). Central visual processing. In M. S. Gazzaniga and C. Blakemore (eds), *Handbook of Psychobiology*, pp. 241–268. New York: Academic Press.

Boder, E. (1971). Developmental dyslexia: Prevailing diagnostic concepts and a new diagnostic approach. In H. Myklebust (ed.), *Progress in Learning Disabilities*. New York: Grune & Stratton.

Bowling, A., and Lovegrove, W. (1980). The effect of stimulus duration on the persistence of gratings. *Perception and Psychophysics*, **27**, 574–578.

Bowling, A., Lovegrove, W., and Mapperson, B. (1979). The effect of spatial frequency and contrast on visual persistence. *Perception*, **8**, 529–539.

Breitmeyer, B. G., and Ganz, L. (1976). Implications of sustained and transient channels for theories of visual pattern masking, saccadic suppression, and information processing. *Psychological Review*, **83**, 1–36.

Cantwell, D. P., and Satterfield, J. H. (1978). The prevalence of academic underachievement in hyperactive children. *Journal of Pediatric Psychology*, **3**, 168–171.

Conners, C. K., and Conry, J. (1987). A double-blind, placebo-controlled, randomized block design study of the effects of four doses of piracetam on visual event-related potentials in children with developmental reading disorders. Final Report, UCB (Brussels).

Conners, C. K., and Reader, M. J. (1987). The effects of piracetam on reading achievement and visual event-related potentials in dyslexic children. *Child Health and Development*, **5**, 75–90.

Conners, C. K., Reader, M. J., Reiss, A., Caldwell, J., Caldwell, L., *et al.* (1987). The effects of piracetam upon visual event-related potentials in dyslexic children. *Psychophysiology*, **24**, 513–521.

Copeland, A. P., and Wisniewski, N. M. (1981). Learning disability and hyperactivity: Deficits in selective attention. *Journal of Experimental Child Psychology*, **32**, 88–101.

Dainer, K. B., Klorman, R., Salzman, L. F., Hess, D. W., Davidson, P. W., and Michael, R. L. (1981). Learning disordered children's evoked potentials during sustained attention. *Journal of Abnormal Child Psychology*, **9**, 79–84.

Denckla, M. B. (1978). Critical review of 'Electroencephalographic and neurophysiological studies in dyslexia'. In A. L. Benton and D. Pearl (eds), *Dyslexia: An Appraisal of Current Knowledge*, pp. 241–249. New York: Oxford University Press.

Denckla, M. B., Rudel, R., Chapman, C., and Krieger, J. (1985). Motor proficiency in dyslexic children with and without attentional disorders. *Archives of Neurology*, **42**, 228–231.

Denney, D. R. (1974). Relationship of three cognitive style dimensions to elementary reading abilities. *Journal of Educational Psychology*, **66**, 702–709.

Dodge, R. (1907). An experimental study of visual fixation. *Psychol. Rev. Monograph*, (Suppl. 8), **37**.

Dykman, R. A., Ackerman, P. T., Clements, S. D., and Peters, J. E. (1971). Specific learning disabilities: An attentional deficit syndrome. In H. Myklebust (ed.), *Progress in Learning Disabilities*, pp. 56–93. New York: Grune & Stratton.

Dykman, R. A., Ackerman, P. T., and Oglesby, D. M. (1979). Selective and sustained attention in hyperactive, learning-disabled and normal boys. *Journal of Nervous and Mental Disease*, **167**, 288–297.

Dykman, R. A., Ackerman, P. T., and McCray, D. S. (1980). Effects of methylphenidate on selective and sustained attention in hyperactive, reading-disabled, and presumably attention-disordered boys. *Journal of Nervous and Mental Disease*, **12**, 745–752.

Dykman, R. A., Ackerman, P. T., and Holcomb, P. J. (1985). Reading disabled and ADD children: Similarities and differences. In D. B. Gray and J. F. Kavanagh (eds), *Biobehavioral Measures of Dyslexia*. Parkton, MD: Your Press.

Eason, R. G., Oakley, M., and Flowers, L. (1983). Central neural influences on the human retina during selective attention. *Physiological Psychology*, **11**, 18–28.

Ford, C. E., Pelham, W. E., and Ross, A. O. (1984). Selective attention and rehearsal in the auditory short-term memory task performance of poor and normal readers. *Journal of Abnormal Child Psychology*, **12**, 127–142.

Freeman, F. N. (1920). Clinical study as a method in experimental education. *Journal of Applied Psychology*, **4**, 126–141.

Geiger, G., and Lettvin, J. Y. (1987). Peripheral vision in persons with dyslexia. *New England Journal of Medicine*, **316**, 1239–1243.

Geschwind, N. (1972). Language and the brain. *Scientific American*, **226**, 76–83.

Goldberg, M. E. (1982). Moving and attending in visual space: Single-cell mechanisms in the monkey. In M. Potegal (ed.), *Spatial Abilities: Development and Physiological Foundations*, pp. 277–300. New York: Academic Press.

Gray, W. S. (1921). The diagnostic value of an individual case in reading. *Elementary School Journal*, **21**, 577–594.

Hallahan, D. P., Kauffman, J. M., and Ball, D. W. (1973). Selective attention and cognitive tempo of low achieving and high achieving sixth grade males. *Perceptual and Motor Skills*, **36**, 579–583.

Harter, M. R., and Aine, C. J. (1984). Brain mechanisms of visual selective attention. In R. Pasuraman (ed.), *Varieties of Attention*. New York: Academic Press.

Harter, M. R., Anllo-Velnto, L., Wood, F. B., and Schroeder, M. M. (1988a). Separate brain potential characteristics in children with reading disability and attention deficit disorder: Color and letter relevance effects. *Brain and Cognition*, **7**, 115–140.

Harter, M. R., Diering, S., and Wood, F. B. (1988b). Separate brain potential characteristics in children with reading disability and attention deficit disorder: Relevance-independent effects. *Brain and Cognition*, **7**, 54–86.

Hatae, T. I., and Hatta, T. (1982). Developmental changes in letter recognition as affected by parafoveal noise. *Perceptual and Motor Skills*, **54**, 888–890.

Hebben, N. A., Whitman, R. D., Milberg, W. P., Andresko, M., and Galpin, R. (1981). Attentional dysfunction in poor readers. *Journal of Learning Disabilities*, **14**, 287–290.

Helfgott, E., Rudel, R. G., and Krieger, J. (1983). Effect of piracetam on the single word and prose reading of dyslexic children. *Psychopharmacology Bulletin*, **20**, 288–290.

Holcomb, P. J., Ackerman, P. T., and Dykman, R. A. (1985). Cognitive event-related brain potentials in children with attention and reading deficits. *Psychophysiology*, **22**, 656–667.

Holcomb, P. J., Ackerman, P. T., and Dykman, R. A. (1986). Auditory event-related potentials in attention and reading disabled boys. *International Journal of Psychophysiology*, **3**, 263–273.

Inhoff, A. W., and Rayner, K. (1980). Parafoveal word perception: A case against semantic preprocessing. *Perception and Psychophysics*, **27**, 457–464.

Knight, R. T., Hillyard, S. A., Woods, D. L., and Neville, H. J. (1981). The effects of frontal cortex lesions on event-related potentials during auditory selective attention. *Electroencephalography and Clinical Neurophysiology*, **52**, 571–582.

Lambert, N. M., and Sandoval, J. (1980). The prevalence of learning disabilities in a sample of children considered hyperactive. *Journal of Abnormal Child Psychology*, **8**, 33–50.

Lesevre, N. (1968). L'organisation du regard chez des enfants d'âge scolaire, lecteurs normaux et dyslexiques. *Revue de Neuropsychiatrie Infant*, **16**, 323–349.

Loiselle, D. L., Stammn, J. S., Maitinsky, S., and Whipple, S. C. (1980). Evoked potential and behavioral signs of attentive dysfunctions in hyperactive boys. *Psychophysiology*, **17**, 193–201.

Lou, H. C., Henriksen, L., and Bruhn, P. (1984). Focal cerebral hypoperfusion in children with dysphasia and/or attention deficit disorder. *Archives of Neurology*, **41**, 825–829.

Lovegrove, W., and Brown, C. (1978). Development of information processing in normal and disabled readers. *Perceptual and Motor Skills*, **46**, 1047–1054.

Lovegrove, W., and Heddle, M. (1980). Visual persistence as a function of spatial frequency and age. *Perception*, **9**, 529–532.

Lovegrove, W., Heddle, M., and Slaghuis, W. (1980). Reading disability: Spatial frequency specific deficits in visual information store. *Neuropsychologia*, **18**, 111–115.

Lovegrove, W. J., Bowling, A., Badcock, D., and Blackwood, M. (1980). Specific reading disability: Differences in contrast sensitivity as a function of spatial frequency. *Science*, **210**, 439–440.

Lovegrove, W. J., Martin, F., Bowling, A., Blackwood, M., Badcock, D., and Paxton, S. (1982). Contrast sensitivity functions and specific reading disability. *Neuropsychologia*, **20**, 309–315.

Lovrich, D., and Stamm, J. S. (1983). Event-related potential and behavioral correlates of attention in reading retardation. *Journal of Clinical Neuropsychology*, **5**, 13–37.

Mattis, W., French, J. H., and Rapin, I. (1975). Dyslexia in children and young adults: Three independent neuropsychological syndromes. *Developmental Medicine and Child Neurology*, **17**, 150–163.

Milberg, W., Whitman, R. D., and Galpin, R. (1981). Selective attention and laterality in good and poor readers. *Cortex*, **17**, 571–582.

Mishkin, M., and Appenzeller, T. (1987). The anatomy of memory. *Scientific American*, June, 80–89.

Pavlidis, G. Th. (1981). Do eye movements hold the key to dyslexia? *Neuropsychologia*, **19**, 57–64.

Pavlidis, G. Th. (1985). Eye movements in dyslexia: Their diagnostic significance. *Journal of Learning Disabilities*, **18**, 42–50.

Pelham, W. E. (1979). Selective attention deficits in poor readers? Dichotic listening, speeded classification, and auditory and visual central and incidental learning tasks. *Child Development*, **50**, 1050–1061.

Pelham, W. E., and Ross, A. O. (1977). Selective attention in children with reading problems: A developmental study of incidental learning. *Journal of Abnormal Child Psychology*, **5**, 1–8.

Peters, J. E., Davis, J. S., Goolsby, C. M., and Clements, S. D. (1973). *Physician's Handbook: Screening for MBD*. Summit, NJ: Ciba.

Petrauskas, R. J., and Rourke, B. P. (1979). Identification of subtypes of retarded readers: A neuropsychological, multivariate approach. *Journal of Clinical Neuropsychology*, **11**, 17–37.

Pirozzolo, F. J. (1979). *The Neuropsychology of Developmental Reading Disorders*. New York: Praeger.

Pirozzolo, F. J., and Rayner, K. (1978). The neural control of EMs in acquired and developmental reading disorder. In H. Avakian-Whitaker and H. A. Whitaker (eds), *Advances in Neurolinguistics and Psycholinguistics*. New York: Academic Press.

Posner, M. I. (1980). Orienting of attention. *Quarterly Journal of Experimental Psychology*, **32**, 3–25.

Prior, M. R., Frolley, M., and Sanson, A. (1983). Language lateralization in specific reading retarded children and backward readers. *Cortex*, **19**, 149–163.

Rayner. K. (1978). Eye movements in reading and information processing. *Psychological Review*, **85**, 618–660.

Rayner, K., McConkie, G. W., and Zola, D. (1980). Integrating information across eye movements. *Cognitive Psychology*, **12**, 206–226.

Ross, A. O. (1976). *Psychological Aspects of Learning Disabilities and Reading Disorders*. New York: McGraw-Hill.

Rothblat, L., and Pribram, K. H. (1972). Selective attention: Input filter or response selection? An electrophysiological analysis. *Brain Research*, **39**, 427–436.

Safer, D. J., and Allen, R. P. (1976). *Hyperactive Children: Diagnosis and Management*. Baltimore: University Park Press.

Santostefano, S., Rutledge, L., and Randall, D. (1965). Cognitive styles and reading ability. *Psychology in the Schools*, **2**, 57–62.

Satterfield, J. H., Schell, A. M., Nicholas, T., and Backs, R. (1988). Topographic study of AERP in ADDH and normal six-year-old boys. *Psychophysiology*, **25**, 591–606.

Shallice, T., and Warrington, E. K. (1977). The possible role of selective attention in acquired dyslexia. *Neuropsychologia*, **15**, 31–41.

Skinner, J. E. (1978). A neurophysiological model for regulation of sensory input to cerebral cortex. In D. A. Otto (ed.), *Multidisciplinary Perspectives in Event-related Brain Potential Research*, pp. 616–625. Chapel Hill, NC: US Environmental Protection Agency.

Skinner, J. E., and Yingling, C. D. (1977). Central gating mechanisms that regulate event-related potentials and behavior: A neural model for attention. In J. E. Desmedt (ed.), *Attention, Voluntary Contraction, and Event-related Potentials*, pp. 30–69. Basel: Karger.

Slaghuis, W. L., and Lovegrove, W. J. (1985). Spatial-frequency-dependent visible persistence and specific reading disability. *Brain and Cognition*, **4**, 219–240.

Stanley, G., and Hall, R. (1973). Short-term visual information processing in dyslexics. *Child Development*, **44**, 841–844.

Stein, J. F., and Fowler, M. S. (1982). Ocular motor dyslexia. *Dyslexia Review*, **5**, 25–28.

Stone, J., Dreher, B., and Leventhal, A. (1979). Hierarchical and parallel mechanisms in the organization of the visual cortex. *Brain Research Reviews*, **1**, 345–394.

Taylor, S. E. (1965). Eye movements while reading: Facts and fallacies. *American Education Research Journal*, **2**, 187–202.

Weingartner, H., Rapoport, J. L., Buchsbaum, M. S., Bunney, W. E., Jr, Ebert, M. H., Mikkelsen, E. J., and Caine, E. D. (1980). Cognitive processes in normal and hyperactive children and their response to amphetamine treatment. *Journal of Abnormal Psychology*, **89**, 25–37.

Wilsher, C. R., Bennett, D., Chase, C. H., Conners, C. K., DiIanni, M., Feagans, L.,

Hanvik, L. J., *et al.* (1987). Piracetam and dyslexia: Effects on reading tests. *Journal of Clinical Psychopharmacology*, **7**, 230–237.

Zambelli, A. J., Stamm, J. S., Maitinsky, S., and Loiselle, D. L. (1977). Auditory evoked potentials and selective attention in formerly hyperactive adolescent boys. *American Journal of Psychiatry*, **134**, 742–747.

Address for correspondence:

Department of Psychiatry, Duke University Medical Center, Durham, North Carolina 27701, USA

Part IV

The Diagnostic Significance of Eye Movements in Dyslexia

10

Detecting Dyslexia through Ophthalmo-kinesis: A Promise for Early Diagnosis

George Th. Pavlidis

George Washington University, Washington D.C.

EYE MOVEMENT AND READING: THEY DEVELOP IN PARALLEL

Since its inception, research on eye movements has been intimately linked to the study of reading. This is a logical relationship, since eye movements constitute an integral part of the reading process. However, most of this research has concentrated on the study of normal readers (Tinker, 1958). Although little has been done to analyze the eye movements of learning-disabled/dyslexic readers, the proven value of eye movements in uncovering the cognitive and perceptual skills of normal readers suggests that it will be useful to apply the ideas and technology of eye movement research to the study of LD/dyslexia and attention deficit hyperactivity disorder. Indeed, this line of research has produced the most promising results for the early objective diagnosis of academic problems (Jost, 1988).

Reading skills develop gradually, improving in precision and speed over the years, and they are clearly reflected in the patterns and characteristics of the readers' eye movements. Most of that development occurs during the first three to four years of schooling. About two-thirds of the total development of readers' eye movements that occurs between the first grade and college level is achieved by 10 years of age (Gilbert, 1953; Taylor *et al.*, 1960). It is noteworthy that the EEG also starts to mature at about the same age (Epstein, 1980).

The overall developmental pattern for eye movements suggests that during both reading and visual search (Lloyd and Pavlidis, 1978; Vurpillot, 1976) an inverse relationship exists between age and duration of fixation, and the number of forward and regressive eye movements (i.e. the older the child the fewer the eye movements and the shorter the duration of fixation). Usually, a shorter fixation is an indication of faster motor system and/or faster information processing and of course reflects efficient word recognition.

THE SIGNIFICANCE OF EYE MOVEMENTS

The functional significance of eye movements is far from being understood. The eyes keep moving during sleep and even during coma and are claimed to be good predictors of the outcome of the coma (Coakley and Thomas, 1977). There are at least five different types of eye movements (saccadic, pursuit, convergent–divergent, vestibular and micromovements). Each type has an independent but interacting neurological control systems which are among the most complex, sophisticated and advanced biological control systems.

The main type of eye movements used during visual scanning and reading are called saccadic eye movements or saccades, which are preceded and followed by pauses or fixations. The brain obtains its information through the eyes only during fixation. Just before and during saccades vision is suppressed. Saccades are the most frequently used and the fastest movements the human body can make. Furthermore, the effectiveness of vision depends on the efficiency of eye movements. It is, however, erroneous to equate eye movements with vision, as the function of eye movements goes well beyond vision and reflects the way the brain functions, including higher brain processes. The importance of eye movements is also reflected in its rich anatomical endowment.

The allocation of the brain's 12 cranial nerves has been made according to the significance of each function. Eye movements are given a great part of the brain's potential as almost three out of the 12 cranial nerves are dedicated to their control. In contrast, only one cranial nerve is allocated to vision itself, which undoubtedly is the most important sense, and it is estimated to provide about 90% of the information that reaches the brain. The one cranial nerve that vision receives is indeed generous as the less functionally important senses, i.e. hearing, smell and touch, receive much less than one nerve. As a rule, the less the significance of a function the lesser part of a cranial nerve it receives.

It would have been a paradox if the sole function of eye movements was to serve vision. How, then, could one explain that vision was given three times less cranial nerves than eye movements? Undeniably, one of the main functions of eye movements is to bring the object of interest onto the fovea, and, hence, to serve vision. What is claimed here, however, is that the function of eye movements goes beyond vision. The following facts make the point as they show the independence of eye movements and vision in a number of conditions and states:

(1) We use eye movements even when we do not use vision, e.g. during sleep, and even when we are not dreaming.

(2) At the beginning of life, although our visual experience is limited, about 60–70% of our prolonged sleeping time is occupied by periods of rapid eye movement (REM). This high percentage declines by adolescence to about 20%.

(3) If eye movements were only to serve vision how could one explain their presence in people who never had vision, such as those who are blind from birth?

The most plausible explanation is that eye movements reflect higher cognitive functions. Recent studies have indeed shown that the way we move our eyes frequently reflects how and what information we process or even what side of the brain initiates and analyzes a thought process.

It is not, therefore, surprising that different types and characteristics of eye movements have been found to be among the first signs and among the most sensitive indices of many neurologically based conditions, including schizophrenia, Alzheimer's, behavioral and other neurological disorders (Corver et al., 1973; Holzman et al., 1976; Shagass et al., 1976; Van Noorden et al., 1964), and hyperactivity–attentional deficit disorder (Bala et al., 1981). In addition, the level of alcohol in the blood, drugs and psychotropic drugs are immediately reflected in the deteriorating eye movement performance. They are also excellent indicators of reading proficiency (Tinker, 1958; Pavlidis, 1981b; 1985a).

EYE MOVEMENTS: A POWERFUL NEUROPHYSIOLOGICAL TOOL

Eye movement efficiency develops almost in parallel with reading. The importance of the use of eye movements as an objective tool for the study of the individual components of the reading process is further enhanced by the fact that during reading the control of eye movements is beyond our consciousness; it is completely automated.

Eye movements are a powerful method for uncovering and understanding the mechanisms involved in the reading process. Unlike other methods that provide only a global picture of the task under study, eye movements can be used to pinpoint and map the specific problems of the reader. By superimposing the location of the eye fixations on the text one can find which word or parts of the text attracted the reader's attention or were very difficult to recognize or understand. This difficulty is reflected in the longer durations of the relevant fixations and the pattern of eye movements around it.

Such information is useful not only for uncovering problems in the different components of reading but also for the development of teaching strategies or methods appropriate for the child's personal strengths or weaknesses. A teacher can even monitor and further adjust his/her teaching strategy by following the child's progress through repeated eye movement measurements over time.

This objective procedure can be complementary to existing educational testing, and because it takes only a few minutes it can be given on an annual or semi-annual basis to all schoolchildren.

Up to now, the relatively high cost of the difficult-to-use eye movement devices, combined with the need for specialized technical skills for their operation, and the laborious, expensive and relatively inaccurate data analysis has restricted their use mainly to universities and other research–clinical institutions. Our device solves all the aforementioned problems. It offers the benefits stemming from simple operation and automated analysis, and can be used by various disciplines including neurology, psychiatry, psychology, ophthalmology, optometry, and education. So non-experts can easily use it in educational and clinical settings.

DYSLEXIA AND ERRATIC EYE MOVEMENTS DURING READING

The relationship between normal reading and eye movements has been known since the beginning of reading research. There are strong developmental trends in the number and duration of fixations, and in the number of regressions, which continue to decrease in normal readers up through high school (Gilbert, 1953; Taylor et al., 1960). In contrast to the eye movements shown by both normal and slow readers, the eye movements of dyslexics are erratic, and show unusual patterns and variability of duration, and size (Figure 1). Regressions often occur in clusters of two or more in succession, whereas advanced, normal and slow readers usually make single regressions whose size is smaller than that of the preceding forward movements (Pavlidis, 1981a,b, 1985b). Similarly, children with attentional hyperactivity problems and with reading problems have abnormal pursuit eye movements characterized by frequent saccades which correct the over- or undershootings of the target (Bala et al., 1981; Pavlidis, 1985a; 1990).

Reading success vitally depends on the proper function of eye movements. Regression during reading has been attributed to comprehension problems (Bayle, 1942), to semantic control (Just and Carpenter, 1978), or to central malfunctions (Zangwill and Blakemore, 1972; Lesevre, 1968). It is a universal finding that dyslexics make significantly more eye movements, more regressions, and have longer and more variable durations of fixation than advanced,

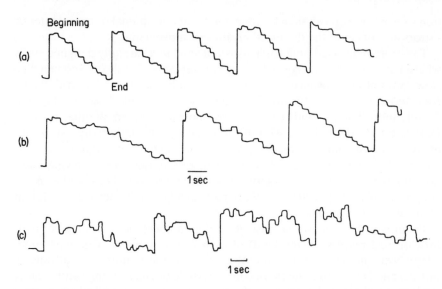

Figure 1. Illustrative eye movement records. The horizontal lines represent fixations. The vertical lines represent eye movements. The sizes of the lines are proportional to the duration of fixation or to the eye movement size. (a) Eye movement record of a normal reader during reading. It consists of successive similar eye movements and fixations which form a repetitive staircase pattern. The regressions are rare and they are invariably smaller in amplitude than the preceding forward saccade. (b) A retarded reader's eye movement record during reading. It is noteworthy that the eyes make more forward and regressive movements than the normal readers, but the amplitude of his regressions is also smaller than the preceding forward saccades. His eye movements form a prolonged staircase pattern. (c) Dyslexics erratic eye movement record. Every line has its own idiosyncratic shape, unlike normal and retarded readers' patterns which are consistent throughout. It is often difficult to distinguish the end of one line from the beginning of the next. The regressions are not only very frequent but they also sometimes occur in clusters of two or more. Their amplitude is frequently bigger than that of the preceding forward saccade.

normal and even slow readers of the same age as dyslexics (for reviews see Pavlidis, 1981b, 1985a, 1986).

What causes the dyslexic's erratic eye movements? To effectively test whether educational and other environmental factors can cause the dyslexics' erratic eye movements, dyslexics and other slow readers, whose reading disability can be attributed to and explained by environmental factors, should be compared. Dyslexics and slow readers should be *of the same age* and *have an equally severe reading disability*. Hence, if educational or environmental factors are the cause of the erratic eye movements, then the two groups should have equally abnormal eye movements. But if dyslexics have significantly worse eye movements than the matched-for-age and reading retardation slow readers, it can then be concluded that educational or environmental factors do not cause the dyslexics' erratic eye movements.

The aforementioned philosophy was reflected in a carefully designed study where Pavlidis (1981b) recorded the eye movements of dyslexics and matched slow, normal and advanced readers while reading text ranging in difficulty from too easy to too difficult. This study showed that dyslexics made significantly more forward and regressive eye movements than all other readers, including the slow readers, who in turn made significantly more eye movements than the normal readers, who made significantly more than the advanced readers (Pavlidis, 1981b). These results raise the following question: do worse readers make significantly more regressions because they make proportionally more of all kinds of eye movements? Or do they make different kinds of eye movements?

To answer these questions, instead of the number, the percentage of their forward and regressive (the kind) of their eye movements were compared. There were no significant differences between the non-dyslexic advanced, normal and backward readers. In contrast, dyslexics had a significantly higher percentage of regressive eye movements than each of the other three groups. These results show that the worse readers make proportionally more forward and regressive movements and that the non-dyslexic readers are part of the same continuum ranging from the best to worst reading ability. In contrast, dyslexics make significantly more eye movements and also have significantly different kinds of eye movements than all other readers. Their number and pattern of regressions was disproportionately high.

The significant differences between dyslexic and slow matched non-dyslexic readers suggest that reading retardation *per se* does not cause the dyslexics' erratic eye movements. But are the eye movement differences, found during reading, still present during non-reading tasks that simulate the sequential, motor and attentional components of reading? If they do so, then such findings would lend support to the hypothesis that dyslexics, unlike normal and slow readers, have a central deficit that manifests itself both during reading and appropriate non-reading tasks that simulate the sequential, oculomotor, attentional and other components of the reading process.

DYSLEXICS' ERRATIC EYE MOVEMENTS IN NON-READING STUDIES

Neurologically based conditions are usually encountered in all socio-economic and psycho-educational backgrounds. In addition, the neurologically impaired part of the brain customarily influences any function that is administered by it. Dyslexia as a neurological condition, unless proven otherwise, is expected to follow the same rules. Namely, dyslexics should have problems performing both reading and non-reading tasks which share with reading the same fundamental components, e.g. automated sequencing, oculomotor control and attention. These shared functions are thought to be administered by the same parts of the brain.

This hypothesis would predict that dyslexics' performance would be worse than normal readers, both during reading and non-reading tasks that simulate/incorporate the vital components of the reading process. Data from a number of studies support the correctness of this hypothesis (Pavlidis, 1981b, 1985b).

In a number of studies words were replaced by a variety of stationary stimuli (Elterman *et al.*, 1980; Gilbert, 1953; Lesevre, 1968; Griffin *et al.*, 1974; Goldrich and Sedgwick, 1982; Jarabek, 1984; Jones and Stark, 1983; Pavlidis, 1981a,b, 1985b; Cizek and Jost, 1984; Mawson, 1984) in order to test the oculomotor performance of learning-disabled children in a task closely resembling reading but free of language, psycho-educational, memory and intelligence factors. These studies have consistently found that LD children, with a varied degree of reading problems, have significantly worse eye movements than their matched normal readers.

In his extensive study, Gilbert (1953) compared the oculomotor performance of his subjects, covering almost the whole reading ability spectrum, while reading prose and in the non-reading task of scanning digits. He found that there was no instance of a pupil who 'was very superior in fixation frequency in reading digits. Rather the data are consistent in pointing out the fact that individuals whose eye movement behavior is most efficient in one type of reading show superiority in the other type also; and very inferior performance in either activity is generally predictive of inferior performance in other type.' Gilbert noted that the above relationship applied to best and worst readers but not to the average readers. From the diagnostic point of view these findings are most promising for the disabled and gifted readers as these are the only groups (not the normal readers) that will profit from the diagnosis of their gift or problem.

In France, Lesevre replicated Gilbert's results and further reported that children younger than 7 years of age have inadequate eye movements, while after that age their eye movements reached a high level of maturity. Lesevre (1968) tested children between 5 and 12 years of age. She asked them to fixate successively, as quickly and as accurately as possible, 48 crosses set out in seven lines, each containing a different number of crosses spaced irregularly. The 5-year-olds were not able to do the task. Most of the 6-year-olds showed a marked improvement, but they were still unable to perform the task accurately. There was a rapid improvement until the seventh year, but after that age improvement slowed down considerably. The functionally important movements (corrective, verification, regressive, etc.) became less and less frequent with age, particularly between 6 and 8 years, while the number of irrelevant (non-functional) movements were the first to disappear. Their number decreased rapidly between 6 and 9 years. A third of the 7-year-olds fixated every single cross and this proportion remained unchanged in adults. It is noteworthy that some very young children's performance surpassed that of much older ones.

In another study, Griffin and his colleagues (1974) asked inadequate readers with a highly variable degree of reading problems, and normal controls, to look sequentially at equidistantly spaced pictures, dots and three-letter words. They concluded that 'inadequate readers seem to have less efficient saccadic eye movements regardless of the type of the material used'. They further suggested that the 'disorder of saccadic eye movement is a problem of microsequencing'.

Elterman and his colleagues (1980) conducted case studies with five young mildly disabled readers and two normal readers. Their subjects were tested in reading and non-reading tasks. Four out of five (80%) of their disabled readers exhibited some degree of sequencing oculomotor problem and erratic eye movements either during reading or non-reading tasks or in both of them. They concluded '. . . that a primary eye movement abnormality may play a contributing role in some cases of developmental dyslexia'.

Further support to the previous finding was provided by the results of Goldrich and Sedgwick (1982), who asked their 16 reading disabled and 15 normal readers to scan a variety of visual non-reading stimuli. They found that the reading-disabled children's eye movements were significantly worse than those of the normal controls. They concluded that '. . . oculomotor control may be a significant factor in reading disability'.

The above studies, as well as those that did not find a significant difference between LD and normal readers (Stanley *et al.*, 1983; see also Pavlidis, 1985a, for comments), have contributed to the understanding of the eye movement characteristics of people with reading problems. However, the selection criteria of the populations used in those studies were either not comprehensive and accurate enough to produce a relatively uniform sample, or researchers did not give adequate descriptions of their populations to allow the evaluation of the possible causes, the kind, degree and severity of the reading and of other problems. In addition, important methodological differences rendered the results of these studies incomparable (Pavlidis, 1985b). The available information suggests that the degree and kind of reading disability of the subjects of the above studies varied considerably either within the same study or across the reported studies.

Pavlidis (1981b) compared the eye movements of advanced, normal, non-dyslexic slow readers and dyslexics in reading and non-reading tasks. The same children who participated in the reading study also took part in the non-reading studies. The retarded non-dyslexic readers and dyslexics were of the same age and had equally severe reading problems (Pavlidis, 1985b).

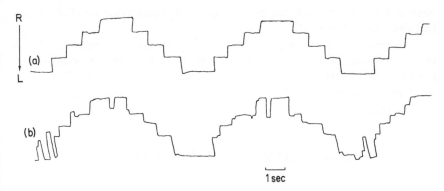

1 sec

Figure 2. Eye movement records of: a) normal reader (boy, 12 years 6 months old, average IQ), and b) severe dyslexic (boy 12 years 6 months old with superior IQ) while following sequentially illuminated LEDs as they proceed left to right and right to left. In contrast to the normal reader, the dyslexic was unable to maintain steady fixation, especially during the longer fixations (2 sec), indicating attentional/concentration and/or prediction/synchronization and/or impulsivity problems between stimulus and eye movements.

They were asked to: (a) follow sequentially illuminated LEDs (Pavlidis, 1981a,b), and (b) sequentially scan equidistantly spaced digits (Pavlidis, 1985b). In both studies the dyslexics made significantly more eye movements than each of the other groups of readers but there was no significant difference between any of the non-dyslexic readers' groups (Figure 2).

The most useful finding was that the eye movement differences between dyslexics and carefully matched controls—made while following the sequentially illuminated LEDs—were so highly significant that they could permit an accurate diagnosis of dyslexic and non-dyslexic readers in 93.2% of cases. Similar percentages were also found in our replication studies, including the latest large study across the USA where the significant eye movement differences were able to differentiate dyslexics and normal readers with an accuracy of about 90%.

The findings of Gilbert (1953) and Lesevre (1968) suggest that maturation of the parts of the brain responsible for the sequential control of the saccadic or possibly the control of other sequential tasks may constitute a prerequisite for the accurate execution of sequential tasks, such as those involved in reading. Thus, it is of interest that worldwide the start of schooling more or less coincides with the period that the oculomotor system becomes mature enough to handle such tasks as reading. The question still remains whether or not dyslexics' eye movements are significantly worse than other children's even before reading age. This possibility is supported both by the recent neurological findings (Galaburda and Kemper, 1979, Gross-Glen *et al.*, this volume) which indicate that the dyslexics' brain malformations occur before birth and also by the fact that dyslexia is an inherited condition (Labuda and DeFries, this volume).

Furthermore, following the author's suggestion in a lecture in 1981 in Prague, Dr Jost conducted a comparative study of the prognostic power of the Pavlidis test in relation to the classic psycho-educational tests. The results were most encouraging. The results of Jost's (1988) important study are summarized below.

PREDICTING ACADEMIC FAILURE

Aims

(1) To examine if the reading development can be predicted by eye movements made during the Pavlidis test of following and scanning lights.
(2) Do eye movements also predict clinical classification of children after two years of schooling?

Predictive Study

Eye movements recorded at the end of the first semester of schooling were highly correlated with other psycho-educational measures (i.e. IQ, reading and performance at various school subjects) taken at the end of the second year or at the beginning of the third grade.

Subjects

All 59 children who entered three different schools in Bohemia, Czechoslovakia, participated in the study. They were 27 male and 32 female children.

Tests

(1) Two of the subtests of the Pavlidis test were given at the beginning of the first semester of schooling.
(2) IQ (WISC) was given at the beginning of the second semester of the first year. It was readministered to 20 underachievers during the first semester of the third year.
(3) *Reading* tests were administered at the end of the second year.
(4) *School achievement* at the end of the first and second year. The score was the sum of all grades in: Czechoslovakian language, mathematics, basic

knowledge, writing, musical education, athletic education and work education.

(5) A variety of psychological and educational tests were also administered at the end of the second or the beginning of the third year. In addition, the teacher's evaluation for each child was also taken into account.

Results

Two groups emerged at the end of the second–beginning of the third year: (1) 35 normals (16 males, 19 females); (2) 24 'underachievers' (11 males, 13 females) for a variety of reasons, including epilepsy, possible mental retardation, speech problems, etc. The high percentage of 'underachievers' is due to the fact that children with mild problems were placed in the 'underachievers' group.

The better the eye movements and the IQ the better the reader.

Correlations of school achievement with eye movements was 0.973/0.872, and with full WISC was only 0.469. Eye movements and IQ had a higher correlation with school performance than socio-economic status.

Sex differences: girls had significantly better eye movements than boys.

PREDICTIVE ACCURACY OF EYE MOVEMENTS

Eye movements recorded during the Pavlidis test at the beginning of schooling proved excellent predictors of subsequent school performance, irrespective of the reason for underachievement. It is noteworthy that if stricter criteria were used for 'underachievement' the discriminating power of eye movements would probably be higher.

The eye movements correctly predicted–classified the children as normal or underachievers in 88.1% of the cases, and if bad eye movement recordings were excluded their classification increased to 91.5% of the cases.

What causes the dyslexics' erratic eye movements? If bad reading habits or other reading problems were the only causes of the dyslexics' erratic eye movements then: (1) the matched—non-dyslexic—slow readers (who were of the same reading and chronological age as the dyslexics) should have had similarly erratic eye movements; and (2) both groups should have had normal eye movements in the non-reading tasks (Pavlidis, 1981b, 1985b). The results of the above studies did not support these hypotheses. On the contrary, the results indicated that the dyslexics' erratic eye movements were relevantly independent of reading and that they were likely to be due to a brain malfunction. As such, they should also be present in non-reading tasks.

EYE MOVEMENTS AND DYSLEXIA: THEIR RELATIONSHIP

Three main interpretative hypotheses have been proposed to explain the dyslexics' erratic eye movements found during reading.

1. Erratic Eye Movements: A Reflection of Reading Problems

Erratic eye movements are just a reflection of bad reading habits or the problems dyslexics have with the reading material (Tinker, 1958; Goldberg and Arnott, 1970) or that they are merely a reflection of the difficulty dyslexics have in decoding and understanding the meaning of the text (Ellis and Miles, 1981). This hypothesis fails to explain the consistent findings that dyslexics and normal readers differ significantly in a variety of non-reading tasks (Dodgen and Pavlidis, this volume; Pavlidis 1985b).

This hypothesis may be true for a certain percentage of dyslexics but there are several lines of evidence against this point of view. For instance, Pavlidis (1981, 1985b) compared advanced, normal, non-dyslexic slow readers, and dyslexics' eye movement performance in reading and non-reading tasks. He found that:

(a) When dyslexics were matched for the severity of their reading problem with other non-dyslexic slow readers of the same chronological age, dyslexics still had significantly more abnormal eye movements in reading and non-reading tasks (Pavlidis, 1981b, 1985b).
(b) When dyslexics read easy text that was one year below their reading age (and many years below their grade level) or when they read 'for fun' without comprehension requirements, their eye movements were still abnormal (Pavlidis, 1981b). So, the text difficulty alone could not have caused their erratic eye movements.
(c) When normal readers read a difficult text for them, they showed some increase in duration of fixation and number of regressions, but neither with the same quantitative and qualitative abnormalities nor to the same extent as dyslexics. In other words, text difficulty does not convert normal readers' eye movements to erratic.
(d) Finally, and most significantly, dyslexics show abnormal eye movements while tracking non-verbal targets but other readers do not.

2. Erratic Eye Movements May Sometimes Cause Dyslexia (Fowler *et al.*, this volume; Gilbert, 1953; Lesevre, 1968; Pavlidis, 1986; Zangwill and Blakemore, 1972)

This could be the case for a certain yet undetermined percentage of dyslexics but this hypothesis, while explaining their eye movement problems, fails to explain the language and other non-reading problems, e.g. the sequential problems consistently found in dyslexics (Vellutino, 1977).

3. Erratic Eye Movements and Dyslexia: Not a Cause–Effect Relationship

Pavlidis (1985a,b) proposed that erratic eye movements and dyslexia do not often have to have a cause–effect relation. Instead I propose that they can both be by-products of brain malfunctions where:

(a) Erratic eye movements can be the symptoms of one or more central neurological deficits commonly shared with dyslexia. In such a case erratic eye movements and dyslexia could share the same common cause, i.e. a malfunctioning part of the brain that causes both dyslexia and erratic eye movements.

(b) They can be the symptoms of independent but parallel central neurological deficits. In other words, two different malfunctioning parts of the brain—one causing dyslexia, and the other causing erratic eye movements—may result from a third common factor that causes the other two different parts of the brain to malfunction.

One such common link was proposed by the late Professor Norman Geschwind (1986). He hypothesized that during pregnancy high levels of testosterone are secreted in males *in utero*. Abnormally high hormonal levels may then affect certain aspects of neurological development and the development of the thymus gland, which plays an important role in the autoimmune system. The same factor responsible for triggering male hormonal secretion *in utero* may thus be responsible for a number of problems, including delaying the growth of the left hemisphere, distorting the functions of the autoimmune system, left-handedness, and certain developmental disabilities such as stuttering and dyslexia, as well as erratic eye movements. By such a common factor, therefore, dyslexia and erratic eye movements would become parallel phenomena.

Parts of Geschwind's theory fit with several known facts about dyslexics, e.g. more frequent allergies, head- and earaches are found in dyslexics, or the fact that more boys than girls are dyslexic (three to five males to one female). Also, strong neurological data indicate that the brains of dyslexics exhibit structural anomalies in the left hemisphere that may be generated in the first months of gestation. Such data are consistent with a hereditary component of dyslexia (LaBuda and DeFries, this volume).

Supporting evidence also comes from the work of Ojemann and his colleagues (1979), who found that reading, phoneme discrimination, naming and automated non-verbal sequential control are administered by the same (left) part of the brain. It is, therefore, likely that sequential eye movements and reading may share some common brain centers. This hypothesis also draws support from clinical findings in patients who developed language problems as a consequence of stroke or brain injury also exhibit other sequential problems (Calvin and Ojemann, 1980).

It is possible that each of the hypotheses claiming a cause–effect relationship could be correct for certain subtypes of dyslexia. In contrast, Pavlidis' hypothesis is strongly supported by data and embraces a significant percentage of dyslexics. It is, however, my prediction that future research may show that what we refer to today as dyslexia is not a unitary entity but a cluster of independent and interdependent conditions with similar psycho-educational profiles but with possibly different causes and prognoses. The first step towards this direction is already made by the subtyping studies (Rourke, this volume). The decisive evidence is likely to be provided from psychophysiological and neuroanatomical studies.

PAVLIDIS TEST: SUBTESTS AND RATIONALE

Eye Movement Testing

During testing, the subjects are seated at right-angles to the tester. Subjects view visual stimuli while wearing fully adjustable spectacle frames with eye movement sensors mounted on them, and with their heads stabilized on a chin and/or head rest. The visual stimuli are displayed on a TV monitor and consist of non-verbal stimuli that simulate the non-verbal aspects of the reading process.

Rationale

The brain malfunction that causes dyslexia (*see* Table 1) should also be affecting other processes sharing the same fundamental skills as reading and which are administered by the same parts of the brain.

There are five subtests and each subtest is designed to test certain constitutional components of the reading process. Their effectiveness is optimized by incorporating into their design critical elements derived from research and clinical experience. The five subtests are:

(1) Following sequentially illuminated spots flashing from left to right (L → R) (Pavlidis, 1981b, 1986).
   Rationale: in this test words are replaced with light spots and it simulates the non-verbal aspects of the reading process such as oculomotor control, visual–spatial and sequential components.

Table 1. Main factors contributing to erratic eye movements

Contributing factors	Sequentially illuminated LEDs Left → Right, R → L	Randomly illuminated LEDs	Synchronously presented LEDs	Pursuit
Oculomotor control	yes	yes	yes	yes
Fast sequencing	yes	no	yes	no
Prediction/ synchronization	yes	no	no	yes
Alternating between 2 'time-sets'	yes	no	no	no
Concentration/ fixation	yes	no/yes	no	yes
Impulsivity	yes	yes	no	no

It differs, however, from the reading task in that during reading when the brain is ready to view new materials it moves the eyes to the next word but, in contrast, in this test the eyes move in response to the movement of the light stimuli.

(2) Following sequentially illuminated spots flashing from right to left (R→L).

Rationale: same as in L→R experiment with the difference that the eyes move in the opposite direction.

(3) Sequentially scanning seven spots synchronously displayed on a horizontal line (Pavlidis, 1985b).

Rationale: same as in L→R and R→L tests but, as during reading, the brain decides when and how fast to move the eyes from one light spot to the next. This test is the closest simulation of the non-verbal aspects of the reading process.

(4) Tracking a slowly moving light spot on a horizontal line.

Rationale: this test detects primary *involuntary* attentional difficulty. Involuntary eye movement abnormality is considered to be those abnormal eye movement characteristics that fail to disappear even when the subject is made to pay full attention to the moving stimulus.

(5) Following randomly illuminated spots.

Rationale: by following randomly moving lights at variable temporal and spatial intervals the sequential and the prediction—synchronization elements were excluded. Any eye movement anomalies in this test would reflect pure oculomotor and possibly impulsivity problems.

The experiments followed each other with an interval of a minute or so. For readers, these non-verbal subtests are supplemented by eye movement recording while reading texts of various levels of difficulty.

Eye Movement Data Analysis

Data analysis is achieved automatically by a set of very advanced hardware and programs developed by the author. The uniqueness of our eye movement system is best exemplified by its ability to accurately and completely automatically analyze all types of eye movements. The software recognizes the exact beginning and end of each eye movement, blink or fixation and times them with an accuracy of 1 ms. It calculates the exact temporal and spatial characteristics of all eye movements, fixations and blinks, such as amplitude, location and velocity.

DISCUSSION

The Advantages of the Ophthalmo-kinetic Diagnostic Method (Pavlidis test)

This method has several important advantages. Because it relies solely on non-verbal tasks and tests involuntary eye movements, it provides objective, quantifiable data about sequencing, attention, timing and control. More important, because it uses a non-reading task, it can be administered to children who have not yet started school or learned how to read. For the first time, an early diagnosis or even a prognosis of dyslexia is possible (Jost, 1988). In addition, the test is simple and easy to administer, lasts only a few minutes, and uses computerized equipment that provides accurate recordings and fully automated data analysis. This expands its use to non-experts such as teachers and nurses.

In contrast, the current exclusionary diagnostic methods of dyslexia are subjective and usually inconclusive. A comprehensive test lasts from 1.5 to 7 hours, and cannot be reliably given before the age of about 7½ years. In addition, a number of the psycho-educational tests used are culturally biased.

The ophthalmo-kinetograph (OKG) incorporates the stimulus control and display unit, sensing, recording, storing, linearizing and automatic analysis systems. With this equipment, we are conducting a prospective study to test preschool-aged children for dyslexia. We will record their eye movements at frequent intervals, and follow their progress in school. Such a developmental study will take two or three years before results are available. As my theory predicts and Dr Jost's data show, those children who later prove to be dyslexic by currently established exclusionary criteria or by our eye movement test will also be the ones who had the worst erratic eye movements before they started school. We have already successfully recorded the eye movements of about 80 4-year-old children in Kansas using our test.

The benefits from a prognostic method for detecting dyslexia early in a child's preschool life are tremendous:

(1) It makes an objective and accurate diagnosis early in life, possibly at pre-school age.
(2) It ameliorates/eliminates psychological problems such as school avoidance stemming from early reading failure, shattered self-esteem and self-confidence.
(3) It allows the diagnosis of dyslexia internationally among children from all socio-economic backgrounds irrespective of intelligence or psychological or educational conditions.
(4) It capitalizes on the plasticity of the young brain to increase the effectiveness of early treatment.
(5) It helps create psychologically healthier, better-balanced individuals and happier families.

The test could be administered to children as young as 3–4 years of age who understand simple instructions. They do not need a long attention span because the actual subtests are very short, lasting about 30 seconds. If, at that early age, we are able to identify children whose erratic eye movements are characteristic of dyslexia, then they can be helped before they even encounter reading problems in school. Even with current methods of treatment, the earlier the diagnosis of dyslexia the better the results (Strag, 1972; Muehl and Forell, 1973).

At present, the diagnostic methods of dyslexia which are based on exclusionary criteria necessitate that a child must fail in reading for at least 18 months to 2 years before the educational system may be able to diagnose it with certainty. By that time, the child could experience continuous reading failure and may have already suffered from emotional problems (Bryan and Bryan, 1990; Pavlidis, 1990).

Another of the main advantages of our diagnostic method is that early diagnosis will forestall the secondary psychological problems common among dyslexics. The psychological problems do not end with the schooling period. About a third of adult dyslexics need some kind of psychological treatment to cope with the problems brought by early reading failure (Johnson, 1986). These problems can be so severe that they frequently prevent bright dyslexics from holding even ordinary jobs.

An important advantage of this method is that it will diagnose dyslexia regardless of a child's intelligence, emotional and educational problems, or poor socio-economic background. Unfortunately, at the moment, children with any of these problems are by definition excluded from the category of dyslexia. They also happen to be the ones most in need of help. The Pavlidis test will enable disadvantaged children also to enjoy the benefits that the US and other educational systems offer to dyslexics, e.g. extra time to take examinations, not to be penalized for spelling errors and to receive free individual tutoring.

In addition, with this fast and objective diagnostic method whole preschool or school populations can be quickly screened to provide an accurate picture of the dimensions of the problem, including its prevalence and distribution by sex, IQ, and socio-economic background.

If we can identify the dyslexic child before he or she starts school and before psychological problems have arisen, it should be possible to institute treatment early in order to minimize or eliminate the devastating effects of dyslexia. Just as stroke patients receive intensive physical therapy to help them partly recover the use of damaged parts of the body affected by neurological deficits, so young children diagnosed as dyslexic may be success-fully treated by 'educational' or biotechnological methods. One encouraging method was recently tested by the author (Pavlidis, 1987).

The brain of the young child is still malleable enough either to correct the malfunctioning circuits of the brain responsible for the deficits or to bypass these circuits by building alternative circuits through proper training. Even current methods of treatment are proven more effective with early diagnosis because they can capitalize on the plasticity of the young brain and on a psychologically intact, motivated child who has not yet developed an aversion to school. Early intervention following early diagnosis or, even better, a prognosis could reduce or eliminate the enormous personal unhappiness that dyslexia brings to individuals and to their families.

CONCLUSIONS

(1) The results of our studies have consistently shown that the Pavlidis test can accurately diagnose as dyslexics 90% or more of those who are diagnosed as such by today's exclusionary criteria. These results establish our method as the most sensitive neurophysiological method that can accurately and objectively diagnose dyslexia.
(2) Dyslexia is caused by an as yet undetermined neurological deficit.
(3) The relation between erratic eye movement patterns and dyslexia, in most cases, is not one simple cause or effect. Either the two share the same common neurological cause(s), or they are epiphenomena of inde-pendent but parallel brain deficits.
(4) Erratic eye movements could possibly be used as a diagnostic biological marker to differentiate dyslexic from normal or slow readers.

(5) Once the cause of erratic eye movements and the relationship between dyslexia and eye movements is established, new effective methods of treatment are likely to be developed.

(6) The fully automated ophthalmo-kinetograph (OKG), when it becomes widely available, will enable non-experts to use eye movements extensively for the objective diagnosis of a variety of neurological conditions such as dyslexia, attentional–concentration problems, multiple sclerosis, Parkinson's, schizophrenia, coma, etc., or states of mind (inebriation, drug usage).

(7) Our non-verbal method can use the diagnostic value of erratic eye movements to provide an early diagnosis of dyslexia, possibly even before children start school. The Jost (1988) data demonstrate that the Pavlidis test can predict at the age of six, with an accuracy of 71.5%, who will develop academic problems by the third grade.

(8) For extending the diagnostic capabilities of our method to younger children, it is necessary to complete a developmental study for ages 4–8, and establish eye movement norms for those ages, and establish differential diagnostic methods to separate the small percentage of non-dyslexic children who have abnormal eye movements for other reasons.

(9) The objective preschool diagnosis of dyslexia by our non-reading test offers dyslexics the hope of more effective treatment and a more balanced and happier life.

ACKNOWLEDGEMENTS

I thank Mr Norman Blackwood of Revlon Inc. for his brilliant contributions to the development of the software and hardware and to the project as a whole. It was a real pleasure to work with him.

My special thanks to the headmasters and pupils of the following schools: Blair Academy, Denver Academy, Gow School, Greenwood School, Lab School, Linden Hill, Putney School and Seton Hall, who made our studies possible through their participation. My greatest pleasure was to work at a personal level with the boys who participated in our study.

REFERENCES

Bala, S. P., Cohen, B., Morris, A. G., Atkin, A., Gittelman, R., and Kates, W. (1981). Saccades of hyperactive and normal boys during ocular pursuit. *Developmental Medicine and Child Neurology*, **23**, 323–336.

Bayle, E. (1942). The nature of causes of regressive movements in reading. *Journal of Experimental Education*, **11**, 16–36.

Bryan, J. H., and Bryan, T. (1990). Social factors in learning disabilities: Attitudes and interactions. In G. Th. Pavlidis (ed.), *Perspectives on Dyslexia, Vol. 2: Cognition, Language and Treatment*. Chichester: Wiley.

Calvin, W. H., and Ojemann, G. A. (1980). *Inside the Brain*. New York: Mentor.

Cizek, O. and Jost, J. (1984). Eye movements, dyslexia, and child development. Manuscript, Praha, Czechoslovakia.

Coakley, D., and Thomas, J. G. (1977). The ocular microtremor record and the prognosis of the unconscious patient. *Lancet*, **1**, 512–515.

Corver, J., Torres-Courtney, G., and Lopez-Rios, G. (1973). The neurotological significance of alterations of pursuit eye movements and the pendular eye tracking test. *Annals of Otology, Rhinology and Laryngology*, **82**, 855–967.

Denckla, M. B., Rudel, R. G., Chapman, C., and Krieger, J. (1985). Motor proficiency in dyslexic children with and without attentional disorders. *Archives of Neurology*, **42**, 229–231.

Ellis, N. C., and Miles, T. R. (1981). A lexical encoding deficiency I: Experimental evidence. In G. Th. Pavlidis and T. R. Miles (eds), *Dyslexia Research and its Applications to Education*, pp. 177–215. Chichester: Wiley.

Elterman, R. D., Abel, L. A., Daroff, R. B., Dell'Osso, L. F., and Bornstein, J. L. (1980). Eye movement patterns in dyslexic children. *Journal of Learning Disabilities*, **13**, 11–16.

Epstein, H. T. (1980). EEG developmental stages. *Developmental Psychobiology*, **13**, 629–631.

Galaburda, A. M., and Kemper, T. L. (1979). Cytoarchitectonic abnormalities in developmental dyslexia: Case study. *Annals of Neurology*, **6**, 94–100.

Geschwind, N. (1986). Dyslexia, cerebral dominance, autoimmunity, and sex hormones. In G. Th. Pavlidis and D. F. Fisher (eds), *Dyslexia: Neuropsychology and Treatment*. Chichester: Wiley.

Gilbert, I. C. (1953). Functional and motor efficiency of the eyes and its relation to reading. *University of California Publications in Education*, **11**, 159–231.

Goldberg, H. K., and Arnott, W. (1970). Ocular motility in learning disabilities. *Journal of Learning Disabilities*, **3**, 160–162.

Goldrich, S. G., and Sedgwick, H. (1982). An objective comparison of oculomotor functioning in reading disabled and normal children. *American Journal of Optometry and Physiological Optics*, **59**, 82 pp.

Griffin, D. C., Walton, G. N., and Ives, V. (1974). Saccades as related to reading disorders. *Journal of Learning Disabilities*, **7**, 310–316.

Holzman, P. S., Levy, D. L., and Proctor, L. R. (1976). Smooth pursuit eye movements, attention, and schizophrenia. *Archives of General Psychiatry*, **33**, 1415–1420.

Jarabek, J. (1984). A contribution to analysis of eye movement disorders in children. Prepublication manuscript, Praha, Czechoslovakia.

Johnson, D. J. (1986). Remediation for dyslexic adults. In G. Th. Pavlidis and D. Fisher (eds), *Dyslexia: Its Neuropsychology and Treatment*. Chichester: Wiley.

Jones, A., and Stark, L. (1983). Abnormal patterns on normal eye movements in specific dyslexia. In K. Rayner (ed.), *Eye Movements in Reading: Perceptual and Language Processes*. New York: Academic Press.

Jost, J. (1988). *Eye Movements and Learning Disabilities: A Timely Diagnosis*. Submitted for publication to the Monograph Series of International Academy for Research in Learning Disabilities.

Just, M. A., and Carpenter, P. A. (1978). Interference processes during reading: Reflections from eye fixations. In J. W. Senders, D. F. Fisher and R. A. Monty (eds), *Eye Movements and the Higher Psychological Functions*, pp. 157–174. Hillsdale, NJ: Erlbaum.

Lesevre, N. (1968). L'organisation du regard chez des enfants d'âge scolaire, lecteurs normaux et dyslexiques. *Reveue Neuropsychiatrie Infant*, **16**, 323–349.

Lloyd, P., and Pavlidis, G. Th. (1978). Child language and eye movements: The relative effects of sentence and situation on comprehension in young children. *Bulletin of the British Psychological Society*, **31**, 70–71.

Mawson, B. (1982). Eye movements and dyslexia. Informal presentation at the British Psychological Society's International Conference on Dyslexia, Manchester University, England, March 1–3. Also personal communication, April 1984.

Miles, T. R., and Ells, N. C. (1981). A lexical encoding deficiency II: Clinical observations. In G. Th. Pavlidis and T. R. Miles (eds), *Dyslexia Research and its Applications to Education*, pp. 217–243. Chichester: Wiley.

Muehl, S., and Forell, E. R. (1973). A follow-up study of disabled readers: Variables related to High School reading performance. *Reading Research Quarterly*, **9**, 110–123.

Ojemann, G., and Mateer, C. (1979). Human language cortex: Localization of memory, syntax, and sequential motor-phoneme identification systems. *Science*, **205**, 1401–1403.

Pavlidis, G. Th. (1981a). Do eye movements hold the key to dyslexia? *Neuropsychologia*, **19**, 57–64.

Pavlidis, G. Th. (1981b). Sequencing, eye movements and the early objective diagnosis of dyslexia. In G. Th. Pavlidis and T. R. Miles (eds), *Dyslexia Research and its Applications to Education*, pp. 99–163. Chichester: Wiley.

Pavlidis, G. Th. (1985a). Eye movements in dyslexia: Their diagnostic significance. *Journal of Learning Disabilities*, **18**, 42–50.

Pavlidis, G. Th. (1985b). Eye movement differences between dyslexics, normal, and slow readers while sequentially fixating digits. *American Journal of Optometry and Physiological Optics*, **62**, 820–832.

Pavlidis, G. Th. (1985c). Eye movements and dyslexia: Factors determining their relationship. *Perceptual and Motor Skills*, **60**, 319–322.

Pavlidis, G. Th. (1986). The role of eye movements in the diagnosis of dyslexia. In G. Th. Pavlidis and D. Fisher (eds), *Dyslexia: Neuropsychology and Treatment*. Chichester: Wiley.

Pavlidis, G. Th. (1987). Reading without eye movements: Dyslexics read fact and comprehend as well as normal readers. Paper presented at the Third World Congress on Dyslexia, Crete, June 28–July 3.

Pavlidis, G. Th. (1990). Conceptualization, symptomatology and research diagnostic criteria for dyslexia. In G. Th. Pavlidis (ed.), *Perspectives on Dyslexia, Vol. 2; Cognition, Language and Treatment*. Chichester: Wiley.

Shagass, C., Roemer, R. A., and Amadeo, M. (1976). Eye-tracking performance and engagement of attention. *Archives of General Psychiatry*, **33**, 121–125.

Stanley, G., Smith, G. A., and Hosell, E. A. (1983). Eye movements and sequential tracking in dyslexic and control children. *British Journal of Psychology*, **74**, 181–187.

Strag, G. A. (1972). Comparative behavioral rating of parents with severely mentally retarded, special learning disability, and normal children. *Journal of Learning Disabilities*, **5**, 52–56.

Taylor, S. E., Franckenpohl, H., and Pettee, J. L. (1960). Grade level norms for components of the fundamental reading skills. *Educational Developmental Laboratories, Information Research Bulletin*, 3, Huntington, NY.

Tinker, M. A. (1958). Recent studies of eye movements in reading. *Psychological Bulletin*, **55**, 215–231.

Vellutino, F. R. (1977). Alternative conceptualizations of dyslexia: Evidence in support of a verbal-deficit hypothesis. *Harvard Educational Review*, **47**, 334–354.

Vurpillot, C. (1976). *The Visual World of the Child*. London: George Allen and Unwin.
Van Noorden, G. K., Thompson, H. S., and Van Allen, M. W. (1964). Eye movements in myotonic dystrophy. An electrooculographic study. *Investigations in Ophthalmology*, **3**, 314–324.
Zangwill, O. L., and Blakemore, C. (1972). Dyslexia: Reversal of eye movements during reading. *Neuropsychologia*, **10**, 371–373.

Address for correspondence:

The Reading Center, George Washington University, 2021 K Street NW, Suite 720, Washington D.C. 20006, USA

11

Sequential, Timing, Rhythmic and Eye Movement Problems in Dyslexics

Charles E. Dodgen* and George Th. Pavlidis

Fair Oaks Hospital, New Jersey, and George Washington University, Washington, D.C.

OVERVIEW

Dyslexia is a syndrome that manifests itself in a wide and varied symptom picture. Because of the diversity of symptoms associated with the syndrome (see Pavlidis, 1990, for a comprehensive list) and the intrinsic complexity of the processes involved, it has remained very difficult to define dyslexia accurately despite active multidisciplinary investigation. The existence of subtypes (Rourke, this volume) complicates the picture further. Attempts to define dyslexia have evolved from unidimensional theoretical approaches (see Benton, 1980, and Sampson, 1975, for historical perspectives) to the more recent trend of neuropsychological definition (Hynd and Hynd, 1984). Interest in sequential, or serial order, processing has grown with the increasing interest in and sophistication of neuropsychological testing. Dyslexics have been found to be deficient in sequential processing across behaviors, sensory systems, and across research procedures as well (Andersen *et al.*, 1987, Atterbury, 1983, 1985; Badian, 1977; Badian and Wolff, 1974; Bryden, 1972; Cohen and Netley, 1981; Corkin, 1974; Denckla and Rudel, 1976; Gaddes, 1978; Hatchette and Evans, 1983; Hooper and Hynd, 1985, 1986; Katz and Deutsch, 1964; Koppitz, 1973; Lindgren and Richman, 1984; Pavlidis, 1981a,b, 1985, 1986, 1990; Richie and Aten, 1976; Sehy, 1984; Tallal, 1980; Vande Voort and Senf, 1973; Wolf, 1986; Wolff *et al.*, 1984; Zurif and Carson, 1970). This convergence of results strongly implies brain dysfunction with respect to sequential processing ability.

Investigators agree that sequential processing is an integral part of the larger reading process (Aaron, 1982; Das *et al.*, 1979; Gaddes, 1978; Pavlidis,

*Adapted from doctoral dissertation at Fairleigh Dickinson University, Teaweck, New Jersey, USA.

1981b, 1986, 1990; Tallal, 1980; Vernon, 1977). Deficits in performing visual-and verbal-sequential tasks are associated with deficits in reading ability (Bakker, 1972; Gaddes and Spellacy, 1977). Gaddes (1985) suggested that serial order processing is an ability with its own functional integrity. In this conceptualization, certain verbal tasks appear to place a load on sequential processing ability which the respondent may possess in varying degrees.

Since Orton's (1925) time, the relative activity of the cerebral hemispheres has been of interest. This interest gained a firm boost in the late 1960s with the work on split-brain individuals (Gazzaniga, 1970; Sperry, 1968). Normal hemispheric differences have been found on anatomical and neuropsychological levels. Dyslexics do not exhibit the typical left hemisphere advantage for verbal material across visual (Marcel *et al.*, 1974), auditory (Sommers and Taylor, 1972) and tactile modalities (Witelson, 1976). The results of these studies seem to indicate the disruption of left hemisphere functioning due to bilateral representation of spatial functions which are normally confined to the right hemisphere (Witelson, 1976).

Sequential-processing demands of reading involve both temporal and spatial components. Studies have linked the left hemisphere with temporal ordering and the right hemisphere with spatial ordering (Bakker and Licht, 1986; Davis and Wada, 1977; Gaddes, 1985; Gaddes and Zaidel, 1978; Hammond, 1982). Visuo-spatial processing appears to be more important in early reading and less important in skilled reading (Gaddes and Spellacy, 1977; Solan and Mozlin, 1986; Vernon, 1977), which has etiological, diagnostic and remedial implications for dyslexia (Bakker and Licht, 1986; Pavlidis and Fisher, 1986). Early reading is heavily dependent upon perceptual skills as the decoding task is of primary importance in unskilled reading. In skilled reading basic perceptual abilities are automated and, hence, less taxing for the brain, permitting it to concentrate on the meaning-deriving process.

DEFINITION

The dyslexics' symptom picture reflects disturbances in many areas: cognitive (sequential), behavioral, attentional, linguistic, emotional and perceptual. The delineation of the associated features and symptoms is one matter; the explanation of their presence is quite another. Herein lies the problem of definition.

Historically, dyslexia was defined from the etiological perspective of the particular researcher (Benton, 1980; Sampson, 1975). The problem that developed over many years of research was quite predictable: many new symptoms were described, and with each researcher claiming to have found 'the cause' of dyslexia the number of definitions grew correspondingly.

Sampson (1975) noted that it was the confusing state of affairs resulting from the above definitional approach that led to the adoption of the use of exclusionary criteria by the Research Group on Developmental Dyslexia of the World Federation of Neurology in 1968. The rationale behind the use of exclusionary criteria can be summed up simply: rule out all external factors known to have a negative effect on reading ability and the unexplained reading failure is called dyslexia. One major advantage of this definitional approach is that it is independent of etiological perspective, and this avoids the problem discussed above concerning etiologically based definition (Sampson, 1975). Also, use of strict, quantifiable exclusionary criteria results in 'purer' (more homogeneous) research groups and a truer picture of the dyslexic can be drawn (Pavlidis, 1985a, 1990). There are problems, however, with the World Federation definition as well as with the employment of exclusionary criteria in general. The criteria do not discriminate between subtypes which may result in heterogeneous populations. A case can be made for the existence of subtypes of dyslexia. On logical grounds, because of the complexity of the reading process, it makes sense that a problem at any given stage would result in a given 'type' of dyslexia. There have been many attempts to classify dyslexics into subgroups (see Rourke, this volume).

Partly as a result of the problems with the use of exclusionary criteria, and partly due to increasing knowledge, there has been a recent trend toward more positive definition of dyslexia as reflected by the National Joint Committee for Learning Disabilities, which states that learning disabilities (of which dyslexia is one type): 'are intrinsic to the individual and presumed to be due to central nervous system dysfunction' (Hynd and Hynd, 1984: p. 484). The difference between this definition and those of the past is that the diagnosis must rest firmly on neuropsychological evidence and not inference and theory.

The future of accurate diagnosis and classification appears to lie within the realm of neuropsychology, neurophysiology and electrophysiology in the forms of electroencephalogram (EEG), computerized tomography (CT), computerized eye movement analysis and other neuropsychological procedures. The use of psycho-educational testing will still be necessary, but these traditional measures will be of secondary importance and devoid of etiological implications.

ETIOLOGICAL THEORIES

Several theories have been proposed in order to account for unexpected reading failure, or dyslexia. The major etiological perspectives may be characterized as those implicating mixed or incomplete dominance/laterality, impaired perceptual processes, problems with intersensory integration, linguistic problems and difficulties in sequential or serial-order processing (Benton, 1980; Sampson, 1975). These approaches will be briefly described below.

As Downing and Leong (1982) note, early investigators (Dearborn, 1931, 1933; Monroe, 1932; Orton, 1925) observed an elevated incidence of poor-reading students demonstrating left, mixed or no dominance. Orton (1925), being particularly impressed by the frequency of reversal errors made by dyslexics, developed a theory to account for reversal phenomena. He posited that dyslexia was caused by incomplete cerebral dominance leading to rivalry between the hemispheres in processing visual stimulation. While the relative importance given to reversals in the study of dyslexia has diminished somewhat since Orton's time, interest in dominance and laterality has continued. Extensive writings by some authors on the development and theoretical importance of laterality gives evidence of the continuation of interest in this area (Ammett, 1976, 1981; Ammett and Kilshaw, 1984; Bertelson, 1982; Geschwind, 1984; Kershner, 1975, 1977). This interest has persisted despite the fact that most studies reveal no significant association between left-handedness and reading disability (Belmont and Birch, 1965; Clark, 1970; Rutter et al., 1970; Satz and Soper, 1986). Interest has also taken the form of neuropsychological studies designed to investigate processing styles of dyslexics when compared to normal readers. Such studies have employed dichotic listening (Bryden, 1970; Kimura, 1961a,b, 1964, 1967; Zurif and Carson, 1970), visual-half field (Bakker, 1979; Witelson, 1977) and dichotomous tactile stimulation (Witelson, 1976) procedures. Results of these studies give evidence of the existence of differences in (hemispheric) processing styles with dyslexics being inferior in the processing of information usually processed efficiently by the left hemisphere; that is, verbal/sequential information (Bakker and Licht, 1986).

Perceptual inefficiencies in reading failure have been investigated in the following areas: figure copying (Brenner and Gillman, 1966; Brenner et al., 1967), directional confusion (Critchley, 1964; Orton, 1937), and spontaneous writing and spelling impairment (Zangwill, 1962). Benton (1980) noted that others have investigated basic visual- and auditory-perceptual processes (Benton, 1962; Fildes, 1922; Hincks, 1926; Nielsen and Ringe, 1969). As Downing and Leong (1982) observe, some investigators have posited that perceptual difficulties may represent a maturational lag rather than enduring deficits (Bender, 1958; Gesell, 1945; Ilg and Ames, 1964; Kinsbourne, 1990; Naylor et al., 1990). Longitudinal studies, however, indicate that problems of the learning-disabled typically last into adulthood (Cooper and Griffith, 1978; Critchley, 1973; Horn et al., 1983; Johnson, 1980; Johnson and Blalock, 1987; Kline and Kline, 1975; Rawson, 1968; Scarborough, 1984). These findings strongly argue against the maturational lag notion.

The intersensory integration model posits that dyslexics are inferior in the ability to integrate information from different sensory systems (Beery, 1967; Birch and Belmont, 1964; Senf, 1969). In the procedure popularized by Birch and Belmont (1964) subjects were required to match auditory patterns with their visual representation. The procedure was based on the theory that reading rests on the ability to transform temporally distributed auditory patterns into spatially distributed visual ones. Birch and Belmont's study has been criticized for sampling and control problems (Muehl and Kremenak, 1966; Sterritt and Rudnick, 1966). Subsequent studies designed to replicate Birch and Belmont's (1964) original results as well as to test all combinations of stimulus presentation (i.e. auditory–visual, visual–auditory, auditory–auditory, visual–visual) have challenged the conclusion that dyslexics are inferior specifically in auditory–visual integration (Badian, 1977; Bryden, 1972; Gaddes, 1978; Hatchette and Evans, 1983; Vande Voort and Senf, 1973; Zurif and Carson, 1970). With dyslexics performing at an inferior level on the inter- and intramodal integration tasks it appears as though they have difficulty with the analysis of any stimulus pattern which is presented serially.

Proponents of the linguistic model contend that language-based problems underlie the dyslexic's difficulties (Mann and Ditunno, 1990; Smith, 1978; Vellutino, 1977, 1978, 1979; see also other chapters, this volume and Volume 2). The crucial chore for the reader is to derive meaning from written words by using the various forms of available information. For example, the reader forms expectations of what is to occur and by using orthographic, semantic and syntactic information he or she can have a good idea of the word(s) before referring to the graphemic aspects of the word(s) in question. Using orthographic, semantic and syntactic information many alternatives are eliminated so that the use of grapheme– (letter or unit with own distinct sound) phoneme (sound associated with grapheme) cues should be the last and simplest step in reading a word. Vellutino (1977) has suggested that all observed difficulties of the dyslexic can be explained in terms of a deficit in verbal processing. More specifically, he states that difficulties in intersensory integration, serial order and visual-perceptual processing can be explained via verbal-encoding deficiencies. This theory, however, fails to explain the findings of the majority of the dyslexia literature showing that dyslexics exhibit non-verbal problems in a variety of tasks and settings.

Temporal-order, sequential processing ability has been investigated with verbal and non-verbal stimuli. The main thesis of this approach is that sequential processes are important to reading at several levels. For example, sequencing is important in putting letters and words in order and moving the eyes in sequence from left to right (Pavlidis, 1981b). In this conceptualization cognitive and linguistic processes involved in reading are seen to be dependent upon more basic sequential processes (Pavlidis, 1981b; Tallal, 1980; Vernon, 1977). Sequential difficulties can account for verbal as well as non-verbal sequential behavioral problems of the dyslexic, while the verbal-deficit hypothesis (Vellutino, 1977) can only account for the former (Pavlidis, 1981b). The data that this theory rests on are presented below.

SEQUENTIAL BEHAVIOR AND DYSLEXIA

Many studies exist comparing normals and disabled readers on sequencing ability. Several studies used verbal tasks (Andersen *et al.*, 1987; Cohen and Netley, 1981; Denckla and Rudel, 1976; Hooper and Hynd, 1985, 1986; Katz and Deutsch, 1964; Koppitz, 1973; Wolf, 1986), two employed spatial tasks (Corkin, 1974; Lindgren and Richman, 1984), six employed tasks that involved the reproduction of sequential patterns by the subjects (Atterbury, 1983, 1985; Badian and Wolff, 1974; Gaddes, 1978; Hooper and Hynd, 1985, 1986; Wolff *et al.*, 1984) and others required judgment of similarity or dissimilarity of sequentially presented stimuli (Badian, 1977; Birch and Belmont, 1964; Bryden, 1972; Gaddes, 1978; Hatchette and Evans, 1983; Richie and Aten, 1976; Sehy, 1984; Tallal, 1980; Vande Voort and Senf, 1973; Willette and Early, 1985; Zurif and Carson, 1970).

Verbal Sequencing

Denckla and Rudel (1976) found that dyslexics were differentiated from normals and other learning-disabled subjects on the test of 'rapid automatized naming' (RAN). Subjects were asked to perform on tests requiring rapid repetitive naming of pictured objects, colors, letters and numbers. Dyslexics' performances were distinguishable from non-dyslexic learning-disabled subjects and normal-reading subjects; that is, dyslexics had a slower naming speed than both other groups. The authors pointed out that this was not due to a generalized slowing of reaction time. Andersen *et al.* (1987) and Wolf (1986) obtained similar results in more recent studies employing the RAN test procedure. Koppitz (1973) found that reading-disabled subjects were inferior to normals on tasks involving the written and oral serial recall of digits presented either visually or aurally. Katz and Deutsch (1964) required subjects to recall serially presented word lists and drawings of common objects, and Cohen and Netley (1981) had subjects recall digits in order. Reading-disabled subjects performed significantly poorer on these recall tasks. Hooper and Hynd (1985, 1986) had dyslexic and normal reading subjects perform two serial recall tests (Number Recall, Word Order) used on the Sequential Processing Scale of the Kaufman Assessment Battery for Children (K-ABC) (Kaufman and Kaufman, 1983). Dyslexics' performance was inferior to normals in both studies. The results of the above-mentioned studies could be interpreted as partly demonstrating the existence of a verbal deficit of some kind, and not necessarily a serial processing problem because of the use of verbal stimuli or a combination of both. The studies discussed below clear this confusion up with the employment of non-verbal stimuli.

Serial-spatial Ordering

Corkin (1974) compared normal and disabled readers on a visual serial-ordering task. Subjects had to tap a linear array of cubes in the same order as the examiner immediately following the examiner's performance and after a short delay. Disabled readers were found to be significantly inferior at this task in the delayed condition. Lindgren and Richman (1984) employed a similar procedure, having reading-disabled and normal children recall the order in which different colored chips were presented. They found that serial order errors occurred significantly more frequently for reading-disabled than normal children.

Production/Reproduction of Temporal Patterns

Atterbury (1983, 1985), Badian and Wolff (1974), Gaddes (1978), Hopper and Hynd (1985, 1986), and Wolff *et al.* (1984) employed procedures which required subjects to perform sequential behaviors. Badian and Wolff (1974) had normal and reading-disabled subjects tap a key in time with a metronome in single-hand and alternating-hand conditions. They found significant differences between normal and disabled readers when alternating hands were used to respond to the metronome. These results were replicated in a later study (Wolff *et al.*, 1984). Atterbury (1983, 1985) found reading-disabled subjects to be inferior in the ability to reproduce rhythmic auditory patterns by clapping their hands. Gaddes (1978) conducted a series of studies designed to investigate the developmental course of serial order abilities. In one study he compared normal-reading second- and fifth-grade students on a task where subjects had to reproduce visual-sequential patterns by tapping on a key which electronically converted taps into light patterns emitted from a lamp. The ability to perform on this task was found to correlate strongly with reading ability. That is, unskilled readers tended to perform more poorly on the serial-order task than skilled readers. Hooper and Hynd (1985, 1986) had dyslexic and normal reading subjects perform a motor test (Hand Movement) which is part of the Sequential Processing Scale of the K-ABC (Kaufman and Kaufman, 1983). Normal-reading subjects performed significantly better than dyslexics in both studies.

Perceptual-discrimination Studies

Many of the studies of interest employed comparative procedures where auditory patterns were compared with visual-spatial patterns (Badian, 1977; Birch and Belmont, 1964; Bryden, 1972; Gaddes, 1978; Hatchette and Evans, 1983; Richie and Aten, 1976; Vande Voort and Senf, 1973; Willette and

Early, 1985; Zurif and Carson, 1970), to auditory patterns (Badian, 1977; Bryden, 1972; Dodgen and Pavlidis, 1989; Gaddes, 1978; Hatchette and Evans, 1983; Sehy, 1984; Tallal, 1980; Vande Voort and Senf, 1973; Willette and Early, 1985; Zurif and Carson, 1970); or, visual to visual comparisons were made (Bryden, 1972; Gaddes, 1978; Hatchette and Evans, 1983; Vande Voort and Senf, 1973; Willette and Early, 1985; Zurif and Carson, 1970). The basic procedure in all of these studies is to present the first stimulus followed by the second stimulus and have the subjects decide whether the two are the same or different; or, the subject has to pick a printed pattern which corresponds to the stimulus patterns. Significant differences were found in all of these studies, with subjects with reading disabilities being consistently inferior.

Eye Movement and Sequence

There is a widespread agreement as to the existence of differences in eye movements between dyslexics and normals on reading tasks (Calvert and Cromes, 1966; Donders and Van der Vlugt, 1984; Elterman et al., 1980; Griffin et al., 1974; Heiman and Ross, 1974; Pavlidis, 1978, 1981b, 1986). In these studies dyslexics have been found to exhibit greater numbers of regressive eye movements, irregular fixations, and greater numbers of eye movements overall. Of course, because the experimental stimuli used were verbal in nature, these studies do little to help determine whether the observed differences reflect difficulties in comprehension, with sequential or oculomotor functioning.

Pavlidis (1981a,b, 1985b) performed a series of studies designed to help answer this question. He conducted three separate studies, the rationales for which were as follows. He reasoned that if dyslexics' erratic eye movements were solely a result of poor reading habits or difficulty with reading material, then: (1) normals' eye movements should become erratic when reading more difficult material; (2) dyslexics' eye movements should become normalized when reading easier text; and (3) dyslexics' eye movements should be indistinguishable from other equally poor readers who are not dyslexic. None of these hypotheses was supported, leading to the conclusion that text difficulty or poor reading habits could not account for dyslexics' erratic eye movements. Rather, brain malfunction was implicated.

Studies have been conducted which have totally removed the comprehension factor present with verbal stimuli by employing tasks with non-verbal stimuli (Adler-Grinberg and Stark, 1978; Bogacz et al., 1974; Black et al., 1984; Elterman et al., 1980; Griffin et al., 1974; Pavlidis, 1981b, 1983; Lefton et al., 1978). Lefton et al. recorded eye movements of dyslexics and normals on a match-to-sample task. On this task subjects were required to choose from one of four five-letter alternatives that matched a sample. On simpler items no differences were found. However, on items which called for sustained attention, dyslexics engaged in unsystematic search strategies, as detected by erratic eye movements. Some of these investigators employed procedures which demanded sequential eye movements similar to those needed while reading (Elterman *et al.*, 1980; Griffin *et al.*, 1974; Pavlidis, 1981b, 1983). Elterman *et al.* and Griffin *et al.* used horizontally arranged stationary stimuli and required subjects to move their eyes from point to point along the horizontal array. On these tasks dyslexics exhibited significantly greater numbers of regressions, longer fixations, and showed a tendency to skip and omit stimuli.

Pavlidis' (1981a,b, 1985b) studies have employed both stationary and moving stimuli. Subjects were required to accurately follow with their eyes a stimulus dot jumping horizontally from point to point (i.e. sequentially) across a screen. On this test dyslexics have consistently been found to exhibit significantly greater numbers of eye movements, greater numbers of regressions and fixation difficulty. Adler-Grinberg and Stark (1978), Black *et al.* (1984) and Bogacz *et al.* (1974) investigated pursuit eye movements (i.e. movements necessary to follow a continuously moving stimulus). They found that dyslexics exhibited a significantly greater number of intruding saccadic eye movements than normals on the pursuit tasks.

As previously discussed, dyslexics have been found to be deficient in sequential processing across behaviors and across procedures as well. Differences have been found with verbal tests, visual tests, tests requiring the reproduction of sequentially presented stimulus patterns and with tests requiring the judgment of similarity or dissimilarity of sequentially presented stimuli. For the long list of sequential processing studies, two variables appear to be of particular importance: the rapidity of presentation of the stimuli, and the variability of the rate of presentation. Many of the above studies presented stimuli with short, variable inter-stimulus intervals (ISIs). Therefore, it is unclear whether the difficulty for dyslexics stemmed from the rapidity or the changing nature of the stimulus pattern. Tallal (1980) and Gaddes (1978) investigated one of these factors. Tallal employed auditory stimuli and found reading-disabled subjects to perform more poorly on serially presented stimulus patterns only at fast speeds (with ISIs of approximately 100 ms or less). Similarly, Gaddes employed visual stimuli and found dyslexics to perform significantly more poorly only for those stimulus patterns presented with ISIs of 100 ms or less. There appears to be a clear trend: the faster the rate of stimulus presentation, the greater the discrimination between dyslexics and normals.

The other factor of concern is the variability of the ISIs. Tallal and Piercy (1974) found that language-delayed children were impaired in discrimination of speech sounds characterized by rapidly changing ISIs, but unimpaired in discriminating speech sounds that were steadily presented. On oculomotor (sequential performance) tasks Pavlidis (1981a,b, 1985b) has reliably discriminated between dyslexics and normals with relatively slow but variable ISIs (of 1 s and 2 s).

Dodgen and Pavlidis investigated these variables in a study in which they attempted to determine whether oculomotor sequential performance difficulties reflected general oculomotor control problems or were yet another manifestation of a general sequencing problem. They reasoned that if the dyslexics' eye movement problems were to be seen as reflecting a sequential performance deficit, and not a general oculomotor control problem, dyslexics should be inferior in temporal (left hemisphere, sequential), but not spatial (right hemisphere, holistic) accuracy when performing eye movements. In their study they also attempted to investigate the relationship between sequential eye movement difficulty and sequential difficulties as measured with more conventional manual performance procedures, and an auditory discrimination test. In order to accomplish this, Dodgen and Pavlidis required dyslexic and carefully matched normal readers to reproduce stimulus patterns of varying speeds and complexity, across two motor-effector systems (manual and oculomotor); also on the discrimination test subjects had to listen to two sets of rhythmically varied auditory patterns to decide whether the two patterns were the same or different. The study is described below.

Subjects

Dyslexics

Subjects used in this study were students at a private residential school for individuals with severe reading difficulties. Only those passing the exclusionary criteria were used in the study. The exclusionary criteria are widely used in dyslexia research and have been established in an attempt to obtain standard, homogeneous research groups (Pavlidis, 1985a). These comprehensive criteria are listed in Pavlidis (1990). Thirty-nine male dyslexic students were used in this study. Their ages ranged from 12 years and 10 months to 18 years and 1 month, with an average of 16 years and 7 months.

Normal readers

Subjects were students at a private high school. Thirty-five normals passed the criteria and were included in the study. Their ages ranged from 16 years and 4 months to 17 years and 6 months, with an average of 16 years and 10 months. The normal readers met the same criteria as the dyslexics, with the exception of the criterion concerned with reading level (Pavlidis, 1990). That is, where dyslexics were required to be at least two years behind in reading, normals were required to be reading on grade level or above.

All testing was conducted in the respective schools. Testing took place in the Spring.

Screening

The screening tests consisted of auditory and visual acuity, lateral dominance questions, a word identification reading test (Woodcock, 1973); possible attention deficit disorder was assessed by the Conners Teacher Rating Scale (Conners, 1973). For normals only a group intelligence test was used (Otis and Lennon, 1967). These tests were performed individually in regular classrooms within the schools, except for the group intelligence test, which was given to the group of normals in a regular classroom.

Test for possible inclusion in the study

Screening tests were always given first. The screening took a total of approximately 5–7 minutes per subject. For both schools, two schooldays were needed in order to screen all prospective subjects. For the normal subjects, an additional day of testing was needed in order to administer the Otis–Lennon Mental Ability Test. This test took approximately 50 minutes to administer.

Experimental Set-up

During testing, the subjects were seated at a table at right-angles to the tester. Subjects viewed visual stimuli with their heads stabilized on a chin rest. The visual stimuli were displayed on a Zenith amber monitor with an 11-inch diagonal screen, which was placed 12 inches away from the subject's forehead. The monitor rested on a portable computer in a dim-light room.

Apparatus

Eye movements were measured by the photoelectric method. Subjects were required to wear spectacle frames on which were mounted an infra-red light source and photo-cells to record from each eye. The computer continuously recorded eye movement position as a function of time with an accuracy of 1 ms, and resolution of better than 10 minutes of arc. All data collection, storing and analysis were automatically performed by computer on a system developed by Dr G. Pavlidis.

Measurement of timing ability

The timing tasks all required the subject to respond by pressing the space bar on the computer keyboard. The computer continuously recorded bar presses as a function of time.

Experimental Procedure

Those students passing the requirements of all the screening tests were given the five experimental tests. These tests were given in one sitting and took approximately 19–22 minutes from start to finish.

Stimulus parameters of tests 1–5

Test 1 (timing–location)   A small dot appeared in seven successive locations across the computer screen which the subjects were facing. The locations were 4° apart on a horizontal line. Each time, the dot appeared for one second before appearing at the next location. To the observer it appeared as though a single dot was 'jumping' from left to right across the screen. One second after reaching the rightmost location, a beep-tone sounded and the dot disappeared. At this time the subject was to look at the screen at the locations where the dot would have been if it had appeared, at the time it would have appeared at each location. In synchrony with eye movements to successive locations subjects were also required to make a bar press. The computer recorded eye location and bar presses as a function of time to perform the test, which would ideally be performed in approximately 7 seconds. The dot locations were placed 4° apart as eye movements of this size typically occur while reading (Pavlidis, 1981b) and are thought to involve only cortical control processes.

Test 2 (location)   A small dot appeared in seven successive locations across the computer screen which the subjects were facing. The locations were 4° apart on a horizontal line. Each time the dot appeared for 1.5 seconds before appearing at the next location. To the observer it appeared as though a single dot was 'jumping' from left to right across the screen. One second after reaching the rightmost location, a beep-tone sounded and the dot disappeared. At this time the subject was to look at the screen at the locations where the dot would have been had it appeared. At 1.5-second intervals a beep-tone sounded, signalling to the subject when he should move his eyes to the next location. The tone sounded seven times (one to signal the subject to move his eyes to the first location, and one more for each successive position). The computer recorded eye location which was also timed.

Test 3 (timing)   A small dot appeared near the centre of the computer screen that the subjects were facing. It remained in position for 2 seconds, then appeared 1.25° to the right of where it was located. It remained in position for 2 seconds, then moved back to the original position. This pattern repeated itself for a total of five jumps. After the fifth jump a tone sounded and the dot disappeared. At this time the subject was to press the space bar each time he thought the dot would have jumped to the other position. The computer recorded the first six bar presses as a function of time to perform the task, which ideally would have been performed in 12 seconds.

Test 4 (rhythm)   Subjects were asked to listen to a set of beep-tones produced by the computer, after which a dot appeared on the computer screen. The dot appeared 2 seconds after the last beep of the set and signalled subjects to begin pressing the space bar in order to reproduce the pattern of beep tones. There were one practice and four test sets. The sets of tones consisted of either four or five beeps separated by some combination of short (0.5-second), medium (1-second) or long (2-second) inter-stimulus intervals. For example, the practice trial consisted of four beeps separated by inter-stimulus intervals of 1 second, 1 second and 2 seconds, respectively. The sets of tones used in this test are similar to those described in Bryden (1972) and Zurif and Carson (1970). The computer recorded bar presses as a function of time for the completion of the tasks, which ideally would have been performed in approximately 6 seconds.

Test 5 (same–different)   Subjects were required to listen to two sets of beep-tones produced by the computer. Two seconds after hearing the first set of beeps the experimenter pointed to the subject to signal the beginning of the second set of beeps. Immediately after listening to both sets of beeps subjects were required to state whether the two sets of beeps were the same or different. There were one practice and five test trials. Sets of tones consisted of five or six beeps separated by some combination of medium (1-second) or very short (0.25-second) inter-stimulus intervals. Two trials had same pairs and three trials had different pairs. All pairs had the same number of beeps; pairs that differed only did so in the pattern of inter-stimulus intervals. For example, a 'different' trial had subjects compare two five-beep sets with the following patterns of inter-stimulus intervals: 0.25 second, 0.25 second, 1 second, 0.25 second; 0.25 second, 0.25 second, 0.25 second, 1 second. The experimenter recorded subjects' verbal responses of either 'same' or 'different'. The sets of tones are similar to those described by Bryden (1972) and Zurif and Carson (1970).

Quantification of Data

Experimental tests 1 (timing–location) and 2 (location)

Of interest on both tests were locational and timing-related characteristics of the eyes. The computer recorded eye location for both eyes, independently, over time. To evaluate locational accuracy the difference between where the eye was looking and position of the actual target location was determined for each of the seven locations across the screen. A subject's score on each test was the sum of the difference scores, in degrees.

To evaluate temporal accuracy the difference between when the eye moved to each successive location and when it should have moved was determined for each of the seven locations across the screen. A subject's score on each test was the sum of difference scores, in milliseconds.

Experimental tests 3 (timing) and 4 (rhythm)

Timing ability on these two tests was measured by bar-press behavior. The computer recorded when each bar press was made over time. The difference, in milliseconds, between when the bar was pressed and when it should have been pressed was computed. A subject's score on each test was the sum of difference scores.

Experimental test 5 (same–different)

The number of correct judgments was recorded for each subject. A total of five correct decisions with a low of zero was possible.

Results

Eye movement temporal–spatial accuracy

The effect of group membership (i.e. dyslexic, normal) upon temporal performance on the eye movement tests (location, timing–location) was analyzed by using a multivariate analysis of variance (MANOVA) procedure. Eye movements were recorded on both eyes for both tests. The dependent variables of interest were dominant and non-dominant eye for each test; the independent variable under investigation was group membership.

The MANOVA was not significant $F(4, 52) = 2.3$. It was determined *a priori* to test the performance of the dominant eye for each test. The data were organized in this way so as to be comparable to the manual timing performance data for which the dominant hand was used. One-way ANOVAs yielded non-significant differences between groups on timing–location, $F(1, 57) = 0.03$, and on location, $F(1, 64) = 2.75$. The means, SDs and uni-variate F statistics for each variable are presented in Table 1.

Since eye movement measurements were taken for both eyes, it was decided *a posteriori* to conduct one-way ANOVAs with the non-dominant data for both tests. In order to control the error rate for *a posteriori* tests, the Bonferroni correction method (Kirk, 1982) was employed. For each test a significance level of 0.025 was employed in order to achieve an overall significance level of 0.05. The one-way ANOVAs yielded a non-significant

Table 1. Mean scores (M), standard deviations (SD), and univariate F statistics (F) for dominant and non-dominant eye on oculomotor timing tests by group

Test	Normal M	Normal SD	Dyslexic M	Dyslexic SD	F
Dominant					
Timing–location	1.26	0.67	1.22	0.83	0.03
Location	1.65	1.03	2.06	0.91	2.75
Non-dominant					
Timing–location	1.16	0.50	1.29	0.94	0.43
Location	1.43	0.92	2.10	0.81	10.38*

*$p < 0.005$.

difference for timing–location, $F(1, 57) = 0.43$, and a significant difference for location, $F(1, 65) = 10.38$, $p < 0.005$. Dyslexics were inferior to normals. Since a significant difference was found between groups for non-dominant eye data but not dominant eye data, a multivariate profile analysis (MPA) was performed in order to test for differences between dominant and non-dominant eyes. The MPA was not significant $F(1, 55) = 0.52$, and neither was the interaction term $F(1, 55) = 2.7$. Improper calibration resulted in the loss of a few records.

Spatial accuracy

The effect of group membership on locational accuracy was analyzed by using a MANOVA procedure. The four dependent variables of interest were dominant and non-dominant eye for both tests; the independent variable of interest was group membership. The MANOVA was not significant $F(4, 32) = 0.97$. It was determined *a priori* to test the dominant eye for each test. One-way ANOVAs for location, $F(1, 54) = 0.00$, and timing–location, $F(1, 47) = 0.19$, were not significant. Since the number of lost records was smaller for the non-dominant eye it was decided to use the data from the non-dominant eye. One-way ANOVAs for location, $F(1, 61) = 2.35$, and timing–location, $F(1, 52) = 0.04$, were not significant (Table 2), indicating no difference in locational accuracy between groups.

Timing

Dyslexics performed significantly worse than normal subjects on the tests which measure timing ability, three of which involve manual performance, and the fourth of which involves only perception. The effect of group

Table 2. Mean scores (M), standard deviations (SD), and univariate F statistics (F) for dominant and non-dominant eye on oculomotor location tests by group

Test	Normal		Dyslexic		
	M	SD	M	SD	F
Dominant					
Timing–location	13.72	8.59	12.68	8.35	0.19
Location	11.19	7.00	11.09	7.41	0.00
Non-dominant					
Timing–location	13.04	6.99	13.55	9.39	0.04
Location	9.37	5.77	11.74	6.47	2.35

membership upon performance on the independent timing tests was analyzed by using one-way ANOVA procedures. Dyslexics were significantly inferior to normals on the test requiring the perception (same–different), $F(1, 70) = 4.9$, $p < 0.05$, and manual reproduction (rhythm) of rhythmic stimulus patterns, $F(1, 66) = 9.9$, $p < 0.01$. There were no group differences on the test requiring the manual reproduction of a relatively slow constant stimulus pattern (timing), $F(1, 62) = 1.1$. On the test requiring the manual reproduction of a relatively fast constant stimulus pattern (timing–location) dyslexics performed worse than normals, $F(1, 65) = 2.8$, although this difference was not significant. Dyslexics were on average inferior on all timing-related tests, although the differences between groups only reached statistical significance for the tests with rapid, changing (i.e. rhythmic, non-constant) stimulus patterns (rhythm, same–different) (Table 3).

Table 3. Mean scores (M), standard deviations (SD), and univariate F statistics (F) on timing tests by group

Test	Normal		Dyslexic		
	M	SD	M	SD	F
Rhythm	4.57	1.84	5.97	1.81	9.9 **
Same–different	4.71	0.67	4.35	0.72	4.9 *
Timing–location	0.73	0.61	1.11	1.14	2.8
Timing	1.28	0.75	1.50	0.95	1.1

$^*p < 0.05.$
$^{**}p < 0.01.$

Timing of eye movements

Dyslexics performed worse than normal readers with respect to the temporal characteristics of the eye movement tests. An *a priori* ANOVA procedure, although not significant at conventional cut-off levels, yielded results in the predicted direction for location. On location the difference between groups approached significance with the dominant eye as the dependent variable. While no firm conclusions can be drawn on the basis of a non-significant trend in the data, it should be considered that a significant group difference was found when the non-dominant eye was used as the dependent variable. The organization of the eye movement data into dominant and non-dominant categories was done so as to be able to compare the oculomotor performance data to the manual performance data which was collected on the dominant hand. Aside from the implication that the eyes do not move in perfect synchrony, the significant difference found when non-dominant eyes were compared indicates that dyslexics had more difficulty than normals with the temporal characteristics of this test. Because a signal was used to tell subjects when to move their eyes, the memory factor was eliminated.

Spatial accuracy of eye movements

With respect to the spatial/locational aspects of the eye movement tests the performance of dyslexics was similar to (not significantly different from) the performance of the normal subjects. That is, dyslexics were no less accurate than normals in visually locating points on the computer screen. Even though a group difference was noted in terms of timing accuracy of eye movements, this did not affect accuracy of location. Basic oculomotor control and good spatial judgment are requisite skills for such an achievement.

Timing

Dyslexics' performance was compared with that of normal readers on the tests which measure timing ability, three of which involve manual performance, and the fourth of which involves only perception. The tests involving stimuli with relatively slow, steady rates of presentation yielded virtually no group differences (timing) or larger differences which did not reach significance (timing–location). The tests with non-constant, more rapid rates of presentation (rhythm, same–different) yielded significant group differences, with dyslexics performing at an inferior level. It appears by the pattern of results that the quicker rate of presentation is more difficult than the slower, and quick and variable stimuli are most difficult for the dyslexic.

Relationship of Sequential Processing to Reading

Given that a basic sequential deficit exists in the ability to process rapid and/or changing stimuli, how does this relate to reading and reading disability? Several authors have noted the association between temporal processing difficulties and reading disability (Aaron, 1982; Bakker, 1972, 1981; Das *et al.*, 1979; Gaddes and Spellacy, 1977; Tallal, 1980). Visual-sequential task performance has been found to correlate with academic ability (reading, writing, and arithmetic) (Gaddes and Spellacy, 1977), as has verbal-sequential task performance (Bakker, 1972; Gaddes and Spellacy, 1977). Tallal (1980) found the ability to process rapidly presented non-verbal auditory stimuli to correlate strongly with reading ability. Jost (1988), using two subtests of the Pavlidis test, which have a strong sequential component, could predict future academic problems with the remarkable accuracy of 91.5%.

Theoretical explanations exist which attempt to explain the association between temporal processing and reading abilities (Ojemann, 1983; Pavlidis, 1981b, and this volume; Tallal, 1983; Vernon, 1977). Vernon describes four basic processes which she feels underlie reading deficiencies: (1) inability to analyze complex sequential visual and/or auditory–linguistic structures; (2) difficulty in the linking of visual and auditory–linguistic structures; (3) inability to establish regularities in variable grapheme–phoneme correspondences; and (4) difficulty grouping words into meaningful phrases. The first two, and most basic, processes appear strongly based on temporal processing abilities (Pavlidis, 1985a). Ojemann (1983) has concluded from his brain stimulation studies, and Tallal (1983) has confirmed with neuropsychological studies, that language skills are intimately related to sequencing skills. Ojemann (1983) speculates that this relationship between sequencing and language skills may be due to a more basic mechanism of the cortex of the left hemisphere, precise timing, which underlies both processes. Ojemann (in Tallal, 1983) has offered a developmental explanation for the proximity of brain sites as well as the functional relationship between language and sequencing skills: 'during the course of human development, the initial role of this common cortex for language production and understanding may be in the decoding of sounds during language acquisition, identifying those significant to speech. The same cortical area later develops the patterns of motor output to generate these significant sounds' (p. 219). On a performance level, Pavlidis (1986) noted that the eyes must move in rapid sequence in order to pick up the visual information necessary to read efficiently. Therefore, a problem exists in obtaining and in processing the information. The importance of the oculomotor demands in reading were recently demonstrated (Pavlidis, 1987). A procedure was used whereby text was flashed on a computer screen on the same spot, one word at a time in sequence. This procedure eliminated or greatly reduced the need for eye movements. On this task dyslexics read at a much higher rate than usual, while maintaining an almost 90% comprehension.

The Brain and Dyslexia

What is needed to support the empirical evidence for the existence of a deficiency in temporal processing is evidence that shows that dyslexics are impaired in left-hemisphere functioning (the side of the brain considered to be more efficient, and preferred in processing time-related information). Ample research exists which places fine temporal discrimination within the domain of the left hemisphere. Hammond (1982) reviewed studies conducted on brain-injured as well as normal subjects from which he concluded that the language-dominant hemisphere shows finer acuity (greater temporal resolution). Gaddes' (1985) review yielded a similar conclusion. Gaddes speculates that the left hemisphere may be language-dominant because of its superiority in processing serially presented information.

Neuropsychological studies designed to tap the functioning of the cerebral hemispheres have revealed differences in functioning between dyslexics and normals. For example, contrary to normals, dyslexics do not show the usual right visual half-field (Marcel *et al.*, 1974), ear (Sommers and Taylor, 1972) or hand (Witelson, 1976) advantage with verbal material. The results of these studies seem to indicate the disruption of left hemisphere functioning due to bilateral representation of spatial functions which are normally confined to the right hemisphere (Witelson, 1977). Also, dyslexics have been shown to exhibit superior visual-spatial scores (and inferior verbal-sequential scores) on standardized intelligence scales (Badian and Wolff, 1974; Bannatyne, 1971). Similarly, Dodgen and Pavlidis (1989) found temporal performance difficulties but unimpaired spatial performance for dyslexics when compared to normal readers on oculomotor tasks. Spatial accuracy would be in the domain of right-hemisphere functioning for most subjects (Davis and Wada, 1977; Gazzaniga, 1970; Sperry, 1968; Springer and Deutsch, 1981). The pattern of results obtained by Dodgen and Pavlidis (1989) resemble those obtained in brain-injury studies (Bakker and Licht, 1986) and brain stimulation studies (Ojemann, 1983). Bakker and Licht cite the fact that right-hemiplegics are accurate and slow in reading, while left-hemiplegics are fast and inaccurate (skipping letters and whole words). In other words, with the left hemisphere intact, time-related performance is not affected, but spatial-locational performance is affected. The reverse is true when the right hemisphere is intact and the left hemisphere is disabled. Ojemann (1983) has demonstrated that electrical stimulation of the brain can be used to selectively disrupt functioning for a given area of the brain, acting as a temporary lesion. Through this stimulation-mapping procedure Ojemann (1983) has shown that the brain is organized for language in discretely localized areas within the cortex. Stimulation of cortical areas of the left hemisphere selectively disrupts language functions, while stimulation of right hemisphere cortical areas selectively disrupts spatial functions. Within the left hemisphere adjacent areas are related but appear to be specialized in specific language functions (e.g. naming, short-term verbal memory, sequencing). One area of particular relevance for the present discussion, the peri-Sylvian area of the left hemisphere, shows selective disruption of the ability to make orofacial gestures in sequence when electrically stimulated, demonstrating anatomical and functional links between non-verbal sequencing and language functioning.

It has been claimed by some researchers (Dodgen and Pavlidis, 1989; Pavlidis, 1986) that the timing difficulty of dyslexics obtained by eye movement measurement reflects difficulty at the level of the left hemisphere. This has not simply been assumed. Evidence for this claim comes from brain stimulation and brain-injury research. While many areas of the brain are involved with the control of eye movements, there are certain oculomotor difficulties which result from disturbances in certain levels of the system. Studies show that amongst others three areas are mainly involved in the control of horizontal eye movements: the frontal lobes, the cerebellum and the parapontine reticular formation (Fox et al., 1985; Henriksson et al., 1984; Shakhnovich, 1977). Dysfunctional brain stem activity results in decreased velocity of saccades, whereas cerebellar disturbances result in gaze nystagmus, saccadic and pursuit abnormalities (Henriksson et al., 1984; Leigh and Zee, 1983). Frontal lobe disease or injury results in disruption of the initiation of saccades. In eye movement studies of dyslexia the presence of nystagmus is reason for exclusion from the study. Also, abnormal performance characteristics such as reduced velocity of saccades are not reported (Adler-Grinberg and Stark, 1978; Leisman et al., 1978; Leisman and Schwartz, 1978). Rather, what are usually found are differences in the number of movements, both forward and backward (Elterman et al., 1980; Griffin et al., 1974; Pavlidis, 1981, 1985). The differences reported in the research more closely resemble those characteristic of disturbance at the level of the frontal lobes rather than at lower brain centers. For example, a study by Pykko et al. (1984) comparing subjects with left frontal lobe lesions and normals found that brain-damaged subjects had differently performing saccades on time command. This finding is similar to the results obtained by Dodgen and Pavlidis (1987) where subjects were required to move their eyes when a tone was sounded.

Diagnostic Implications

The typical diagnostic course is a multi-level process which usually begins with an informal observation made by the classroom teacher. Once a child is designated as being a poor reader, a more formal assessment process is set into motion. Formal assessment usually involves various standardized reading tests, physical assessment and comparison of IQ to reading level (Bond *et al.*, 1979). Such an assessment necessitates multi-disciplinary involvement and, more importantly, time. As Hawkins (1985) notes, often children are not referred for help until the end of the primary grades because there is a reluctance to label children and a hope that the children are going through a passing phase. Therefore there is a tendency to under-identify potential dyslexic readers.

The unfortunate implications of the above typical scenario are highlighted by results reported by Strag (1972) and Muehl and Forell (1973). Strag (1972) reported that the percentage of poor-reading children reaching normal reading levels dropped dramatically the later the diagnosis was made. For example, when the diagnosis was made by grade 2, 82% of the children were brought up to normal classroom work. This percentage is to be compared to only 46% of those identified by the third grade. Similarly, Muehl and Forell (1973) found that early diagnosis, regardless of the amount of subsequent remediation, was associated with better reading performance at a five-year follow-up.

What is needed is the early application of short, easy-to-administer, objective and accurate diagnostic tools. To the extent that temporal/successive processing ability is thought to be involved with reading at all stages, tests which measure this ability may be useful in the early objective diagnosis of dyslexia. For example, Jost (1988) conducted a study in which eye movement performance on the Pavlidis test given during the first semester of schooling was used to predict academic ability in the second and third grades. Using the Pavlidis eye movement test, Jost was able to correctly predict with an accuracy of 91.51% which of his 6-year-olds would develop academic problems by the end of the second grade. Jost also noted that eye movement efficiency was more highly correlated with reading ability than the more conventional measures of socio-economic status and (Wechsler) IQ. The youngest age at which the group differences can be reliably measured needs to be further investigated. Jost's (1988) study is a good starting point but its applicability for early diagnosis needs to be replicated and expanded.

Remedial Implications

Many remedial approaches are discussed in the literature. Zigmond (1978) classified them into three categories: those which focus on requisite skills; blanket approaches applied to all dyslexics; and those identifying strengths and weaknesses and matching the appropriate treatment. Those in the first category (e.g. Frostig and Horne, 1964) typically involve visual and motor perceptual training. Those in the second category (e.g. Orton–Gillingham approach) usually involve sensory training, multi-sensory training and phonics instruction. Those in Zigmond's third category work on the assumption that a match can be made between deficiencies of a given child and a given type of instruction (e.g. Naidoo, 1981).

Remedial efforts with dyslexics have yielded equivocal results at best. Spache (1981) reviewed over 30 remedial studies and concluded that 'remedial treatment apparently does not affect school progress appreciably over time' (p. 397). He noted that most studies found significant gains during the treatment period which were dissipated over time. This observation suggests that the obtained skills were not generalizable and reading did not advance any further once the programs stopped. However, Dumont (1990) reaches a different conclusion, claiming that remediation of dyslexia can be successful.

Given that temporal processing difficulties have been shown to reliably discriminate dyslexics from normals, some remedial implications follow. From the literature review two areas of difficulty have been identified: in the picking up of the written information (due to the oculomotor-attentional problem) and in the processing of serially presented information (left-hemisphere processing). Interventions have been proposed to increase dyslexics' abilities to employ successive (left-hemisphere) processing strategies. For example, Gunnison et al. (1982) have suggested exercises which involve the rehearsal of strategies designed to improve successive processing abilities. McCarthy (1985) has proposed a novel approach which involves employment of time-based components of music (i.e. rhythm). For example, he suggests that reading words to music may be helpful to dyslexics.

Another approach involves the stabilization of the eyes or removing the need to move the eyes during reading. Larger-scale, well-controlled studies need to be conducted before firm conclusions can be drawn, although the Pavlidis (1987) results are encouraging.

Pavlidis (1987) eliminated the need for eye movements during reading. He presented words on a computer screen, one after another, at the same central spot. Dyslexics were able to read at a much faster rate than normally, while retaining near 90% comprehension. This method produced very promising results and deserves further investigation.

Direct implications for remedial training

Whatever the source of the dyslexics' erratic eye movements, they disturb the reading process. If eye movements are found to be temporally or spatially inaccurate, or both, this will provide appropriate information for specific remediation. The more clearly eye movement characteristics are understood, the clearer are the remedial implications. Procedures to train the eyes in timed movement or accurate distance estimation could be implemented as needed. However, the effectiveness of such training will depend on whether any gains in eye movement efficiency transfer to reading performance as well.

Several studies have actually applied successive processing strategies discussed above (Kaufman and Kaufman, 1979; Kirby and Robinson, 1987; Klein and Schwartz, 1979). All three studies reported academic improvement which was particularly encouraging because the subjects were not specifically trained in reading. Therefore the potential to generalize and apply these skills after the training period is increased. This is important, as the previously noted review by Spache (1981) revealed that progress in reading usually dissipated after treatment stopped. Of course, long-term, well-designed studies are needed to substantiate empirically the long-range effectiveness of this type of training.

CONCLUSIONS

(1) The manifestation of temporal/serial order difficulties across procedures and modalities in the research literature strongly implies central nervous system (i.e. brain) dysfunction. The finding of oculomotor difficulty in timing, but not locational accuracy (Dodgen and Pavlidis, 1987), is in agreement with other neuropsychological studies implicating left-hemisphere dysfunction (Marcel *et al.*, 1974; Sommers and Taylor, 1972; Witelson, 1976). Brain stimulation (Calvin and Ojemann, 1980; Ojemann and Mateer, 1979) and cytoarchitectonic analysis of the brain of the dyslexic (Galaburda and Kemper, 1979) also locate dysfunction in the left hemisphere. Temporal order processing difficulties appear to be related to verbal and non-verbal difficulties of the dyslexic due to the proximity of location of brain areas responsible for these respective processes (Ojemann, 1983; Pavlidis, 1986, and Chapter 10, this volume).

(2) Oculomotor measurement appears to be more sensitive than manual performance methods in detecting differences in time-related behavior.

(3) Eye movement analysis holds promise for the early objective diagnosis of dyslexia.

(4) Deficiencies of the dyslexic can be remediated in a number of ways, some of which are currently being applied. Reduction of the need for reading eye movements (Pavlidis, 1987) and training in successive processing strategies (Kaufman and Kaufman, 1979; Kirby and Robinson, 1987; Klein and Schwartz, 1979) have yielded encouraging results.

In order to achieve maximum discrimination between dyslexic and non-dyslexic readers (for maximum diagnostic accuracy) certain parameters need to be more systematically investigated. The rate of stimulus presentation which yields maximum discrimination needs to be found, as well as the optimal variability of the inter-stimulus intervals. The modality of presentation (i.e. visual, auditory) which best exploits timing differences, as well as the most sensitive measurement procedure, need to be further explored. In order to achieve the important goal of early diagnosis, studies should be conducted with younger children. The predictive value of these tests can then be tested empirically.

The investigation of intervention strategies should be undertaken in long-term studies. While a few studies have reported positive results (Dumont, 1990; Kaufman and Kaufman, 1979; Kirby and Robinson, 1987; Klein and Schwartz, 1979; Pavlidis, 1987; Punnett and Steinhaur, 1984; Solan, 1985), the meaningfulness of these results can only be evaluated in terms of their long-range effectiveness.

Computerized, automatically analysed eye movements will play a vital role both for the early diagnosis/prognosis of dyslexia and also in the initiation and objective evaluation of various methods of treatment.

REFERENCES

Aaron, P. G. (1982). The neuropsychology of developmental dyslexia. In R. N. Malatesha and P. G. Aaron (eds), *Reading Disorders: Varieties and Treatments*. New York: Academic Press.

Adler-Grinberg, D., and Stark, L. (1978). Eye movements, scanpaths, and dyslexia. *American Journal of Optometry and Physiological Optics*, **55**, 557–570.

Ammett, M. (1976). Handedness and the cerebral representation of speech. *Annals of Human Biology*, **3**, 317–328.

Ammett, M. (1981). The right shift theory of handedness and developmental language problems. *Bulletin of the Orton Society*, **31**, 103–121.

Ammett, M., and Kilshaw, D. (1984). Lateral preference and skill in dyslexics: Implications of the right shift theory. *Journal of Child Psychology and Psychiatry*, **25**, 357–377.

Andersen, S. W., Podwall, F. N., and Jaffe, J. (1987). Timing analysis of coding and articulation processes in dyslexia. *Annals of the New York Academy of Sciences*, **433**, 71–86.

Atterbury, B. W. (1983). A comparison of rhythm pattern perception and performance in normal and learning disabled readers, age seven and eight. *Journal of Research in Music Education*, **31**, 259–270.

Atterbury, B. W. (1985). Musical differences in learning-disabled and normal-achieving readers, aged seven, eight, and nine. *Psychology of Music*, **13**, 114–123.

Badian, N. A. (1977). Auditory–visual integration, auditory memory, and reading in retarded and adequate readers. *Journal of Learning Disabilities*, **10**, 49–55.

Badian, N. A., and Wolff, P. H. (1974). Manual asymmetries of motor sequencing in boys with reading disability. *Cortex*, **13**, 343–349.

Bakker, D. J. (1972). *Temporal Order in Disturbed Reading*. Rotterdam: Rotterdam University Press.

Bakker, D. J. (1979). Hemispheric differences and reading strategies: two dyslexias? *Bulletin of the Orton Society*, **29**, 84–100.

Bakker, D. J., and Licht, R. (1986). Learning to read: Changing horses in mid-stream. In G. Th. Pavlidis and D. F. Fisher (eds), *Dyslexia: Its Neuropsychology and Treatment*. New York: Wiley.

Bakker, D. J. (1990). Alleviation of dyslexia by stimulation of the brain. In G. Th. Pavlidis (ed.), *Perspectives on Dyslexia, Volume 2, Cognition, Language and Treatment*. Chichester: Wiley.

Bannatyne, A. (1971). *Language, Reading, and Learning Disabilities*. Springfield, IL: Thomas.

Beery, J. W. (1967). Matching of auditory and visual stimuli by average and retarded readers. *Child Development*, **38**, 827–833.

Belmont, L., and Birch, H. G. (1965). Lateral dominance, lateral awareness, and reading disability. *Child Development*, **36**, 57–71.

Bender, L. (1958). Problems in conceptualization and communication in children with developmental alexia. In P. H. Hoch and J. Zubin (eds), *Psychopathology of Communication*. New York: Grune & Stratton.

Benton, A. L. (1962). Dyslexia in relation to form perception and directional sense. In J. Money (ed.), *Reading Disability: Progress and Research Needs in Dyslexia*. Baltimore: Johns Hopkins Press.

Benton, A. L. (1980). Dyslexia: evolution of a concept. *Bulletin of the Orton Society*, **30**, 10–26.

Bertelson, P. (1982). Lateral differences in normal man and lateralization of brain function. *International Journal of Psychology*, **7**, 173–210.

Birch, H. G., and Belmont, L. (1964). Auditory–visual integration in normal and retarded readers. *American Journal of Orthopsychiatry*, **34**, 852–861.

Black, J. L., Collins, W. K., DeRoach, J. N., and Zubrich, S. R. (1984). Dyslexia: Saccadic eye movements. *Perceptual and Motor Skills*, **58**, 903–910.

Bogacz, J., Mendilaharsu, C., and Mendilaharsu, S. A. (1974). Electro-oculographic abnormalities during pursuit movements in developmental dyslexia. *Electroencephalography and Clinical Neurophysiology*, **36**, 651–656.

Bond, G. L., Tinker, M. A., and Wasson, B. B. (1979). *Reading Difficulties: Their Diagnosis and Correction* (4th edn). Englewood Cliffs: Prentice Hall.

Brenner, M. W., and Gillman, S. (1966). Visuomotor ability in school children: A survey. *Developmental Medicine and Child Neurology*, **8**, 686–703.

Brenner, M. W., Gillman, S., Farrell, M., and Zangwill, O. L. (1967). Visual-motor disability in school children. *British Medical Journal*, **4**, 259–262.

Bryden, M. P. (1970). Laterality effects in dichotic listening: Relations with handedness and reading ability in children. *Neuropsychologia*, **8**, 443–450.

Bryden, M. P. (1972). Auditory–visual and sequential–spatial matching in relation to reading ability. *Child Development*, **43**, 824–832.

Calvert, J. J., and Cromes, G. F. (1966). Oculomotor spasms in handicapped readers. *The Reading Teacher*, **20**, 231–237.

Calvin, H., and Ojemann, G. A. (1980). *Inside the Brain*. New York: Mentor.

Clark, M. M. (1970). *Reading Difficulties in Schools*. Harmondsworth: Penguin.

Cohen, R. L., and Netley, C. (1981). Short-term memory deficits in reading disabled children in the absence of opportunity for rehearsal strategies. *Intelligence*, **5**, 69–76.

Conners, C. K. (1973). Rating scales for use in drug studies with children. *Psychopharmacological Bulletin* (Special Issue), 24–29.

Cooper, J., and Griffith, P. (1978). Treatment and prognosis. In M. Wyke (ed.), *Developmental Dysphasia*. New York: Academic Press.

Corkin, S. (1974). Serial-ordering deficits in inferior readers. *Neuropsychologia*, **12**, 347–354.

Critchley, M. (1964). *Developmental Dyslexia*. London: Heinemann.
Critchley, M. (1973). Some problems of the ex-dyslexic. *Bulletin of the Orton Society*, **23**, 7–14.
Das, J. P., Kirby, J. R., and Jarman, R. F. (1979). *Simultaneous and Successive Cognitive Processes*. New York: Academic Press.
Davis, A. E., and Wada, J. A. (1977). Hemispheric asymmetries in human infants: Spectral analysis of flash and click evoked potentials. *Brain and Language*, **4**, 23–31.
Dearborn, W. F. (1931). Ocular and manual dominance in dyslexia. *Psychological Bulletin*, **28**, 704.
Dearborn, W. F. (1933). Structural factors which condition special disability in reading. *Proceedings of the American Association on Mental Deficiency*, **38**, 266–283.
Denckla, M. B., and Rudel, R. G. (1976). Rapid automatized naming (R.A.N.): Dyslexia differentiated from other learning disabilities. *Neuropsychologia*, **14**, 471–479.
Dodgen, C. E., and Pavlidis, G. Th. (1989). A neuropsychological investigation of temporal and spatial processing abilities of dyslexic and normal reading high school males (manuscript in preparation).
Donders, J., and Van der Vlugt, H. (1984). Eye-movement patterns in disabled readers at two age levels: A test of Bakker's balance model. *Journal of Neuropsychology*, **6**, 241–256.
Downing, J., and Leong, C. K. (1982). *Psychology of Reading*. New York: Macmillan.
Dumont, J. J. (1990). Effectiveness of dyslexia treatment. In G. Th. Pavlidis (ed.), *Perspectives on Dyslexia, Volume 2, Cognition, Language and Treatment*. Chichester: Wiley.
Elterman, R. D., Abel, L. A., Daroff, R. B., Dell'Osso, L. F., and Bornstein, J. L. (1980). Eye movement patterns in dyslexic children. *Journal of Learning Disabilities*, **13**, 16–21.
Fildes, L. G. (1922). A psychological inquiry into the nature of the condition known as congenital word-blindness. *Brain*, **4**, 286–307.
Fox, P. J., Fox, J. M., Raichle, M. E., and Burde, R. M. (1985). An investigation of voluntary saccades: A positron emission tomographic study. *Journal of Neurophysiology*, **54**, 348–364.
Frostig, M., and Horne, D. (1964). *The Frostig Program for the Development of Visual Perception*. Chicago: Follett.
Gaddes, W. H. (1978). *A Review of Some Research in the Area of Serial Order Behavior*. Amsterdam: International Academy For Research in Learning Disabilities.
Gaddes, W. H. (1985). *Learning Disabilities and Brain Function: A Neuropsychological Approach* (2nd edn). New York: Springer-Verlag.
Gaddes, W. H., and Spellacy, F. J. (1977). *Serial order perceptual and motor performances in children and their relation to academic achievement*. Research Monograph no. 35. Victoria, BC, Canada: Department of Psychology, University of Victoria.
Gaddes, W. H., and Zaidel, E. (1978). An examination of visual temporal sequential perception in two commissurotomy patients. Unpublished.
Galaburda, A. M., and Kemper, T. L. (1979). Cytoarchitectonic abnormalities in developmental dyslexia: A case study. *Annals of Neurology*, **6**, 94–100.
Gazzaniga, M. S. (1970). *The Bisected Brain*. New York: Appleton-Century-Crofts.

Geschwind, N. (1984). The biology of cerebral dominance: Implications for cognition. *Cognition*, **17**, 193–208.

Gesell, A. (1945). *The Embryology of Behavior*. New York: Harper & Row.

Griffin, H. C., Walton, H. N., and Ives, V. (1974). Saccades as related to reading disorders. *Journal of Learning Disabilities*, **7**, 310–316.

Gunnison, J., Kaufman, N. L., and Kaufman, A. S. (1982). Reading remediation based on sequential and simultaneous processing. *Academic Therapy*, **17**, 297–307.

Hammond, G. R. (1982). Hemispheric differences in temporal resolution. *Brain and Cognition*, **1**, 95–118.

Harris, A. J. (1982). How many kinds of reading disability are there? *Journal of Learning Disabilities*, **15**, 456–460.

Hatchette, R. K., and Evans, J. R. (1983). Auditory–visual and temporal–spatial pattern matching performance of two types of learning-disabled children. *Journal of Learning Disabilities*, **16**, 537–541.

Hawkins, S. (1985). Early intervention in preventing reading problems. *Academic Therapy*, **21**, 193–197.

Heiman, J. R., and Ross, A. O. (1974). Saccadic eye movements and reading difficulties. *Journal of Abnormal Child Psychology*, **2**, 53–61.

Henriksson, N. G., Pyykko, I., Schalen, L., Magmusson, M., and Wennmo, C. (1984). Interpreting eye-movements: An eye motor model. *Acta Otolaryngologica*, **412**, 55–57.

Hincks, E. M. (1926). Disability in reading and its relation to personality. *Harvard Monographs in Education*, No. 7.

Hooper, S. R., and Hynd, G. W. (1985). Differential diagnosis of subtypes of developmental dyslexia with the Kaufman Assessment Battery for Children (K-ABC). *Journal of Clinical Child Psychology*, **14**, 145–152.

Hooper, S. R., and Hynd, G. W. (1986). Performance of normal and dyslexic readers on the Kaufman Assessment Battery for Children (K-ABC): A discriminant analysis. *Journal of Learning Disabilities*, **19**, 206–210.

Horn, W., O'Donnell, J., and Vitulano, L. (1983). Long-term follow-up studies of learning-disabled persons. *Journal of Learning Disabilities*, **14**, 542–553.

Hynd, G. W., and Hynd, C. R. (1984). Dyslexia: Neuroanatomical/neurolinguistic perspectives. *Reading Research Quarterly*, **19**, 483–498.

Ilg, F. L., and Ames, L. B. (1964). *School Readiness: Behavior Tests Used at the Gesell Institute*. New York: Harper & Row.

Johnson, D. (1980). Persistent auditory disorders in young dyslexic adults. *Bulletin of the Orton Society*, **30**, 268–276.

Johnson, D. J., and Blalock, J. W. (eds). (1987). *Adults with Learning Disabilities*. New York: Grune & Stratton.

Jost, J. (1988). *Eye Movements and Learning Disabilities: A Timely Diagnosis*. Submitted for publication to the Monograph Series of the International Academy for Research in Learning Disabilities.

Katz, A. P., and Deutsch, M. (1964). Modality of stimulus presentation in serial learning for retarded and normal readers. *Perceptual and Motor Skills*, **19**, 627–633.

Kaufman, A. S., and Kaufman, N. L. (1983). *K-ABC Interpretive Manual*. Circle Pines, MN: American Guidance Service.

Kaufman, D., and Kaufman, P. (1979). Strategy training and remedial techniques. *Journal of Learning Disabilities*, **12**, 63–66.

Kershner, J. R. (1975). Reading and laterality revisited. *Journal of Special Education*, **9**, 269–279.

Kershner, J. R. (1977). Cerebral dominance in disabled readers, good readers, and gifted children: Search for a valid model. *Child Development*, **48**, 61–67.

Kimura, D. (1961a). Some effects of temporal-lobe damage on auditory perception. *Canadian Journal of Psychology*, **15**, 156–165.

Kimura, D. (1961b). Cerebral dominance and the perception of verbal stimuli. *Canadian Journal of Psychology*, **15**, 166–171.

Kimura, D. (1964). Left–right differences in the perception of melodies. *Quarterly Journal of Experimental Psychology*, **16**, 355–358.

Kimura, D. (1967). Functional asymmetry of the brain in dichotic listening. *Cortex*, **3**, 163–178.

Kinsbourne, M. (1990). Cognitive deficits concomitant with adult dyslexia. In G. Th. Pavlidis (ed.), *Perspectives on Dyslexia, Volume 2, Cognition, Language and Treatment*. Chichester: Wiley.

Kirby, J. R., and Robinson, G. L. W. (1987). Simultaneous and successive processing in reading disabled children. *Journal of Learning Disabilities*, **20**, 243–251.

Kirk, R. E. (1982). *Experimental Design* (2nd edn). Monterey: Brooks/Cole Publishing Co.

Klein, P. S., and Schwartz, A. A. (1979). Effects of training auditory sequential memory and attention on reading. *Journal of Special Education*, **13**, 365–374.

Kline, C., and Kline, C. (1975). Follow-up study of 216 children. *Bulletin of the Orton Society*, **25**, 127–144.

Koppitz, E. M. (1973). Visual–aural digit span test performance of boys with emotional and learning problems. *Journal of Clinical Psychology*, **29**, 463–466.

Lefton, L. A., Lahey, B. B., and Stagg, D. I. (1978). Eye movements in reading disabled and normal children: A study of systems and strategies. *Journal of Learning Disabilities*, **11**, 22–31.

Leigh, R. J. and Zee, D. S. (1983). *The Neurology of Eye Movements*. Philadelphia: F. A. Davis Co.

Leisman, G., and Schwartz, J. (1978). Aetiological factors in dyslexia: I. Saccadic eye movement control. *Perceptual and Motor Skills*, **47**, 403–407.

Leisman, G., Ashkenazi, M., Sprung, L., and Schwartz, J. (1978). Aetiological factors in dyslexia: II. Ocular–motor programming. *Perceptual and Motor Skills*, **47**, 667–672.

Lindgren, S. D., and Richman, L. C. (1984). Immediate memory functions of verbally deficient reading-disabled children. *Journal of Learning Disabilities*, **17**, 222–225.

McCarthy, W. G. (1985). Promoting language development through music. *Academic Therapy*, **21**, 131–139.

Marcel, T., Katz, S., and Smith, M. (1974). Laterality and reading proficiency. *Neuropsychologia*, **12**, 131–139.

Monroe, M. (1932). *Children Who Cannot Read*. Chicago: University of Chicago Press.

Muehl, S., and Forell, E. R. (1973). A follow-up study of disabled readers: Variables related to high school reading performance. *Reading Research Quarterly*, **9**, 110–123.

Muehl, S., and Kremenak, S. (1966). Ability to match information within and between auditory and visual sense modalities and subsequent reading achievement. *Journal of Educational Psychology*, **57**, 230–239.

Naidoo, S. (1981). Teaching methods and their rationale. In G. Th. Pavlidis and T. R. Miles (eds), *Dyslexia Research and its Applications to Education*. Chichester: Wiley.

Naylor, C. C., Felton, R. H., and Wood, F. B. (1990). Adult outcome in developmental dyslexia. In G. Th. Pavlidis (ed.), *Perspectives on Dyslexia, Volume 2, Cognition, Language and Treatment*. Chichester: Wiley.

Nielsen, H. H., and Ringe, K. (1969). Visuo-perceptive and visuo-motor performance of children with reading disability. *Scandinavian Journal of Psychology*, **10**, 225–231.

Ojemann, G. (1983). Brain organization for language from the perspective of electrical stimulation mapping. *Behavioral and Brain Sciences*, **6**, 189–230.

Ojemann, G., and Mateer, K. (1979). Human language cortex: Localization of memory, syntax, and sequential motor-phoneme identification systems. *Science*, **205**, 1401–1403.

Orton, S. T. (1925). Word blindness in school children. *Archives of Neurology and Psychiatry*, **14**, 581–615.

Orton, S. T. (1937). *Reading, Writing, and Speech Problems in Children*. New York: Norton.

Otis, A. S., and Lennon, R. T. (1967). *Otis–Lennon Mental Ability Test*. New York: Harcourt, Brace, & World, Inc.

Pavlidis, G. Th. (1978). The dyslexic's erratic eye movements: Case studies. *Dyslexic Review*, **1**, 22–28.

Pavlidis, G. Th. (1981a). Do eye movements hold the key to dyslexia? *Neuropsychologia*, **19**, 57–64.

Pavlidis, G. Th. (1981b). Sequencing, eye movements and the early objective diagnosis of dyslexia. In G. Th. Pavlidis and T. R. Miles (eds), *Dyslexia Research and its Application to Education*. Chichester: Wiley.

Pavlidis, G. Th. (1983). Erratic sequential eye movements in dyslexics: Comments and reply to Stanley *et al. British Journal of Psychology*, **74**, 189–193.

Pavlidis, G. Th. (1985a). Eye movements in dyslexics: Their diagnostic significance. *Journal of Learning Disabilities*, **18**, 42–50.

Pavlidis, G. Th. (1985b). Eye movement differences between dyslexics, normals and slow readers while sequentially fixating digits. *American Journal of Optometry and Physiological Optics*, **62**, 820–832.

Pavlidis, G. Th. (1986). The role of eye movements in the diagnosis of dyslexia. In G. Th. Pavlidis and D. F. Fisher (eds), *Dyslexia: Its Neuropsychology and Treatment*. New York: Wiley.

Pavlidis, G. Th. (June, 1987). Reading without eye movements: Dyslexics read fast and comprehend as well as normal readers. Paper presented at the 3rd World Congress on Dyslexia, Crete.

Pavlidis, G. Th. (ed.) (1990). *Perspectives on Dyslexia, Volume 2, Cognition, Language and Treatment*. Chichester: Wiley.

Punnett, A. F., and Steinhaur, G. D. (1984). Relationship between reinforcement and eye movements during ocular motor training with learning disabled children. *Journal of Learning Disabilities*, **17**, 16–19.

Pyykko, I., Dahlen, A. I., Schalen, L., and Hindfelt, B. (1984). Eye movements in patients with speech dyspraxia. *Acta Otolaryngologica*, **98**, 481–489.

Rawson, M. (1968). *Developmental Language Disability: Adult Accomplishments of Dyslexic Boys*. Baltimore: Johns Hopkins Press.

Richie, D. J., and Aten, J. L. (1976). Auditory retention of nonverbal and verbal sequential stimuli in children with reading disabilities. *Journal of Learning Disabilities*, **9**, 54–60.

Rourke, B. P. (1989). Learning disabilities subtypes: a neuropsychological perspective. In G. Th. Pavlidis (ed.), *Perspectives on Dyslexia, Volume 1, Neurology, Neuropsychology and Genetics*. Chichester: Wiley.

Rutter, M., Tizard, J., and Whitmore, K. (1970). *Education, Health, and Behavior*. London: Longman.

Sampson, O. C. (1975). Fifty years of dyslexia. A review of the literature, 1925–75. I. Theory. *Research in Education*, **14**, 15–32.

Satz, P., and Soper, H. V. (1986). Left-handedness, dyslexia, and autoimmune disorder: A critique. *Journal of Clinical and Experimental Neuropsychology*, **8**, 453–458.

Scarborough, H. S. (1984). Continuity between childhood dyslexia and adult reading. *British Journal of Psychology*, **75**, 329–348.

Sehy, D. M. (1984). An investigation of the intermodal and cross modal temporal and spatial–temporal abilities of normal and learning-disabled children. *Dissertation Abstracts International*, **44**, 3356.

Senf, G. M. (1969). Development of immediate memory for bisensory stimuli in normal children and children with learning disorders. *Developmental Psychology*, **1**, Part 2.

Shakhnovich, A. R. (1977). *The Brain and Regulation of Eye Movement*. New York: Plenum Press.

Smith, F. (1978). *Understanding Reading: A Psycholinguistic Analysis of Reading and Learning to Read*. New York: Holt, Rinehart & Winston.

Solan, H. (1985). Deficient eye-movement patterns in achieving high school students: Three case histories. *Journal of Learning Disabilities*, **18**, 66–70.

Solan, H., and Mozlin, R. (1986). The correlations of perceptual-motor maturation to readiness and reading in kindergarten and the primary grades using multivariate analysis. *Journal of the American Optometric Association*, **57**, 28–35.

Sommers, R. K., and Taylor, M. L. (1972). Cerebral speech dominance in language-disordered and normal children. *Cortex*, **8**, 224–232.

Spache, G. D. (1981). *Diagnosing and Correcting Reading Disabilities* (2nd edn). Boston: Allyn & Bacon.

Sperry, R. W. (1968). Hemispheric deconnection and unity in conscious awareness. *American Psychologist*, **23**, 723–733.

Springer, S. P., and Deutsch, G. (1981). *Left Brain Right Brain*. San Francisco: Freeman.

Sterritt, G. M., and Rudnick, M. (1966). Auditory and visual rhythm perception in relation to reading ability in fourth grade boys. *Perceptual and Motor Skills*, **22**, 859–864.

Strag, G. A. (1972). Comparative behavioral ratings of parents with severe mentally retarded, special learning disability and normal children. *Journal of Learning Disabilities*, **5**, 52–56.

Tallal, P. (1980). Auditory temporal perception, phonics, and reading disabilities in children. *Brain and Language*, **9**, 182–198.

Tallal, P. (1983). A precise timing mechanism may underlie a common speech perception and production area in the peri-Sylvian cortex of the dominant hemisphere. *Behavioral and Brain Sciences*, **6**, 219–220.

Tallal, P., and Piercy, M. (1974). Developmental aphasia: Rate of auditory processing and selective impairment of consonant perception. *Neuropsychologia*, **12**, 83–93.

Vande Voort, L., and Senf, G. M. (1973). Auditory–visual integration in retarded readers. *Journal of Learning Disabilities*, **6**, 49–57.

Vellutino, F. R. (1977). Alternative conceptualizations of dyslexia: Evidence in support of a verbal-deficit hypothesis. *Harvard Educational Review*, **47**, 334–354.

Vellutino, F. R. (1978). Toward an understanding of dyslexia: Psychological factors in specific reading disability. In A. Benton and D. Pearl (eds), *Dyslexia: An Appraisal of Current Knowledge*. New York: Oxford University Press.

Vellutino, F. R. (1979). *Dyslexia: Theory and Research*. Cambridge: MIT Press.

Vernon, M. D. (1977). Varieties of deficiency in the reading processes. *Harvard Educational Review*, **47**, 396–410.

Willette, T. L., and Early, G. H. (1985). Abilities of normal and reading-disabled children to combine the visual and auditory modalities with dimensions of space and time. *Perceptual and Motor Skills*, **61**, 1295–1298.

Witelson, S. F. (1976). Abnormal right hemisphere functional specialization in developmental dyslexia. In R. M. Knights and D. J. Bakker (eds), *Neuropsychology of Learning Disabilities: Theoretical Issues*. Baltimore: University Park Press.

Witelson, S. F. (1977). Early hemisphere specialization and interhemispheric plasticity: An empirical and theoretical review. In S. J. Segalowitz and F. A. Gruber (eds), *Language Development and Neurological Theory*. New York: Academic Press.

Wolf, M. (1986). Rapid alternating stimulus naming in the developmental dyslexias.

Wolff, P. H., Cohen, C., and Drake, C. (1984). Impaired motor timing control in specific reading retardation. *Neuropsychologia*, **22** (5), 587–600.

Woodcock, R. W. (1973). *Woodcock Reading Mastery Tests*. Minnesota: American Guidance Service.

Zangwill, O. L. (1962). Dyslexia in relation to cerebral dominance. In J. Money (ed.), *Reading Disability: Progress and Research Needs in Dyslexia*. Baltimore: Johns Hopkins University Press.

Zigmund, N. (1978). Remediation of dyslexia: a discussion. In A. L. Benton and D. Pearl (eds.), *Dyslexia: An Appraisal of Current Knowledge*. New York: Oxford University Press.

Zurif, E. B., and Carson, G. (1970). Dyslexia in relation to cerebral dominance and temporal analysis. *Neuropsychologia*, **8**, 351–361.

Addresses for correspondence:

Dr Charles E. Dodgen; Fair Oaks Hospital, Summit, New Jersey 07902, USA

Professor George Th. Pavlidis; The Reading Center, George Washington University, 2021 K Street NW, Suite 720, Washington, D.C. 200, USA

12

Vergence Eye Movement Control and Spatial Discrimination in Normal and Dyslexic Children

M. S. Fowler[1], P. M. Riddell[1] and John F. Stein[2]

[1]*Royal Berkshire Hospital, Reading, and* [2]*University of Oxford*

INTRODUCTION

The first workers to suggest that different subtypes of dyslexia might exist were Kinsbourne and Warrington (1963). They differentiated two groups of dyslexics having a 20-point or more difference in their performance or verbal subtests of the WISC. The children with higher performance than verbal IQ seemed to have language deficits, while the children with higher verbal than performance IQ showed a form of Gerstmann syndrome with finger agnosia and visuoperceptual difficulties. Since then many other workers have defined dyslexic subgroups with either language or visuoperceptual deficits (Boder 1973; Mattis, 1978).

There is a natural temptation to link the dichotomy of language versus visuoperceptual difficulties with left versus right hemisphere processing (Duane, 1985). Children whose reading difficulties are associated with language deficits are then classified as having left hemisphere deficiencies, whereas visuoperceptual problems are attributed to right hemisphere dysfunction. There is some evidence to support the idea that children with language-based difficulties might have microlesions of the left hemisphere. Galaburda and Kemper (1979) reported the results of an autopsy which had been carried out on a known dyslexic after a fatal accident. The planum temporale was found to be the same size on each side. Such symmetry is found in only 24% of the normal population (Geschwind and Levitsky, 1968). Also polymicrogyria and cortical dysplasias were found, mostly in the left hemisphere. This subject had a known history of late language development and dyslexia. These findings have since been confirmed in several more dyslexic brains (Geschwind and Galaburda, 1987).

Fewer anatomical abnormalities which could be linked to visuospatial dysfunction have been found in the right hemisphere. However, there appears to be a larger number of dyslexic children with language-based rather than visuoperceptual problems, so it may be that the small number of brains so far examined has not included a dyslexic subject with mainly visuoperceptual difficulties.

Our research has been concentrated on an attempt to find a clinical means of differentiating dyslexic children with mainly visuoperceptual—or visuomotor—difficulties from those with mainly language problems. Many dyslexic children complain of symptoms of a visual nature. Letters appear to move about or blur, they lose their place on the page and their eyes get tired. On standard tests, their vision is usually found to be normal, however. Refractive errors or pathological problems are rarely found.

Why should letters appear to move around for these children? Normally, our visual world remains stationary when our eyes move because the oculomotor system provides signals indicating how far and in which direction our eyes have moved. This information is used to determine visual direction each time we fixate an object of interest. Combining this with retinal signals which identify what is being inspected allows the brain to build up a representation of where objects are in space. This helps to stabilize the visual world despite frequent eye movements.

If, however, the position of the eyes were to vary unpredictably, successful integration of retinal and oculomotor signals would be difficult; hence small objects, like letters on a page, might appear to move about when the eyes move. For the high resolution required to read small print therefore, the eyes must maintain steady foveal fixation.

We have suggested that it is the integration of eye movement and position signals with retinal information which breaks down in some dyslexic children when they are viewing small targets in near space with the eyes held in a convergent position (Stein and Fowler, 1981; Stein *et al.*, 1989). If the links between the oculomotor and retinal systems are not properly developed, these children could experience instability of their visual world leading to confusion not only when they try to read but also when they attempt to localize small targets.

When a child is learning to read, the eyes have to be maintained in a convergent position. This position has to be continually adjusted to cope with the small changes in distance between the eyes and the text. The problems so far described might therefore arise as a result of some abnormality in the development of fine control of vergence eye movements.

Although gross vergence movements are known to be present in young infants (Fox *et al.*, 1980), very little is known about the development of fine

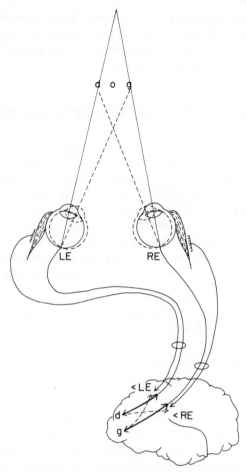

Figure 1. Calculation of visual direction sense during reading. LE, left eye; RE, right
eye

vergence control after this time. Our investigations suggest that some children
fail to develop accurate vergence control even by the age of 8 years or more.
We believe that this delay can lead to learning difficulties because unstable
bifoveal fixation results in difficulties in accurately localizing small letters on
the page.

Consider a beginning reader looking at the word 'dog' (Figure 1). The
normal child can maintain fixation on the 'o'. The position of the 'o' is then
given by the angle of the eyes, which is supplied by the oculomotor system.
However, a child with unstable vergence control may relax his convergence to
a position behind the plane of the word, so that one eye may foveate the 'd'
and the other the 'g'. A moment later he may converge in front of the word

and the situation will reverse. Even this would not be disastrous if the child's oculomotor system were able to provide an accurate indication of the movements of the eyes. However, it is possible that these eye movements are not accurately registered by the child's brain.

VERGENCE CONTROL AND READING ABILITY

We started our investigation into binocular control using a subjective test of vergence stability: the Dunlop test. In the 1970s, Dunlop and co-workers (1972, 1973a,b, 1974, 1975, 1981) suggested that some dyslexic children may experience problems when learning to read as a result of difficulties with accurate binocular control. They thought that this control would depend upon the use of a controlling or 'reference' eye, so that lack of development of this reference eye might disturb normal binocular function.

In order to test this hypothesis, Patricia Dunlop developed a test to assess the reference eye in binocular situations. The test had to fulfil several criteria:

(1) The visual information had to be similar enough to allow full binocularity at all times, but each eye also had to have some unique information to allow the test operator to ensure that the subject was maintaining binocularity.
(2) The visual information had to be restricted to the central retina.
(3) The test had to involve some means of demonstrating the eye which controls binocular function.

The test which she developed is based on experiments on the appreciation of fixation disparity when the eyes are moved disconjugately (Ogle, 1962). Small visual targets (3° of arc) are projected separately to each eye using a synoptophore or major amblyoscope (Figure 2). The optical properties of the synoptophore ensure that the slides are viewed at infinity. The slides used to perform the test show a house with a central front door. In one slide, there is a post with an arrow on one side of the door, while on the other slide a post with a circle appears at the other side of the door. These posts are projected to the nasal retinae of each eye. The slides are viewed at the angle of fusion so that the subject sees a binocular image of a house with a post on either side of a central front door.

By abducting the synoptophore tubes, the targets are slowly moved disconjugately across the retinae, thus stimulating a vergence movement of the subject's eyes as they attempt to track the targets. Since vergence depends on retinal disparity as an error signal to provide the stimulus for movement there is a disparity between the image of the post in one eye and that in the other eye. This means that the posts are displaced with reference to the house seen by the opposite eye. The houses remain fused, however, since the extent of

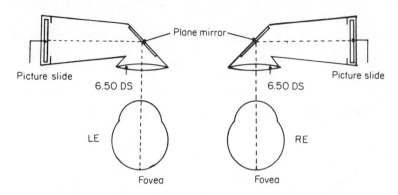

Figure 2. Diagram of the major amblyoscope or synoptophore

the retinal disparity does not exceed the bounds of Panum's fusional area—the elliptical area on one retina which corresponds to a single point on the other. This allows points in space just in front or behind the plane of focus to be fused, despite the retinal disparities existing between the retinal images.

Since the eyes move disconjugately, the target appears to move in depth. All movement should therefore appear to be towards or away from the subject. However, when the test is performed using normal, fully binocular subjects, there is an impression of lateral movement of one post towards the door. This movement suggests that the correct association between the movement of the target across the retina and the movement of the eyes is being made for one eye only. This eye will not see a lateral movement of the post. The Dunlops define this eye as the 'reference' eye.

When using this test, we ensure that the child is maintaining steady fixation on the foveal target and then diverge the tubes of the synoptophore slowly (at about 0.5°/second). This forces the child's eyes to diverge also, in order to maintain foveal fusion of the target. The child is asked to report which of the two posts appears to move towards the door before the door breaks into two when fusion fails. The test is repeated ten times to see whether the side of movement is the same on each testing. A child is said to have stable Dunlop test responses if the apparent movement of the post is seen by the same eye on at least eight out of ten testings.

In order to investigate how the eyes moved, we started to record the children's eye movements during the Dunlop test (Figure 3). This showed us that children who found the Dunlop test confusing were virtually unable to make any vergence movements in response to divergence or convergence of the tubes if small (<3°) fusion targets were used. But their responses were better when we used larger (7°) targets. Thus it seemed that the size of target used to test for stable vergence control was an important variable. Using small targets, children with unstable Dunlop test responses

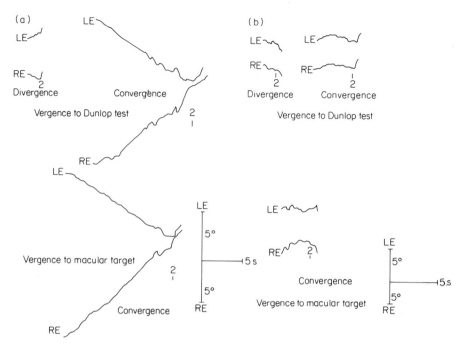

Figure 3. Vergence eye movements during divergence and convergence to Dunlop test slides and convergence to macular sized slides recorded from: (a) a 10-year-old normal reader; (b) a 10-year-old disabled reader. LE, left eye; RE, right eye; 2, time at which subject reported diplopia

appeared to make mainly version movements: they were slow to recognize diplopia and they tended to suppress alternately one eye then the other. Such visuomotor problems could result in confusion of the apparent position of letters on the page, as explained earlier. The child may not only be confused when he is trying to read a word but may also find difficulty when trying to recall the exact position of letters in words. Hence abnormal vergence control may cause major problems with learning to read successfully.

Children with stable Dunlop test responses have good vergence movements in response to all sizes of targets, whereas children with unstable responses show reduced amplitude of movements, both in convergence and divergence. The smaller the target the poorer the vergence control in these children. This may help to explain why some children have greater problems when the size of print is reduced.

Do all beginning readers show this pattern of poor binocular control? In order to assess this, we tested the vergence control of 750 primary school children between the ages of 5 and 12, using the Dunlop test. Figure 4 shows the developmental trend for the acquisition of stable Dunlop test responses.

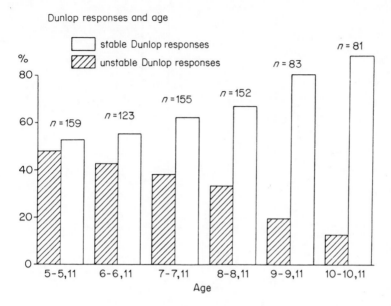

Figure 4. Developmental trend for the acquisition of stable Dunlop test responses in 755 unselected primary school children

It can be seen that at 5 years of age only about 50% of children had acquired binocular stability, while at 11 years old about 90% of children had stable Dunlop test responses.

This result shows that many children have stable Dunlop test responses and good control of vergence, even before they start to learn to read. Hence stable vergence control is not a skill which is necessarily dependent upon the ability to read.

The natural history of the development of stable binocular control might help to explain why some investigators have failed to find visuomotor perceptual problems in groups of dyslexic children. Two variables are important: the age of the children tested and the size of the targets used. Since our research suggests that there is a developmental trend in the acquisition of stable vergence control then visuomotor perceptual problems are more likely to reach statistical significance in unselected groups of dyslexics when the average age of the children tested is low. Our research also suggests that the size of the targets used to test for these problems is important. Targets need to be small before significant effects will be found.

In Figure 5, the relationship between stable Dunlop test responses and reading ability is shown for a selection of the normal children described previously. Children with stable Dunlop test responses are found to be significantly better readers than children with unstable responses.

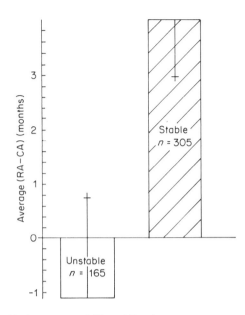

Figure 5. Relationship between stability of Dunlop test responses and reading ability measured as reading age minus chronological age

We have now carried out a longitudinal study with the cooperation of a local infant school. The children were first seen during their first week at the school, when they were 4–5 years old. Vision, binocular vision, ocular movements, convergence and accommodation (using the RAF rule) were tested. All children performed the Dunlop test. Attempts to measure their eye movements at this point failed. The first child burst into tears at the sight of the glasses, and so that was the end of that! Eye movements were recorded successfully at the end of the first year, however.

The reading ability of this population was first measured at 7 years old. Dunlop test measurements were made at both 6 and 7 years old. In Figure 6, the results of the Dunlop test at both 6 and 7 years has been plotted against the reading ability measured at 7 years. For both years, the reading ability of the children who were found to have unstable responses was significantly lower than those with stable responses. Thus these results show that the Dunlop test can be used to detect children with potential reading difficulties at least a year before their reading can be assessed. This shows the predictive ability of the Dunlop test in a normal population.

Having identified this problem, is there anything we can do to help these children? In our study published in the *Lancet* in 1985 we showed the efficacy of treating dyslexic children with unstable Dunlop test responses by occluding one eye during reading, writing and number work. Our argument was that

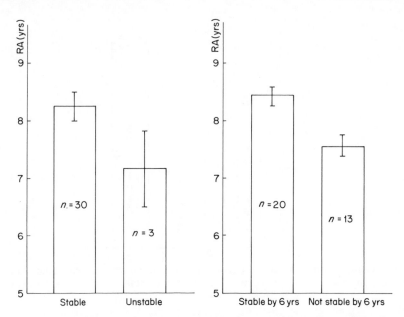

Figure 6. Comparison between the reading ability of normal 7-year-old children with or without stable Dunlop test responses: (a) selection on the results of the Dunlop test results at 7 years old; (b) selection on the results of the Dunlop test results at 6 years old

some children experience confusion because the two eyes supply conflicting information about the location of small targets. If this is true, then occluding one eye should alleviate this problem. In our 1985 study of about 150 children, we defined our dyslexic population using the word reading test from the British Abilities Scale (BAS). Scores on this test were compared with scores in the Similarities and Matrices subtests from the BAS. Performance in these two subtests has been shown to be relatively unaffected by dyslexic problems (Thomson, 1982) and hence are likely to give a fair representation of the basic level of intelligence of these children. Normative data relating the IQ subtest scores to the word-reading ability are available for these tests. Children who scored 2 SDs lower on the reading score than the level expected from their IQ and chronological age were defined as 'dyslexic'.

We found that twice as many children developed stable Dunlop test responses while wearing occlusion than would have been expected of un-assisted children from our developmental studies (Figure 7). Children who gained stability during the trial were found to improve their reading ability significantly faster than those who did not (Figure 8). To ensure that this difference was independent of the IQ of the children, the results were regressed against IQ. Figure 9 shows the results. It is clear that, although

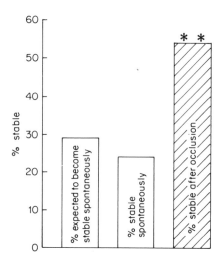

Figure 7. Comparison between the percentage of children who gained stable Dunlop test responses as a result of occlusion or who gained stability without treatment

there was a slightly better prognosis for children with high intelligence, the increase in reading ability resulting from the treatment is true for all IQ levels.

We also recorded vergence movements both before and after occlusion therapy (Figure 10). These measurements showed that it is possible to improve some children's ability to converge and diverge in response to small targets, using occlusion therapy.

Our hypothesis is that poor vergence control is associated with reduced accuracy of visual localization, which, in turn, leads to learning difficulties. It might be argued that learning difficulties lead to poor vergence control, i.e. that cause and effect are reversed. We have therefore compared the vergence abilities of dyslexics with younger normal children matched for reading age rather than using the normal chronological age match. If good reading ability leads to good vergence control then the younger children who read normally for their age should have as poor vergence control as older dyslexics. If, however, good vergence control results in good reading ability then there should be no evidence of poor control in the younger normal readers.

Thirty-one normal readers were matched to a dyslexic group defined as described above by age and IQ. The normal group were then split into those who were dyslexic because their reading age was 2 SDs below their IQ, and those who read at or above that expected for their IQ. There were 11 dyslexic 'normals' matched to dyslexics from the clinical population, and 20 younger normal readers who were matched with the dyslexics by reading age. Figure 11 shows the percentage of children in each of the groups with (a) unstable

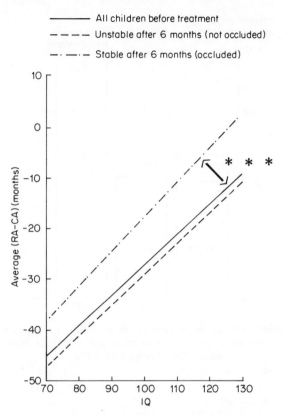

Figure 8. Comparison between the reading age improvement in three groups of reading-disabled children: (a) UOU, children who had monocular occlusion treatment for 6 months but failed to develop stable Dunlop test responses; (b) UNU, children who were untreated for 6 months and failed to develop stable Dunlop test responses; (c) UOS, children who had monocular occlusion treatment for 6 months and developed stable Dunlop test responses during that period

Dunlop test responses and (b) unstable vergence eye movement control. No significant differences were found between the dyslexics from the normal population and the dyslexics from the clinical population. However, we did find a significant difference in both stability of responses to the Dunlop test and stability of eye movement responses between the dyslexics and the normal readers. This shows that the differences in stability of vergence control were not due to better reading ability. Instead the poor reading ability of the dyslexic group seemed to be dependent on their ability to maintain accurate vergence control.

Do all children with poor vergence control have learning difficulties? No. Many children with squints have poor vergence control. Those who show

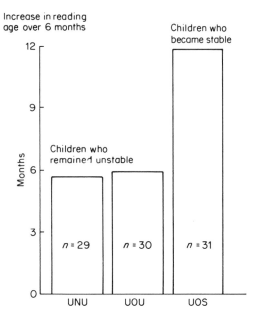

Figure 9. Comparison of the improvement in reading age regressed against IQ between children who developed stable Dunlop test responses with occlusion and those who remained unstable

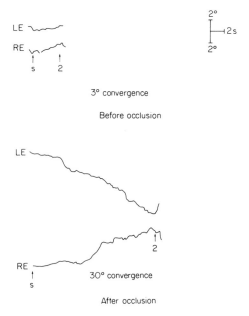

Figure 10. Comparison of the convergence eye movements to a macular target recorded before and after 6 months of monocular occlusion therapy

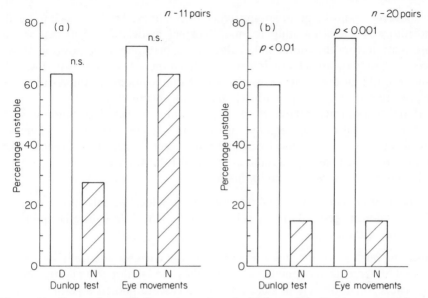

Figure 11. Comparison of the percentage of children with Dunlop test and eye movement stability in: (a) dyslexics from a clinical population matched with dyslexics from a 'normal' population by reading age and IQ; (b) dyslexics from a clinical population matched with younger readers from a 'normal' population by reading age and IQ

suppression as a result of the squint rarely show reading difficulties, however. As stated earlier, reading with one eye seems to be easier than reading with two. Some kinds of squint may well result from poor vergence control. Some families contain one child who squints and another with no squint, but learning difficulties. Thus both conditions may be due to defects in vergence control.

It is important to stress that not all learning difficulties are due to visuomotor problems. Many dyslexics suffer from a delay in the development of specific language faculties or have problems with auditory discrimination. There are likely to be more children falling into these latter categories than children with purely visuomotor problems. But up to two-thirds of children with learning difficulties may suffer from inaccurate fine vergence control. However, in less than one-third is this their main problem. These visuomotor problems could lead to inaccuracies in the localization of small visual targets, such as letters, thus proving an obstacle in learning to read.

DOT LOCALIZATION AND VERGENCE CONTROL

We have suggested that children with unstable vergence control fail to learn to read at the same rate as their peers because this instability causes their eyes to converge and diverge in an unpredictable manner. This is associated with difficulties when attempting to make correct associations between visual information from the retina and oculomotor signals about the position of the eyes. It is only by associating information from these two sources that we are able to build up a spatial representation of the positions of objects in space relative to ourselves—especially when the objects are very small.

If this hypothesis is correct, then we would predict that children with unstable control of fine vergence movements, as measured by the Dunlop test, would be poorer at localizing all small objects in near visual space—not just letters. The results presented here support this theory.

Two populations were used in this study:

(1) 80 'normal' children aged 4;6 to 6;6 seen at a local infant school;
(2) 82 children aged 6;0 to 18;0 referred to the Royal Berkshire Hospital for learning difficulties.

Since the purpose of the study was to assess the correspondence between the control of vergence movements as assessed by the Dunlop test and the ability to localize small objects in space, all subjects were pooled together for the analysis.

All the children were assessed orthoptically. No children with poor visual acuity or squints were included in the sample. The children all performed the Dunlop test and this was used to determine the stability of vergence control. In order to confirm that the results of the Dunlop test correlated with the accuracy of their vergence control, some of the children also had their eye movements recorded while performing the test. The concordance between the Dunlop test and eye movement recordings in this group was high (80%).

The children performed a computer game which was designed to test their ability to localize small objects accurately in visual space. In this task, a priming spot appeared in a random position on a television screen. The children were asked to fixate it. When the spot disappeared, a second probe spot appeared to the left or right of the previous position of the first spot. The child had to indicate which side of the priming spot the probe spot had appeared. This task was referred to as a random left–right discrimination (RLRD) task.

The protocol for the task was as follows: the subject sat 30 cm (reading distance) away from a television screen with the head restrained to minimize head movements. The subject looked at a black bordered area (14.5 cm × 14.5 cm). He was instructed that a small spot would appear somewhere within this area and that when the spot appeared he should watch it carefully. The priming spot (1 mm × 2 mm) stayed on the screen for 1 second. This time was made deliberately long to enhance the chances of uncontrolled eye movements occurring. There was then a delay of 200 ms, after which the test spot (1 mm × 2 mm) appeared in a position slightly to the left or right of the priming spot for 100 ms. The distance between priming spot and test spot averaged 2 mm. Eye movements were recorded during the test to ensure that the subjects fixed the priming spot continually. Each subject performed the task at least 20 times. The subject was instructed to indicate on which side of the priming spot the test spot had appeared by pointing to the left or right. This ensured that difficulties in naming right and left did not produce a confounding effect on the results. The results were stored on computer by the experimenter. The computer made a comparison of the subject's response with the true test spot position and scored 0 for an error, or 1 for a correct response. Analysis of the results of this forced two-choice paradigm was performed using the χ^2 test.

It was expected that children who showed poor control of vergence movements would be less able to localize small objects in space. Figure 12 shows the percentage errors made by children with stable versus unstable Dunlop test responses on this task of dot localization. The children with stable Dunlop test responses made on average 21.8% errors, whereas those with unstable responses made 29.7% errors. Both groups are performing well above the level of chance (50% errors). There was a significant difference between these two groups ($\chi^2 = 31.04$, DOF = 1, $P < 0.001$). Hence it was clear that children with unstable Dunlop test responses made more errors on this test involving localization of small objects in space.

A developmental trend was found for the acquisition of stable Dunlop test responses. If the ability to localize dots in space is correlated with stability of

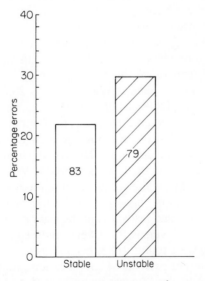

Figure 12. Comparison of the percentage errors made on a dot localization task between children with stable Dunlop test responses and those with unstable responses

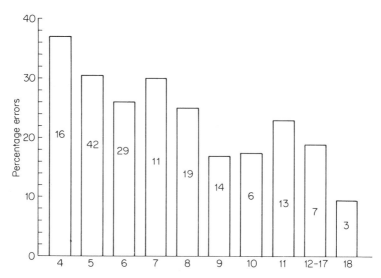

Figure 13. Developmental trend in the ability to perform a dot localization task
accurately

vergence control, then there should also be a developmental trend for this
skill. Figure 13 shows the percentage errors made by children from 4 to 18
years old. In general there was a trend for older children to perform more
accurately on the test, although all groups perform better than chance. This
trend was maintained even after the subjects were grouped according to the
stability of their vergence control.

There is evidence to suggest that males perform better than females on tests
of a visuospatial nature (McGee, 1979). Figure 14 shows the percentage
errors for males and females on this task. The males were indeed found to
make fewer errors than the females (24.2% versus 28.2%). This difference
was significant ($\chi^2 = 6.70$, DOF = 1, $P < 0.01$).

Since the subjects were required to fix a central spot and then process dots
appearing to the right or left of this spot, the ability of each hemisphere to
perform this task could be investigated. The visual pathways are organized in
such a way that stimuli seen in the left visual field (LVF) are processed first in
the right hemisphere (RH), while stimuli seen in the RVF are first processed
in the LH. Hence test spots appearing to the left of the priming spot are
processed first by the RH and test spots to the right by the LH.

When errors in the LVF versus RVF were analysed across all subjects, no
significant differences were found. It has been suggested, however, that males
and females have different patterns of lateralization. Males have been shown
to be superior at LVF–RH processing of spatial tasks, whereas females
showed no difference between LH and RH (Witelson, 1976). Figure 15 shows

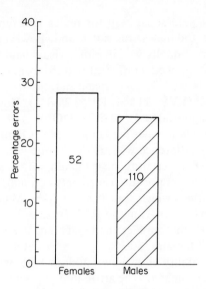

Figure 14. Comparison of the percentage error rate on a dot localization task between males and females

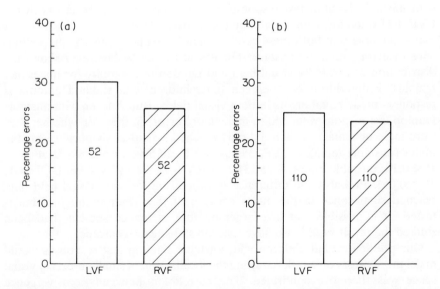

Figure 15. Comparison of the percentage error rate on a dot localization task in the left visual field (LVF) or right visual field (RVF) between (a) females and (b) males

the effects by visual field separately for males and females. The expected LVF–RH advantage for males was not found, however. Instead the males were found to perform equally well in either visual field (LVF, 25.0%; RVF, 23.5%). Females also showed a different pattern from that expected. Instead of performing equally well in each visual field, a trend towards RVF–LH superiority was found (LVF, 30.1%; RVF, 25.8%). However, this trend did not reach statistical significance ($\chi^2 = 2.77$, DOF = 1, $P < 0.1$).

Figure 14 suggests that females made more errors than males in this task. It was possible that this difference was greater in one visual field. So the errors made by males and females were investigated with respect to visual field. Figure 15 shows that the major difference between males and females was in their processing of targets which appear in the LVF. Males and females made almost equal numbers of errors in the RVF (males, 23.5%; females, 25.8%) whereas, in the LVF, the females made significantly more errors than the males (males, 25.0%; females, 30.1%; $\chi^2 = 5.59$, DOF = 1, $P < 0.02$).

The difference in ability shown by children with stable versus unstable Dunlop test responses might also be attributed to poorer processing by one or other hemisphere. Figure 16 shows the percentage errors by visual field for children with stable versus unstable Dunlop test responses. Children with stable responses performed equally well regardless of visual field (LVF, 21.5%; RVF, 21.9%). However, children with unstable Dunlop test responses made significantly more errors in the LVF (LVF, 32.8%; RVF, 26.7%, $\chi^2 = 7.92$, DOF = 1, $P < 0.01$). Hence both females and children with unstable Dunlop test responses made significantly more errors in the LVF–RH when localizing small objects in space.

It is possible that both these results might be explained by the preponderance of errors made by unstable females in the LVF. Figure 17 shows the distribution of errors by visual field and Dunlop test stability for males and females. From this it can be seen that children with stable Dunlop test responses made equal errors in both visual fields. But children with unstable Dunlop test responses tended to make more errors in the LVF whether they were male or female. This trend only reached statistical significance for the males (unstable females: LVF, 35.8%; RVF, 29.5%; $\chi^2 = 2.83$, DOF = 1, $P < 0.10$; unstable males: LVF, 31.1%; RVF, 25.3%; $\chi^2 = 4.96$, DOF = 1, $P < 0.05$). Probably the difference in processing for each visual field only reached significance in the males because of the larger number of males tested. It is possible that if a larger number of female subjects had been studied the result would also have reached statistical significance.

Our prediction that children with unstable Dunlop test responses would make more errors on a task requiring the localization of small objects in visual space was therefore confirmed. The correlation between poor vergence control and poor dot localization was strengthened by the finding that both skills showed a developmental trend. Although these results do not prove a

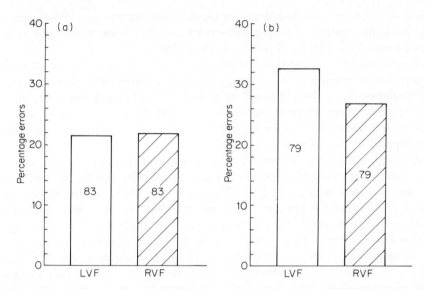

Figure 16. Comparison of the percentage error rate on a dot localization task in the LVF or RVF between (a) children with stable Dunlop test responses and (b) children with unstable responses

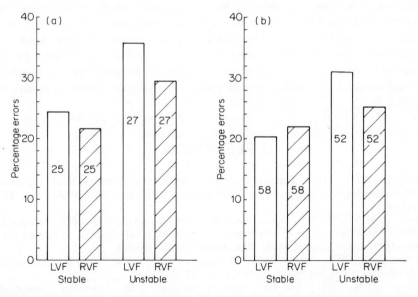

Figure 17. Comparison of the percentage error rate on a dot localization task in the LVF or RVF for children with stable or unstable Dunlop test responses between (a) females and (b) males

causal relation between the ability to localize dots accurately in visual space and accurate control of vergence movements, they suggest that this relationship would be worthy of further investigation.

The results also suggest that females are poorer at tasks requiring accurate localization of objects in space than their male counterparts. However, this difference could not be explained by male LVF–RH superiority. Instead, it was found that females performed more poorly in their LVF. This result was mostly accounted for by the poor performance of females with unstable Dunlop test responses in the LVF.

Although children with unstable Dunlop test responses made more errors than children with stable responses in either visual field, significantly more of the errors were found in the LVF. This trend was found in both males and females with unstable Dunlop test responses. Only in males was this trend statistically significant, but many more males were studied.

Overall, the results suggest that accurate dot localization can be performed by either hemisphere, but that processing in the right hemisphere is less reliable in children with unstable vergence control. Since our results suggest that adequate control of fine vergence movements is a necessary prerequisite for learning to read, it is possible that children with a reading difficulty resulting from poor vergence control are exhibiting some kind of right hemisphere dysfunction. The deficit in LVF–RH processing found in these children suggests that the overall control of vergence movements and spatial relationships is normally controlled by the right hemisphere. A dysfunction of normal right hemisphere processing might then lead to visuomotor difficulties which could interfere with the development of reading abilities. Thus, as impairment of the left hemisphere may lead to learning difficulties by its effect on language functions, impairment of the right hemisphere may affect learning to read by interfering with correct spatial localization of letters in words.

REFERENCES

Boder, E. (1973). Developmental dyslexia: A diagnostic approach based on three atypical reading–spelling patterns. *Developmental Medicine and Child Neurology*, **15**, 663–687.

Duane, D. (1985). Written language underachievement: An overview of the theoretical and practical issues. In F. H. Duffy and N. Geschwind (eds), *Dyslexia: A Neuroscientific Approach to Clinical Evaluation*. Boston: Little, Brown.

Dunlop, D. B. (1972). An interdisciplinary approach to dyslexia. II. The binocular basis for dyslexic confusion. *Austral. Orthopt. J.*, **12**, 4–15.

Dunlop, D. B. (1981). On the origin of visual dyslexia. *Australian Journal of Ophthalmology*, **9**, 193–198.

Dunlop, D. B., and Dunlop, P. (1974). New concepts of visual laterality in relation to dyslexia. *Australian Journal of Ophthalmology*, **2**, 101–112.

Dunlop, D. B., and Dunlop, P. (1975). *A new orthooptic technique in learning disability due to visual dyslexia*. Paper presented to Dyslexia Conference, Boston.

Dunlop, D. B., Dunlop, P., and Fenelon, B. (1973). Vision-laterality analysis in children with reading disability: The results of new techniques of examination. *Cortex*, **9**, 227–236.

Dunlop, P. (1973). An interdisciplinary approach to dyslexia. III. Dyslexia: The orthoptic approach. *Austral. Orthopt. J.*, **12**, 16–20.

Fox, R., Aslin, R. N., Shea, S. L., and Dumais, S. T. (1980). Stereopsis in human infants. *Science*, **207**, 233–234.

Galaburda, A. M., and Kemper, T. L. (1979). Cytoarchitectonic abnormalities in developmental dyslexia: A case study. *Annals of Neurology*, **6**, 94–100.

Geschwind, N., and Galaburda, A. M. (1987). *Cerebral Lateralization: Biological Mechanisms, Associations and Pathology*. Cambridge, MA: MIT Press.

Geschwind, N., and Levitsky, W. (1968). Human brain: Left–right asymmetries in temporal speech region. *Science*, **161**, 186–187.

Kinsbourne, M., and Warrington, E. (1963). Developmental factors in reading and writing backwardness. *British Journal of Psychology*, **54**, 145–156.

McGee, M. G. (1979). Human spatial abilities: Psychometric studies and environmental, genetic, and neurological influences. *Psychological Bulletin*, **86**, 889–918.

Mattis, S. (1978). Dyslexia syndromes: A working hypothesis that works. In A. L. Benton and D. Pearl (eds), *Dyslexia: An Appraisal of Current Knowledge*. Boston: Little, Brown.

Ogle, K. N. (1962). The optical space sense. In H. Davson (ed.), *The Eye* (Vol. IV). New York: Academic Press.

Stein, J. F. and Fowler, M. S. (1981). Visual dyslexia. *Trends in Neuroscience*, **4**, 77–80.

Stein, J. F., Riddell, P. M., and Fowler, M. S. (1989). Disordered right hemisphere function in developmental dyslexia. In C. van Inler, I. Lundberg and G. Lennerstrand (eds), *Brain and Reading*; Wenner Gren International Symposium Series Vol. 54. London: Macmillan.

Thomson, M. E. (1982). The assessment of children with specific reading difficulties (dyslexia) using the British Ability Scales. *British Journal of Psychology*, **73**, 461–478.

Witelson, S. (1976). Sex and the single hemisphere: Specialisation of the right hemisphere for spatial processing. *Science*, **193**, 425–427.

Addresses for correspondence:

Mr M. S. Fowler and Dr P. M. Riddell; Royal Berkshire Hospital, Reading, Berkshire, UK

Dr John F. Stein; Department of Physiology, University of Oxford, Parks Road, Oxford OX1 3PT, UK

Index